easy entertaining
darina allen

darina allen

easy entertaining

over 250 stress-free recipes and sensational styling ideas

photography by peter cassidy

kyle cathie limited

For Rosalie, who has helped to make my life EASY for the past 21 years.

No book is ever the work of just one person but this book has had input from more than most. Twenty years later I still can't type or use a word processor so every syllable is written in long hand and then has to be typed by a team of long-suffering keen-sighted people who struggle to read my scrawl. So for this I am deeply grateful to Truus Boelhouwer, Robin Bryant, Patrick Treacy, Adrienne Forbes, Sharon Hogan and Dorothee Krien.

Emer Fitzgerald and her team at the Ballymaloe Cookery School helped to test recipes in the midst of a hectic work schedule.

I would also like to acknowledge my friend Mary Dowey whose idea it originally was to do an easy entertaining book. We planned to do this book together but I was so slow and hopeless about meeting my deadlines that Mary understandably had to honour her other engagements.

A huge thank you also to the many guest chefs and friends who have shared their recipes with me over the years which has greatly enhanced our repertoire.

Tom Doorley's inspired wine and food pairings have added a wonderful extra dimension to this book – thank you Tom.

I especially asked for Peter Cassidy to do the photos for this book and his gorgeous images have not disappointed.

Thank you also to Linda Tubby for her wonderful food styling, Charis White and Roisin Nield for their stylish props and Geoff Hayes for his inspired design.

My editor Muna Reyal is some kind of saint, a brilliant strategist who manages to extract manuscripts from busy authors by a myriad of clever subtle devices. Thank you Muna for your brilliant editing, and most of all, for your patience.

My agent Jacqueline Korn and my publisher Kyle Cathie have been unflinching in their encouragement and support as have my truly wonderful family and staff – for this I am ever grateful.

This paperback edition published in 2008

First published in Great Britain in 2005 by
Kyle Cathie Limited
122 Arlington Road
London NW1 7HP
general.enquiries@kyle-cathie.com   www.kylecathie.com

ISBN: 978 1 85626 761 8

Text © 2005 by Darina Allen, except for p10–11 and wine notes © Tom Doorley
Photography © 2005 by Peter Cassidy

Senior editor **Muna Reyal**
Designer **Geoff Hayes**
Photographer **Peter Cassidy**
Food stylist **Linda Tubby**
Props stylists **Charis White** (pp 24–27, 32, 36, 46–49, 52, 60, 102–105, 107, 190–195, 260–263, 274, 291) and **Roisin Nield**
Copyeditor **Marion Moisy**
Editorial assistant **Cecilia Desmond**
Production **Sha Huxtable and Alice Holloway**

Printed in Singapore by Tien Wah Press

contents

introduction

Entertaining is one of the easiest and most pleasurable things in the world. All it means is that you and some friends or family gather together, share some food and generally enjoy yourselves. But somehow the word seems to invoke more fear than fun. So what I want to do is to show you that that pleasure can come without pain.

The first place to start is with the thought that you are probably more experienced in it than you think you are. If you have friends round for a coffee or a quick drink with a bite to eat, then you are entertaining. Inviting friends to lunch, having an impromptu barbecue on a sunny day or an evening in watching films are all types of entertaining and they don't differ in principle from the more ceremonious social events such as parties or formal dinners.

So whatever the occasion, the *raison d'etre* is to get everyone together and have lots of fun and good conversation. And whether it is a multi-course meal or, in the words of the legendary Elizabeth David, 'an omelette and a glass of wine', you need only follow a few key guidelines.

● Firstly, keep it simple, keep it simple, keep it simple.

● Secondly, and I can't stress this enough, be prepared. Make shopping lists, plan the preparation and cooking time and check that you have enough cutlery and glasses.

● And finally, relax. This is not just so that you can have fun – it's crucial that the hosts are not tense or stressed, as the tension will easily transmit itself to the guests.

So this is my mantra, and while I readily admit that I don't always practise what I preach, I have written this book because I firmly believe that with a little forethought, some good food and a few special touches, anybody can entertain effortlessly and memorably.

choosing food

Because there are as many ways to entertain as there are ways to eat, I have divided this book into styles of party, so that you can choose the food to match your event.

The first chapter is devoted to brunch, because I think this is a brilliant way to entertain a large group of people, particularly families – and it takes care of breakfast and lunch. The chapter on Finger Food will be helpful for drinks parties or buffet meals, but you should also take a look in Starters for more ideas. The recipes in Soups and Salads complement the Starters chapter, but they also make great light meals by themselves.

Then come lots of Quick and Easy Meals, perfect for when you are short of time or need to prepare something with little notice. The recipes in Prepare-ahead Suppers, on the other hand, will help when you have more time to plan but less on the day. Then there are chapters on Slow Food and Festive Meals for special occasions, as well as some fantastic recipes for Formal Suppers, not to forget yummy ideas for a children's party. Portable Food will be useful for barbecues and picnics; this and Foraging are two of my favourite ways to entertain, so you'll find many of my best-loved recipes here. Another chapter is devoted to irresistible Sweet Things, to finish a meal and perfect for a tea party: and there are many lovely options to encourage you to serve A Cheese Course.

Tom Doorley, an inspired wine writer and a good friend, has suggested delicious wines to serve with some tempting menus for each chapter, and I've also included a Drinks chapter with a few suggestions for aperitifs.

I hope you will find all you need in these chapters, but please remember that nothing is carved in stone. You can enjoy experimenting, but the most important thing of all is to pick up the phone, invite people round and have fun.

feel free to mix and match

When you flick through this book you will discover that it includes an eclectic mix of recipes – everything from Irish stew to Moroccan Tagine, from sushi to fajitas, so pick and choose what appeals to you. Having said that, don't throw caution to the wind altogether, be careful not to be too random or your guests will end up with serious indigestion! In general stick to a particular style, be it Asian, Mexican, Moroccan or European. Fajitas followed by Irish stew followed by Tira Misu would clash quite strongly, but you would be safe to mix Thai and Japanese or French with Italian. Or be a bit more adventurous and plan an Asian starter and main course, to be followed by Western dessert.

achieving the 'wow' factor!

Taste at the beginning, taste in the middle and taste at the end – that's the secret of really good food. That and starting off with the finest-quality ingredients. I personally seek out as much organic and free-range

produce as I can get my hands on. Freshness is of paramount importance. Locally produced is also a priority with me – it makes no kind of sense to use jet-lagged food which has travelled halfway across the world, arriving on our shelves days, weeks or in some cases months after it was produced or harvested and therefore containing less flavour and fewer nutrients. When you begin with mass-produced, denatured food you need to be a magician to get it to taste good – and that's when life gets complicated and you have to add twiddles, bows and smarties on top to compensate for the fact that the flavour wasn't there in the first place.

So why not make your job easier and spend a little time sourcing really good, fresh, naturally produced, local food in season? Then it's easy to achieve the 'wow' factor. When you start off with a piece of spanking fresh fish or freshly picked vegetables you have only to cook them simply and they will taste sublime.

how many people?

If you are not planning to use outside help (which is the premise behind this book), six to eight people is the optimum number for a dinner party. Once the numbers go to twelve or fourteen, it is almost essential to have help with the serving and clearing, otherwise the food will be cold and service too slow. You don't have to hire professional help – a local teenager may be thrilled to earn some pocket money and learn some extra skills, or you can rope in your own children. The size of your dining room and table will also dictate the numbers you invite. Don't ask more people than you can seat easily. Alternatively, a buffet or fork supper will remove the problems of service as well as reducing the amount of crockery and cutlery needed.

Choose a menu that can be served easily whatever the circumstances. A mezze or selection of bruschetta can double as finger food and starter, with maybe a little pâté or salmon rillettes. Soup can be served in espresso or cappuccino cups, so – with a bit of strategic washing up between courses – the cups could be used for starter and then for coffee.

cooking for large numbers

Recipes like Tagine of Lamb (see p112) and Spiced Chicken and Red Peppers (p113) are easy to serve for big numbers with rice, cous cous or orzo followed by a big green salad. To finish, it's nice to serve a selection of farmhouse cheese and a dessert buffet. Choose puds that complement each other so that your guests can try them all .

Lots of other recipes in this book are suitable for big numbers, just multiply up the quantities (but note the guidelines under **How much food?** on p9).

cutting corners

Here are a few tips to make entertaining easier.

● Numero uno is to keep your store cupboard well stocked, so that you always have something in reserve in case someone turns up unexpectedly. A number of my recipes can be made using such ingredients; others need only the addition of a few fresh veg or herbs. See p299 for my suggestions on standby ingredients.

● My big break-through came on the day I started to freeze soups, stews, curries and various vegetables and bean stews in small containers. Previously I froze everything in large quantities, but spontaneous entertaining is out of the question if you are faced with a solid iceberg to defrost – stress free it is not. If you know you have a selection of little pots of this and that, it doesn't matter who breezes into your kitchen – you wont be fazed. Simply fill the sink with hot water and pop the sealed containers in to defrost for 8–10 minutes. The contents will slip out of the containers and you can then pop them into a saucepan or casserole on a gentle heat – Thai green or red curry, Italian beef stew, spicy chicken with almonds, mild madras curry are all favourites. By the time the rice is cooked the stew will be bubbling. Scatter with freshly chopped herbs and presto, instant meal.

● Put your most frequently used recipes in a ring binder – divide into starters, mains, puddings and make notes as necessary. In the same folder keep a list of useful contacts – where to get ice or hire glasses as well as carpet cleaners!

● Write quantities for mayonnaise, soda bread, French dressing, frittata, chocolate mousse on the inside of cupboards for when you want to whizz up something in a hurry.

● A herb garden or at least a window box brimming with fresh herbs is a must for easy entertaining. Snip and scatter freshly chopped herbs to transform basic grub instantly into posh nosh.

● Keep a few hens in your garden. Friends will be so enchanted by collecting the eggs that they will be happy to have boiled eggs and soldiers for supper.

● A visit to your local Farmer's Market can yield a variety of delicious foods. You don't have to cook everything from scratch – smoked fish, cured meat, pâtés, farmhouse cheese, crusty bread, homemade cakes and tarts are perfect for easy entertaining.

● If you are entertaining with someone, agree responsibilities ahead of time – who is getting the fish or buying the flowers. On the day, decide who will take coats and offer drinks. Knowing who is supposed to clear the table glaring across the table or kicking under it! If you are entertaining single-handedly, ask a friend if they would mind arriving early to take charge of pouring wine. It is also ok to ask for help in chopping garnishes or bringing plates through.

planning a menu

A good menu is about well-chosen food, but part of that is based on careful thought and preparation.

First decide what sort of event you are hosting. Hopefully the chapters of this book will simplify the process, but here is a summary of the most likely scenarios:

● A formal affair, where you have plenty of time to plan and plenty to prepare.
● A meal where some or all can be prepared in advance, good for post-work dinners.
● An impromptu meal that you can whizz up in minutes using storecupboard ingredients.
● Slow-cooked dishes – these cook long and slowly (in your absence if necessary) to produce a robust, comforting and trouble-free meal.
● A meal specific to an occasion, be it Christmas Day, a children's party or picnic.

Next you need to consider whether you want to serve three courses, all in individual plates, or begin with, say, a mezze where people can help themselves. At the end of many of the chapters I have put together a selection of menu plans in the hope that they will form a good base for you.

With each recipe, I have also given guideline timings for preparation (P) and cooking (C), as well as time required for chilling or marinating. These should help you plan your schedule, but bear in mind that it is difficult to prepare all three courses at the same time. However if one dish needs to go into the oven for an hour, this will give space to prepare another.

If you have small children, it can be a huge effort to get the house ship-shape. If you've got a long list of 'must haves' why not entertain two nights in a row – the flowers will last, the house is looking good and you can prepare twice the amount of food ahead of time and serve the same menu.

menu considerations

The words 'menu planning' strike terror in many people. It sounds complicated and mysterious, but in lots of ways it is just common sense. Here are a few guiding principles to save you from potential pitfalls. In general, it is easiest to decide on a main course first, then choose a starter and dessert to complement it.

The Occasion
This is an important factor when choosing a menu and laying the table. For anniversaries or romantic evenings, you might incorporate a heart-shaped tart or a dish to share. Foreign guests will be intrigued if you cook them a traditional meal. It can also be fun to plan a meal on a particular colour scheme – for example, the colours of your favourite sports team at a victory dinner.

Pleasing Your Guests
For formal or large dinners you may have to do a little subtle research to avoid dishes that your guests are unable to eat, whether for religious, moral or health reasons. As our understanding of food allergies and intolerances grows, it's good to have a repertoire of gluten-free or dairy-free dishes ready to go. Keep a few cartons of beans or vegetable stews in your freezer for emergencies. If you are sending formal invites or emails, ask guests to let you know if they have any dietary restrictions when they RSVP.

Similarly, it is not usually wise to present anything too challenging or unusual to first-time guests. The golden rule is to be considerate: if you are unsure of your guests' tastes, or think that they might be unfamiliar with certain foods, avoid them. Many people find offal off-putting; other don't appreciate very hot curries and other spicy foods. Corn on the cob might present problems for older people and some of my favourite dishes like squid, sea urchins, prawns in the shell and globe artichokes can all be a challenge to tackle.

Pot-luck Parties
New York hostesses have become so frustrated by trying to cater for their guests' specific requirements that they now ask each guest to bring a dish – brilliant idea! This works particularly well for buffet meals, barbecues or participation parties (see p102–107). Among close friends, you could ask each guest to bring a separate course, which not only makes entertaining easy, but also, depending on how tightly it is planned, can produce a completely unexpected menu.

Season and Weather
People need and can digest much heartier meals in winter than in summer, so keep rich soups, stews and cassoulets for chilly days. Cold soups and sunny Mediterranean salads will delight in the summer. I let the seasons choose the ingredients and use locally produced food. In addition to having a better flavour, it helps to narrow the choice and it is usually cheaper than imported food.

Don't forget about simple, everyday foods that are seldom found on restaurant menus, but which lots of people love, e.g. rhubarb, carrigeen moss, swede and turnips.

Budget

Given a bit of imagination it is perfectly possible to prepare exciting meals on a small budget. There is no need to splash out on all three courses — lots of posh nosh can be created with ingredients from your storecupboard. Cheaper cuts of meat make succulent braises and slow-cooked dishes. Egg-based dishes such as frittatas are inexpensive and amazingly versatile.

Consider the Number of Dishes

The number of dishes you choose will depend on various factors. The first is the skill of the cook: don't be over-ambitious and don't cook anything new and complicated for guests. Make sure the menu is realistic. I know it sounds very 'back to school' but it's a terrific idea to jot down an order of work. Think through the menu to see whether you need any special equipment. If you are entertaining single-handed or with very little help, plan the menu so that you can prepare as much as possible in advance, particularly any complex dishes. The number of dishes you need will also depend on how you plan to serve the meal, whether formal or informal plate service or a buffet.

Balance

This is often the most perplexing element of planning a menu. Try to provide a contrast of ingredients, texture and flavour. This sounds obvious but it's surprisingly easy to unwittingly repeat foods in your menu, particularly common ingredients such as eggs. On the face of it, this menu below looks balanced enough:
Cheese Souffle
French Onion Tart
Tomato and Mint Salad, Green Salad
Crème Caramel with Caramel Shards
but each guest will be consuming about five eggs in the course of the meal!

The idea of a starter is to whet the appetite with something light and delicious. It sets the mood for the rest of the meal, but it ought not to be so substantial as to fill people up before the main course.

It's also easier on the cook and more practical to use different cooking methods, so, for example, avoid grilling everything. Another easy pitfall is serving sauces which seem to be different but have the same basis, such as a starter containing mayonnaise followed by fish and tartare sauce.

Serve a green salad with lunch and dinner. It has magical properties and makes people feel less full — leaving room for pud! If the first two courses are rich or creamy, consider a lighter dessert, perhaps something citrus-based to wake things up.

Colour and Contrast

In addition to the 'balance' factors mentioned above, don't overlook the question of colour. Try not to repeat colours unless you are deliberately working to a colour scheme. In particular, guard against an all-white plate e.g. Haddock with Dijon Mustard Sauce, Buttered Cucumber and Scallion Champ — sounds delicious but it will look bland. A little Tomato Fondue or at least a sprig of chervil, fennel or watercress would make all the difference.

It also makes for more interesting eating if there is a juxtaposition of texture in the food — crisp with creamy, e.g. buttered crumbs on fish pie or croûtons, with creamy soup.

Contrasts of flavour are also important, e.g. mild with spicy — Cucumber raita with curry. Sharp with bland — Blue cheese sauce on pasta or salad. Sweet with sour — Carrot and apple cruditées with sweet-sour dressing.

Seasonings

Try not to get carried away with chillies and spices unless you feel like a hot fest! You may want to confine strong flavouring or spices to one dish in the menu unless you are cooking a specifically Indian or Chinese meal, in which case make sure not to repeat the same spices in each course.

Garnishing

We 'eat' with our eyes, so it is crucial to present a meal well. A herb garden will mean edible herb flowers, but remember the maxim — flavour is of paramount importance and any garnish should be relevant and edible.

cheat

As I said earlier, don't feel you have to cook everything from scratch. A plate of good charcuterie with olives with piquillo pepper and country bread followed by a tart or chocolate confection, bought from your local deli, will look and taste great!

how much food?

All the recipes indicate the number of servings. For large numbers just multiply up. If you're doing four or five times a recipe, for soup for example, you can usually cut down on the butter or olive oil for sweating the vegetables; otherwise calculate carefully, stick to the recipe and don't forget to taste.

timing

Planning is everything and lists are crucial. Think about when you need to buy your ingredients, particularly the ones that need to be fresh. Fish, herbs and flowers should always be bought on the day if possible.

Little Touches

● Look out for tiny containers for butter, salt and pepper — little night light holders, tiny ramekins, even teeny terracotta flower pots. Oyster shells also look great.

● Serve tiny tapenade or pesto fingers or square sandwiches as an accompaniment with each bowl of soup.

● Offer a wedge of nougat, halva or fudge with an espresso at the end of the meal.

choosing wine and drinks

by Tom Doorley

'Red with carpet, white with lino,' was the wine advice given in Katherine Whitehorn's *Cooking in a Bedsit*, and it remains sound. A great deal of nonsense is spouted about matching food and wine, while most normal human beings tend to resort to the time-honoured formula of using whatever happens to be in the house.

That is not to say that our enjoyment of food and of wine will not be enhanced by using a bit of logic. It stands to reason, for example, that if you serve a dish with a wine from the same region, it has a good chance of being a pleasant combination; in Europe, regional food and regional wines have grown up together over centuries.

It also stands to reason that rich food will respond well to a crisp, acidic wine, just as mackerel, say, goes with gooseberries. And big, hearty, spicy stews and casseroles taste good with wines that are…well, big and hearty and spicy. Nobody is going to win the Nobel prize for pointing this out.

Having said that, in most cases, matching food and wine is a rather hit and miss affair, or, at best a question of getting it as right as possible. Marriages made in heaven are few, but there are some worth bearing in mind. Sauvignon Blanc wines work brilliantly with very ripe goat's cheese, and sweet dessert wines are superb with Roquefort. The Thai flavours of ginger, galangal and coriander seem to be even more vibrant with a dry Australian Riesling.

Roast lamb or beef, especially if cooked rare, takes the edge off red Bordeaux and Burgundy, while pork needs something crispier and juicier like a good Beaujolais or a Chianti. Roast chicken and turkey often work better with a ripe Chardonnay (either from the New World or from the more expensive bits of Burgundy) than with many reds.

And while I might prefer salmon with a Chablis or a dry Alsace wine there's no doubt that some light red wines go well with it (especially Chinon and others from the Loire); so let's just forget all the old 'rules'

For white wines that are crisp enough to cut richness – say in oysters – it's probably best to look to Europe because New World examples tend to be riper; that's part of their appeal. A good Muscadet or Chablis will work a treat but so will any dry, zesty white wine from Verdicchio to Albarinho.

what of the new world?

New World whites, especially the new wave ones made from Viognier, Verdelho, Marsanne and other off-beat grape varieties are often bigger on fruit than acidity but while they might not cut rich dishes they seem very much at home with fusion and Pacific Rim cooking.

New World reds, generally speaking, are rich, robust and packed with fruit, a style that suits them to equally robust food. In addition to the more familiar Cabernets and Shirazes, Malbec from Argentina, Carmanere from Chile and Pinotage from South Africa all seem expressly made for a steaming casserole. Many of them not only go well with rare roast beef but can also tackle a dollop of horseradish head-on.

organic wines

While organic meat, vegetables and fruit are becoming almost commonplace, the wine world is lagging behind. In fact, organic wines are much the same as conventionally produced wines: there are some good ones and some bad ones. The world's largest producer of (very good) organic wines is Bonterra of Medocino, California, which is owned by Fetzer. Bonterra wines are widely available. If you are concerned about sustainability, concentrate on small producers.

champagne vs. sparkling

Non-vintage Champagne, especially the famous brands, is generally over-priced (although Darina has a fondness for Veuve Clicquot). Sparkling wines, often made in exactly the same way, can offer more for less. Prosecco, from Italy, is possibly the best value of all – and if you add a dash of peach juice you have a Bellini! Cava from Spain can be great too, but if you want something made from the same grapes as Champagne, try Australia, New Zealand or California. Names to watch include Green Point, Lindauer, Deutz, Jansz and Mumm. Champagne from individual growers is often half the price of the grandes marques and most traditional wine merchants will stock at least one.

but does it have to be wine?

We are gradually waking up to the fact that beer and cider can be worthy accompaniments to food. Steak and kidney pudding could not have a better companion than traditional English bitter or other dark ales, and these go well with roast meats too. Lagers – not the bland, big brand ones – can tackle hot spices but will also work with seafood, especially crab. Guinness, the doyen of stouts, is as good with oysters as the best Chablis. And it's a great deal cheaper. A fresh, citrus-scented beer like Hoegaarden is excellent with simply cooked fish.

Cider has a well-known affinity with pork, both in the pot and on the table, but its refreshing sharpness (especially if it's a dry version) can often have an almost wine-like quality. Again, seafood is a good companion, especially if the dish features coriander, lime or ginger. Cider from artisan producers, in the West Country or Normandy, is what to look for, not the strictly commercial stuff.

calculating quantities

Choosing wine, beer or cider for entertaining will always be an art rather than a science.

The same could be said of judging how much you are going to need, but it is a little simpler.

It is always best to err on the side of generosity, so although you don't want to assume that all your guests are dipsomaniacs, have too much rather than just enough. As a rough guide, allow a half bottle of wine per head for the main course (a bottle equates to five glasses) and a single glass of whatever is being served with the starter. Dessert wines are a different matter; some guests simply don't like them and those who do usually have a small glass and perhaps a modest top-up. This means that a bottle will serve five or six people comfortably. However, one of the secrets of stress-free entertaining is to calculate as outlined above but to buy more as a precaution.

what about budget?
As to budget, this will depend on the occasion, but broadly speaking I think we can divide entertaining with food and wine into three categories. For the informal supper around the kitchen table, there is no need to go above £7 a bottle, although a dessert wine might merit a couple of pounds extra. The rather more formal lunch or dinner, provided you don't feel the need to show off, weighs in at around £10 to £12 a bottle, while the very special occasion will merit as much as you want to spend. However, as a guide, I would suggest pushing the boat out to around £20 or £25. Although wine does indeed often taste better the more you spend (simply because the winemaker is getting a bigger cut), there are limits. Above this kind of price wine can simply get silly.

standby wines
If you want to be prepared for all eventualities, consider putting together a mini-cellar. You will need a bottle of fizz (Champagne, if you wish, but a good sparkler such as Lindauer or Green Point will do fine). Then a couple of dependable whites which will cover most of the bases: Macon, Chablis or a dry Riesling perhaps. Then a couple (or more) of red: a really good Côtes du Rhone is suitably flexible. Or you may want a contrast of styles: some fleshy young Beaujolais cru such as Brouilly or Moulin-à-Vent on the one hand, and maybe a Chilean Carmanere Reserva or Oz Grenache/Syrah blend on the other. Bear in mind, incidentally, that a good, fruity, dry rosé will go with just about anything. Cover the dessert wine possibilities with a Late Harvest Riesling or Semillon and a bottle of good tawny port that won't need decanting (Taylor or Fonseca 20 Year Old are superb and will keep).

bear in mind
Entertaining with wine is pretty simple. Take some care in choosing and don't talk much about it. Wine, for most people, is great to drink but mind-numbingly boring to discuss. If someone asks about a wine they want to know where to buy it, not the details of the vineyard.

There are some things that no wine can take: horseradish, cranberries, excessive sweetness and the vindaloo end of the curry scale are all beyond the ability of wine to cope.

Remember to chill the white in good time, but don't over-chill; you want to be able to taste the wine. Room temperature is fine for red.

Decanting is only necessary for aged wines with sediment, but it can make other wines taste better simply because it aerates them. Odd as it may seem, this applies to whites as well as reds, so if you have both the time and the decanters it may be worth doing.

Pulling corks in advance is a good idea from the point of view of convenience but, contrary to common belief, it won't make the wine taste any different.

Provide lots of bottled water (sparkling and still) and have something, such as elderflower cordial or homemade lemonade, for the drivers and teetotallers. Almost everyone enjoys food but wine is a different matter.

notes on wine
Wine is a very personal thing so do please bear in mind that the suggestions I make in this book are just that: suggestions. I think they are worth trying, and they certainly work for me. If you cannot easily get hold of the suggested wine, try something in a similar style. Wine shops, as distinct from supermarkets, can appear a little daunting but most of them will respond very well to a request for advice and some of them really do enjoy discussing menus. You may end up with something quite different from what you were looking for but a good wine merchant will want you to come back and their suggestions may well be very sensible. Needless to say, if you have time for a dry run (not, perhaps, the most appropriate phrase in the circumstances) there is no substitute for trying out wine and food matches before springing them on your guests.

tom's top tips
● Don't be a perfectionist. There's no need to strive for the perfect match. Good food and good wine is what it's all about.

● Be bountiful. Err on the side of generosity. Buy too much wine rather than too little. It will keep.

● Get in the pink. A good dry rosé makes a perfect aperitif and goes well with virtually anything savoury.

creating atmosphere

Once you have chosen the food, it's time to think about creating an atmosphere. This is another mysterious subject, but actually is nothing more than a few simple touches. The individual chapters of this book have suggestions specific to each occasion, but here are some general tips.

ornamentation

Make an effort to dress up a room or table. Look around for inspiration – lots of night lights surrounded by pretty shells or pebbles collected from the beach are adorable. Take inspiration from the seasons – dried autumn leaves, nuts, berries and fruit are easy to arrange expressively; Spanish chestnuts in their shells look wonderfully dramatic. Spices such as star anise and cinnamon also smell delicious in the winter months. Use the natural beauty of globe artichokes, pomegranates (whole or halved) and figs. For a party, hang twists of ribbon along a picture rail or around window frames.

If you collect knick-knacks from trips abroad, you could use them to recreate a holiday dinner – tin figures from Mexico, pottery chickens from Guatemala, pewter and bamboo from south-east Asia.

Flowers

To me, flowers are the simplest way to add colour, scent and glamour to an evening. There is so much to choose from, and the right flower can instantly change the mood of a room. Be creative about what you use as vases – try empty jam jars, glass bottles or recycled tins – and where you place them. Tie posies with raffia for a table centrepiece or use single stems as place settings.

In summer, a bowl of gorgeous fragrant old roses in full bloom is irresistible but petals floating in a bowl or scattered on the table also create a sensuous and slightly decadent effect. Float a few flower heads or blossoms in a low dish; hellebores are particularly lovely and last much longer this way.

Check out florists' websites for inspiration. For formal arrangements, your local florist should be able to create something spectacular for your table.

Lighting

Flickery candles create a magical atmosphere in a way that no other lighting can. A tall candelabra on a long table looks wonderfully elegant but even cheap and cheerful tea lights arranged in a line, circle or diamond draw gasps of admiration and you can get funky holders in different shapes and formations. Resist the temptation to have scented candles – most are overpoweringly fragrant.

Look out for candleholders – tin, enamel, pottery, glass or edible containers such as pumpkins or squashes. Outdoor lighting along an avenue or path creates excitement and anticipation – at its simplest just night lights in jam jars or thick candles in brown paper bags with some sand in the base look great Fairy lanterns slung from trees are pretty in any season. Make your own by piercing holes in tin cans to form a pattern.

Remember never to leave candles unattended either indoors or outdoors.

Strings of fairy lights now come in a range of shapes and colours – flowers, chillies, stars, bulbs – and you can drape them around tables, chairs, walls, trees and plants.

If your indoor lighting is a bit harsh, try bringing in lamps from your bedroom or simply replacing the bulb with a softer light.

Table Cloths

One of the funkiest table settings I've ever seen consisted of a 'cloth' of newspapers with flowers arranged in a line of fruit tins down the centre. Lots of coloured glasses, tin plates and mismatched cutlery gave a cool look.

Plain white or coloured sheets can solve the problem of an oversized table, while overlays of pretty materials, scarves, shawls, sari fabric or sarongs make attractive 'camouflage'.

place settings

These can be as formal or subversive as you like. Fabric, paper, glass and slate all make brilliant table mats and if they are home made, you can scribble or elegantly calligraph each guest's name or a witty, or rude, message. Some friends of mine made round place mats from cardboard and drew brilliant cartoon pics of each of the guests, which have now become collector's items. Bake cup cakes or shortbread biscuits and ice the guest's name on each. And simplest of all, tie a luggage label with the guest's name on around wine glasses.

crockery and cutlery

In this day and age you certainly don't need to have matching crockery and cutlery to have fun. Hunt out antiques, or pieces from around the world. Pile them into a funky container or terracotta pot so that your guests can help themselves.

getting the party going

when the guests arrive

What if, despite your best intentions, the guests arrive before you are fully prepared or even dressed? If you are running late it's a smart idea to get dressed and lay out some glasses, drinks and nibbles in plenty of time. Then, when the doorbell rings, take a slow, deep breath, welcome your guests into the kitchen, pour some drinks (don't forget yourself) and drink a toast to the yummy dinner which is underway!

Spend money on the aperitifs. Something bubbly always gets the evening going – Champagne, sparkling wine or Prosecco are divine. For a really special occasion, why not splash out and hire a portable bar, complete with bar tenders, to create a range of cocktails especially for you? Or send your partner to a cocktail class the weekend before.

Passing around some nibbles helps guests to relax and feel comfortable. If the nibbles are reasonably substantial they can double up as a first course.

If you need to introduce your guests to each other, give them a snippet of interesting info to get the conversation started: *'This is my accountant friend Ben who climbed Carrantwohill last week, meet Clarissa who is crazy about chickens, but is an airline pilot in real life…'*

Keep an eye out for people looking a little lonely and reintroduce as required. Asking them to top up glasses or pass around nibbles for you is a good way to get them talking to people.

Provide a room as a cloakroom and make sure it has a mirror. If children arrive unexpectedly, don't bat an eyelid. Dig out magic markers or crayons and paper. Better still, involve them – ask them to help you to pass around nibbles. If all else fails, pop them in front of the TV with a film or cartoon.

music

Try to find some time before the event to choose a stack of CDs so that you don't spend all evening hunting for the next one. If you have an MP3 player, set up some playlists for the occasion.

party games

Parties are the perfect opportunity to play some old-fashioned games. Charades and spin the bottle are always fun and there are lots of traditional games like Cluedo and poker. But how about a few more physical games to burn off some dinner.

The Cereal Box Game

For this test of agility you will need a light cardboard box, preferably taller than it is wide – an old cereal box is perfect. The box is placed on the floor and guests must pick the box up with their teeth, with the following limitations:

1 They must not touch the ground with any part of their body other than the soles of their feet.

2 They must not touch the box with any part of their body other than their mouth.
3 If they knock the box over, they're out!

Once all the guests have made their attempt, a strip is torn off the box – the depth of the strip depends on how challenging the previous round was. The field is whittled down to the most elastic and persevering of your guests!

a theatre supper

Some opera-buff friends invite us occasionally to what they call a 'Theatre Supper'. It goes like this.

Guests are requested to arrive at 6.30pm, not before and certainly not after! Everyone dresses in black tie, theatre hats etc. We have an aperitif before curtain up, then we repair to the drawing room where we watch the first act of some wonderful opera on our hosts' large-screen TV, seated in comfortable sofas and armchairs. At the interval we go to the dining room for our first course. Another act, another course and so on, four courses and coffee. The finale is at 11.30pm – a fun way to entertain music-loving friends and a formula that could easily be adapted to show a film, play or sporting event.

finishing touches

Make sure you have the number of a local, licensed cab firm to hand.

If a guest becomes tiresome, be polite but firm. Draw him or her away from the rest of the party to avoid drawing attention. A walk outside always helps to calm people down.

If you need to wrap up the party, the most subtle way is to stop filling people's glasses. Other more blatant tactics include turning off the music, turning up the lighting or simply asking if anyone wants to help with the washing up. Failing all else, yawn and pretend to fall asleep in an armchair.

a big brunch

Brunch is a great meal for family get-togethers and it combines two meals in one – the epitome of easy entertaining. It's also perfect for entertaining children – I feed them first and let them run off and play, before we adults settle down to our coffee and newspapers. The recipes in this chapter are a tempting mix of hearty dishes like kedgeree and eggs benedict as well as fruity compotes and sinful chocolate and orange muffins, and should see you through till teatime.

Crunchy Granola

MAKES 20 SERVINGS   (**P**: 5 MINS/**C**: 30 MINS)

350g (12oz) honey
225ml (8fl oz) sunflower oil
450g (1lb) oat flakes
200g (7oz) barley flakes
200g (7oz) wheat flakes
110g (4oz) rye flakes
150g (5oz) raisins or sultanas
150g (5oz) hazelnuts or cashew nuts, split
  and roasted
25g (1oz) sunflower seeds, toasted
50g (2oz) dried apricots, chopped
50g (2oz) dates, stoned and chopped (optional)
75g (3oz) wheat germ and/or millet flakes

Preheat the oven to 180°C/350°F/gas mark 4.

In a saucepan, mix the honey and oil together and heat just sufficiently to melt the honey. Mix the oat, barley, wheat and rye flakes together and then pour in the honey/oil mixture. Stir until the grains are coated. Spread thinly on two baking trays.

Bake for 20–30 minutes, turning frequently, until just golden and toasted, not roasted – ensure the edges don't burn. Leave the mixture to cool.

Mix in the raisins or sultanas, nuts, seeds, apricots, dates (if using) and wheat germ and/or millet flakes.

The granola will keep for 1–2 weeks, stored in a screw-top jar or sealed plastic container.

Crunchy Granola Layered in a Glass

SERVES 2   (**P**: 5 MINS)

225ml (8fl oz) homemade yogurt (see p33)
2 tablespoons honey
110g (4oz) granola (see recipe above)
110g (4oz) blueberries, raspberries,
  strawberries or even sliced banana
sprigs of mint (optional)

2 straight squat glasses, 13cm (5in) tall

This is a cool way to serve breakfast in a glass – bursting with goodness and totally yummy.

Mix the yogurt and honey together. Divide about half the granola between the two glasses, then top with half of the yogurt. Sprinkle the berries over the top, retaining a few for garnish, then add the remaining granola and finally add the rest of the yogurt.

Garnish with the reserved berries, and perhaps a sprig of mint. Provide long-handled spoons and tuck in.

Fruity Smoothies

Mix and match to your heart's content.

Banana and Yogurt Smoothie
SERVES 1–2   (**P**: 5 MINS)

1 ripe banana
225ml (8fl oz) natural yogurt (see p33)
1 teaspoon honey (optional)

Peel the banana, chop coarsely, then blend with the other ingredients in a liquidiser until smooth.

Pour into glasses and serve immediately.

Mango Smoothie
SERVES 1–2   (**P**: 5 MINS)

Follow the recipe above, but use mango instead of banana. You'll need about 150g (5oz). For a more Indian flavour, add ¼ teaspoon freshly ground cardamom pods. Or add the seeds from 1 passion fruit for a marriage made in heaven.

Mango and Banana Smoothie
SERVES 2–3   (**P**: 10 MINS)

350ml (12fl oz) freshly squeezed orange juice
1 chopped mango
1 banana
225ml (8fl oz) natural yogurt

Put all the ingredients in a liquidiser and whizz until smooth. Taste and add a little honey if necessary.

Raspberry and Nectarine Smoothie

Another delicious combination – add 25–50g (1-2oz) fresh raspberries and 1 ripe nectarine.

Glebe House Eggs Benedict

SERVES 4   (P: 5 MINS/C: 20 MINS)

Jean Perry's cafe, Glebe House near Baltimore in West Cork, is a gem. The spinach come from the organic garden, the eggs from his happy, lazy hens.

8 free-range, organic eggs
4 thick slices of homemade white yeast bread
  (see p34)
butter

For the creamed spinach:
900g (2lb) fresh spinach
225–350ml (8-12fl oz) cream
salt and freshly ground pepper
freshly grated nutmeg

roux, optional (see p139)

First make the creamed spinach. Put the leaves into a heavy saucepan on a very low heat and cover tightly. After a few minutes, stir and replace the lid. When the spinach is cooked, after about 5–8 minutes, strain off the copious amount of liquid that has been released and press between two plates until almost dry. Chop roughly and return to the pan. Increase the heat, add the cream to the spinach and bring to the boil, stir well and thicken with a little roux if desired (see p139); continue stirring until the spinach has absorbed most of the cream. Season with salt, pepper and freshly grated nutmeg to taste. (If you wish, the creamed spinach may be cooked ahead of time and reheated.)

Next poach the eggs. Bring a small pan of water to the boil. Reduce the heat, swirl the water with a ladle, crack open an egg and slip it gently into the centre of the whirlpool. Cook for 3–4 minutes until the white is set and the yolk still soft and runny – the water should not boil again, but bubble very gently just below boiling point.

Toast and butter the bread and place on four warm plates. Spread the creamed spinach over the toast and top each portion with two poached eggs. Serve with freshly ground pepper and a few flakes of Maldon sea salt – divine.

Scrambled Eggs and Variations

SERVES 4   (P: 5 MINS/C: 5 MINS)

Simple scrambled eggs are always an option for a stress-free brunch or supper, when one has unexpected guests, or when one feels like plain, comforting food. You can add a huge variety of ingredients – chopped and seasoned tomatoes, pieces of freshly cooked asparagus and smoked bacon or prosciutto cooked in olive oil. Cold scrambled egg with chives makes the best egg sandwiches.

8 free-range, organic eggs
4 tablespoons creamy milk
salt and freshly ground pepper
generous knob of butter
To serve: warm buttered toast or fresh soda
  bread (see p36)

Break the eggs into a bowl, add the milk and season. Whisk well until the whites and yolks are thoroughly mixed. Put a knob of butter into a cold saucepan, pour in the egg mixture and cook over a low heat, stirring continuously with a flat-bottomed wooden spoon, until the egg has scrambled into soft, creamy curds. Serve immediately on warm plates, with lots of warm buttered toast or fresh soda bread.

Scrambled Eggs with Wild Smoked Salmon
A few seconds before the scrambled egg is fully cooked, add 4–6 tablespoons diced smoked salmon, stir once or twice, and sprinkle with a little chopped parsley.

Scrambled Eggs with Tarragon and Basil or Chives
A few seconds before the scrambled egg is fully cooked, add 2 teaspoons chopped tarragon and basil or 1–2 teaspoons chives and stir once or twice.

Scrambled Eggs with Chorizo
Cook 50g (2oz) diced chorizo in 1 tablespoon extra virgin olive oil until it begins to become crispy and the fat runs. Drain. A few seconds before the scrambled egg is fully cooked, add the chorizo and 2 teaspoons chopped parsley and stir once or twice.

Indian Scrambled Eggs

SERVES 4   (P: 10 MINS/C: 10 MINS)

25g (1oz) butter
1 small onion, finely chopped
1/2–1 teaspoon peeled and finely grated
  fresh ginger
1 green chilli, deseeded and chopped
1/4 teaspoon ground turmeric
2 teaspoons ground cumin

2 very ripe tomatoes, chopped
8 large free-range, organic eggs
salt and freshly ground black pepper
2 tablespoons chopped coriander leaves
To serve: paratha, naan bread or toast

Melt the butter in a medium sauté pan over a medium heat. Add the onion and cook for 2 minutes or until soft. Add the ginger, chilli, turmeric, cumin and tomatoes. Stir and cook for 3–4 minutes or until the tomatoes soften.

Meanwhile whisk the eggs and season. Add to the pan and stir gently until the eggs scramble, then add the coriander. Serve immediately with paratha, naan bread or toast.

Pinhead Oatmeal Porridge

SERVES 8   (P: OVERNIGHT/C: 10 MINS)

Pinhead oatmeal, or steel-cut oats, is quite simply a feast and a perfect GI breakfast. We eat it with rich creamy organic milk from our Jersey cows, and some soft brown sugar.

310g (11oz) pinhead oatmeal
1/2 teaspoon salt
To serve: pouring cream or rich milk, and soft
   brown sugar

The night before, soak the oatmeal in 225ml (8fl oz) of cold water in a saucepan. On the day, bring 675ml (23fl oz) water to the boil, then add to the oatmeal. Cook on a low heat, stirring continuously, until the water comes to the boil. Cover and simmer for 15–20 minutes, stirring occasionally. Stir in the salt. Cover again and set aside overnight; the oatmeal will absorb all the water.

The next morning, reheat over a low heat, adding a little more water if necessary to make it smooth. Serve with cream or rich milk, and some soft brown sugar.

Ballymaloe Strawberry Muesli

SERVES 8   (P: 20 MINS)

This is a huge favourite with all our family and friends – it's delicious, made in minutes and will keep you going through the morning. We vary the fruit through the seasons – in the summer strawberries, raspberries, loganberries and blueberries and grated Cox's Orange or Egremont Russet apples in the autumn.

6 heaped tablespoons rolled oatmeal
225g (8oz) fresh strawberries
2 teaspoons honey

To serve: pouring cream and soft brown sugar

Soak the oatmeal in 8 tablespoons water for 10–15 minutes. Mash the strawberries roughly with a fork and mix with the oatmeal. Sweeten to taste with honey; a couple of teaspoons is usually enough but it depends on how sweet the strawberries are.

Serve with pouring cream and some soft brown sugar.

Freshly Squeezed Juices

It goes without saying that fresh juices come from freshly squeezed fruit, not from freshly opened packets or cans! Drink the juice soon after making it as the amount of vitamin C decreases after being exposed to air. If the juice has to be made ahead, pour it into dark bottles and fill right to the top.

Choose from:
orange juice
mandarin or tangerine juice
citrus orange juice: a mixture of grapefruit,
   orange, tangerine, blood orange, ugli fruit, etc.
apple* juice
ruby grapefruit juice
carrot* and orange juice
carrot,* apple and ginger juice
pineapple** and orange juice
beetroot, orange and ginger juice

Cut the citrus fruit around the equator and juice by hand or in an electric citrus juicer. Many other types of fruit will need to be chopped and then juiced in a centrifuge.

Experiment with different combinations.

* Use a centrifuge
** Use a liquidiser and strain

Breakfast Burrito with Tomato and Coriander Salsa and Home Fries

MAKES 6   (P: 15 MINS/C: 5 MINS)

6 large (25cm/10in diameter) flour tortillas
175g (6oz) Cheddar cheese, grated
3-6 mushroom and chorizo omelettes
   (see p108 and add some mushrooms and
   chorizo that have been lightly cooked in
   extra virgin olive oil)
Frijoles de Olla , see below
6 tablespoons Tomato and Coriander Salsa
   (see p294)
salt and freshly ground pepper
To serve: soured cream, tomato and coriander
   salsa (see p294), roughly chopped fresh
   coriander leaves, and home fries (see below)

Preheat the oven to 180°C/350°F/gas mark 4. Wrap the tortillas in aluminium foil and warm them in the oven while you make the omelettes. Alternatively, heat them for a few seconds on each side in a hot frying pan.

Just before you assemble the burrito, sprinkle a small handful of grated cheese over the centre of each warm tortilla. Top with half an omelette – if someone is really hungry, go for it and give them a whole omelette. Add a generous tablespoon of Mexican beans and some salsa. Season to taste. Fold over the sides and roll into a sausage-like wrap.

Transfer to a warm plate, spoon a generous portion of soured cream on top, scatter generously with tomato and coriander salsa and sprinkle with some fresh coriander leaves. Serve a portion of home fries on the side.

Frijoles de Olla (Mexican Beans)

SERVES 6–8   (P: OVERNIGHT/C: 2 HOURS)

Beans cooked simply like this and the Frijoles Refritos (Refried Beans) that are made from them are virtually a staple in Mexico, served at almost every meal including breakfast. They keep well and taste even better next day or the day after.

450g (1lb) dried black beans, red kidney or
pinto beans
1–2 tablespoons. good-quality lard or butter
1 small onion, chopped
1 teaspoon salt approximately (may take more
   depending on the beans)

The day before, cover the beans generously with cold water and soak overnight. Alternatively if you are in a hurry, bring the beans to the boil for 3–4 minutes, then take off the heat and leave aside for 1 hour or so. Drain the beans, cover with fresh water, add the lard or butter and onion. Bring to the boil and simmer gently for 1–2 hours depending on the beans. About 30 minutes before the end of the cooking time add the salt. Keep an eye on the beans while they cook, they should always be covered with liquid. When they are cooked the beans should be completely soft and the liquid slightly thick and soupy.

Refried Beans

These can accompany many snacks including tacos and Mexican Scrambled Eggs. The texture can be soupy or a thickish purée.

50–75g (2–3oz) best-quality pork lard or butter
1 medium onion, finely chopped
225g (8oz) Mexican beans

Heat the lard or butter in a heavy frying pan and cook the onion until soft and brown. Increase the heat and add about a third of the beans and their broth to the pan and cook over a high heat mashing them as you stir with a wooden spoon, or you could even use a potato masher. Gradually add the rest of the beans little by little until you have a soft or thick purée. Taste and season with salt if necessary. Although this sounds as though it might be a lengthy business it only takes about 5–6 minutes. Refried Beans keep well and may be reheated many times.

Home Fries

SERVES 6   (P: 5 MINS/C: 10 MINS)

3 tablespoons sunflower oil
1 medium onion, coarsely chopped
700g (1½lb) potatoes, chopped in 6mm (⅓in)
   dice (no need to peel new potatoes)
salt and freshly ground pepper
1 teaspoon freshly roasted and ground cumin
   seeds (optional)

Heat the oil in a wide non-stick frying pan, add the onion and cook on a low heat until soft and slightly coloured. Transfer to a plate.

Increase the heat, add the potatoes to the pan (add more oil if necessary to stop them sticking) and fry, turning frequently, for 10–15 minutes until cooked and slightly crispy.

Season well with salt, freshly ground pepper and ground cumin seeds (if using). Return the onion to the pan and mix well through the potatoes.

Serve with the burrito or with other brunch dishes.

Breakfast Panini

SERVES 4   (**P:** 10 MINS/**C:** 40 MINS)

1 frittata (see p117) omelette or 4 fried eggs
4–8 rashers of organic bacon
4–8 flat mushrooms
salt and freshly ground pepper
4 very ripe tomatoes
pinch of sugar
4 panini rolls, focaccia or ciabatta

Alternative fillings:
crispy bacon and baked beans
sausage, mushrooms and apple sauce
kipper and scrambled egg or frittata
mature Cheddar cheese, smoky bacon and
  sun-blush tomatoes
crispy bacon, black pudding and apple sauce

First make the frittata or fry the eggs.

Cook the bacon rashers until crisp and golden (I prefer to cook them on a frying pan rather than under the grill), then transfer to a plate and keep warm.

Fry the flat mushrooms in the bacon fat and season with salt and freshly ground pepper.

Slice the tomatoes and season with salt, freshly ground pepper and a pinch of sugar.

Preheat a sandwich toaster. Cut the panini in two, but do not slice all the way through – keep them attached at one side. Put a slice of frittata, omelette or fried egg on the base of each one, top with a few slices of tomato, then some bacon and finally 1–2 mushrooms. Close the panini and toast for 3–4 minutes.

Alternatively, warm the panini, then fill and eat immediately.

French Toast Fingers with Citrus Marmalade Butter

SERVES 4–6   (P: 10 MINS/C: 5 MINS)

4 free-range, organic eggs
225ml (8fl oz) full-cream milk
2 tablespoons sugar
1 teaspoon vanilla extract
12 thick slices of best-quality white yeast bread
clarified butter (see p108), for frying
icing sugar, for dusting

For the marmalade butter:
110g (4oz) butter, slightly softened
2–3 tablespoons marmalade, chopped

First make the marmalade butter. Cream the butter and mix in the marmalade.

To make the French toast, whisk the eggs well in a bowl with the milk, sugar and vanilla extract. Cut the bread into rectangular pieces and soak in batches in the eggy milk until well saturated but not falling apart.

Heat a large, preferably non-stick frying pan over a medium heat and add a little clarified butter. Cook the soaked bread fingers in batches until golden brown, about 1 minute per side. Serve immediately, or keep warm in the oven.

Serve the French toast on a warmed plate, sprinkled with a little sieved icing sugar and accompanied with the marmalade butter.

Other good things to serve with French toast
Summer berries and crème fraîche or sugared strawberries
Sliced bananas and chopped walnuts
Crispy bacon and maple syrup or honey

American Buttermilk Pancakes with Crispy Bacon and Maple Syrup

Makes 14 x 7.5cm (3in) pancakes
          (P: 5 MINS/C: 10 MINS)

These are incredibly moreish and it's so difficult to know when to stop!

225ml (8fl oz) buttermilk
1 free-range, organic egg
10g (1/2oz) butter, melted
75g (3oz) plain white flour
good pinch of salt
1 teaspoon bicarbonate of soda
clarified butter (see p108)

To serve: butter, 12–18 pieces of crispy streaky bacon, maple syrup

Mix the buttermilk, egg and butter in a large bowl until smooth and blended. Sift the flour, salt and bicarbonate of soda together, then stir into the buttermilk until the ingredients are just combined – don't worry about the lumps. Do not overmix or the pancakes will be heavy.

Heat a heavy iron or non-stick frying pan until medium hot. Grease with a little clarified butter. Spoon 2 generous tablespoons of batter on to the centre of the pan and spread slightly with the back of the spoon to a round about 17.5cm (3in) across. Cook until bubbles rise and break on the top of the pancake (about a minute). Flip over gently and cook the other side until pale golden. Transfer to a plate, cover with a tea towel or aluminium foil and continue making pancakes in the same way until all the batter is used up.

Spread each pancake with butter. Serve a stack of three with crispy streaky bacon and maple syrup. Alternatively, serve the pancakes with loganberry jam, soured cream and sausages.

Cornmeal Pancakes
Follow the above recipe, but substitute 25g (1oz) cornmeal for 25g (1oz) of the plain flour.

a family brunch

I adore serving brunch. This is a leisurely meal for me and I like to have lots of food ready so we can munch our way through hot savoury dishes, warm fresh bread and flaky pastries, all the while catching up with the week's events.

Mid-morning I pop a couple of loaves of soda bread and a Spotted Dog into the Aga. I lay the table and fill little bowls with homemade jam, marmalade and local honey. Then I arrange some strawberry muesli, toasted granola, maybe a breakfast fruit salad with a bowl of thick unctuous yogurt out on the old marble work top in the kitchen.

I like to present the muesli in a large glass bowl, showing off the lovely fruit colours and tempting those who might normally refuse such healthy fare – often I mash the strawberries into the oatmeal so it becomes lovely and juicy. Next I make lots of freshly squeezed juices, so when people arrive, they can begin the day with plenty of good vitamins.

Once everyone is tucking into muesli and juice, I start taking orders for a hot breakfast and cook rashers and eggs, American pancakes, waffles or even a big pot of softly scrambled eggs.

Then some sweet pastries and muffins, with lots of bread warm from the oven, are always welcome and I like to have a selection of fresh seasonal fruit to finish off the meal.

relaxed and informal

Even a big brunch should be a relaxed affair, so there is no need for elaborate styling or table decoration. I like to set individual places, but you could simply lay out rows of plates and bowls for people to help themselves. Encourage your guests to raid your cupboards for sauces and condiments, but I do think that it is worth pouring the milk into a pretty jug and sculpting little pats of butter in a small saucer.

A posy of fresh flowers will bring some morning sunshine into the room. Pick some from your garden or pick up a bunch when you pop out for the papers, but do buy those that are in season rather than imported exotics.

For a bit of fun for the kids, comics and colourful papers make great napkin rings and can line a basket of bread or muffins.

Photographs are actually a fab way to decorate the table and will make a great talking point, especially if you have not seen each other for a while. Use photographic corners to hold them in place and then cover with a protective PVC oil cloth – which also wipes clean easily! With the advent of digital cameras and home printing, it is easy to create a personal touch for each guest – for example, if it is a birthday breakfast, make mini flags or placemats using photos of the guest of honour – they also make sweet keepsakes.

Mary Jo's Waffles

MAKES 6 (P: 10 MINS/C: 25 MINS)

Mary Jo McMillan worked with us at the cookery school on several occasions – she was a passionate and perceptive cook. This is her recipe for waffles, which I enjoy much more than mine. They can be served in a variety of ways, both sweet and savoury. You will need a waffle iron.

175g (6oz) plain white flour
10g (1/2oz) sugar
pinch of salt
2 teaspoons baking powder
350ml (12fl oz) milk, slightly warmed
50g (2oz) butter, melted
2 free-range, organic eggs, separated
icing sugar for dusting

Preheat a waffle iron. Sift all the dry ingredients into a deep bowl and make a well in the centre.

Mix the warm milk and melted butter, then whisk in the egg yolks. Pour the milky mixture into the well in the flour and stir together to form a batter. Whisk the egg whites until stiff peaks form and gently fold into the batter.

Pour a 75ml (3fl oz) ladle of batter on to the waffle iron and cook for 3–4 minutes until crisp and golden. Sprinkle with icing sugar and serve hot.

Good things to serve with waffles
Crispy bacon and honey or maple syrup
Crispy bacon and slices of Gruyère or Emmental cheese
Crispy bacon with sliced banana
White peaches with raspberries

Waffles with Fresh Fruit and Berries
Ripe fruit and berries of all kinds are delicious with waffles: sliced peaches, nectarines, apricots and bananas, strawberries, raspberries, loganberries, boysenberries. Pile the fruit on top of hot waffles, or serve it on the side of the plate. A dollop of softly whipped cream doesn't go amiss either!

Waffles with Bananas, Toffee Sauce and Chopped Walnuts

SERVES 6 (P: 5 MINS/C: 10 MINS)

2–3 bananas, sliced
6 waffles (see recipe above)
110g (4oz) walnuts, coarsely chopped

For the toffee sauce:
110g (4oz) butter
175g (6oz) dark soft brown Barbados sugar
110g (4oz) granulated sugar
275g (10oz) golden syrup
225ml (8fl oz) double cream
1/2 teaspoon vanilla extract

To make the toffee sauce, put the butter, both sugars and the golden syrup into a heavy-bottomed saucepan and melt gently over a low heat. Simmer for about 5 minutes, then remove from the heat and gradually stir in the cream and the vanilla extract. Return to the heat and stir for 2–3 minutes until the sauce is absolutely smooth.

Put some banana slices on top of the waffles, pour toffee sauce over and sprinkle with the chopped walnuts.

Top Tip: Toffee sauce is also delicious with ice cream. It will keep for several weeks, stored in a screw-top jar in the fridge.

Breakfast Fruit and Berry Plate

A serving of seasonal fruit and berries provides a delectable vitamin-rich and totally guilt-free breakfast. Use a selection of ripe and juicy fruit and berries, such as melon or pineapple, strawberries, red or yellow raspberries, loganberries or tay-berries, boysenberries, blackcurrants... All are divine, just mix and match according to availability.

All of the fruit listed in the introduction to this recipe benefit from a squeeze of lime or lemon juice.

Serve with a bowl of homemade natural yogurt (see p33) and some local honey. I sometimes sprinkle over a little snipped mint, lemon balm or sweet cicely.

Compote of Plums or Greengages

SERVES 4   (P: 1 MIN/C: 10 MINS)

Poach the fruit whole — they'll taste better. Serve for breakfast or dessert.

400g (14oz) sugar, or a bit less if the fruit are
  very sweet
450ml (16fl oz) cold water
900g (2lb) plums (Victoria, Opal or those dark
  Italian plums that come into the shops in
  autumn) or greengages

To serve: whipped cream

Put the sugar and water into a saucepan on a medium heat and bring to the boil. Tip in the fruit, cover and simmer until they begin to burst (about 4–5 minutes).

Turn into a bowl and serve warm, with a dollop of lightly whipped cream. Exquisite!

Top Tip: Poached plums or greengages keep very well in the fridge for weeks and are delicious for breakfast without the cream!

Poached Apricots with Sweet Geranium Leaves

SERVES 4   (P: 5 MINS/C: 30 MINS)

4–6 large leaves of lemon-scented geranium
  (*Pelargonium graveolens*)
225g (8oz) sugar
225ml (8fl oz) cold water
450g (1lb) fresh apricots, left whole or cut in
  half and stoned

To serve: pouring cream or Sweet
  Geranium Cream (see recipe below)

Put the geranium leaves into a saucepan with the sugar and water and bring slowly to the boil over a moderate heat.

Meanwhile, add the whole apricots to the syrup, or, if you prefer, halve and stone them first. Cover the saucepan and simmer until the apricots are soft (about 15–30 minutes, depending on ripeness). Turn into a bowl and leave to cool, then store in the fridge. Serve chilled, with pouring cream or sweet geranium cream.

Variation: Try this with 4 pears, halved and cored, instead of the apricots.

Sweet Geranium Cream

(C: 30 MINS)

600ml (1 pint) cream
3–4 leaves of lemon-scented geranium
  (*Pelargonium graveolens*)

Pour the cream into a saucepan, add the geranium leaves and heat gently until the surface begins to shiver. Allow to cool. Whip lightly and serve.

A Great Kedgeree

SERVES 6–8   (P: 5 MINS/C: 30 MINS)

The word kedgeree immediately conjures up images of country-house breakfasts, which were often a veritable feast. Usually it would be served on a silver dish set on the polished sideboard, so that guests could help themselves. Easy-peasy to make and delicious for brunch.

450g (1lb), raw wild salmon or
   225g (8oz) raw salmon and 225g (8oz)
   cooked smoked haddock
salt and freshly ground pepper
225g (8oz) white long-grain basmati rice
3 free-range, organic eggs
225ml (8fl oz) cream
40g (1^1/$_2$oz) butter
^{1}/$_2$ teaspoon chilli flakes
3 tablespoons chopped parsley
1^1/$_2$ tablespoons chopped chives
good pinch of cayenne pepper

To serve: freshly baked bread or warm
   buttered toast

Put the salmon in a saucepan just large enough to fit it and cover with boiling salted water – use 1 dessertspoon salt to every 600ml (1 pint) water.* Bring to the boil, cover and simmer for 20 minutes. Remove the pan from the heat, leave covered and allow to sit for a few minutes before removing the salmon from the water, then leave to cool.

Meanwhile, cook the rice in boiling salted water for about 8-10 minutes.

Hard-boil the eggs in boiling salted water for 10 minutes, then drain off the water and run under a cold tap to cool and stop the cooking. Peel and chop roughly.

Remove the skin and any bones from the salmon (and haddock, if using) and flake into small pieces.

Heat the cream and butter in a saucepan and add the chilli flakes, parsley and chives. As soon as the mixture bubbles, add the cooked rice, flaked fish and hard-boiled eggs. Season well with salt and freshly ground pepper and a pinch of cayenne pepper. Mix very gently. Taste, adjust the seasoning to taste, pile into a hot dish and serve with freshly baked bread or warm buttered toast.

* Note: If using fillet use 1 teaspoon salt to 600ml (1 pint) water and cook for just 8-10 minutes.

Congee with Chicken, Shrimps and Mushrooms

SERVES 4–6   (P: 15 MINS/C: 45 MINS)

Congee is a rice porridge – a staple breakfast food in China and Hong Kong, often eaten with dough sticks to dunk. I also love it as a soup – increase the amount of water. Feel free to add some extra tasty titbits at the table.

250g (9oz) jasmine rice, well washed and
   drained
2 litres (3^1/$_2$ pints) water
100g (3^1/$_2$oz) raw chicken, very finely sliced
100g (3^1/$_2$oz) raw or cooked shrimps
1 teaspoon peeled and grated fresh ginger
a little vegetable oil, for frying
1 chilli, thinly sliced (optional)
100g (3^1/$_2$oz) mushrooms, thinly sliced
salt and freshly ground pepper
1–2 tablespoons sesame oil
2 tablespoons thinly sliced spring onion
2 tablespoons roughly chopped
   coriander leaves

Put the rice into a saucepan, add the water and bring to the boil, then cover and simmer for 30–40 minutes until the rice is cooked and the consistency is slightly soupy. Add the chicken and shrimps, ginger and chilli (if using), and cook for a further 4–5 minutes.

Meanwhile heat a pan, add a very little oil vegetable oil and sauté the mushrooms. Season with salt and freshly ground pepper and add to the congee and coriander. Taste and adjust the seasoning if necessary, then drizzle with sesame oil and sprinkle with the spring onion.

Dark Chocolate and Seville Orange Muffins

MAKES ABOUT 10   (**P:** 15 MINS/**C:** 40 MINS)

vegetable oil, for greasing
110g (4oz) butter
175g (6oz) caster sugar
finely grated zest of 1 unwaxed lemon
2 free-range, organic eggs
225ml (8fl oz) buttermilk
75g (3oz) Seville orange marmalade
75g (3oz) dark chocolate, chopped
275g (10oz) plain white flour
pinch of salt
3/4 teaspoon bicarbonate of soda

Preheat the oven to 200ºC/400ºF/gas mark 6. Grease a tray of muffin tins or line with non-stick muffin cases.

Cream the butter and mix in the sugar and lemon zest. Add the eggs one at a time, beating well between each addition.

Next add the buttermilk, marmalade and chopped chocolate. Blend well. Finally stir in the flour, salt and bicarbonate of soda, until just mixed.

Fill the muffins tins with the batter and bake for 30–40 minutes until golden. Serve warm.

Mini muffins are an adorable option and great for kids of all ages.

Breakfast Fruit Salad

SERVES 8   (**P:** OVERNIGHT/**C:** 20 MINS)

Breakfast fruit salads that can be made ahead and kept in the fridge are a terrific standby. We love this one and also often eat it as a winter dessert, with a few pistachio nuts or toasted almonds added.

185g (6½oz) prunes
175g (6oz) dried apricots
handful of raisins
grated zest of 1/2 unwaxed lemon
1–2 tablespoons pure honey

To serve: 3–4 bananas, sliced
250ml (9fl oz) freshly squeezed orange juice,
    and pouring cream or natural yogurt

Soak the prunes and apricots in lots of cold water overnight.

Next day, drain the fruit and retain the soaking water. Put the prunes, apricots, raisins and grated lemon zest into a flameproof casserole.

Mix the honey with 125ml (4fl oz) warm water, pour over the fruit and add enough of the fruit soaking water to cover. Bring to the boil and simmer for 20 minutes.

Allow to cool, transfer to a Kilner jar or other sealed glass jar and store in the fridge; it will keep for 1–2 weeks.

Just before serving, add some banana slices and a little freshly squeezed orange juice to each bowl. Serve with pouring cream or natural yogurt.

Divine Homemade Yogurt

MAKES 1.8 LITRES (3 PINTS)
     (**P:** 5 MINS/**C:** 45 MINS + OVERNIGHT)

Making one's own yogurt is a very simple and satisfying thing to do. Don't try using low-fat milk as the result will have only a fraction of the flavour.

2.4 litres (4 pints) full-cream milk
150ml (1/4 pint) double cream
225g (8oz) live natural yogurt

Put the milk into a large saucepan and bring to the boil. Reduce the heat to low and simmer, stirring occasionally, until reduced by at least half — better still, two thirds. Remove the pan from the heat and pour the milk into a thick pottery bowl. Add the cream and stir well. Allow to cool.

When the milk has cooled enough that you can hold your clean finger in it for a count of 10, add the yogurt and stir well. If the milk is too hot when the yogurt is added, it will kill the live bacteria.

Cover with a tea towel or clingfilm and leave to thicken in a warm, dark place. We leave it beside the Aga or put it in the cupboard over the boiler in the office. Sometimes it takes days to thicken. Once the yogurt has thickened, it will keep in the fridge for 7–10 days.

We serve this with apple blossom honey and toasted hazelnuts.

Ballymaloe White Yeast Bread

MAKES 2 LOAVES   (**P:** 15 MINS/**C:** 3 HOURS)

Making white yeast bread from scratch may not be your idea of easy entertaining, but the mixing takes just a few minutes, the kneading can be done in a food mixer, and the rising takes no effort on your part except a glance every now and then to check its progress. When the dough is risen, the fun begins: you can make one loaf or several, simple shapes or elaborate plaits, or a variety of rolls in every shape and form from simple knots, coils and clover leaves to snails, hedgehogs and wiggly worms to amuse the younger guests.

20g (^{3}/$_4$oz) non-GM fresh yeast
425ml (^{3}/$_4$pint) lukewarm water
700g (1^1/$_2$lb) strong white flour, plus extra for
   dusting (optional)
2 teaspoons salt
10g (^{1}/$_2$oz) sugar
25g (1oz) butter
beaten egg and poppy or sesame seeds, for
   topping (optional)

2 loaf tins 13 x 20cm (5 x 8in)

Mix the yeast with 150ml (^{1}/$_4$ pint) of the lukewarm water and leave in a warm place for about 5 minutes.

In a large, wide mixing bowl sift the flour, salt and sugar. Rub in the butter and make a well in the centre. Pour in the soaked yeast and most of the remaining lukewarm water. Mix to a loose dough, adding the remaining water or a little extra flour if needed.

Turn the dough on to a lightly floured work surface, cover with a tea towel and leave to relax for about 5 minutes. Then knead in a food mixer with a dough hook for about 5 minutes or until smooth, springy and elastic; if kneading by hand, knead for 10 minutes.

Put the dough in a large pottery bowl. Cover the top tightly with clingfilm and set aside in a warm place for about 1^1/$_2$–2 hours until the dough has more than doubled in size (yeast dough rises best in a warm, moist atmosphere).

Knock back the dough (force out all the air) by kneading again by hand for about 2–3 minutes. Leave to relax for 10 minutes.

Shape the dough into loaves, plaits (see below) or rolls, transfer to the loaf tins or a baking tray and cover with a light tea towel. Allow to rise again in a warm place, until the shaped dough has again doubled in size (about 20–30 minutes). The dough is ready for baking when a small dent remains after it is pressed lightly with a finger.

Meanwhile, preheat the oven to 230°C/450°F/gas mark 8.

If you like, brush the dough with beaten egg and sprinkle with poppy or sesame seeds, or dust lightly with flour for a rustic-looking loaf. Bake for 25–35 minutes depending on size. When it is cooked, the bread should sound hollow when tapped underneath. Cool on a wire rack.

To make a plait:
After the dough has been knocked back, take half the dough and divide into three pieces. With both hands, roll each one into a rope — the thickness depends on how fat you want the plait. Pinch the three ropes together at one end, then bring each outside strand into the centre alternately to form a plait. Pinch the ends together and tuck in neatly. Transfer to a baking tray, cover and allow to double in size. Brush with beaten egg or dredge with flour and bake.

Tear-and-share Bread

MAKES 1 LOAF (SEE PHOTOGRAPH ON P210.)
                     (**P:** 15 MINS/**C:** 3 HOURS)

A fun bread for a dinner party or family supper – just tear and share.

450g (1lb) Ballymaloe White Yeast Bread
   dough (see recipe above)
cornmeal or flour, for dusting
poppy seeds (optional)

Roll out the dough into a round about 20cm (8in) across. Sprinkle a baking tray with cornmeal or flour and lay on the dough, then allow it to rest for about 5 minutes. Brush with water and sprinkle with cornmeal or flour.

Press a 7.5cm (3in) diameter cutter or small glass into the centre of the dough to make a circular indent, but do not cut through. Sprinkle the centre with poppy seeds (if using). With a pastry cutter or knife, divide the dough on the outside of the circle into half, then quarters, then eighths, and then into sixteenths, so you are left with 'petals' around the centre circle.

Give each 'petal' a quarter turn so part of the cut side faces upwards. Cover with a tea towel and allow to rise in a warm place until doubled in size (about 20–30 minutes). Meanwhile preheat the oven to 230°C/450°F/gas mark 8.

Bake for 10–15 minutes, then reduce the heat to 180°C/350°F/gas mark 4 and continue baking until the bread is crusty and golden. Cool on a wire rack.

Brown Yeast Bread

MAKES 1 LOAF   (P: 20 MINS/C: 1½ HOURS)

I know the word 'yeast' conjures up thoughts of kneading, rising and knocking back, but don't be afraid – the Ballymaloe Brown Yeast Bread is a doddle to make. It takes time – about 1½ hours from start to finish – but only 10 minutes of preparation: the rest of the time is spent allowing the bread to rise or bake. The main ingredients – wholemeal flour, treacle and yeast – are highly nutritious.

450g (1lb) wholemeal flour, or 400g (14oz)
    wholemeal flour and 50g (2oz) strong
    white flour
1 teaspoon salt
1 teaspoon black treacle or molasses
425ml (¾ pint) water, at blood heat
20–25g (½–1oz) non-GM fresh yeast (Dried
    yeast may be used instead of baker's (fresh)
    yeast: follow the same method but use only
    half the weight given for fresh yeast, and
    allow longer to rise. Fast-acting yeast may
    also be used: follow instructions on packet.
sunflower oil, for greasing
sesame seeds (optional)

1 loaf tin, about 13 x 20cm (5 x 8in)

The ingredients should all be at room temperature. In a large bowl, mix the flour with the salt. In a small bowl or jug, mix the treacle or molasses with 150ml (¼ pint) of the warm water and crumble in the yeast. Set the bowl in a warm place (such as close to the aga or oven or near a radiator) for 4–5 minutes to allow the yeast to start to work; it is ready when it looks creamy and slightly frothy. Meanwhile brush the tins with sunflower oil.

Preheat the oven to 230°C/450°F/gas mark 8.

When the yeasty water is ready, stir and pour it, along with the remaining warm water, into the flour to make a loose wet dough. The mixture should be too wet to knead. Pour the dough into the greased tin and sprinkle the top with sesame seeds if you like. Cover with a tea towel and leave to rise in a warm place (about 10–15 minutes). Just before the dough reaches the top of the tin, remove the tea towel and bake for 50–60 minutes, until the bread looks nicely browned and the base sounds hollow when tapped. During cooking the bread will rise a little further; this is called 'oven spring'. If the dough has reached the top of the tin before it goes into the oven it will continue to rise and flow over the edges.

We usually remove the loaf from the tin about 10 minutes before the end of cooking and put it back into the oven to crisp all round, but if you like a softer crust there's no need to do this. Cool on a wire rack.

Variation: To make Russian Village Bread, use 400g (14oz) wholemeal flour, 50g (2oz) rye flour and 50g (2oz) strong white flour. When the dough is ready, brush the tin with sunflower oil, sprinkle a layer of coriander seeds onto the base of the tin and another layer over the top of the bread. Cook as above.

Breadsticks

(P: 20 MINS/C: 15 MINS)

These are great for cocktail parties and go well with dips, soups and salads. Breadsticks wrapped in a slice of Parma or Serrano ham make delicious nibbles, to serve with an aperitif. They don't need to be perfectly even in shape – you could form the dough into wriggly worms to great effect!

Ballymaloe White Yeast Bread dough (see
    recipes on page 34 and above)
selection of sprinkles: coarse sea salt and/or
    ground black pepper, chopped rosemary,
    crushed cumin seeds, sesame seeds, poppy
    seeds, chilli flakes, grated Parmesan cheese
    (optional)

When the dough has been 'knocked back', preheat the oven to 220°C/425°F/gas mark 7.

Sprinkle the work surface with coarse sea salt and black pepper if you wish and/or your chosen flavouring.

Pull off small pieces of dough, 10–25g (½–1oz) in weight. Roll into very thin, medium or fat breadsticks with your hands, but bear in mind that they will double in size.

Roll in the chosen 'sprinkle' (you may need to brush the dough lightly with cold water first). Place on a baking sheet. Repeat this process until all the dough has been used.

Bake for 8–15 minutes, depending on size, until golden brown and crisp. Cool on a wire rack.

Top Tip: Breadsticks are usually baked without a final rising, but for a slightly lighter result let the shaped dough rise for about 10 minutes before baking.

White Soda or Buttermilk Bread

MAKES 1 LOAF   (**P**: 10 MINS/**C**: 45 MINS)

Soda bread uses bicarbonate of soda instead of yeast to leaven the bread as well as an acidic ingredient – buttermilk or sour milk. It also requires plain flour, not strong flour. This soda or buttermilk bread takes only 2–3 minutes to make and 45 minutes to bake. You can also add olives, sun-dried tomatoes or caramelised onions to suit your menu, which makes this an infinitely useful bread.

450g (1lb) plain white flour, preferably
  unbleached
1 teaspoon salt
1 teaspoon bicarbonate of soda
400ml (14fl oz) buttermilk

Preheat the oven to 250ºC/475ºF/gas mark 9.

Sift all the dry ingredients into a large, wide bowl and make a well in the centre. Pour in the milk. Using the fingers of one hand, stiff and outstretched like a claw, stir from the centre to the edge of the bowl in concentric circles. The dough should be softish, but not too wet and sticky. When it all comes together, turn out on to a well-floured work surface.

Wash and dry your hands. Pat the dough into a tidy shape and flip over gently, then pat it into a round about 4cm (1½in) thick. Gently transfer to a floured baking tray. Cut a deep cross into the loaf and prick the centre of each quarter to 'let the fairies out!'

Bake for 15 minutes, then reduce the heat to 200ºC/400ºF/gas mark 6 and bake for a further 30 minutes or until cooked. If you are in doubt, tap the bottom of the bread: it should sound hollow. Cool on a wire rack. Soda bread is best eaten on the day it is made.

For spotted dog, add 1 tablespoon sugar, 110g (4oz) sultanas and 1 free-range, organic egg to the above recipe. Reduce the buttermilk to 350ml (12fl oz).

West Cork Cheddar Cheese 'Focaccia'

MAKES 1 LOAF   (P: 10 MINS/C: 30 MINS)

Here we bake the buttermilk bread flat with a bubbly Cheddar cheese topping.

1 quantity White Soda Bread dough (see recipe on p36)
extra virgin olive oil, for greasing
110–175g (4–6oz) mature Cheddar cheese

1 Swiss Roll tin, 31 x 23cm (12 x 9 in)

Preheat the oven to 230ºC/450ºF/gas mark 8.

Make the bread in the usual way. Flatten the dough into a rectangle approximately 30 x 23cm (12 x 9in). Brush the tin with extra virgin olive oil. Press the dough gently into the tin. Scatter the grated cheese evenly over the top.

Bake for 5 minutes, then turn down the oven to 200ºC/400ºF/gas mark 6 and bake for about 20–25 minutes more or until just cooked and the cheese is bubbly and golden. Transfer to a wire rack to cool. Cut into squares and serve with drinks or with a steaming bowl of soup.

Wheaten Bread

MAKES 1 LOAF   (P: 10 MINS/C: 40 MINS)

225g (8oz) plain white flour
225g (8oz) wholemeal flour, plus extra for dusting
1 teaspoon salt
1 barely rounded teaspoon bicarbonate of soda
450ml (16fl oz) buttermilk

Preheat the oven to 200°C/400°F/gas mark 6.

Mix the flours in a large bowl, add the salt and sift in the bicarbonate of soda. Lift the flour up with your fingers to distribute the salt and bicarbonate of soda.

Make a well in the centre and pour in the buttermilk. With your fingers stiff and outstretched, stir from the centre to the edge of the bowl in ever-increasing concentric circles. When you reach the edge of the bowl, the dough should be made – it will be soft, but not too wet or sticky. Sprinkle a little flour on a work surface and turn the dough out on to it. Wash and dry your hands.

Sprinkle a little flour on your hands and gently tidy the dough around the edges. Tuck the edges underneath with the inner edge of your hands and gently pat the dough with your fingers into a loaf about 4cm (1½in) thick.

Cut a deep cross into the bread (this is called 'blessing the bread') and then prick it in the centre of each quarter to 'let the fairies out'.

Sprinkle some flour on to a baking tray and put the dough on it. Bake for 30 minutes, then turn the bread over and bake for a further 5–10 minutes until cooked (the bottom should sound hollow when tapped). Cool on a wire rack.

Teeny Weeny Rolls

MAKES 40   (P: 15 MINS/C: 20 MINS)

Three teeny weenies, with different toppings and threaded on to a satay stick, look great with a bowl of steaming soup.

1 quantity Wheaten Bread dough (see recipe above) or White Soda Bread dough (see recipe p36)
flour, for dusting
buttermilk or beaten egg, to glaze (optional)
toppings: sesame seeds, rolled oatmeal, kibbled wheat, poppy seeds, pumpkin seeds, grated Cheddar cheese (optional)

Preheat the oven to 230ºC/450ºF/gas mark 8.

Make the dough as per your chosen recipe. Turn out on to a floured work surface. Roll out into a round or square, 2.5cm (1in) thick. The quickest and least wasteful way to make teeny weenies is to cut the dough into 2.5cm (1in) squares. Alternatively, stamp the dough into rounds with a floured 4cm (1½in) cutter so there is a minimum of waste, then gently roll the scraps and stamp out more shapes.

If you like, brush the tops with buttermilk or beaten egg and dip the pieces into one or a selection of the suggested toppings. Transfer to a baking sheet.

Bake for 15–20 minutes – when cooked they should sound hollow when tapped. Transfer to a wire rack and allow to cool.

Wholemeal Soda Bread

MAKES 1 LARGE LOAF OR 3 SMALL LOAVES
(**P**: 20 MINS/**C**: 60 MINS)

This is a modern version of soda bread, and it couldn't be simpler. Just mix and pour into a well-greased tin. This bread keeps very well for several days and is also great toasted.

400g (14oz) stone-ground wholemeal flour
75g (3oz) plain white flour, preferably
  unbleached
1 teaspoon salt
1 teaspoon bicarbonate of soda, sifted
1 free-range, organic egg
1 tablespoon peanut or sunflower oil, plus
  extra for greasing
1 teaspoon honey
425ml (³/₄ pint) buttermilk or sour milk,
  plus a little extra if necessary
sunflower or sesame seeds (optional)

loaf tin, 23 x 12.5 x 5cm (9 x 5 x 2in)

Preheat the oven to 200°C/400°F/gas mark 6.

Put all the dry ingredients, including the bicarbonate of soda, into a large bowl and mix well.

Whisk the egg, then add the oil and honey and the buttermilk or sour milk. Make a well in the centre of the dry ingredients and pour in all the liquid; mix well and add more buttermilk if necessary. The mixture should be soft and slightly sloppy.

Pour into an oiled tin or tins. Sprinkle some sunflower or sesame seeds on the top, if using. Bake for about 60 minutes, or until the bread is nice and crusty and sounds hollow when tapped. Remove from the tin and cool on a wire rack.

Top Tip: For a healthy seed bread, add to the dry ingredients 1 tablespoon each sunflower seeds, sesame seeds, pumpkin seeds and kibbled wheat. Keep a little aside to scatter over the top before baking.

Fougasse (Provençal Flat Bread)

MAKES 4-6   (**P**: 20 MINS/**C**: 60 MINS)

This is wonderful-looking bread with its ragged holes and lovely crust.

1 quantity Ballymaloe White Yeast Bread dough
  (see p34)
extra virgin olive oil, for brushing
sea salt
chopped rosemary (optional)

Make the dough and knead it. Oil a large bowl and put in the dough. Cover with a light tea towel and allow to rise as described on p34. Knock back the dough by kneading for 2–3 minutes and divide it into 4–6 pieces. Preheat the oven to 230°C/450°F/gas mark 8.

Gently roll each piece of dough into an oval shape at least 18cm (7in) long and 10cm (4in) wide. Using a very sharp knife or a razor blade, make 3 or 5 angled cuts in the dough. Brush a baking tray with olive oil. Transfer the dough to the baking tray, pulling the cuts apart to open holes in the dough.

Allow to rise in a warm place until doubled in size, about 30 minutes. Brush the surface with olive oil, then sprinkle with sea salt and rosemary (if using). Bake for 5 minutes, then reduce the temperature to 200°C/400°F/gas mark 6 and continue baking for a further 20–25 minutes until golden. Cool on a wire rack.

Heart-shaped Bread

MAKES SEVERAL   (**P**: 20 MINS/**C**: 20 MINS)

1 quantity Ballymaloe White Yeast Bread
  dough (see p34) or White Soda Bread dough
  (see p36)
whole Kalamata olives
fresh rosemary sprigs
extra virgin olive oil, for brushing

heart-shaped cutter

Make the dough as given in the recipe and roll out to a 2cm (³/₄in) thickness. Preheat the oven to 230°C/450°F/gas mark 8.

Using a heart-shaped cutter, stamp out heart shapes from the dough. Press a whole olive into the centre of each one and tuck in a tiny sprig of rosemary behind it.

Bake for 15–20 minutes depending on size. Brush with a little extra virgin olive oil and serve.

Pitta Bread

MAKES 8 LARGE OR ABOUT 48 MINI PITTA
BREADS   (**P**: 15 MINS/**C**: 30 MINS)

Pitta bread is readily available to buy, but it's easier to make than you might imagine and once you have tasted homemade pitta bread it's difficult to settle for less. It's terrifically versatile: you can stuff it with salad, cured meats or cheese or simply eat it on its own, and mini pitta breads make a great base for hummous and dips.

400g (14oz) strong white flour
1 teaspoon salt
1 tablespoon sugar
10g (^{1}/$_2$oz) non-GM fresh yeast
2 tablespoons extra virgin olive oil
225ml (8fl oz) hot water

8 x 18cm (7in) piece of aluminium foil

Put 110g (4oz) of the flour into the bowl of an electric mixer, add the salt and sugar and crumble in the yeast. Mix the oil with the hot water. Using the paddle and with the mixer on a low speed, mix the liquid with the dry ingredients for 30 seconds. Now change to the dough hook and add the balance of the flour 2 tablespoons at a time, keeping the motor running. When all the flour has been added, continue to knead for a further 4–5 minutes. The dough will be a shaggy mass. Continue to knead until the dough comes easily away from the sides of the bowl.

Turn the dough out on to a lightly floured work surface. Knead by hand for a further few minutes. The dough will be slightly sticky. Divide the dough into 8 or 48 pieces. Roll into balls, cover and leave to rest for 20 minutes.

Preheat the oven to 250ºC/475ºF/gas mark 9.

With the palm of your hand, gently flatten each ball and roll out to an oval shape about 15cm (6in) across (2.5cm/1in for mini pittas) and about 5mm (^{1}/$_2$in) thick. Don't worry too much about getting a perfect shape, but it is important to make the discs thin. Put each piece of dough on to a piece of aluminium foil and leave to rest for a further 5 minutes. Meanwhile, put a baking sheet to warm in the oven.

Carefully put 2 or 3 of the breads on to the hot baking sheet and bake for 8 minutes (6 minutes for mini pittas) or until they have puffed up and are slightly golden – if you allow them get too dark they will have a hard crust. Remove the breads from the oven and wrap them in aluminium foil or a tea towel; the tops will fall and there will be a pocket that you can fill. Bake and wrap the remaining breads in the same manner. Serve warm or cold.

Indian Paratha Bread

MAKES 16   (**P**: 20 MINS/**C**: 40 MINS)

These roughly triangular flat breads are eaten all over India. They are easy to make at home – all you need is a cast-iron frying pan. In India ghee (clarified butter) is used instead of vegetable oil. Parathas can be reheated in the oven: wrap 3 or 4 at a time in foil and warm through at 180°C/350°F/gas mark 4 for 5–10 minutes.

175g (6oz) sifted wholemeal flour (weigh the flour after sifting and return the bran to the remainder in the bag)
185g (6^1/$_2$oz) plain white flour, plus extra for dusting
^{1}/$_2$ teaspoon salt
2 tablespoons vegetable oil or clarified butter (see p108), plus extra for brushing and frying
200ml (7fl oz) water

Put the wholemeal flour, white flour and salt into a bowl and mix. Sprinkle the vegetable oil or clarified butter over the top and rub in with your fingertips. The mixture will resemble coarse breadcrumbs. Add the water and gradually mix together with your fingers to form a softish ball of dough.

Knead the dough on a clean work surface for about 10 minutes. Rub the ball of dough with a little oil, put it into a bowl, cover with clingfilm and allow to rest for 30 minutes.

Knead the dough again for 1–2 minutes, shape into a cylinder and divide into 16 pieces. While you work with each piece, keep the remainder covered with a light tea towel.

Flatten a piece of dough and dust with a little plain flour. Roll out to a round 15cm (6in) across. Brush a little oil over the top and fold in half. Brush with oil again, then fold again to form a triangle. Roll out this triangle towards the point into a larger triangle with 18cm (7in) sides. Dust with flour if necessary to prevent it from sticking during rolling. Cover and set aside. Repeat with the remaining dough.

Heat a cast-iron frying pan until it is really hot, slap a paratha on to it and cook for a minute or so. Brush the top generously with oil, then turn the paratha over and cook the other side for a minute or so. Both sides should have brownish spots. Move the paratha around as you cook so all parts are exposed evenly to the heat. Transfer the cooked paratha to a plate and cover with a saucepan lid or a piece of aluminium foil. Cook the remaining parathas in the same way. Serve warm.

Grilled Fremantle Flat Bread

MAKES 5 OR 6

(**P**: 5 MINS + OVERNIGHT/**C**: 50 MINS)

This flat bread is great served with dips or simply with good-quality extra virgin olive oil.

500g (1lb 2oz) plain white flour
250ml (9fl oz) water
40g (1¹/₂oz) butter
pinch of sugar
salt and freshly ground pepper
rice flour or cornmeal, for rolling
extra virgin olive oil, for brushing

Put the flour, water and butter into the bowl of an electric mixer. Add the sugar and 1 teaspoon salt. Mix together at a slow speed with a dough hook for about 5 minutes until the dough is really smooth and shiny.

Turn out on to a lightly floured work surface and knead lightly for a couple of minutes. Roll the dough into a cylinder and wrap in clingfilm or greaseproof paper. Refrigerate overnight.

The following day, allow the dough to come back to room temperature for about 30 minutes. Divide into 5 or 6 pieces. Dust the work surface with rice flour or cornmeal and roll out each portion into a very thin round – don't worry too much about the shape as long as it is thin. Cover and leave to rest for about 20 minutes.

The breads can be either grilled or cooked in a frying pan: either preheat the grill to its highest setting, or heat a heavy, wide frying pan over a medium heat.

Brush the dough pieces with olive oil and sprinkle with freshly ground pepper. If using the grill, grill 1 or 2 pieces at a time for 2–3 minutes on both sides. They will puff up almost immediately. Be careful not to overcook or they will become crisp and brittle. If you are using a frying pan, slap a dough round directly on to the hot pan, cook for a few minutes on one side, then turn over and continue to cook for 2–3 minutes on the other side.

Wrap in a warm tea towel until needed. Brush with extra virgin olive oil. Sprinkle with salt and serve.

Yufka (Turkish Flat Bread)

MAKES 12

(**P**: 15 MINS/**C**: 50 MINS)

Bread is a staple in Turkey, as in so many cultures. According to the Koran, bread was sent to Earth by God's command, hence it is revered and not a crumb should be wasted. There are many delicious ways to use up stale bread but I rarely have any left over to experiment with.

110g (4oz) strong white flour
110g (4oz) plain white flour
50g (2oz) wholemeal flour
1 scant teaspoon salt
200–225ml (7–8fl oz) warm water

Mix all the flours and the salt together in a bowl. Add 200ml (7fl oz) warm water, mix to a dough and knead well for a couple of minutes. Add more water if necessary. Shape into a roll, divide into 12 pieces, cover with a tea towel and leave to rest for at least 30 minutes, preferably 45 minutes.

Roll out each piece of dough into a thin round no more than 8mm (¹/₃in) thick.

Heat a griddle or large non-stick iron frying pan. Cook the yufka quickly on both sides until brown spots just start to appear. The bread can be eaten immediately; alternatively, it can be stacked in a box for several days, even weeks, in a dry place

Before eating, sprinkle a little warm water over the breads, fold them in half, wrap in a cloth and allow to soften for about 30 minutes. Eat with cheese or butter and honey, or fill with your chosen filling of roasted vegetables, cured meat or salad – they are then called *durum*, meaning roll.

throwing a good brunch

When planning a menu, make sure you have a good mix of bread, fruit and hot dishes. If it is more breakfast than lunch, French toast, muffins and a good porridge or crunchy granola go down well. For a mid-morning meal, provide a couple of hot dishes and you may even want to add a drop of champagne to the orange juice.

If you have time, a basket of breads (soda bread, a brown yeast loaf, tear and share, wheaten bread and teeny-weeny rolls) is a wonderful thing and perfect for nibbling on through the morning. As brunch turns into lunch, bring out some local cheese, succulent ham and pickle and a good green salad. What could be easier?

Brunch is a meal to linger over, to make any plans for the rest of the day. Turn the radio on for some background news or music, provide a selection of newspapers, then sit down, relax and let your guests help themselves to whatever they want.

A light breakfast (see p24–27)
Ballymaloe Strawberry Muesli (see page 20)
French Toast Fingers with Citrus Marmalade Butter (see page 23)
Dark Chocolate and Seville Orange Muffins (see page 33)
White Soda Bread with Olives or Spotted Dog (see page 36)
A selection of fresh fruit

To drink
Breakfast is not really the time for wine but some inexpensive sparkling Cava added to freshly squeezed orange juice will add just a little kick to all that healthy vitamin C. If you want something with more of a hit, then a Bloody Mary will do the trick, or a few drops of elderflower syrup added to Champagne or sparkling wine. If breakfast is early, consider serving a Virgin Mary (just leave out the vodka) and your guests may not know the difference.

Healthy breakfast menu
Pinhead Oatmeal Porridge (see p20)
Breakfast Fruit Salad with Divine Homemade Yogurt (see p33)
Healthy Seed Bread (see Wholemeal Soda Bread, page 38)

To drink
Mango and banana smoothie (see page 16) will provide an instant hit of vitamins and energy, as will freshly squeezed juice (see page 20). For a fizzy refresher, add some elderflower cordial to sparkling water.

A hearty brunch
A Great Kedgeree (see p30)
Breakfast Panini (see p22)
Compote of Plums and Greengages (see p28)

To drink
A simple and fairly inexpensive white Burgundy, such as a Macon-Villages, will partner the kedgeree very effectively, and tackle the panini. Good alternatives include Pinot Grigio and Verdicchio. The relatively low alcohol Moscatel de Valencia is ideal with the compote.

finger food

When I was little, a neighbour gave a cocktail party and I was so intrigued that I went around to help her prepare the food. I was amazed to find little chunks of cheese and grapes on cocktail sticks sticking out of a melon. I thought it was the most exciting and sophisticated thing I'd ever seen. Canapés have come a long way since then. Nowadays we can let our imaginations run riot and come up with delicious bites, from soup served in shot glasses to tapas, sushi and spring rolls.

Isaac's Sushi Rice

(P: 20 MINS/C: 1 HOUR, 15 MINS)

450g (1lb) sushi rice 'No. 1 Extra Fancy'
600ml (1 pint) water

For the vinegar water:
125ml (4fl oz) rice wine vinegar
3 tablespoons sugar
5 teaspoons salt

Rinse the rice in a colander or sieve under cold running water for 10 minutes or until the water runs clear.

'Wake up' the rice by sitting it in 600ml (1 pint) cold water for 30–45 minutes. In the same water, bring it to the boil, cover and cook for 10 minutes until all the water has been absorbed. Do not stir: do not even remove the lid. Turn up the heat for 10 seconds before turning the heat off. Remove the lid, place a tea towel over the rice, replace the lid and leave for 20 minutes.

Mix the rice wine vinegar, sugar and salt together in a bowl until dissolved. Turn the rice out on to a big flat plate (preferably wooden). While the rice is still hot pour the vinegar solution over it and mix the rice and vinegar together in a slicing action with the aid of a wooden spoon. Don't stir. You must mix quickly, preferably fanning the rice with a fan at the same time. (This is much easier if you have a helper!) Allow the rice to cool on the plate, covering it meanwhile with kitchen paper or a tea towel. (It will soak up the liquid as it cools.)

Norimaki

MAKES 7–8 ROLLS, 6–8 PIECES IN EACH
(P: 30 MINS)

packet of nori seaweed
vinegar water (see recipe above)
1 quantity Isaac's Sushi Rice (see recipe above)

For the filling:
3–4 basil leaves per roll
6–8 strips of raw wild or smoked salmon or tuna
   cut into 5mm ($1/4$in) strips
2 avocado slices, of similar size to the fish
$1/2$ cucumber, deseeded and cut into 5mm
   ($1/4$in) strips
25g (1oz) Cheddar cheese, cut into 5mm
   ($1/4$in) strips

To serve: wasabi paste, soy sauce and pickled
   ginger

bamboo sudari mat for rolling

Place a bamboo sudari mat on the worktop. Wave a sheet of nori seaweed over a gas flame to freshen up the flavour and make it more pliable. Lay on a bamboo sudari mat, with the shiny side down and grain running horizontally. Dip your hand in the vinegar water.

Spread a layer of rice over it, keeping it 2.5cm (1in) from the top of the sheet of nori. Make a shallow indentation in the rice and put in the filling. You can use whatever you fancy for the filling – smoked salmon and basil, avocado, cucumber, even strips of Cheddar cheese. Roll the mat tightly and press to seal, then unroll the mat.

To serve, cut the norimaki with a razor-sharp knife into 6 pieces (dip the knife in the vinegar water each time). Arrange on a plate, together with a blob of wasabi paste about the size of a small pea, a little dish of soy sauce and a few slivers of pickled ginger. For perfection, sushi should not be refrigerated.

Note: sudari mats are available from Japanese or Asian shops as well as many health-food shops and now even some supermarkets. If you can't find one, just use a clean tea towel as though you were making a Swiss roll.

Nigiri Sushi

MAKES 48–50   (P: 30 MINS)

1 quantity Isaac's Sushi Rice (see recipe above)
vinegar water (see recipe above)
6–8 strips of raw wild or smoked salmon or tuna
   (raw fish must be spanking fresh)
fennel leaves or packet of nori seaweed

To serve: wasabi paste, soy sauce and pickled
   ginger

First dip your hand in the vinegar water. Make a little oblong ball from the rice, moulding it gently in a lightly clenched hand.

Put a slice of salmon or tuna on top. Garnish with fennel leaves or a strip of nori. Serve with wasabi paste, soy sauce and pickled ginger.

Shermin Mustafa's Californian Roll (Inside-out Sushi)

MAKES 7–8 ROLLS (6–8 PIECES IN EACH)
(**P:** 30 MINS)

packet of nori seaweed
1 quantity Isaac's Sushi Rice (see p44)
110g (4oz) wild smoked salmon, cut into
   oblong pieces about 1cm (1/2in) wide
1 firm but ripe avocado, cut into long pieces of
   a similar size to the salmon
50g (2oz) sesame seeds, lightly toasted

To serve: wasabi paste, soy sauce and pickled
   ginger

bamboo sudari mat for rolling

Wave a sheet of nori seaweed over a gas flame until soft and pliable, about 8–10 seconds. Place the seaweed on a bamboo sudari mat, shiny side down and with the grain running horizontally.

Wet your hands to prevent the rice from sticking to them. Using your fingertips, press enough rice on to the seaweed to cover it as evenly and as thinly as possible. Lift up the seaweed and the rice, turn the whole thing upside down and place back on to the bamboo mat. Arrange the strips of salmon and pieces of avocado horizontally across the seaweed and rice, tucking the end in. Carefully roll up, pressing firmly on the bamboo mat, then remove the mat.

Sprinkle some sesame seeds on a clean work surface and roll the sushi roll in the seeds until evenly covered. Wet a sharp knife and cut the roll into 6–8 even-sized pieces, using a sawing motion. Serve with wasabi paste, soy sauce and pickled ginger.

Temari Sushi (Clingfilm Sushi)

MAKES 20–30 PIECES   (**P:** 20 MINS)

20–30 sprigs of dill
1/2 quantity Isaac's Sushi Rice (see p44)

For the filling:
50g (2oz) smoked salmon, cut into 2.5cm
   (1in) squares *or*
20–30 cooked prawns or shrimps *or*
1/2 cucumber, sliced wafer-thin and cut into
   2.5cm (1in) squares *or*
50g (2oz) rare roast beef, thinly sliced and cut
   into 2.5cm (1in) squares
To serve: wasabi paste and pickled ginger

Lay a piece of clingfilm, about 10cm (4in) square, on a clean work surface and place a sprig of dill and then a piece of smoked salmon or other filling of your choice at the centre of it. Mould a teaspoonful of sushi rice into a loose ball and place on top of the dill and salmon.

Pick up all four corners of the clingfilm and gather them in the middle. Twist the clingfilm to compact the rice and form a small ball. Repeat the process with the remaining salmon and other fillings.

Keep each piece of sushi wrapped in the clingfilm until just before serving and keep cool but not refrigerated. You may want to put a dab of wasabi under the rice if served as finger food. For a starter arrange on a plate and serve with pickled ginger and a little wasabi.

a cocktail party

A cocktail party is a brilliant way to entertain lots of guests, especially if they don't know each other very well. Handing round food and sipping cocktails will help people to mingle and get the conversation flowing.

Start by serving savoury canapés with your cocktails, wine or champagne. Variety is essential, and there are so many exciting choices from mini poppadoms to bloody mary jellies to mussels served in their shells. Haphazard combinations can work really well, but give some thought to the order you bring them out. Balance is also crucial – you will need a combination of hot and cold canapés as well as a mix of meat, fish and vegetarian. Choose the canapés carefully so you have a contrast of flavours and texture – some mild, some hot and spicy, some perennial favourites. You may also want to balance expensive canapés which include prawns or lobster with classics like Cheddar cheese croquettes and mixed bruschetta.

Try to bring out a new dish every 20 minutes or so – timing is everything because you don't want to overwhelm your guests – they will only be able to manage one at a time, but you don't want too big a gap, especially if the wine is good!

About two-thirds of the way through the evening, you may want to switch to a good dessert wine and replace your savoury selection with delicious sweet canapés such as petit fours, little lemon tartlets, glazed strawberries or ice creams served in egg cups.

sleek and stylish

Be creative when choosing serving plates – they don't have to be conventional. Improvise using old glass mirrors, a large slate tile, brie boxes and flat, wicker baskets. Sea shells and banana leaves can be a great way to present food, as are antique spoons, Moroccan tea glasses, lemongrass stalks and small tin plates or espresso cups.

Arrange each item dramatically on its serving plate – long lines or a symmetrical pattern are striking, but random displays can be equally dramatic – the trays should turn people's heads as it circulates, whetting their appetite. Although you can prepare a lot of food in advance (see individual recipes for advice), always garnish at the last moment.

Strew surfaces with grass, flowers, petals, glass beads or even sweets. Keep the lighting bright enough so that guests can see what they are eating and move around confidently, but place tea lights on reflective surfaces for extra sparkle.

Provide lots of bright paper napkins and cocktails sticks, and make sure that whoever is handing round the food also has a small bag or bowl to collect them; otherwise you will find them in your flower pots for months afterwards. Take turns handing round food and working in the kitchen, so that you can enjoy the party. Turn your guests into waiters – it's a good trick for shy friends or those that don't know many people.

Tomato and Coconut Milk Soup in Espresso Cups with Tiny Breadsticks

SERVES 6   (P: 10 MINS/C: 15 MINS)

Tinned tomatoes and coconut milk are must-have store-cupboard ingredients. This recipe can be put together in a few minutes or made well ahead and frozen. For a drinks party, serve in espresso cups, accompanied by tiny breadsticks.

1 small onion, finely chopped

10g (1/2oz) butter

850ml (11/2 pints) homemade tomato purée
   (see p294) or 2 x 400g (14oz) tins tomatoes,
   liquidised and sieved

400g (14oz) tin coconut milk

250ml (9fl oz) homemade chicken stock or
   vegetable stock (see p295)

2 tablespoons chopped coriander leaves

salt and freshly ground pepper

sugar

To serve: crème fraîche, fresh coriander leaves
and tiny breadsticks (see p35)

6 espresso cups

Sweat the onion in the butter over a gentle heat until soft but not coloured.

Add the tomato purée (or liquidised tinned tomatoes plus juice), coconut milk and stock. Add the chopped coriander and season with salt, pepper and sugar to taste. Bring to the boil and simmer for a few minutes.

Liquidise, taste and dilute further with stock if necessary. Bring back to the boil and correct the seasoning. Taste carefully: the final result depends on the quality and balance of the homemade ingredients.

Pour into espresso cups. Garnish with a tiny dollop of crème fraîche and some coriander leaves. Serve 1 or 2 tiny breadsticks on the saucer as an accompaniment.

Top Tip: Tinned tomatoes need a surprising amount of sugar to counteract their acidity. Fresh milk cannot be added to the soup – the acidity in the tomatoes will cause it to curdle.

Thai Chicken on Chinese Spoons with a Leaf of Fresh Coriander

MAKES 30   (P: 10 MINS/C: 20 MINS)

This is also delicious as a starter or main course, served with Thai fragrant rice.

450g (1lb) skinless and boneless free-range,
   organic chicken breasts

50g (2oz) butter

40g (11/2oz) fresh ginger, peeled and
   finely chopped

2 garlic cloves, crushed

1/4 teaspoon green peppercorns

1 lemongrass stalk, finely chopped

2 red chillies, finely chopped

2 teaspoons lime juice

1/2 teaspoon ground coriander

400ml (14fl oz) tin coconut milk

2 teaspoons chopped coriander leaves

salt and freshly ground pepper

30 coriander leaves, to garnish

30 Chinese porcelain spoons

Cut the chicken into 30 evenly sized cubes. Heat half the butter in a large frying pan and sauté the chicken pieces until lightly browned on all sides.

Melt the remaining butter in the frying pan and sauté the ginger, garlic, peppercorns, lemongrass and chillies. Add the lime juice and ground coriander. Gradually stir in the coconut milk, bring to the boil, then reduce the heat and simmer for 8 minutes.

Add the chicken pieces and continue to simmer for 2–3 minutes. Stir in the chopped coriander leaves and season to taste. The recipe can be prepared ahead up to this point.

Serve on porcelain Chinese spoons, each garnished with a coriander leaf.

Top Tip: Also delicious as a starter with fresh coriander leaves or as a main course with Thai fragrant rice.

Mixed Bruschetta Plate

(**P:** 20 MINS/**C:** 65 MINS)

Great for a casual party. Ensure each topping is well seasoned. Good bread is essential – you'll need lots of sour dough bread and plenty of napkins.

Making the bruschetta

1 loaf of sour dough or country bread
whole garlic cloves, cut in half
extra virgin olive oil

First prepare the toppings (see below). Slice the bread 1cm (¹/₂in) thick (cut in half if the slices are too large) and chargrill the bread. Alternatively cook on a preheated, ridged grill pan until nicely marked on both sides. Rub each piece with a cut clove of garlic, drizzle with extra virgin olive oil and coat with the chosen topping. Arrange a selection of bruschettas on a large platter or pass round on separate plates.

Roast Sweet Pepper and Flat Parsley Topping

5 tablespoons extra virgin olive oil
1–2 garlic cloves, crushed
Roasted red and yellow peppers (see p298), peeled, deseeded and cut into strips
2 tablespoons coarsely chopped flat parsley or basil
salt and freshly ground pepper

Heat the olive oil in a pan over medium heat. Add the garlic and cook for a few seconds. Add the peppers, toss and cook for 5–6 minutes. Add the parsley or basil and season to taste. Spoon over the warm bruschettas and serve immediately.

Spicy Roast Pepper Topping

Add ¹/₂–1 teaspoon chilli flakes to the garlic in the pan and proceed as above.

Olive, Chilli and Caper Topping

225g (8fl oz) tapenade (see p75)
¹/₄ teaspoon chilli flakes
1 tablespoon capers, rinsed
1 tablespoon chopped flat parsley

Whizz all the ingredients together in a food processor. Taste – you may need to add a little salt. Spoon on to warm bruschettas and serve as soon as possible.

Kale and Parsley Pesto Topping

450g (1lb) fresh kale
1 garlic clove, crushed
¹/₂ teaspoon sea salt
75ml (3fl oz) extra virgin olive oil
2 tablespoons chopped parsley (optional)

Remove the stalks from the kale leaves and wash well, then dry. Put all the ingredients in a food processor and whizz to a thick paste. This can be made ahead and stored in a covered jar in the fridge for several days.

Tip: If you prefer a more mellow flavour, blanch the kale in boiling, salted water for 3–4 minutes, refresh, drain well and proceed as above.

Broad Bean and Mint Topping

Best made with fresh young broad beans, but frozen ones will do at a push.

450g (1lb) shelled fresh broad beans
leaves from 6–8 sprigs of mint, plus extra to garnish
3–4 tablespoons extra virgin olive oil
2 tablespoons freshly squeezed lemon juice
salt and freshly ground pepper

Cook the broad beans in boiling water until tender (just a few minutes). Drain, reserving the cooking liquid. Rinse the beans under running cold water, then blend in a food processor. Add the mint, olive oil and lemon juice and mix to a purée, adding enough of the reserved cooking liquid to give a soft consistency. Season to taste with salt and pepper. Taste and adjust the levels of lemon and oil, if necessary. Garnish with mint.

More Toppings for Bruschetta or Crostini (see p74)

1   Rocket leaves, mozzarella cheese, roasted red and yellow peppers
2   Potato, olives and Provençal herbs
3   Smashed broad beans, extra virgin olive oil and freshly grated Pecorino cheese
4   Artichoke hearts with olive oil and Parmesan cheese
5   Poached pear, Gorgonzola cheese and rocket leaves
6   Sautéed wild or flat mushrooms with marjoram and shavings of Parmesan cheese
7   Spiced aubergine (see p243)
8   Gravadlax with mustard and dill mayonnaise (see p140)
9   Goat's cheese with onion marmalade (see p298) and watercress
10 Buffalo mozzarella cheese, vine-ripened tomatoes and basil leaves
11 Warm cannellini beans with extra virgin olive oil and rosemary
12 Pata Negra, Serrano or Parma ham and rocket leaves
13 Goat's cheese, home-roasted tomatoes, crispy Parma ham and rocket leaves
14 Spiced aubergine (see p243), goat's cheese and rocket leaves
15 Manchego cheese and membrillo (quince paste)
16 Soft goat's cheese with tapenade oil (see p75) or caramelised onion
17 Avocado, tomato, chilli and coriander
18 Ruffles of fresh prosciutto and rocket leaves
19 Thinly sliced raw tuna with picked ginger and wasabi

Croustade with Goat's Cheese, Chestnut Honey and Thyme Leaves

SERVES 2   (**P:** 5 MINS/**C:** 5 MINS)

A delicious speedy snack.

2 slices of good bread, cut into 5mm
  (¹/₄in) slices
50–75g (2–3oz) fresh goat's cheese
¹/₂ teaspoon thyme leaves
2 dessertspoons chestnut honey (or another
  strongly flavoured honey)

To serve: thyme flowers (optional)

Preheat the grill. Toast or chargrill the slices of bread. Spread thickly with goat's cheese. Sprinkle generously with fresh thyme leaves.

Pop under the hot grill for 2–3 minutes. Drizzle with chestnut honey and serve immediately, sprinkled with thyme flowers if available.

Rory's Spicy Popcorn

SERVES 10   (**P:** 5 MINS/**C:** 5 MINS)

An irresistible munchie to nibble with drinks.

50g (2oz) butter
1 teaspoon salt
¹/₂ teaspoon chilli flakes (optional)
¹/₂ teaspoon cracked black pepper
¹/₂ teaspoon ground cumin
¹/₂ teaspoon curry powder (hot)
1 tablespoon fresh ginger, grated
1 garlic clove, finely chopped
3 tablespoons sunflower oil
110g (4oz) popcorn, still unpopped of course

In a small saucepan, melt the butter and add all the seasonings. Do not let this mixture fry but keep it very hot.

In a large heavy bottomed saucepan, heat the vegetable oil over a very high heat until it is nearly smoking. Add the corn and shake. Wait until you hear the first few pops, then quickly toss in the spiced butter, cover and shake. Shake the pot continuously in a front to back motion until the corn stops popping. Quickly tip into a funky serving bowl or better still serve in paper cornets.

Mini Poppadoms with Spicy Chicken, Banana and Cardamom Raita

MAKES 30   (**P:** 10 MINS + 30 MINS
TO MARINATE/**C:** 15 MINS)

All of the prep for these yummy canapés can be done ahead, but they taste best if the chicken is warm.

3 chicken breasts, preferably free-range organic
30 mini poppadoms
sunflower oil, for frying and roasting

For the spice marinade:
2 teaspoons ground cumin
2 teaspoons paprika
1/2 teaspoon cayenne pepper
2 teaspoons ground turmeric
1 teaspoon caster sugar
1/2 teaspoon freshly ground black pepper
1 teaspoon salt
1 large garlic clove, crushed
2 tablespoons freshly squeezed lemon juice

To serve: Banana and Cardamom Raita
(see p294) and coriander leaves

First make the spice marinade by mixing all the ingredients in a bowl.

Cut the chicken breasts into cubes or small slices, toss in the marinade and refrigerate for at least 30 minutes.

Next make the Banana and Cardamom Raita.

Cook the poppadoms in batches in sunflower oil in a deep-fat fryer at 200°C/400°F or in a frying pan with oil to a depth of 2.5cm (1in). When the oil is almost smoking, cook for just a few seconds. Drain well and set aside.

Preheat the oven to 200°C/400°F/gas mark 6.

Spread the chicken cubes on a baking tray just large enough to hold them in a single layer. Drizzle with sunflower oil. Cook for 10–15 minutes or until fully cooked but still succulent and juicy. Toss regularly while cooking.

Arrange the poppadoms on a plate – square or rectangular plates look particularly good, but round is fine too. Place a teaspoonful of the spicy chicken on each one. Top with a little Banana and Cardamom Raita and garnish with a coriander leaf. Serve as soon as possible.

Tiny Yorkshire Puddings with Pink Lamb, Tapenade Mayo and Rocket Leaves

MAKES ABOUT 28   (**P:** 10 MINS + 1 HOUR
TO STAND/**C:** 15 MINS)

110g (4oz) plain white flour
2 free-range, organic eggs
300ml (1/2 pint) milk
10g (1/2oz) butter, melted and cooled
sunflower oil, for greasing

Tapenade Mayo (see p297)

175–225g (6–8oz) slightly pink roast lamb (or chargrill a thick chump chop until medium rare, rest and slice thinly as needed)

To serve: 50g (2oz) membrillo (quince paste; optional) and rocket, mint or flat parsley

Sift the flour into a bowl. Make a well in the centre of the flour and drop in the eggs. Using a small whisk or wooden spoon, stir continuously, gradually drawing the flour from the sides into the eggs, while adding the milk to the central well in a steady stream. When all the flour has been incorporated, whisk in the remainder of the milk and the butter. Alternatively put all the ingredients into a blender and whizz for a few seconds. Leave to stand for 1 hour.

Preheat the oven to 230°C/450°F/gas mark 8.

Heat two mini-muffin tins in the oven, grease with sunflower oil and half-fill with the batter. Return to the oven and bake for 15 minutes or until crisp, golden and bubbly.

Remove from the tins. Fill each pudding with a tiny blob of tapenade mayo. Top with a thin sliver of lamb and a little cube of membrillo (if available). Garnish with a rocket leaf, sprig of fresh mint or flat parsley. Serve as quickly as possible.

Other serving suggestions
Rare roast beef, horseradish sauce (see p158) and wild rocket leaf
Rare roast beef, onion marmalade (see p298) and watercress leaves
A ruffle of Lollo Rosso lettuce, pink trout, dill mayo (see p297) and horseradish sauce (see p158)

Bocconcini, Olives, Sun-blush Tomatoes and Pesto on Skewers

MAKES 20

(P: 50 MINS + 10 MINS TO MARINATE)

Bocconcini are baby mozzarella cheeses – great for salads, finger food and some pasta dishes. They do however need a little bit of help with flavour, which is where the pesto comes in.

20 bocconcini
extra virgin olive oil
pesto (see p297)
20–40 basil leaves
20 Kalamata olives, stoned
20 sun-blush tomatoes

bamboo cocktail sticks or satay sticks

Drain the bocconcini and pop them into a bowl, drizzle with extra virgin olive oil and add a generous tablespoon of homemade pesto. Toss to coat. Cover closely and leave to marinate for at least 10 minutes.

Thread a bocconcino, a basil leaf, an olive and a piece of sun-blush tomato on to each of 20 bamboo cocktail sticks.

Dill Potato Cakes with Gravadlax and Sweet Mustard Mayo

SERVES 8   (P: 30 MINS/C: 5 MINS)

900g (2lb) unpeeled main-crop potatoes, such as Golden Wonder or Kerrs Pink
25g–50g (1–2oz) butter
25g (1oz) plain flour
2 tablespoons chopped dill
creamy milk, as required
salt and freshly ground pepper
seasoned flour
clarified butter (see p108) or olive oil, for frying

To serve: Mustard and Dill Mayonnaise (see p140), Gravadlax (see p140) and sprigs of dill

Cook the potatoes whole in their jackets, in well-salted boiling water to cover. Drain, pull off the peel and mash right away with the butter, flour and chopped dill, adding a few drops of creamy milk if the mixture is too stiff. Season with lots of salt and pepper. Taste and adjust the seasoning if needed, adding more dill if necessary.

Shape into potato cakes 2cm ($^3/_4$in) thick. Coat the cakes in seasoned flour and fry in clarified butter or olive oil until golden on one side, then flip over and cook on the other side, about 4–5 minutes in total. They should be crusty and golden. Serve on very hot plates.

Put a dollop of Mustard and Dill Mayonnaise on top of each potato cake. Top with slivers of gravadlax and tiny sprigs of dill. Serve immediately.

Other good things to serve with the potato cakes
Use smoked salmon, mackerel or trout instead of gravadlax and substitute crème fraîche for the mustard mayo.
Use hot crispy bacon or chorizo instead of gravadlax, with crème fraîche.
Top the dill potato cakes with smoked haddock, a fried quail's egg and some flat parsley.

Cheddar Cheese and Thyme Leaf Croquettes

MAKES 25–30   (P: 10 MINS/C: 20 MINS)

425ml ($^3/_4$ pint) milk
1 sprig of thyme
200g (7oz) roux (see p139)
salt and freshly ground pepper
2 free-range, organic egg yolks
200g (7oz) mature Cheddar cheese, grated and 25g (1oz) Parmesan or Gabriel cheese, grated
1 tablespoon thyme leaves
olive oil, for deep-frying
To serve: Sweet Chilli Sauce (see p296) or Spicy Tomato Jam (see p298)

For the coating:
seasoned white flour, preferably unbleached
beaten egg,
fine white breadcrumbs

Put the cold milk into a saucepan, add the sprig of thyme, bring slowly to the boil and simmer for 3–4 minutes. Strain, bring the milk back to the boil and whisk in the roux bit by bit – it will get very thick but persevere. (The roux always seems like a lot too much, but you need it all, so don't decide to use less.)

Season with salt and freshly ground pepper. Cook for 1–2 minutes on a gentle heat, then remove from the heat. Stir in the egg yolks, cheese and thyme leaves. Taste and correct the seasoning. Spread out on a flat tray to cool.

When the mixture is cold or at least cool enough to handle, shape into balls about the size of a walnut or about 25g (1oz). Roll first in seasoned flour, then in beaten egg and then in fine breadcrumbs. Chill until firm but bring back to room temperature before cooking otherwise they may burst. Heat olive oil in a deep fryer to 150°C/300°F and cook the croquettes until crisp and golden. Drain on kitchen paper and serve hot with Sweet Chilli Sauce or Spicy Tomato Jam.

Note: Cooked Cheddar Cheese and Thyme Leaf Croquettes can be kept warm in the oven for up to 30 minutes. They can also be frozen and reheated in the oven.

Alicia's Cheese Straws

MAKES ABOUT 12   (P: 20 MINS/C: 15 MINS)

Alicia Wilkinson from Silwood Kitchens in Capetown gave me this delicious recipe.

250g (9oz) puff or rough puff pastry
1 free-range, organic egg white, lightly whisked
100g (3¹/₂oz) Parmesan cheese
100g (3¹/₂oz) Cheddar cheese
pinch of cayenne pepper

Preheat the oven to 190°C/375°F/gas mark 5.

Roll the chilled puff pastry into a large rectangle on a floured marble slab. Brush the lower half of the pastry with lightly beaten egg white.

Finely grate the two cheeses and mix with a good pinch of cayenne pepper. Sprinkle half the cheese and spice mixture liberally over the egg white, and press down gently.

Fold the upper half of the pastry down over the lower half and press with a rolling pin to seal. Roll out the pastry to the size of the first rectangle. Paint the entire sheet with egg white and cover with the remaining cheese and spice.

Chill for approximately 10 minutes. Cut the pastry into thin strips 1cm (¹/₂in) wide and twist into straws. Bake for 10–15 minutes or until golden brown and cooked through. Cool on a wire rack.

Serve in a tall glass or beaker. We use a tall, scalloped zinc pot or children's tin sand buckets depending on the occasion.

Top Tip: The raw prepared cheese straws can be laid on silicone paper and frozen. The silicone paper can be lifted on to a baking sheet with the cheese straws direct from the freezer and baked as above, allowing a little extra cooking time.

Alicia's No-cook Chorizo con Marmalada de Sevilla

MAKES 36   (P: 5 MINS)

When Alicia Rios came to Ballymaloe to teach a tapas course with me, she created this unlikely but delicious tapa using our Seville orange marmalade – perfect for easy entertaining. Your guests will need paper napkins!

110g (4oz) Seville orange marmalade
225g (8oz) chorizo sausage
To serve: small rounds of bread (optional)

Chop the peel in the marmalade into short chunks. Cut the chorizo into slices and top each slice with a little Seville orange marmalade.

Serve as is or on little rounds of bread.

Chorizo with Sherry

SERVES 4   (P: 5 MINS/C: 5 MINS)

Don't forget this simple tapa – it's one of our favourites. Enjoy it with a chilled fino or manzanilla sherry.

200g (7oz) chorizo (the semi-cured type
   suitable for cooking is perfect)
75ml (3fl oz) fino or medium-dry sherry
a drizzle of extra virgin olive oil
To serve: crusty bread
cocktail sticks

Cut the chorizo into slices about 6mm (¹/₃in) thick.

Heat a frying pan over medium heat and add a drizzle of olive oil. When the oil begins to smoke, add the chorizo and fry until it starts to crisp. Turn over and fry the other side. When both sides are crisp, add the sherry. It will splutter but keep the pan over the heat for a few seconds to burn off the alcohol. Transfer the contents of the pan to a dish and tuck in immediately. Provide a few cocktail sticks, and some crusty bread to mop up the juices.

Melon and Spearmint Soup with Crispy Parma Served in Shot Glasses

MAKES 600ML (1 PINT) – 12 SHOT GLASSES
(**P:** 10 MINS/**C:** 10 MINS)

1 really ripe Ogen or Galia melon
juice of 1 large lemon
2–3 tablespoons caster sugar
2 tablespoons chopped spearmint
110g (4oz) sliced Parma ham

To serve: 12 sprigs of mint

Peel and deseed the melon. Liquidise or purée the flesh with the lemon juice and spearmint, and add sugar to taste. Chill.

Meanwhile preheat the oven to 180ºC/350ºF/gas mark 4.

Spread the Parma ham slices in a single layer on a baking tray. Lay another tray on top. Cook for 5–8 minutes or until the ham is crisp and the fat has melted. Allow to cool, then break the ham into long slivers.

To serve, pour the melon 'soup' into shot glasses. Top with a splinter of ham and a sprig of fresh mint.

Mussels with Dill Mayo and Cucumber, Red Onion and Fennel Salsa

MAKES 60   (P: 20 MINS/C: 5 MINS)

60 large fresh mussels
coarse sea salt

For the Cucumber, Red Onion and Fennel Salsa:
1 crisp cucumber seeded and finely diced
1½ small red onion finely diced
3–6 tablespoons finely chopped fresh fennel
  (dill may be used instead)
A few drops of white wine vinegar
Salt, freshly ground pepper and sugar

To serve: Dill Mayonnaise (see p297)

Check that all the mussels are closed. If any are open, tap each mussel on the worktop, and discard all that do not close within a few seconds. (A good maxim with shellfish: 'If in doubt, throw it out.') Wash the mussels well in several changes of cold water.

Spread them in a single layer in a pan, cover with a lid and cook over a gentle heat. As soon as the shells open the mussels are cooked – this usually takes 2–3 minutes. Remove from the pan immediately or they will shrink in size and become tough.

Remove the beard and discard one shell from each mussel. Loosen the mussel from the other shell, but leave it in the shell. Open the rest in the same way. Set aside until quite cold. Coat a serving dish evenly with coarse salt. Arrange the mussels in their half shells on the salt.

Next make the salsa. Mix all the ingredients together. Taste and correct the seasoning. It should taste sweet and sour. If dill is used instead of fennel in this recipe, use half the quantity. Spoon the salsa over half of the mussels and put a blob of dill mayo on the others. Serve at room temperature or chilled.

Parmesan Toasts

MAKES 20   (P: 10 MINS/C: 30 MINS)

What began as a way to use up leftover bread has become a delicious nibble to serve with drinks or as an accompaniment to tomato, onion, cauliflower, pumpkin or kale soups.

day-old yeast or sour dough bread, or
  good-quality baguette, cut into 3mm (⅛in)
  thick slices (cut the baguette diagonally)
extra virgin olive oil
Parmesan cheese, grated

Preheat the oven to 150°C/300°F/gas mark 2.

Brush one side of each slice of bread with olive oil. Sprinkle with Parmesan.

Arrange in a single layer on a baking tray and bake slowly until golden brown and crisp, about 30 minutes. Serve warm.

Cheat's Tarts with Various Fillings

MAKES 20   (P: 5 MINS/C: 10 MINS +
                        TIME TO PREPARE FILLING)

I'm frightfully snooty about sliced bread but this is a brilliant trick shown to us by one of my favourite cookery writers and joint-owner of 'Books for Cooks' in London, Eric Treuille, when he came to teach at the school a few years ago. I've listed a number of fillings you could use. Look in your fridge, experiment and use fresh herbs and herb flowers. Unfilled Cheat's Tarts will keep in an airtight tin for several days.

ready-sliced white bread
filling of your choice (see suggestions, right)

rolling pin
mini muffin tray
4.5cm (1¾in) cutter

Preheat the oven to 200°C/400°F/gas mark 6.

Cut the crusts off the bread. Roll the bread out very thinly with a rolling pin – it should be completely flat. Stamp out rounds with the cutter. Fit into the mini muffin tins and press down hard.

Bake for 5–7 minutes until crisp and pale golden in colour. Remove from the tray while hot. Cool on a wire rack and add your chosen filling.

Suggested fillings
Wild salmon pâté (Salmon Rillettes, see p74) with Cucumber Pickle (see p73) and dill
Chicken liver pâté with sun-blush tomatoes
Goat's cheese and Kumquat Compote (see p267)
Goat's cheese with pesto and cherry tomatoes
Prawns or shrimps with guacamole and coriander
Crab mayonnaise (white crab meat mixed with a little mayo)
Smoked mussels with mayo
Goat's cheese, piquillo pepper and basil leaves
Smoked Mackerel and Dill Pâté (see p73)
Crab, ginger and lime (see p60)

Ragged Filo Tartlets

MAKES 20   (P: 20 MINS/C: 65 MINS)

110g (4oz) filo pastry
110g (4oz) butter, melted

mini muffin tins, bun trays or muffin trays

For the crab, ginger and lime filling:
250g (9oz) white crab meat, drained
1/2–1 tablespoon peeled and grated fresh
   ginger
juice and finely grated zest of 1 lime
1/2 unpeeled cucumber, cut into 5mm
   (1/4in) dice
1 avocado, diced
4 tablespoons homemade mayonnaise
   (see p296–297)
tabasco sauce
sea salt
coriander leaves, to garnish

Preheat the oven to 180°C/350°F/gas mark 4.

Using a wide pastry brush, brush 1 sheet of filo pastry with the melted butter. Cut into 10–15cm (4–6in) pieces – adjust the size to fit your tartlet trays or mini muffin tins. Butter the muffin tins and line each one with 3 buttered filo pastry squares placed at slightly different angles. (It is easier to assemble the stacks before pressing into the tin.) Repeat until all the filo pastry has been used. Bake to a rich golden brown, about 6–8 minutes.

Carefully remove the tartlets from the tins and leave to cool completely on a wire rack. These tartlets can be baked a few days in advance. Store in an airtight container at room temperature.

To make the filling, mix the crab meat with the ginger, lime zest, cucumber, avocado and mayonnaise. Add a few dashes of Tabasco, a little lime juice and salt. Taste and adjust the seasoning if needed. Close to the time of serving divide the crab mixture among the ragged filo tartlet cases. Garnish with coriander leaves.

Top Tip: Keep the filo pastry covered with a damp cloth until ready to use otherwise it will become dry, brittle and unusable.

Quesadillas with Tomato Salsa and Guacamole and Various Fillings

SERVES 8   (**P:** 5 MINS/**C:** 5 MINS
+ TIME TO PREPARE FILLING)

Quesadillas are a favourite snack in Mexico. On Sundays in Oaxaca there are little stalls on the streets and squares with women making and selling these delicious stuffed tortillas. They flavour them with an aromatic leaf called hoja santa. Cut into 6 or 8 wedges, they make delicious finger food. There are masses of delicious filling combinations. Experiment and have fun! Serve with Guacamole, Tomato and Coriander Salsa and refried beans.

16 corn tortillas or 4 wheat flour tortillas
225–450g (8oz–1lb) mild Cheddar cheese,
   grated, or a mixture of Cheddar and
   mozzarella
1 onion or 8 spring onions, sliced
4 green chillies, sliced (optional)

To serve: Guacamole (see p294), Tomato and
   Coriander Salsa (see p294), Refried Beans
   (see p21)

Heat a wide, heavy, iron pan, griddle or non-stick pan. Lay a tortilla on the hot pan. Sprinkle about 25g (1oz) grated cheese on top, depending on size, keeping it a little from the edge, then add a few onion rings and some sliced chilli (if using). Cover with another tortilla. Cook for a minute or two. As soon as the cheese begins to melt, carefully turn the assembly over. Cook for 1–2 minutes on the other side.

Serve just as it is or cut into wedges, accompanied by Guacamole, Tomato and Coriander Salsa and, if you like, Refried Beans.

Quesadillas with Cheese and Courgette Blossoms
A favourite filling for quesadillas in Oaxaca is simply grated Oaxacan string cheese (mozzarella is our nearest equivalent) and fresh courgette blossoms. Thinly sliced green chilli is sometimes added for extra excitement!

Quesadillas with Spicy Pork or Chicken and Slices of Avocado
Add spicy pork or chicken and slices of avocado to the basic recipe.

Quesadillas with Shredded or Smoked Chicken, Mango, Brie and Lime
Substitute slices of Brie for the Cheddar cheese in the basic recipe and add some cooked shredded chicken, diced mango and lime.

Quesadillas with Pappadew Peppers, Mozzarella and Basil Leaves
Sprinkle some sliced pappadew peppers over the grated mozzarella cheese in the basic recipe. Top with a layer of basil leaves.

Quesadillas with Chorizo
Add some diced or thinly sliced chorizo to the basic recipe.

Seafood Quesadillas
Shrimps, prawns or strips of smoked salmon can also be delicious.

Quesadillas with Spicy Chicken, Mozzarella and Coriander
Spread some cooked spicy chicken, mozzarella, chopped spring onions and fresh coriander leaves over the tortilla and continue as in the basic recipe.

Quesadillas with Mozzarella and Tapenade or Pesto
Spread tapenade (see p75) or pesto (see p297) on a tortilla and top with grated mozzarella. Top with another tortilla, cook and serve as before.

Quesadillas with Anchoïade and Mozzarella
Substitute anchoiade for tapenade or pesto in the above recipe.

Quesadillas with Ballymaloe Country Relish and Cheddar Cheese
Spread a tortilla with Ballymaloe Country Relish, top with grated Cheddar cheese and sprinkle with chopped parsley and spring onions. Cook and serve as before.

Marinated Black Olives

SERVES 10 (P: 10 MINS)

Marinated olives are so easy to make – we always have some ready to nibble with drinks. Prepare at least a few days ahead of serving.

225g (8oz) black olives, such as Kalamata
1 garlic clove, crushed
1/2 teaspoon smoked paprika
1 tablespoon sherry vinegar or red wine vinegar
pinch of freshly ground cumin
a little grated orange zest (optional)
65ml (2¹/₂fl oz) extra virgin olive oil

Stir all the ingredients together and store in a Kilner jar. Cover the olives completely with oil and they will keep for several weeks.

Marinated Green Olives

SERVES 10 (P: 5 MINS)

225g (8oz) Spanish green olives
2–4 garlic cloves, lightly crushed
65ml (2¹/₂fl oz) extra virgin olive oil
1 tablespoon finely chopped oregano or annual marjoram
To serve: wild garlic or chive flowers

Stir everything together and store in a Kilner jar. Serve at room temperature, sprinkled with wild garlic or chive flowers.

Roasted Kalamata Olives

SERVES 20 (P: 5 MINS/C: 15 MINS)

500g (1b 2oz) black olives, such as Kalamata
5 large garlic cloves, bashed
1 teaspoon chopped rosemary or thyme
3–4 strips lemon or orange zest (scrub the fruit if not organic)
extra virgin olive oil, for drizzling

Preheat the oven to 180°C/350°F/gas mark 4.

Mix the olives, garlic, chopped herb and citrus zest in a small roasting tin and drizzle with olive oil. Roast for 10–15 minutes. Serve warm.

Spicy Candied Nuts

SERVES 6–8 (P: 5 MINS/C: 10 MINS)

100g (3¹/₂oz) walnut halves
75g (3oz) sugar
1/2 teaspoon ground cinnamon
1/2 teaspoon ground coriander
1/4 teaspoon ground star anise

Preheat the oven to 180°C/350°F/gas mark 4. Spread the walnuts in a single layer on a baking tray and toast them for 4–5 minutes until they smell rich and nutty.

Meanwhile, mix the sugar with the spices and spread this mixture over the base of a frying pan in an even layer. Scatter the walnut halves on top. Cook over a medium heat until the sugar melts and starts to colour. Carefully rotate the pan until the walnuts are completely coated with the amber-coloured spicy caramel. Turn out on to non-stick, silicone paper or an oiled baking tray. Allow to cool and harden. Store in an airtight container until needed.

Edamame with Sea Salt

SERVES 4–8 (P: 20 MINS/C: 65 MINS)

These fresh soya beans in their pods are one of our favourite nibbles – they are not widely available fresh, but can be found frozen and then cooked in minutes.

1.2 litres (2 pints) water
450g (1lb) edamame
3 teaspoons sea salt

Bring the water to the boil and add the edamame beans. Return to the boil and cook for 3–4 minutes. Taste. If sufficiently cooked, they'll have a slight bite. Drain and sprinkle with the sea salt. Serve cold.

tips on finger food

The essence of good finger food is fantastic ingredients. Find a good deli or farmer's market and buy lots of top-quality bocconcini, heirloom tomatoes, salami, juicy olives and a really good smoked fish and that will happily make up half of your menu.

Finger food does not need to be complicated – a fat prawn on some brown bread with a dollop of mayonnaise and a sprig of parsley or dill – what could be more delicious, but the quality of ingredient is key to this simplicity, and will also make it easier. If the tomatoes and mozzarella taste good to start with, you don't have to work so hard. Or serve miniature portions of your favourite recipes with a saucy herb garnish or dollop of crème fraîche and jazz up the presentation – sprigs of woody herbs, such as rosemary, make creative alternatives to the usual cocktail sticks and skewers and Virginia creeper leaves, vine leaves and even fig leaves are also very effective.

Food should be no larger than single mouthfuls and you should reckon on 5–7 pieces per person, less if this is a starter. Make sure that there are at least two vegetarian choices and if one of your guests cannot eat gluten, for example, do take care to explain the ingredients as you pass. Consider what will be popular dishes and make more of them than, for example, something containing tapenade, which not everybody likes.

Put the toppings on at the last-possible minute otherwise they will melt through, especially when using porous bases such as prawn crackers. Nonetheless you can do a little preparation: arrange the bases on serving trays and have the garnish ready to go. Then it's just a simple matter of warming up the topping, loading up the tray and off you go.

Cocktail party (see p46–49)

Bloody Mary Jellies (see p66)
Melon and Spearmint Soup with Crispy Parma Ham (see p57)
Mussels with Salsa Cruda, Dill Mayo and Cucumber (see p59)
Mixed Bruschetta (see p52)

To drink

A classic margarita (p290) will work here but if you want to provide a wine alternative the most effective choice is probably a New World sparkler wine with plenty of ripe fruit character. Champagne or even Prosecco would be a little too austere. Go for something that combines elegant bubbles with a touch of tropical fruits. Names like Lindauer, Deutz, Jansz and especially Pelorus (from Cloudy Bay in New Zealand) are worth seeking out.

Round the world menu

Sushi (see p44)
Thai Chicken on Chinese Spoons (see p51)
Mini Poppadoms with Spicy Chicken, Banana and Cardamom Raita (see p54)
Teeny Yorkshire Puddings (see p54)
Quesadillas with Tomato Salsa (see p61)
Marinated Black Olives (see p62)

To drink

Sushi goes brilliantly with two starkly contrasting wines: Australian dry Riesling and fino or manzanilla sherry. The Riesling will also work with Thai chicken – and everything else on this menu with the possible exception of the quesadillas. These ideally need something with more fruit, perhaps a New World Chardonnay. If you must have one wine, stick to a fresh Chilean Sauvignon Blanc, it will do a pretty good job.

Vegetarian party

Tomato and Coconut Milk Soup in Espresso Cups (see p51)
Crostini with Spiced Aubergine (see p53)
Bocconcini, Olive, Sun-Blush Tomato and Pesto on Skewers (see p55)
Cheddar Cheese and Thyme Leaf Croquettes (see p55)
Alicia's Cheese Straws (see p56)
Cruditées with Hummus and Aubergine Purée (see pp213, 118, 119)

To drink

Both the crostini and the croquettes need a fruity red with a bit of bite: Montepulciano d'Abruzzo will fit the bill perfectly. Although a lot of people turn their noses up at it, Retsina works magically well with both hummus and aubergine. But chill it very thoroughly and do bear in mind that some people think it's the wine equivalent of turpentine!

starters

A taste of things to come, a starter should tempt your tastebuds but leave your guests wanting more. Here are ideas for crostini, dips and pâtés as well as ceviche and spring rolls. Many other recipes can double up as starters, so do also have a look in Soups and Salads as well as Finger Food – just remember to keep portions small. Starters don't have to be served at the dinner table – if you want to introduce people informally, choose dishes that can be passed around with an aperitif.

Campari and Blood Orange Granita

SERVES 10   (P: 10 MINS + FREEZING TIME)

An irresistible and deliciously non-fattening appetiser. Of course it can be made with juicy oranges at any time of the year, but keep an eye out for blood oranges from January to March. A non-alcoholic version with blood orange juice alone is also perfectly delicious.

1 litre (1³/₄ pints) freshly squeezed blood
  orange juice, or a mixture of blood orange
  juice and ordinary orange juice
350g (12oz) caster sugar, plus extra if needed
125ml (4fl oz) Campari
1 free-range, organic egg white (optional)
1–2 blood oranges, segmented, and mint
  leaves, to garnish (optional)

Mix the orange juice with the sugar and Campari. Stir and taste, and add more sugar if needed. Make the granita in one of the following three ways:

1 Pour the mixture into a stainless-steel or plastic container and put into the freezer or the freezing compartment of a fridge. After about 4–5 hours, when the mixture is semi-frozen, remove from the freezer and whisk until smooth; then return to the freezer. After a few hours, whisk again. Return to the freezer until needed.

2 Allow the mixture to freeze completely in a stainless-steel or plastic container, then break into large pieces and whizz in a food processor for a few seconds. Add the slightly beaten egg white, whizz again for further few seconds, then return to the bowl and freeze until needed.

3 Pour into the drum of an ice-cream maker or sorbetière and freeze for 20–25 minutes. Scoop out and serve immediately, or store in a covered bowl in the freezer until needed. This method produces a less granular texture, which might be called a sorbet rather than a granita.

To serve, scoop out the granita and serve just as it is in chilled cocktail glasses, white bowls or plates, or, if you wish, garnished with segments of blood orange and some mint leaves.

Bloody Mary Jellies

SERVES 8   (P: 10 MINS +SETTING TIME)

1 tablespoon vodka
dash of tabasco
10g (¹/₂oz) gelatine
4 tablespoons water
micro greens and a few tender celery stalks,
  diced, to garnish

8 shot glasses

For the fresh tomato juice:
450g (1lb) very ripe tomatoes, skinned, halved
  and deseeded
1 spring onion with a little green leaf or
  1 slice onion 5cm (2in) in diameter,
  8mm (¹/₃in) thick
3 fresh basil or spearmint leaves
2 teaspoons white wine vinegar
125ml (4fl oz) cold water
1 teaspoon salt
1 teaspoon sugar
freshly ground black pepper

First make the fresh tomato juice. Blend all the ingredients together in a liquidiser, then strain. Taste and correct the seasoning if necessary.

Add the vodka and a dash of Tabasco to the fresh tomato juice. Taste.

Sponge the gelatine with the water in a bowl, then place the bowl over a saucepan of simmering water until the gelatine melts completely.

Stir some of the tomato juice into the gelatine, then mix with the remainder of the juice, stirring well. Pour into 8 shot glasses or oiled moulds. Allow to set in the fridge for several hours.

Serve with some micro greens and a little dice of tender stalks from the heart of celery.

Warm Mushroom and Rocket Salad with Shavings of Desmond Farmhouse Cheese

SERVES 8   (P: 10 MINS/C: 10 MINS)

This is a poshed-up version of mushrooms on toast. Virtually all fungi are delicious on toast, so this can be a very humble or very exotic dish depending on the variety chosen.

extra virgin olive oil, for frying
900g (2lb) flat mushrooms or oyster
   mushrooms, or better still a mix of shiitake,
   enoki, oyster and beech mushrooms, sliced
   into biggish chunks (leave the enoki whole)
salt and freshly ground pepper
6 tablespoons coarsely chopped marjoram
1 garlic clove, crushed (optional)
lots of rocket leaves
shavings of Desmond farmhouse cheese
   or Parmesan

To serve: crostini or chargrilled bruschetta
   (see p52)

Heat a little olive oil in a hot frying pan. Cook the mushrooms in batches and keep warm while you cook the rest. Season each batch with salt and freshly ground pepper, and sprinkle with chopped marjoram and some crushed garlic if you like. When all are cooked, taste and adjust the seasoning if needed.

Arrange a fistful of rocket leaves on each plate and top with the mushrooms. Sprinkle on a few shavings of Desmond farmhouse cheese or Parmesan and serve immediately with crostini or chargrilled bruschetta.

This salad is just as good if the mushrooms have cooled to room temperature.

Peach, Gorgonzola and Watercress Salad

SERVES 8   (P: 20 MINS)

A gorgeous summer starter salad that can be made in minutes. For a light lunch, add a few strips of pangrilled chicken breast.

4 ripe peaches or nectarines
2–3 tablespoons lemon juice
sugar to taste
watercress sprigs or rocket leaves
225g (8oz) Gorgonzola cheese, or Crozier or
   Wicklow Blue
110g (4oz) shelled walnuts, coarsely chopped
4 spring onions, thinly sliced

For the dressing:
2 tablespoons white wine vinegar
6 tablespoons walnut oil
1 teaspoon wholegrain mustard
1 teaspoon honey
sea salt and freshly ground pepper

First make the dressing. With a fork, whisk all the ingredients together in a little bowl. Taste and adjust the seasoning as needed.

Cut the fruit in half and remove the stones, then slice into 6–8 pieces. If you are not serving immediately, sprinkle the fruit with some lemon juice and sugar and toss gently.

Scatter a few watercress sprigs or rocket leaves on each plate, tuck a few peach or nectarine slices in here and there, and crumble some gorgonzola or other blue cheese over the top. Drizzle on some dressing, and sprinkle over the walnuts and thinly sliced spring onions. Serve soon.

Top Tip: Add a few strips of pangrilled chicken breast for a light lunch.

Salad of Goat's Cheese with Rocket, Figs and Pomegranate Seeds

SERVES 8   (P: 10 MINS)

1 fresh pomegranate
32 fresh walnut or pecan halves
enough rocket leaves for 8 helpings
a few radicchio leaves
4 small fresh goat's cheeses
8–12 fresh figs or plump dried figs (try to find
 the Turkish ones on a raffia string)

To serve: crusty bread

For the dressing:
125ml (4fl oz) extra virgin olive oil
3 tablespoons freshly squeezed lemon juice
1/2–1 teaspoon honey
salt and freshly ground pepper

Cut the pomegranate in half and break each side open. Flick out the glistening, jewel-like seeds into a bowl, avoiding the bitter, yellowy pith. Alternatively, if you are in a hurry, put the cut side down on the palm of your hand over a bowl and bash the skin side firmly with the back of a wooden spoon – this works really well but it tends to be a bit messy, so be sure to protect your clothes with an apron as pomegranate juice really stains.

Next make the dressing. Just whisk the oil, lemon juice and honey together in a bowl. Season well with salt and freshly ground pepper.

Toast the walnut or pecan halves in a dry pan over a medium heat until they smell sweet and nutty.

Just before serving, toss the rocket leaves and radicchio in a deep bowl with a little of the dressing. Divide between 8 large white plates. Cut each cheese into 6 pieces. Cut the figs into quarters from the top, keeping each one still attached at the base. Press gently to open out. Divide the cheese between the plates, 3 pieces per plate, and place a fig in the centre.

Sprinkle with pomegranate seeds and freshly roasted nuts. Drizzle with a little extra dressing and serve immediately with crusty bread.

Ciabatta Stuffed with Good Things

MAKES 12 SMALL PIECES
          (**P:** 10 MINS/**C:** 15 MINS)

Serve as a starter, finger food, or for a yummy snack.

1 loaf ciabatta bread
extra virgin olive oil, for brushing
12 thin slices Parma or Serrano ham
Roasted red and yellow peppers (see p298)
125ml (4fl oz) Pesto (see p297) or
 Tapenade (see p75)
225g (8oz) soft white cheese, such as
 mozzarella, sliced
rocket leaves

Preheat the oven to 230ºC/450ºF/gas mark 8.

Cut the bread in half lengthways and remove some of the soft bread from both the top and bottom with your fingers (save it for making breadcrumbs). Brush the base with olive oil. Lay the slices of ham on the bottom, allowing them to drape over the sides of the bread.

Top with roasted red and yellow peppers and drizzle with pesto or tapenade. Cover with slices of cheese and drizzle with more pesto or tapenade. Top with some rocket leaves and fold over the ham to enclose the filling. Lay the other half of the bread on top and press gently.

Place the stuffed ciabatta on a baking tray and cook for 10–15 minutes. Transfer to a chopping board and cut into pieces about 4cm (1 1/2in) wide. Serve warm.

Other yummy fillings
Tapenade, mozzarella cheese and rocket leaves
Tomato, mozzarella cheese, balsamic vinegar and basil leaves
Chorizo sausage, mozzarella cheese, roasted red and yellow pepper and marjoram leaves

Salmon Spring Rolls with Coriander Dipping Sauce

MAKES 12   (P: 20 MINS/C: 10 MINS)

450g (1lb) wild salmon, about 2.5cm (1in)
  thick, skinned
12 rice paper wrappers (*bahn trang*),
  16cm (6¹/₂in) square
48 coriander leaves
4 tablespoons finely chopped spring onion
  greens
salt and freshly ground pepper
vegetable oil, for frying
coriander sprigs, to garnish

For the marinade:
4 tablespoons extra virgin olive oil
4 tablespoons fresh lime juice
2 tablespoons chopped coriander leaves
1 teaspoon peeled and grated fresh ginger

For the coriander dipping sauce:
Juice of 2 limes
2 tablespoons rice vinegar
1 tablespoon soy sauce
2¹/₂ teaspoons sugar, or to taste
2 teaspoons peeled and grated fresh ginger
2 tablespoons chopped coriander leaves

Whisk the marinade ingredients together in a large bowl and season with salt and pepper to taste.

Cut the salmon crossways into 12 pieces, each about 10 x 2.5cm (4 x 1in) and add them to the marinade. Leave to marinate, turning the pieces occasionally, for 30 minutes.

Meanwhile make the dipping sauce. Whisk all the ingredients together except the chopped coriander, and add 1 tablespoon water.

Remove the salmon from the marinade and pat dry. Fill a wide, shallow bowl with hot water. Soak a rice paper wrapper for about 10 seconds, until very pliable. Drain. Lay on a chopping board and arrange a salmon piece on the bottom half of the wrapper, leaving a 2.5cm (1in) border on the bottom edge and on each side. Top the salmon with about 4 coriander leaves, 1 teaspoon spring onion greens and salt and pepper to taste. Roll up the rice paper wrapper around the filling, folding in the sides after the first roll to enclose the filling completely. Make the remaining spring rolls in the same way.

In a deep 30cm (12in) non-stick pan or a deep fryer, heat 5mm (¹/₄in) oil over a moderately high heat until hot but not smoking. Fry 4 spring rolls at a time, turning once, until they are golden brown and the salmon is cooked through, about 3 minutes. Drain on kitchen paper. Repeat the procedure with the remaining spring rolls.

Stir the chopped coriander into the dipping sauce. Garnish the spring rolls with sprigs of coriander, and serve as a first course or as finger food, accompanied by the dipping sauce.

Mexican Ceviche

SERVES 10–12
      (P: 10 MINS + 5¹/₂ HOURS TO MARINATE)

The fish is 'cooked' by the action of the lime juice.

900g (2lb) fillets of very fresh white fish, such
  as monkfish, cod or plaice
2 lemons
4 limes
salt and freshly ground pepper
2 garlic cloves, finely chopped
3–4 tablespoons chopped coriander leaves
75g (3oz) onion, finely sliced
1–2 fresh, red or green chillies
1 red pepper, finely diced
1 green pepper, finely diced
To serve: crusty white bread

For the garnish:
crisp lettuce, such as Little Gem
2 ripe avocados, sliced
4 spring onions, sliced at an angle

Skin the fish, slice or cube it into 1cm (¹/₂in) pieces and put them into a deep, stainless-steel or china bowl. Squeeze the juice from the lemons and limes and pour over the fish. Sprinkle with salt, freshly ground pepper and chopped garlic. Cover, put in the fridge and leave to marinate for 3–4 hours.

Add the chopped coriander, sliced onion, chillies and half of the diced red and green peppers. Cover and return to the fridge for 1¹/₂ hours. Then serve or keep covered in the fridge until later

To serve, arrange a few crisp lettuce leaves on each plate and place a tablespoon of ceviche in the centre. Decorate with slices of avocado, the remaining diced peppers and the sliced spring onions. Serve with crusty white bread.

Vine-ripened and Sun-blush Tomato Salad with Mozzarella, Prosciutto and Basil

SERVES 8   (**P**: 10 MINS/**C**: 15 MINS)

The mozzarella can be wrapped in the prosciutto ahead of time and refrigerated until needed.

8 small balls of buffalo mozzarella
8 slices of Parma ham (prosciutto)
8 large or 16 small vine-ripened tomatoes
salt and freshly ground pepper
24 sun-blush tomatoes
extra virgin olive oil, for drizzling
balsamic vinegar, for drizzling,
sugar or honey, to taste
pesto (see p297)
lots of fresh basil leaves

To serve: crusty bread

Wrap the mozzarella balls in prosciutto, cover loosely with clingfilm and keep chilled in the fridge until needed. This can be done ahead of time.

Preheat the oven to 250ºC/475ºF/gas mark 9.

Slice the fresh tomatoes into 5mm (¼in) thick slices and season with salt and freshly ground pepper. Drizzle over a little olive oil and balsamic vinegar, taste and add a little sugar or honey if needed.

Put the prosciutto-wrapped mozzarella onto a baking tray and place in the oven until the prosciutto is beginning to crisp and the mozzarella is starting to melt, about 10 minutes. Meanwhile arrange a circle of slightly overlapping tomato slices on individual serving plates (we like to use wide, deep soup bowls). Arrange 3 pieces of sun-blush tomatoes on top. Heat some balsamic vinegar and reduce it to make it a little syrupy and concentrate the flavour. Drizzle a little pesto and balsamic vinegar around the edges and over the top.

When the prosciutto and mozzarella balls are ready, pop them on top of the tomatoes. Scatter over lots of fresh basil leaves, and drizzle on some olive oil. Serve with crusty bread.

Baja-style Fish Tacos with Chipotle Mayonnaise

SERVES 10   (**P**: 20 MINS/**C**: 10 MINS)

10 small fillets of fresh white fish, such as
  haddock, brill, plaice or lemon sole
seasoned flour
oil, for deep-frying

For the chilli beer batter:
225g (8oz) plain white flour
2 teaspoons mustard powder
2 teaspoons chilli powder
1 teaspoon salt
2 teaspoons sugar
3 free-range, organic eggs, beaten
225ml (8fl oz) lager

For the chipotle mayonnaise:
225ml (8fl oz) homemade mayonnaise
  (see p296)
1¹/₂ tablespoons puréed chipotle chillies in
  adobo
juice of 1 lime
1 tablespoon chopped coriander leaves

For the accompaniments:
10 flour tortillas
20 lettuce leaves
Guacamole (see p294)
Tomato and Coriander Salsa (see p294)

First make the chilli beer batter. Sift the flour into a bowl and add the mustard powder, chilli powder, salt and sugar. Make a well in the centre, drop in the eggs, and gradually add the beer, whisking all the time from the centre to the edge of the bowl in ever-increasing concentric circles until all the flour is incorporated. Cover and leave to stand.

Make the mayonnaise in the usual way, then add the chillies in adobo, lime juice and chopped coriander.

Preheat the oven to 180°C/350°F/gas mark 4. Wrap the tortillas in an aluminium foil parcel and heat through in the oven for 5–10 minutes. Meanwhile, prepare the rest of the accompaniments.

Heat the oil in a deep-fat fryer to 190°C/375°F. Dip each fish fillet in the batter, cook until crisp and drain on kitchen paper.

Put a few lettuce leaves on to half a warm tortilla, top with a piece of crispy fish, some chipotle mayonnaise, Guacamole and Tomato and Coriander Salsa, fold over and enjoy!

Carpaccio with Slivers of Parmesan, Rocket and Truffle Oil

SERVES 12   (P: 15 MINS)

Carpaccio is a brilliant recipe to make a little really good beef go a very long way. For this I use our own organically reared free-range Aberdeen Angus, or some Pol Angus beef from our local butcher.

450g (1lb) fillet of beef, preferably Aberdeen
    Angus, Hereford or Shorthorn (fresh not
    frozen)
about 5 rocket leaves per person, depending
    on the size
4–5 very thin slivers Parmesan cheese per
    person
Maldon or Halen Mon sea salt
freshly cracked pepper
truffle oil or extra virgin olive oil
24–36 black Kalamata olives (optional)

To serve: focaccia or ciabatta bread

Chill the meat. Slice the beef fillet with a very sharp knife to 5mm ($\frac{1}{4}$in) thick. Place each slice on a piece of oiled parchment paper and cover with another piece of oiled parchment paper. Roll gently with a rolling pin until the meat is almost transparent and has doubled in size. Peel the parchment paper off the top, turn the meat on to a chilled plate and gently peel away the other layer of paper.

Arrange the rocket leaves on top of the beef and scatter a few very thin slivers of Parmesan over the leaves. Sprinkle with sea salt and freshly cracked pepper. Drizzle with truffle oil or with your very best extra virgin olive oil.

Scatter a few black olives (if using) over each portion and serve immediately with crusty bread – focaccia or ciabatta is best.

A little drizzle of Tapenade (see p75) is delicious instead of truffle oil and olives.

Smoked Mackerel and Dill Pâté with Cucumber Pickle

SERVES 8   (P: 10 MINS + 1 HOUR IN FRIDGE)

225g (8oz) undyed smoked mackerel, skinned,
    boned and flaked
75g (3oz) unsalted butter, softened
75g (3oz) full-fat cream cheese
juice of $\frac{1}{2}$ lemon
2 tablespoons chopped dill
1 tablespoon chopped parsley
sea salt and freshly ground pepper
sprigs of dill and dill flowers, to garnish

For the accompaniments:
generous amount of watercress leaves
extra virgin olive oil
white wine vinegar
angular toast

For the cucumber pickle (serves 10–12):
1kg (2$\frac{1}{4}$lb) unpeeled, cucumber, thinly sliced
3 small onions, thinly sliced
350g (12oz) sugar
2 tablespoons salt (be very accurate with salt)
225ml (8fl oz) cider vinegar

Put the flaked mackerel in a liquidiser and add the butter, cream cheese and lemon juice. Whizz to a smooth purée. Transfer to a bowl and fold in the dill and parsley. Add salt and pepper to taste.

Divide between ramekins or small bowls. Top each with a sprig of dill and a dill flower. Cover and chill for at least an hour.

To serve, toss the watercress leaves in a little olive oil and a dash of white wine vinegar. Sprinkle with salt and pepper and toss. Put some of the leaves on each plate, along with a ramekin of pâté; serve with angular toast and the cucumber pickle.

To make the pickle, put the cucumber and onion slices in a large pyrex or stainless-steel bowl. In a separate bowl, mix together the sugar, salt and vinegar and pour over the cucumber and onion; toss well. Cover tightly and chill in the fridge for at least 1 hour or, ideally several hours to overnight before using. The pickle keeps well for up to a week in the fridge.

A Dozen Oysters and a Pint of Murphy's or Guinness

SERVES 1–2 (P: 10 MINS)

What could be easier or more delicious than freshly shucked oysters with Irish wheaten bread and a pint of gorgeous creamy stout? If you come from County Cork, Murphy's is the sacred drop – Guinness is not quite the same, but we have to admit it makes a good substitute.

12 native Irish oysters

For the accompaniments:
seaweed or sea salt
1 lemon wedge
Wheaten Bread (see p37) or Ballymaloe Brown
  Yeast Bread (see p35)
600ml (1 pint) Murphy's stout or Guinness

First wash the oysters if necessary, then open with a shucking knife or stubby, short-tipped knife. When opening oysters, it's wise to protect your hand with a folded tea towel. Wrap the tea towel round your hand, then set the deep shell on it with the wide end on the inside. Grip the oyster firmly in your protected hand, insert the tip of the knife into the hinge and twist to lever the two shells apart; you'll need to exert quite a lot of pressure, so protect your hand well. Then slide the blade of the knife under the top shell to detach the oyster from the shell. Discard the top shell, then loosen the oyster from the deep shell and flip it over to reveal the plump side – don't lose the precious briny juice.

Make a bed of seaweed or sea salt on a plate and arrange the oyster shells over the top. Serve with a lemon wedge, some wheaten bread and a pint of the black stuff!

Salmon Rillettes with Piquillo Pepper Crostini

SERVES 12–16 (P: 20 MINS/C: 5 MINS)

As well as a fine starter this also makes great finger food.

40g (1¹/₂oz) butter, plus 350g (12oz) butter,
  softened
350g (12oz) smoked wild or organic Irish
  salmon
350g (12oz) fresh salmon, cooked
pinch of grated nutmeg
lemon juice, to taste
chopped fennel (optional)
salt and freshly ground pepper

For the crostini:
extra virgin olive oil, for frying
3–5 thick slices of really good-quality French
  baguette per person, cut diagonally

For the accompaniments:
400g (14oz) tin piquillo peppers
brocco shoots (if you can't find these, use
  mustard or cress, or small rocket leaves or
  sprigs of purslane
sea salt

Melt the 40g (1¹/₂oz) butter in a saucepan over a low heat; add the smoked salmon and 1 tablespoon water. Cover and cook for 3–4 minutes or until the salmon no longer looks opaque. Allow it to get quite cold.

Cream the 350g (12oz) softened butter in a bowl. With two forks, shred the smoked and cooked fresh salmon and mix well together. Still using a fork (not a food processor), mix them with the creamed butter. Sprinkle in some grated nutmeg and season with salt and pepper. Taste and add lemon juice as necessary, and some chopped fennel if you have it. Salmon rillettes will keep perfectly in the fridge for 5–6 days, provided they are sealed with clarified butter (see p108).

Not long before serving, make the crostini. Add olive oil to a frying pan to a depth of 5mm (¹/₄in) and heat until very hot. Cook the crostini a few at a time, turning them as soon as they are golden. Drain on kitchen paper.

To serve, spoon a dollop of salmon rillettes on a warm crostini and top with a strip or twirl of piquillo pepper. Top with brocco shoots or a tiny rocket leaf or sprig of purslane and a few flakes of sea salt.

Other good things to do with salmon rillettes:
1 Serve in individual pots or in a pottery terrine with cucumber pickle (see p73).
2 Use to fill pappadew peppers, and serve with a salad of rocket leaves.
3 Serve as a starter or a light lunch.

Dips

Choose from these delicious dips and eat with grilled flat bread (see p40).

Beetroot and Ginger Relish

SERVES 8–20   (P: 10 MINS/C: 30 MINS)

This sweet-and-sour relish is particularly good with cold meats and coarse country terrines, or used simply as a dip.

40g (1¹/₂oz) butter
225g (8oz) onions, chopped
3 tablespoons sugar
salt and freshly ground pepper
450g (1lb) raw beetroot, peeled and grated
30ml (1fl oz) sherry vinegar
125ml (4fl oz) red wine
2 teaspoons peeled and grated fresh ginger

Melt the butter in a pan and, over a very low heat, cook the onion until very soft. Add the sugar and salt and pepper to taste, and add all the remaining ingredients and cook over a low heat for 30 minutes. Leave to cool then pour into a sterilised screwtop jar and refrigerate until needed (the relish will keep for ages). Serve cold.

Tapenade

MAKES 200ml (7fl oz)   (P: 5 MINS)

The strong, gutsy flavour of tapenade can be an acquired taste – however, the black olive paste becomes addictive and has become a 'new basic' for me.

175g (6oz) stoned black olives (do not buy ready stoned olives)
4 tinned anchovy fillets
2 garlic cloves, chopped
4 tablespoons extra virgin olive oil

In a food processor, whizz together the olives, anchovy fillets and garlic, gradually adding the olive oil (alternatively, use a pestle and mortar.) Process to a coarse or smooth purée, as you prefer. It will keep for months in the fridge.

Serve with crudités, bruschetta and crostini, lamb dishes, pasta, goat's cheese…

Tapenade Oil

Add lots of extra virgin olive oil and store in a sterilised jar. Use to drizzle over goat's cheese, etc.

Tuna and Olive Tapenade

Flake one tin Ortiz tuna and add tapenade to taste. Serve with flat bread, tiny pitta breads, hot crusty bread or toast.

Dukkah

MAKES 150g (5oz)   (P: 10 MINS/C: 15 MINS)

This Middle Eastern mix of spices and nuts can be served with crudités, warm pitta bread and a bowl of best olive oil. Just dip a piece of crisp vegetable or a strip of bread into the olive oil and then into the dukkah. It is also delicious with all manner of things such as hard-boiled eggs or sprinkled over grilled meats as seasoning.

50g (2oz) shelled hazelnuts
4 tablespoons sesame seeds
2 tablespoons whole coriander seeds
1¹/₂ tablespoons whole cumin seeds
¹/₂ tablespoon black peppercorns
1 teaspoon ground cinnamon
pinch of salt

Preheat the oven to 200ºC/400ºF/gas mark 6. Put the hazelnuts on a baking tray and roast for 10 minutes or until the skins start to loosen. Allow to cool and rub off the loose skins. Chop finely or whizz them in a food processor for just a few seconds. Be careful not to overprocess or the nuts will blend into a paste.

Heat a small, heavy frying pan over a medium heat and add the sesame seeds. Shake gently until they turn a shade darker and release a nutty aroma. Tip into a bowl. Repeat with the coriander and cumin seeds.

Place the roasted seeds and peppercorns in a clean spice grinder or coffee grinder and whizz quickly to give a coarse, dry powder. Mix with the cinnamon and salt, then add the chopped nuts. Taste and adjust the seasoning if needed.

Store in a screw-top jar or airtight container. It will keep for months but loses its fragrance and oomphf over time.

soups and salads

Perfect as a starter or light meal, there are endless variations of soups and salads, so feel free to play around with ingredients and garnishes. Soups can be hot or cold, thin, thick or solid, and a basic soup can be livened up with a few fresh herbs or spices. Salads rely on the best-quality ingredients and a great dressing. Think about the balance of colour and texture. But don't just think of them as starters. Soup can be served as a canapé in miniature cups, bowls or shot glasses or in a chunky mug for a cheering winter lunch or late-night snack. A salad can be beefed up into a summer lunch by adding some boiled potatoes, croûtons or delicious cold meat.

Thai Chicken, Galangal and Coriander Soup

SERVES 8   (P: 10 MINS/C: 10 MINS)

A particularly delicious example of how fast and easy to make a Thai soup can be. Serve in Chinese porcelain bowls if available. The kaffir lime leaves and galangal (a type of ginger used in Thai cooking) are served but not eaten. The chilli may of course be nibbled. Prawns and shrimps can be substituted for the chicken in this recipe with equally delicious results.

900ml (1¹/₂ pints) homemade chicken stock
   (see p295)
4 kaffir lime leaves
5cm (2in) piece of galangal, peeled and sliced,
   or smaller piece of fresh ginger
4 tablespoons fish sauce (*nam pla*)
6 tablespoons freshly squeezed lemon juice
225g (8oz) free-range organic chicken breast,
   very finely sliced
225ml (8fl oz) coconut milk
1–3 Thai red chillies
5 tablespoons coriander leaves

Put the chicken stock into a saucepan and add the lime leaves, galangal or ginger, fish sauce and lemon juice. Bring to the boil, stirring continuously, then add the finely sliced chicken and coconut milk. Continue to cook over a high heat for 1–2 minutes until the chicken is just cooked.

Crush the chillies with a knife or Chinese chopper, add to the soup along with the coriander leaves and cook for just a few seconds. Ladle into hot Chinese rice bowls and serve immediately.

Noodle Soup
Blanched and refreshed rice noodles are a great addition to this soup – hey presto, you have a main course. Serve in wide pasta bowls, with lots of fresh coriander scattered over the top.

Top Tip: Fresh lime leaves are not available in every shop, so buy them any time you spot them and pop them into a bag and freeze.

Bacon and Cabbage Soup

SERVES 6   (P: 15 MINS/C: 15 MINS)

Bacon and cabbage are a quintessential rustic meal, and a favourite flavour combination of mine. Cabbage soup is also delicious. Spinach or watercress, chard or kale can be substituted for cabbage.

50g (2oz) butter
150g (5oz) potatoes, chopped into 8mm (¹/₃in)
   dice
110g (4oz) onions, chopped into 8mm (¹/₃in)
   dice
salt and freshly ground pepper
1.2 litres (2 pints) light chicken stock or
   vegetable stock (see p295)
250g (9oz) Savoy cabbage leaves (stalks
   removed), chopped
50–125ml (2–4fl oz) cream or creamy milk
225g (8oz) streaky bacon, in 1 piece, boiled
a little oil, for frying
2 tablespoons chopped parsley

Melt the butter in a heavy saucepan. When it foams, add the potatoes and onion and turn them in the butter until well coated. Sprinkle with salt and freshly ground pepper. Cover and sweat on a low heat for 10 minutes.

Add the stock and boil, covered, until the potatoes are soft, then add the cabbage and cook with the lid off until the cabbage is cooked (keeping the lid off will preserve the green colour of the cabbage). Do not overcook or the vegetables will lose both their fresh flavour and their colour.

Remove from the heat and stir in the cream or creamy milk to thin to required texture. Purée the soup in a liquidiser or blender. Taste and adjust the seasoning if needed.

Just before serving, cut the bacon into strips. Heat a very little oil in a frying pan and toss in the bacon to heat through and get a little crispy. Add to the soup and sprinkle on some parsley.

Cabbage and Caraway Soup
Add 1–2 teaspoons freshly crushed caraway seeds to the potatoes and onions in the frying pan. Omit the bacon garnish.

Top Tip: If this soup is not served immediately, reheat until it just boils and serve. Prolonged boiling spoils the colour and flavour of green soups.

Mediterranean Fish Soup with Rouille

SERVES 6–8   (P: 1 HOUR/C: 30 MINS)

I can't pretend that this gutsy fish soup is either quick or easy to make – it is a labour of love but worth every minute. Fish soups can be made with all sorts of combinations of fish. Don't be the least bit bothered if you haven't got exactly the fish I suggest, but use a combination of whole fish and shellfish. In my opinion the crab adds almost essential richness.

2.5kg (5^1/$_2$lb) mixed fish, such as 1 whole
   plaice, ^{1}/$_2$ cod and 2 small whiting
150ml (^{1}/$_4$ pint) extra virgin olive oil
275g (10oz) onions, chopped
1 large garlic clove, crushed
5 large very ripe tomatoes, sliced, or
   400g (14oz) tin tomatoes
5 sprigs of fennel
2 sprigs of thyme
1 bay leaf
3 swimming crabs or 1 common crab,
6–8 mussels and 8–10 shrimps or prawns,
   including heads
1.2 litres (2 pints) fish stock or water, to cover
^{1}/$_4$ teaspoon saffron strands
pinch of cayenne pepper
salt and freshly ground pepper
chopped parsley, to garnish

Prepare the fish. Remove the gills and cut the fish into chunks, bones, heads and all.

In a large, deep pan, heat the olive oil until smoking, add the onions and garlic and stir for a minute or two. Add the tomatoes, fennel, thyme and bay leaf, then the fish and shellfish and cook, stirring occasionally, for 10 minutes. Pour over enough fish stock or water barely to cover, boil and cook for a further 10 minutes. Add more liquid if it reduces too much.

Soak the saffron strands in a little fish stock or water. Pick out the mussel shells and crab shells. Remove the crab meat from the shells and add to the soup. Add cayenne, salt and pepper to taste, then add the saffron and its soaking liquid.

Push the soup through a mouli or sieve. This may seem like an impossible task but you'll be surprised how effective it is – there will be just a mass of dry bones left, which you discard.

Next make the rouille.

Rouille

SERVES 8   (P: 10 MINS)

This is a spicy mayonnaise from the Mediterranean.

1 piece of French baguette bread,
   about 5cm (2in) long
4 garlic cloves
1 free-range, organic egg yolk
pinch of saffron strands
6 tablespoons extra virgin olive oil
salt and freshly ground pepper

Cut the bread into cubes and soak in 5–6 tablespoons of the hot fish soup. Squeeze out the excess liquid and mix to a mush in a bowl.

Crush the garlic to a fine paste, preferably using a pestle and mortar, then add it to the soggy bread along with the egg yolk and saffron. Season with salt and freshly ground pepper. Mix well and whisk in the oil drip by drip, as if making mayonnaise. If the mixture looks too thick or oily, add 2 tablespoons of hot fish soup and continue to stir.

Croûtons

(P: 10 MINS/C: 10 MINS)

8 thin slices of French baguette bread
75–110g (3–4oz) Gruyère cheese, grated

Mouli legume (food mill)

Toast the bread until the slices are dry and crisp. Spread the croûtons with rouille and sprinkle with the Gruyère cheese.

Bring the soup back to the boil. Serve each guest a bowl of fish soup garnished with some parsley and 3–4 croûtons, a little bowl of rouille and a little bowl of freshly grated gruyère cheese.

To eat, spread the croûtons with rouille, sprinkle with gruyère cheese and float in your bowl of soup – exquisite.

Cauliflower Cheese Soup with Cheddar and Walnut Crisps

SERVES 6–8   (P: 20 MINS/C: 25 MINS)

1 medium organic cauliflower, with green
  leaves retained
850ml (1¹/₂ pints) chicken or vegetable stock
  (see p295), plus a bit extra if needed

For the mornay sauce:
600ml (1 pint) milk, with a dash of cream
1 slice of onion
3–4 slices of carrot
6 peppercorns
sprig of thyme or parsley
roux (see p139)
150g (5oz) Cheddar cheese, grated or
  a mixture of Gruyère, Parmesan and Cheddar
¹/₂–1 teaspoon Dijon mustard, to taste
salt and freshly ground pepper

To serve: Cheddar and Walnut Crisps
  (see recipe below) or cubes of Cheddar
  cheese, chopped parsley and croûtons

Remove the cauliflower's outer leaves and wash both the vegetable and the leaves well. In a saucepan just large enough to take the cauliflower, put 2.5cm (1in) water and add a little salt. Chop the leaves into small pieces and break the cauliflower into florets. Put the leaves into the pan, then the cauliflower pieces on top of the leaves, cover and simmer for about 10–15 minutes until the cauliflower is cooked. Test by piercing a stalk with a knife; it should be quite soft. Remove the cauliflower and the leaves to an ovenproof serving dish.

While the cauliflower is cooking make the mornay sauce. Put the milk into a large saucepan with the slice of onion, carrot slices, peppercorns and the thyme or parsley. Bring to the boil, simmer for 3–4 minutes, then remove from the heat and leave to infuse for 10 minutes.

Strain out the vegetables from the milk, bring the milk back to the boil and thicken with roux to a light coating consistency. Add the grated cheese and a little mustard, salt and freshly ground pepper, then taste and adjust the seasoning if needed. Add the cauliflower, its cooking water and the chicken or vegetable stock. Liquidise the soup in batches, adding more stock if necessary to create your desired consistency. Taste and adjust the seasoning if needed.

Serve with Cheddar and Walnut Crisps or cubes of Cheddar cheese, chopped parsley and croûtons.

Cheddar and Walnut Crisps

MAKES ABOUT 50   (P: 10 MINS/C: 5 MINS)

**Yummy to serve with Cauliflower Cheese
Soup or as a nibble with drinks.**

70g (2³/₄oz) mature Cheddar cheese, grated
70g (2³/₄oz) Parmesan cheese, grated
50g (2oz) walnuts, chopped
1 tablespoon thyme leaves

2 baking sheets lined with Bakewell paper

Preheat the oven to 280C/350F/gas mark 4.

Mix the cheeses in a bowl with the chopped walnuts and thyme leaves.

Drop spoonfuls of the mixture on to the lined baking sheets. Flatten with the back of a spoon. Bake for about 5 minutes or until bubbling and golden around the edge.

Remove the baking sheets from the oven and allow to cool for a few minutes. Lift off the crisps with a palette knife and cool on a wire rack.

Potato Soup with Harissa Oil and Coriander Seed Grissini

SERVES 6 (P: 10 MINS/C: 20 MINS)

Most people would have potatoes and onions in the house even if the cupboard were otherwise bare, so one could make this simply delicious soup at a moment's notice. It can be served completely unadorned, or it can be embellished with a variety of garnishes: wild garlic, parsley pesto, melted leeks, sizzling garlic butter or chorizo and flat parsley. We sometimes pile homemade potato crisps on top and pour over some sizzling garlic butter at the last moment!

50g (2oz) butter
425g (15oz) potatoes, cut into 8mm (1/3in) dice
110g (4oz) onions, cut into 8mm (1/3in) dice
salt and freshly ground pepper
1 litre (13/4 pints) homemade chicken stock or vegetable stock (see p295)
125ml (4fl oz) creamy milk, or to taste
harissa oil (see recipe below)
flat parsley leaves, to garnish
coriander seed grissini (Breadsticks, see p35, rolled in crushed coriander seeds before baking) to serve

Melt the butter in a heavy saucepan. When it foams, add the potatoes and onions and toss them in the butter until well coated. Sprinkle with salt and a few grinds of pepper. Cover with a paper lid and then the saucepan lid. Sweat on a low heat for about 10 minutes.

Meanwhile bring the stock to the boil. When the vegetables are almost soft but have not yet coloured, add the hot stock and cook until the vegetables are soft.

Purée the soup in a blender. Taste and adjust the seasoning if needed. Thin with creamy milk to the required consistency. Serve in warm bowls, with a drizzle of harissa oil and a few flat parsley leaves on top, accompanied by coriander seed grissini.

Harissa Oil

MAKES 225ML (8FL OZ) (P: 5 MINS)

My brother Rory O'Connell gave me this delicious recipe. Serve with grilled meat, fish and vegetables, and drizzle into soups.

6 chillies, roasted, peeled and seeded
6 tablespoons tomato purée
8 garlic cloves, crushed
3 teaspoons cumin seeds, toasted and ground
3 teaspoons coriander seeds, toasted and ground
6 tablespoons extra virgin olive oil, plus extra if needed
1 teaspoon red wine vinegar
3 tablespoons chopped coriander leaves
salt, freshly ground pepper and sugar, to taste

Place the prepared chillies, tomato purée, garlic and ground spices in a food processor. Purée until smooth and continue processing while you drizzle in the olive oil and vinegar.

Transfer to a lidded jar and add the coriander leaves. Add salt, pepper and a little sugar to taste, and add a little more olive oil if needed. It keeps for several weeks or longer in the fridge.

Chilled Cucumber, Melon and Mint Soup

SERVES 8 (P: 20 MINS + TIME TO CHILL)

1 large or 2 small organic cucumbers,
1 ripe melon (Galia or Honeydew)
450ml (16fl oz) natural yogurt (not low-fat)
4 tablespoons chopped mint, plus extra leaves to garnish
4 tablespoons lime juice
sugar, to taste (4–5 tablespoons depending on the sweetness of the melon)
salt

Peel the cucumber and the melon and cut into chunks. Working in batches, put some cucumber and melon in a liquidiser, and add yogurt, chopped mint and lime juice. Add some sugar and a pinch of salt. Purée, taste and add more sugar if needed.

When all has been puréed, place in the fridge to chill until needed.

Serve in little bowls, with a few mint leaves scattered on top.

Gazpacho

SERVES 4–6   (P: 40 MINS)

We love to make this cold soup in the summer, when the vine-ripened tomatoes in the greenhouses are bursting with flavour. Serve it as a starter or as a refreshing drink for picnics.

700g (1¹/₂lb) very ripe tomatoes, skinned and finely chopped
3 thick slices of good-quality stale bread, crusts removed and roughly chopped
1 tablespoon red wine vinegar
2–3 garlic cloves, crushed
425ml (³/₄pint) fresh tomato juice (see p66)
110g (4oz) onions, chopped
2 red peppers, roasted and peeled
1 medium cucumber, chopped
4 tablespoons extra virgin olive oil
2 tablespoons homemade Mayonnaise (see p296; optional)
salt, freshly ground black pepper and sugar, to taste

For the garnishes:
2 red peppers, deseeded and finely diced
1 small cucumber, finely diced
4 very ripe tomatoes, finely diced
4 slices of bread, cut into small dice and fried in extra virgin olive oil
2 tablespoons diced black olives, or small whole olives
1 small onion, diced
1–2 tablespoons chopped mint
extra virgin olive oil, for drizzling
ice cubes (optional)

Put the chopped tomatoes into a food processor or blender and add the chopped bread, red wine vinegar, crushed garlic, tomato juice, chopped onions, roasted red peppers, chopped cucumber, olive oil and mayonnaise. Season with salt, freshly ground pepper and sugar and whizz until smooth. Dilute with water if necessary to loosen up the soup – how much you need depends on how juicy the tomatoes are.

While the soup is chilling in the fridge, you can prepare the garnishes.

Before serving, taste the soup and adjust the seasoning if needed. Serve the garnishes on separate plates and everybody can help themselves – the soup should be thick with garnishes.

Drizzle with olive oil, and on a very hot day, add an ice cube or two if you wish.

Gazpacho Smoothie
Make as above, adding a little iced water if necessary. Serve chilled as a delicious drink.

Cannellini, Chorizo and Cabbage Soup

SERVES 6   (P: 10 MINS/C: 15 MINS)

Assorted cans of beans, tinned tomatoes, and chorizo or kabanossi sausages are brilliant secret ammunition to have in your larder. Salads, omelettes and bean stews can all be whipped up literally in minutes. For this recipe, if you don't have fresh or frozen stock, use stock cubes – Kallo are best.

2 tablespoons extra virgin olive oil
175g (6oz) onions, chopped
175g (6oz) chorizo or kabanossi sausage, sliced
400g (14oz) tin tomatoes
salt, freshly ground pepper and sugar, to taste
1.2 litres (2 pints) homemade chicken stock, (see p295)
400g (14oz) tin cannellini, haricot beans or black-eyed beans, drained
¹/₄ Savoy cabbage
4 tablespoons chopped parsley
1 teaspoon thyme leaves

To serve: crusty bread

Heat the oil in a sauté pan over a medium heat, add the onions, cover and sweat over a low heat until soft but not coloured. Add the chorizo or kabanossi slices and toss for 2–3 minutes until they begin to become slightly crisp – the fat should run. Transfer to a large saucepan.

Chop the tomatoes fairly finely in the tin and add them with all the juice to the large pan, then season with salt, freshly ground pepper and a little sugar. Bring to the boil and cook on a high heat for 5–6 minutes. Meanwhile, bring the stock to the boil in another pan.

Add the boiling stock and tinned beans to the large pan and bring back to the boil. Thinly slice the cabbage and add it to the pan. Cook for a further 2–3 minutes, then add the chopped parsley and thyme leaves. Taste and adjust the seasoning if needed, and serve with lots of crusty bread.

Moroccan Harira Soup

SERVES 6–8

(**P**: OVERNIGHT + 10 MINS/**C**: 2 HOURS)

In Morocco this soup is served as an important part of the festivities of Ramadan. It's the traditional soup to break the fast. My brother Rory O'Connell shared this particularly delicious version with us.

110g (4oz) dried chickpeas, soaked overnight
  and drained
110g (4oz) dried Puy lentils
450g (1lb) leg or shoulder of lamb, cut into
  1cm (1/2in) cubes
175g (6oz) onions, chopped
1 teaspoon ground turmeric
1/2 teaspoon ground cinnamon
1/4 teaspoon each ground ginger, saffron
  strands and paprika
salt, freshly ground pepper and sugar, to taste
50g (2oz) butter
110g (4oz) long-grain rice
4 large ripe tomatoes, skinned, deseeded
  and chopped
2 tablespoons chopped coriander leaves
4 tablespoons chopped flat parsley

To serve: lemon quarters

Tip the soaked chickpeas and dry lentils into a large saucepan. Add the lamb, onions, turmeric, cinnamon, ginger, saffron strands and paprika, then pour in 1.5 litres (2 1/2 pints) water. Season with salt and freshly ground pepper.

Bring to the boil, skimming all the froth from the surface as the water begins to bubble, then stir in half the butter. Reduce the heat and leave to simmer, covered, for 1 1/2–2 hours until the chickpeas are tender, adding a little more water from time to time if necessary.

Towards the end of the cooking time, cook the rice. Bring 850ml (1 1/2 pints) water to the boil in a saucepan, sprinkle in the rice and add the rest of the butter and salt to taste. Cook until the rice is tender. Drain, reserving 3 tablespoons of the liquid.

To finish the soup, put the chopped tomatoes in a small pan, add the reserved rice-cooking water and season with salt, pepper and sugar. Cook over a medium heat for 5 minutes or until the tomatoes have 'melted'. Add this and the drained rice to the soup and simmer for a further 5 minutes to allow the flavours to mix.

Taste and adjust the seasoning if needed. Add the chopped herbs, stir once or twice, and serve accompanied by lemon quarters.

Roast Red Pepper Soup with Tapenade Fingers

SERVES 4   (**P**: 10 MINS/**C**: 10 MINS)

4 onions
6 red peppers
3 ripe tomatoes
salt and freshly ground pepper
1 chilli (optional)
4 tablespoons extra virgin olive oil, plus extra
  to serve
2 tablespoons balsamic vinegar
1.2 litres (2 pints) homemade chicken or
  vegetable stock (see p295)
a few basil leaves

For the tapenade fingers:
4 slices of good white bread
Tapenade (see p75)

Preheat the oven to 200°C/400°F/gas mark 6.

Peel the onions and cut each into 4 pieces, cut each pepper into 4 pieces and deseed them, and cut the tomatoes in half.

Put the vegetable pieces into a stainless-steel roasting tin and season well with salt and pepper. Add the chilli (if using) and drizzle with the olive oil and balsamic vinegar. Roast for 15–20 minutes, until the vegetables are roasted and soft. Meanwhile, heat the stock over a low heat.

Remove the skins from the peppers and tomatoes, and remove the stalk and seeds from the chilli (if using). Put the contents of the roasting tin and all the juices into a liquidiser and add the basil leaves, then whizz until smooth. Transfer to a saucepan and mix in the hot stock. Taste and adjust the seasoning if needed.

To make the tapenade fingers, cut the crust off the bread, spread the slices with tapenade, and cut into thick fingers.

To serve, reheat the soup if necessary, drizzle a little olive oil over each bowl and serve with a few tapenade fingers.

You could use aubergine purée (see p119) instead of tapenade. Pesto fingers or breadsticks are also delicious with this soup.

A Retro Salad with Traditional Cream Dressing

SERVES 4   (P: 30 MINS)

This simple, old-fashioned salad is one of my absolute favourites. It is the sort of thing you would have had for tea during a visit to your granny on a Sunday evening, perhaps served with a slice of meat left over from the Sunday lunch joint. It can be quite delicious when it's made with a crisp lettuce, good home-grown tomatoes and cucumbers, free-range eggs and home-preserved beetroot. If on the other hand you make it with pale battery eggs, watery tomatoes, tired lettuce and aged cucumber – and, worst of all, vinegary beetroot from a jar – you'll wonder why you bothered. The salad cream dressing was popular before the days of mayonnaise. The recipe comes from Lydia Strangman, the previous occupant of our house.

2 free-range, organic eggs
1 butterhead lettuce (the ordinary lettuce that is available everywhere)
4 tiny spring onions
2–4 ripe tomatoes
16 cucumber slices
4 radishes, thinly sliced
8 slices home-pickled beetroot (see recipe below)

For the traditional cream dressing:
2 free-range, organic eggs
1 tablespoon dark soft brown sugar
pinch of salt
1 teaspoon English mustard powder
1 tablespoon brown malt vinegar
50–125ml (2–4fl oz) cream

For the garnish:
chopped spring onion
watercress
chopped parsley

Hard-boil the eggs for the salad and the dressing. Bring a small saucepan of water to the boil, gently slide in the eggs and boil for 10 minutes (12 minutes if they are very fresh). Strain off the hot water and cover with cold water to cool them, then peel them.

Wash and dry the lettuce and spring onions, and set aside.

Next make the dressing. Cut 2 of the eggs in half. Remove the yolks, place in a bowl, add the sugar, a pinch of salt and the mustard powder. Blend in the brown malt vinegar and cream to make a pouring consistency. Chop the egg whites and add some to the sauce, setting the rest aside to scatter over the salad. Cover the dressing until needed.

To assemble the salad, arrange a few lettuce leaves on each plate. Cut the tomatoes into quarters and arrange on the salad. Cut the remaining 2 hard-boiled eggs into quarters and add to the plates, then place a few slices of cucumber, some sliced radish and 2 slices of beetroot on each plate. Garnish with some chopped spring onion and watercress, scatter on the reserved chopped egg white (from the dressing) and some chopped parsley.

Put a tiny bowl of traditional cream dressing in the centre of each plate and serve immediately, while the salad is crisp and before the beetroot starts to run.

Pickled Beetroot

SERVES 5–6   (P: 10 MINS/C: 2 HOURS)

This is a brilliant storecupboard standby and is great with goat's cheese.

450g (1lb) raw beetroot
salt
450ml (16fl oz) water
225g (8oz) sugar
225ml (8fl oz) white wine vinegar

To prepare the beetroot, leave 5cm (2in) of the leaf stalks on top and the whole root on the beet. Hold the beetroot under cold running water and gently wash off the mud with the palms of your hands; ensure you don't damage the skin, otherwise the beetroot will bleed during cooking.

Put the beetroot in a pan, cover with cold water and add a little salt and sugar. Cover the pan, bring to the boil and simmer on top of the stove, or in the oven, for 1–2 hours depending on size.

Beetroot are usually cooked when the skin rubs off easily and when they dent when pressed. If in doubt, test with a skewer or the tip of a knife. Drain, allow the beetroot to cool, then gently peel and slice them, and transfer to a bowl.

Pour the measured water into a saucepan and add the sugar. Stir to dissolve, then bring to the boil. Remove from the heat, stir in the vinegar, pour over the sliced beetroots and leave to cool. Refrigerate until needed.

A Salad of Crozier Blue Cheese with Ripe Pears and Spicy Candied Nuts

SERVES 8   (P: 25 MINS/C: 5 MINS)

Much of this salad can be made in advance: the prepared salad leaves can be stored in the fridge, the spicy candied nuts in an airtight container, and the dressing in a sealed jar. Cashel Blue, Bellingham Blue, Stilton or Gorgonzola cheese would be delicious alternatives to Crozier Blue.

selection of salad leaves, including curly
  endive and watercress
Spicy Candied Nuts (see p62)
ripe Crozier Blue cheese
3–4 ripe pears (Bartlet or Anjou)
sprigs of chervil, to garnish

For the dressing:
2 tablespoons red wine vinegar
6 tablespoons extra virgin olive oil
salt and freshly ground pepper

Preheat the oven to 180°C/350°F/gas mark 4.

Gently wash the salad leaves and dry them, then transfer to a bowl, cover and refrigerate.

Prepare the candied nuts.

To make the dressing, whisk the vinegar and oil together and season to taste.

To serve the salad, cut the cheese into cubes or small wedges. Sprinkle the salad leaves with the dressing and toss gently until the leaves glisten. Taste and add more seasoning if needed. Divide the salad leaves between the plates, making a little mound in the centre. Slice the pears and tuck 3–4 slices in between the leaves on each plate. Scatter with a few cubes of cheese and some Spicy Candied Nuts. Sprinkle with a few sprigs of chervil and serve.

Clair McSweeney's Wakame Seaweed Salad

SERVES 8   (P: 40 MINS/C: 10 MINS)

I first tasted this delicious salad at a meeting of the Cork Free Choice Consumer's Group on using seaweed. Clair McSweeney gave me the recipe and it has become a favourite – it's great with fried fish or tempura. Seaweeds are full of goodness and trace elements not found in other foods.

40g (1¹/₂oz) dried wakame seaweed
1 large cucumber
1 tablespoon salt
1 handful of pickled ginger
¹/₂ pickled daikon, finely diced

For the dressing:
6 tablespoons rice wine vinegar
3 tablespoons soy sauce
2 tablespoons sugar

Put the wakame seaweed into a large bowl, pour lots of cold water over it and leave to rehydrate for about 15 minutes.

Peel the cucumber in strips along the length, cut it in half lengthways, scoop out the seeds and slice thinly. Put about 250ml (9fl oz) water into a bowl and add the salt and the sliced cucumber. Leave to soak for 20 minutes.

In a saucepan, mix the ingredients for the dressing and warm over a low heat until the sugar has dissolved.

Drain the seaweed, rinse in cold water, then drain again thoroughly. Drain the cucumber and press out any excess water. Mix the cucumber and seaweed together, and add the pickled ginger and diced daikon. Refrigerate for about 30 minutes before serving, so the salad becomes cool and crisp.

Mexican Chicken Salad with Chilli and Coriander Cream

SERVES 12   (P: 45 MINS/C: 15 MINS)

A delicious recipe from The Tante Marie's Cooking School Cookbook by Mary Risley, one of my great heroes who owns the Tante Marie's Cooking School in San Francisco.

4 chicken breasts
1 large Cos lettuce, torn into 2.5cm (1in) strips
400g (14oz) cooked black beans or 2 x 225g (8oz) tins black beans
350g (12oz) fresh sweetcorn kernels
12 cherry tomatoes, cut in half
2 medium red onions, chopped
4 small ripe but firm avocados, chopped
350g (12oz) Cheddar cheese, grated
225g (8oz) tortilla chips

For the spicy dressing:
175ml (6fl oz) cider vinegar
1 tablespoon sea salt
4 teaspoons freshly ground black pepper
4 tablespoons Worcestershire sauce
2 teaspoons English mustard powder
2 tablespoons honey
juice of 1/2 lemon
4 garlic cloves, crushed
110g (4oz) tomato puree
1 teaspoon chilli flakes
175ml (6fl oz) extra virgin olive oil
225ml (8fl oz) sunflower oil
1 tablespoon cumin seeds, toasted and ground

For the chilli and coriander cream:
225g (8oz) soured cream or crème fraîche
1 tablespoon chopped jalapeño chilli
2 tablespoons roughly chopped fresh coriander leaves
salt and freshly ground pepper

First pangrill the chicken until cooked. Leave to cool and cut into 1cm (1/2in) dice.

Make the spicy dressing (this recipe makes more than you need but it keeps very well in a covered jar in the fridge). Whisk all the ingredients together in a bowl, taste and add a little water if the flavour is too intense.

Make the chilli and coriander cream by mixing all the ingredients together in a bowl. Keep chilled until needed.

Put the lettuce, chicken, beans, sweetcorn, tomatoes, onion, avocado, Cheddar cheese and tortilla chips in a large bowl. Add 1/2–2/3 of the spicy dressing and toss gently. Serve on individual plates, with a dollop of chilli and coriander cream, a sprinkle of spring onions and some fresh coriander leaves.

Pasta, Bocconcini and Tomato Salad

SERVES 6–8   (P: 20 MINS/C: 10 MINS)

450g (1lb) penne pasta (spirals) or tiny shells
450g (1lb) cherry tomatoes, preferably vine-ripened and organic
450g (1lb) bocconcini (baby mozzarella cheeses)
lots of fresh basil or mint or marjoram leaves
4 spring onions, sliced diagonally
salt and freshly ground pepper
12–18 Picholine or Kalamata olives (green or black)

For the dressing:
175ml (6fl oz) extra virgin olive oil
50ml (2fl oz) balsamic vinegar or white wine vinegar
2 garlic cloves, crushed
Pesto (optional; see p297)

Cook the pasta in a large pot of boiling salted water until al dente (still slightly firm).

Meanwhile, cut the tomatoes in half. Whisk together all the dressing ingredients in a bowl, then add the tomatoes, bocconcini, herbs and spring onions. Season to taste with salt and freshly ground pepper. Drizzle some of the dressing over the salad and toss gently.

When the pasta is ready, drain it, toss immediately in the remaining dressing and allow to cool. Then combine the pasta with the salad and add the olives. Taste and adjust the seasoning and add more herbs and pesto if you wish.

Tomato and Mint or Basil Salad

SERVES 8   (P: 10 MINS)

12 very ripe firm tomatoes
12 leaves, coarsely chopped mint or torn basil,
salt, freshly ground black pepper and sugar
Ballymaloe French Dressing (see p94)

Remove the core from each tomato and slice into 3–4 rounds (around the equator) or into quarters. Arrange in a single layer on a flat plate. Sprinkle with salt, sugar and several grinds of black pepper. Toss immediately in just enough French dressing to coat the fruit and sprinkle with coarsely chopped mint or basil. Taste for seasoning. Tomatoes must be dressed as soon as they are cut to seal in their flavour.

Chicken Salad with Pomegranate, Pine Nuts and Raisins

SERVES 8   (P: 25 MINS/C: 5 MINS)

Use up leftover morsels of chicken in a delicious way.

700–900g (1¹/₂–2lb) roast chicken
1 pomegranate
75–110g (3–3¹/₂oz) pine nuts, pecans or
  walnuts
selection of salad leaves, including watercress,
  frisée and rocket leaves
lots of fresh mint leaves
50g (2oz) raisins, Lexia if possible
salt and freshly ground pepper

To serve: crusty bread

For the dressing:
6 tablespoons extra virgin olive oil or walnut
  oil
2 tablespoons best-quality white wine vinegar
1–2 teaspoons honey
¹/₂ teaspoon wholegrain mustard

If the chicken has been refrigerated, bring it to room temperature.

Whisk all the ingredients for the dressing together. Taste and adjust the seasoning if needed. Cut the pomegranate in half and flick the seeds into a bowl, ensuring you do not include any of the pith.

Toast the nuts briefly, then chop them coarsely.

Just before serving, put the salad leaves and mint in a deep bowl. Sprinkle over a little of the dressing and toss gently – there should be just enough dressing to make the leaves glisten. Add a little dressing to the pomegranate seeds and toss.

Slice the chicken into chunky pieces and place in a shallow dish. Sprinkle a little dressing over and toss gently.

Combine the salad, pomegranate seeds, chicken pieces, raisins and salt and pepper to taste. Divide pleasingly between the plates and sprinkle with the chopped nuts. Serve immediately, with some crusty bread.

Variation
Pheasant, guinea fowl or free-range turkey instead of chicken would also be delicious in this salad; a few green grapes also make a good addition. A combination of walnut and sunflower oil may be used for the dressing if you wish.

Red Cabbage with Dried Cranberries, Walnuts and Apple

SERVES 6   (P: 15 MINS)

3 Cox's Orange Pippin apples
75g (3oz) dried cranberries
450g (1lb) red cabbage
small handful of flat parsley leaves
50g (2oz) shelled walnuts, halved

For the dressing:
6 tablespoons red wine vinegar
2 tablespoons walnut oil
1 small teaspoon honey
salt and freshly ground pepper

First make the dressing. Whisk the vinegar, oil and honey together and season with salt and pepper.

Cut the apples, unpeeled, into dice. Transfer to a bowl, toss in a little of the dressing and add the dried cranberries.

Cut the red cabbage into quarters and slice thinly crossways. Transfer to a large serving bowl, add the diced apples and cranberries, the flat parsley and some more dressing. Toss gently to coat evenly and add the walnut halves. Taste and adjust the seasoning if needed.

Serve on its own or as an accompaniment to cold duck, goose, pork or ham.

Basmati Rice, Pea, Broad Bean and Dill Salad

SERVES 6–8   (P: 5 MINS/C: 20 MINS)

225g (8oz) basmati rice
salt and freshly ground pepper
extra virgin olive oil, for drizzling
freshly squeezed juice of 1–2 lemons
110g (4oz) peas (shelled weight)
110g (4oz) broad beans (shelled weight)
4 tablespoons chopped dill

Cook the rice in lots of boiling salted water. Drain, transfer to a wide bowl and drizzle with olive oil and some freshly squeezed lemon juice. Leave to cool.

Meanwhile, cook the peas and broad beans separately in boiling salted water, then drain them. Allow to cool.

Combine the rice, peas, broad beans and dill. Toss, taste and adjust the seasoning as necessary.

Spicy Green Salad

SERVES 4   (P: 10 MINS/C: 10 MINS)

1 handful coriander leaves
1 handful parsley leaves
1/2 handful mint leaves
4 spring onions, white and green part,
   sliced diagonally
4 kaffir lime leaves, finely shredded (optional)
1–2 red chillies, deseeded and thinly sliced

For the sweet-and-sour dressing:
2 tablespoons soft brown sugar
2 tablespoons caster sugar
2 tablespoons fish sauce (*nam pla*)
2 tablespoons lime juice

First make the dressing. Put all the sugar into a small saucepan and add 2 tablespoons water. Place over a medium heat and stir to dissolve, then bring to the boil and continue to boil for a minute or two, or until it becomes liquid. Remove from the heat and mix in the fish sauce and lime juice. Pour into a jar or small bowl.

Put the coriander, parsley and mint leaves into a bowl, then add the sliced spring onions, shredded kaffir lime leaves (if using) and sliced chillies.

Just before serving, toss the leaves with enough dressing to make them glisten. Serve as soon as possible.

Shrimp and Rice Noodle Salad

SERVES 8   (P: 20 MINS)

450g (1lb) vermicelli noodles or fine rice
   noodles
1 small organic cucumber
48 shrimps or 32 prawns, cooked and peeled
8 spring onions, sliced diagonally
10g (1/2oz) coriander leaves
10g (1/2oz) mint leaves
110g (4oz) peanuts or cashew nuts,
   roasted and chopped

To serve: lime wedges

For the dressing:
125ml (4fl oz) soy sauce
50ml (2fl oz) rice vinegar or cider vinegar
50ml (2fl oz) extra virgin olive oil
1 red chilli, deseeded and thinly sliced
1 teaspoon peeled and grated fresh ginger
2 tablespoons brown sugar or palm sugar

Put the noodles into a large bowl. Cover with boiling water and leave to stand for 5–7 minutes or until just tender.

Meanwhile, make the dressing by combining all the dressing ingredients in a bowl. Stir until the sugar has dissolved.

Drain the noodles well and toss in the dressing while still warm.

Cut the cucumber in half lengthways. Scoop out the seeds with a melon baller or a sharp spoon and discard. Cut the cucumber into thin diagonal slices.

Add the cucumber slices to the noodles, along with the shrimps or prawns, the sliced spring onions and the coriander and mint. Toss well. Taste and adjust the seasoning if needed. Scatter with the coarsely chopped nuts and serve with wedges of lime.

Top Tip: Noodles of all types are a must-have for your store cupboard – there are a million delicious salads you can make. They are also great added to soup, or as an extra something in spring rolls.

Puy Lentil and Walnut Salad with Pomegranate Molasses

SERVES 6–8   (P: 15 MINS/C: 15 MINS)

350g (12oz) dried Puy lentils
1/2–1 pomegranate (optional)
25–50g (1–2oz) shelled walnuts, halved
3–4 spring onions, sliced diagonally
4 tablespoons chopped flat parsley leaves
salt and freshly ground pepper

For the dressing:
1 tablespoon pomegranate molasses
2 tablespoons extra virgin olive oil
freshly squeezed juice of 1/2 lemon
1/2 teaspoon cumin seeds, toasted and ground

Cook the lentils in boiling salted water for 10–15 minutes or until just cooked.

Meanwhile, cut the pomegranate (if using) into pieces and flick the seeds into a bowl.

Drain the lentils and place in a large bowl. Whisk all the ingredients for the dressing together and pour over the warm lentils. When cool, add the walnut halves, chopped spring onions and parsley; scatter with the pomegranate seeds (if using). Taste and add salt and freshly ground pepper as needed.

Sticky Asian Pork with Herb and Roasted Peanut Salad

SERVES 6   (P: 10 MINS/C: 20 MINS)

You can cook the meat without marinating, but it is better marinated. This recipe would also work well with chicken or duck.

50g (2oz) unsalted peanuts
500g (1lb 2oz) pork fillet, preferably free-range
3 teaspoons five-spice powder
sunflower oil, for frying
enough salad leaves for 6 (include 1/2 large Cos
   lettuce, some rocket and other crisp leaves)
handful each of basil, mint and coriander
   leaves
1 organic cucumber, cut lengthways,
   deseeded and sliced
3 tablespoons Asian Dressing (see p95)
4 spring onions, diagonally sliced

For the marinade:
1 tablespoon fish sauce (*nam pla*)
3 tablespoons soy sauce
1 lemongrass stalk, trimmed and shredded
3 large mild red chillies, deseeded and chopped
2 large garlic cloves, crushed
3 shallots, finely chopped
2 tablespoons soft brown sugar

Preheat the oven to 200°C/400°F/gas mark 6.

Spread the peanuts into a roasting tray and roast for about 15 minutes, shaking once or twice. Take the tray outdoors and blow off the loose skins (sounds very odd but it's exactly what everyone does in Asia). If the peanuts are not already golden brown all over, return them to the oven briefly. Chop coarsely.

Slice the pork fillet into 1cm (1/2in) thick pieces and put into a bowl, then toss with the five-spice powder.

To make the marinade, mix all the ingredients together in a bowl. Add the pork and toss well. Leave to marinate for 30 minutes, better still 1 hour.

Heat a little sunflower oil in a heavy frying pan. Drain the marinated pork, retaining the marinade. Fry the meat for about 1 minute on each side, then add the remaining marinade and cook for a further few minutes.

Meanwhile, tear any large salad leaves in 3–4 pieces. Put them into a large, wide salad bowl with the other leaves and herbs, and add the cucumber. Sprinkle on the Asian dressing and toss well. Add the pork with all the sticky caramelised bits. Scatter on the spring onions and roasted peanuts and serve as soon as possible.

Top Tip: Chicken breasts work brilliantly in this recipe instead of pork.

Panzanella

SERVES 8   (P: 20 MINS)

Every culture has a variety of recipes for using up leftover bread in a delicious way. This is a Tuscan bread salad, but don't attempt it unless you have really good yeast or sour dough bread.

700g (1 1/2lb) very ripe tomatoes
450g (1lb) 2-day-old country bread
125ml (4fl oz) extra virgin olive oil,
2 tablespoons lemon juice or red wine vinegar
3 garlic cloves, crushed
1 large red onion, sliced or coarsely chopped
sea salt and freshly ground black pepper
sugar, if needed
24 basil leaves, roughly torn, or 3 tablespoons
   marjoram or tarragon leaves
rocket leaves (optional)
slivers of Parmesan cheese (optional)

Cut the tomatoes into 1cm (1/2in) dice or small chunks. Transfer to a colander, sprinkle with a little salt and leave to drain while you prepare the remainder of the ingredients.

Cut the bread into slices about 1cm (1/2in) thick, then tear or cut into uneven cubes. (I sometimes pop them into the oven for a few minutes just to crisp the edges.)

In a bowl, mix the olive oil, lemon juice or vinegar and garlic. Add the drained tomatoes and sliced or chopped red onion. Season with salt, pepper and a little sugar if the tomatoes are not sweet enough. Add lots of torn basil leaves or marjoram or tarragon. Toss gently, then add the stale bread and toss well. Taste and adjust the seasoning if needed.

A few peppery rocket leaves on the base of each plate, and slivers of Parmesan on top, make delicious additions to this rustic salad.

Top Tip: Although in Tuscany panzanella is a summer salad, there's no reason why one can't have fun during the other seasons. For instance, we make a delicious autumn version with sautéed wild mushrooms. Large flat mushrooms or portabellos are also great with lots of marjoram or thyme leaves, chopped rocket or watercress leaves, and shavings of Parmesan – it tastes as good as it sounds! In winter we add cubes of roast butternut squash or Jerusalem artichoke, kale and pecorino cheese; in late spring asparagus and broad beans.

A Green Salad for Every Season

The herb and vegetable gardens beside the Ballymaloe Cookery School are bursting with a myriad of lettuce and salad leaves and edible flowers. We eat a green salad with lunch and dinner. The lettuces, salad leaves and wild things vary throughout the seasons.

Spring Green Salad

For this salad, use a selection of organic
   lettuces and salad leaves:
Butterhead lettuce, Iceberg lettuce, radicchio,
   chicory, endive…
Watercress
Buckler leaf sorrel
Rocket leaves
Claytonia
Mysticana
Wild garlic leaves and flowers

Summer Green Salad

A selection of fresh organic lettuces and
   salad leaves:
Butterhead lettuce, Oakleaf lettuce, Iceberg
   lettuce, Lollo Rosso, frisée, Little Gem…
Mesclum or Saladisi
Red Orach
Mizuna
Mibuna
Rocket
Edible chrysanthemum leaves
Green pea shoots or broad bean tips
Tiny chard and beetroot leaves
Wild sorrel leaves or buckler leaf sorrel
Salad burnet
Fresh herb leaves such as lemon balm, mint,
   flat parsley, golden marjoram, annual
   marjoram, tiny sprigs of dill, tarragon
   or mint
Edible flowers such as chive flowers,
   marigold petals, young nasturtium leaves
   and flowers, borage or hyssop flowers,
   courgette or squash blossoms

Autumn and Winter Green Salad

A selection of autumn and winter lettuces:
Butterhead lettuce, Oakleaf lettuce, Lollo
   Rosso, radicchio, chicory, endive…
Watercress
Buckler leaf sorrel, lamb's tongue and wood
   sorrel leaves
Rocket leaves
Lamb's lettuce or mache
Tender leaves of kale

Winter purslane
Mysticana
Tips of purple sprouting broccoli are also delicious, and if you feel like something more robust use some finely shredded Savoy cabbage and maybe a few shreds of red cabbage. Finely shredded stalks of fresh chard are also good.

How to Make a Green Salad

A good green salad should have a contrast of texture, colour and flavour. The mixture of lettuce and salad leaves should ideally reflect the seasons. Seek out salad leaves that have been grown in rich, fertile soil rather than hydroponically; they will not only have more flavour but will also be more nutritionally complex.

Wash and carefully dry the lettuce and salad leaves. Leave the leaves whole or, if too large, tear into bite-sized pieces. Put them into a deep salad bowl, then add the herb sprigs and edible flowers. Toss, cover and store in the fridge until needed. Washed organic salad leaves seem to keep perfectly in a plastic bag in the fridge for 4–5 days.

Immediately before serving, toss the salad in just enough dressing to make the leaves glisten, then taste and add a little more seasoning if needed.

Note: It is really worth investing in a good salad spinner to dry the leaves, otherwise the residual water will dilute the dressing and spoil the salad.

Salad Dressings

Green salad must not be dressed until just before serving, otherwise it will look tired and unappetising. The flavour of the dressing totally depends on the quality of the oil and vinegar. We use best-quality, cold-pressed oils and superb wine vinegars to dress the precious organic lettuce and salad leaves. The quantity needed is so small it's really worth spending as much as you can afford on best quality – it makes all the difference. All salad dressings need a good shake before serving.

Simple French Dressing

MAKES ENOUGH TO DRESS A SALAD FOR
8 PEOPLE

6 tablespoons extra virgin olive oil
2 tablespoons white or red wine vinegar
sea salt and freshly ground pepper

Just before the salad is to be eaten, put all the ingredients into a small bowl or jar. Whisk with a fork until the dressing has emulsified.

Ballymaloe Cookery School Dressing for Salad Leaves

MAKES 150ML (1/4 PINT)

125ml (4fl oz) extra virgin olive oil
2 teaspoons balsamic vinegar
1 teaspoon honey
1 garlic clove, crushed
1/2 teaspoon English mustard powder or
   1/2 teaspoon Dijon mustard
sea salt and freshly ground pepper

Just before the salad is to be eaten, put all the ingredients into a small bowl or jar. Whisk with a fork until the dressing has emulsified.

Honey and Wholegrain Mustard Dressing

MAKES 250ML (9FL OZ)

175ml (6fl oz) extra virgin olive oil or a
   mixture of olive and other oils, such as
   sunflower
50ml (2fl oz) white wine vinegar
2 teaspoons honey
2 heaped teaspoons wholegrain honey
   mustard
2 garlic cloves, crushed
sea salt and freshly ground pepper

Mix all the ingredients together in a small bowl or jar. Taste and adjust the seasoning if needed. Whisk well before use.

Verjuice Dressing

MAKES 250ML (9FL OZ)

Verjuice is made from the juice of tart fruit e.g. apples or grapes and was a popular medieval flavouring in the days before lemon juice was available. It is not technically a vinegar because it does not ferment. Verjuice is still used today in Middle Eastern Cookery and in the making of commercial mustard.

50ml (2fl oz) verjuice
1 tablespoon lemon juice
175ml (6fl oz) extra virgin olive oil
1 teaspoon honey
sea salt and freshly ground pepper

Mix all the ingredients together in a small bowl or jar. Taste and adjust the seasoning if needed. Whisk well before use.

Yogurt and Mint Dressing

MAKES 150ML (1/4 PINT)

125ml (4fl oz) natural yogurt
1 tablespoon freshly squeezed lime or
  lemon juice
1 tablespoon extra virgin olive oil
1 teaspoon honey
1 tablespoon chopped mint
sea salt and freshly ground pepper

Mix all the ingredients together in a small bowl or jar. Taste and adjust the seasoning if needed. Whisk well before use.

Herbed Vinaigrette Dressing

MAKES 250ML (9FL OZ)

175ml (6fl oz) extra virgin olive oil
4 tablespoons cider vinegar
1 teaspoon Irish honey
1 garlic clove, crushed
2 tablespoons chopped mixed herbs,
  such as parsley, chives, mint, watercress and
  thyme
sea salt and freshly ground pepper

Put all the dressing ingredients into a screw-topped jar, adding salt and freshly ground pepper to taste. Shake well. Alternatively whizz all the ingredients together in a food processor or liquidiser for a few seconds.

As a variation you could use 4 tablespoons lemon juice or wine vinegar instead of cider vinegar.

Asian Dressing

MAKES ABOUT 300ML (1/2 PINT)

2 Thai chillies, deseeded and finely sliced
1 large garlic clove, crushed
3 tablespoons caster sugar
4 tablespoons fish sauce (*nam pla*)
4 tablespoons lime juice
4 tablespoons rice wine vinegar
3 tablespoons extra virgin olive oil

Mix all the ingredients together in a small bowl or jar. Taste and adjust the seasoning if needed. Whisk well before use.

Use to dress salad leaves or omit the olive oil and use as a dip.

quick and easy meals

If you have a well-stocked storecupboard and a folder of recipes you can whip up in minutes, unexpected visitors need not faze you. The recipes in this chapter are perfect for when you have very little time to prepare – mussels, for example, make a wonderful meal in an instant and meat or fish can be pangrilled in minutes.

Bowl of Warm Cockles or Mussels with Homemade Mayonnaise or Asian Mayonnaise

ALLOW 600ML (1 PINT PER PERSON)
(**P:** 20 MINS/**C:** 5 MINS)

This is one of our favourite simple suppers. Just pop a few teeny weeny rolls into the oven, whizz up a bowl of mayonnaise and cook the shellfish – the entire feast will be on the table in less than 30 minutes.

600ml (1 pint) per person
cockles or mussels
homemade Mayonnaise (see p296) or
  Asian Mayonnaise (see p297)

To serve: Wheaten Bread or rolls (see p37)
  and green salad

Check that all the cockles or mussels are tightly shut. Tap any that are slightly open on the worktop: if they refuse to close, discard them. Wash them under lots of cold running water.

Preheat a wide sauté pan. Put a batch of cockles or mussels in a single layer in the pan, cover with a lid and cook on a moderate heat for 1–2 minutes. As soon as they open, turn the whole lot into a serving bowl, discarding any that have not opened. Continue cooking in batches in the same manner. They are most delicious while still warm, but they're also good cold or at room temperature. Cockles are eaten just as they are but you will need to remove the 'beard' from the mussels before eating.

Serve with freshly baked wheaten bread, a bowl of homemade mayonnaise and a good green salad.

Spicy Omelette Sambo with Tomato and Red Onion Salsa

SERVES 1   (**P:** 15 MINS/**C:** 5 MINS)

1 portion of focaccia bread or 1 crusty roll
butter
1 tablespoon extra virgin olive oil
2 free-range, organic eggs
$1/4$–$1/2$ teaspoon cumin seeds, toasted and
  ground
1 teaspoon snipped flat parsley
salt and freshly ground pepper
a few rocket leaves
Tomato and Red Onion Salsa (see p294)

Preheat the oven to 200°C/400°F/gas mark 6.

Warm the piece of focaccia or roll in the oven. Split it in half and smear with butter.

Heat the olive oil in a non-stick pan on a high heat and warm a plate. Whisk the eggs in a bowl, add the cumin and parsley and season with salt and pepper.

Pour the egg mixture into the hot pan. It will start to cook instantly, so quickly pull the edges of the omelette towards the centre with a plastic spoon or spatula, tilting the pan so that the uncooked egg runs to the sides; repeat this process 4–5 times, until most of the egg is set and will not run any more; the centre will still be soft and uncooked but will continue to cook on the plate. To fold the omelette, flip the edge just below the handle of the pan into the centre, then hold the pan almost perpendicular over the plate so that the omelette will flip over again; finally half roll, half slide the omelette on to the plate so that it lands folded in three. (It should not take more than 30 seconds in all to make the omelette.)

Scatter a few rocket leaves over the base of the bread, top with the omelette and finally a generous spoonful of Tomato and Red Onion Salsa. Serve immediately.

Roast Chicken Pasta with Portobello Mushrooms and Pancetta

SERVES 8   (**P**: 15 MINS/**C**: 15 MINS)

Bubbly superchef Merrilees Parker did this yummy recipe when she came to teach at the school in 2004. We have adapted it somewhat, but it was really her idea. It's a great recipe for using up delicious morsels of roast chicken – be sure to include the crispy skin. Alternatively use pangrilled chicken breasts.

salt

500g (1lb 2oz) spaghetti or linguine

sea salt and freshly ground black pepper

2 tablespoons extra virgin olive oil

225g (8oz) pancetta or smoked streaky bacon, rind removed and cut into 5mm (¹/₄in) wide strips

225g (8oz) Portobello or field mushrooms, sliced

2 tablespoons thyme leaves (preferably lemon thyme) or annual marjoram leaves

350g (12oz) leftover roast chicken or pangrilled chicken breast, coarsely shredded

150ml (¹/₄ pint) double cream

110g (4oz) mixed salad leaves, such as rocket or baby spinach, roughly chopped

110g (4oz) Parmesan cheese, grated

Bring 6 litres (10 pints) water to the boil in a large saucepan and add 2 tablespoons salt. Curl in the pasta and stir gently. Bring back to the boil and cook for 2 minutes. Turn off the heat, cover with a tight-fighting lid and leave to continue cooking in the hot water for about 5 minutes until al dente (cooked but still slightly firm).

Meanwhile, heat a wok or a large, heavy frying pan. Add 1 tablespoon of the olive oil and then the bacon strips. Cook over a high heat for 4–5 minutes until really crispy. Remove to a plate. Add the remaining oil to the wok or frying pan and toss in the sliced mushrooms. Cook over a high heat for 3–4 minutes, stirring frequently.

Drain the pasta. Tip into the wok or frying pan on top of the mushrooms. Add the crispy bacon, thyme or marjoram leaves and chicken and toss really well. Season with salt and pepper. Pour the cream into the pan and bring to the boil. Taste and adjust the seasoning if needed, then toss thoroughly again.

Finally add the fresh leaves and half the Parmesan, mixing gently. Serve immediately, in warmed deep bowls, with the remaining Parmesan sprinkled over the top.

Pasta with Mushrooms and Ginger

SERVES 6   (P: 5 MINS/C: 30 MINS)

450g (1lb) penne pasta
4.5 litres (8 pints) water
2 tablespoons salt

Mushroom à la Créme with Ginger (see p241)

Cheat's Method of Cooking Dried Pasta
We developed this method of cooking pasta when we taught a 'survival course' for students in bedsits or small apartments with limited cooking facilities. Italians are usually shocked, but it works perfectly.

Choose a large, deep saucepan; two handles are an advantage for ease of lifting. To cook 450g (1lb) pasta, bring 6 litres (10 pints) water to the boil and add 2 tablespoons salt. Tip the pasta in all at once, stir well to ensure the strands or shapes are separate and cover the pan to bring the water back to the boil quickly.

Cook for 2 minutes for spaghetti and tagliatelli, or 4 minutes for penne, small shells and so on. Keep the pan covered. Then turn off the heat and allow the pasta to continue to cook in the hot water for the time indicated on the packet. Test, drain and proceed as usual.

Add the drained penne to the Mushroom à la Créme and toss well. Taste and adjust the seasoning if needed. Serve immediately.

Pasta with Garlic and Herbs

SERVES 4–6   (P: 10 MINS/C: 20 MINS)

This is a terrific standby recipe and a brilliant basic no-cream sauce for pasta. Really fresh herbs are a must. If you haven't got a herb garden to pick and snip at, pop down to your local garden centre and plant up a hanging basket or window box right away.

450g (1lb) spaghetti or thin noodles
salt
50–110g (2–4oz) Parmesan cheese, grated
chive flowers and wild garlic in season (use
   both leaves and bulbs), to garnish

For the herb butter:
50–75g (2–3oz) butter, or half butter and half
   extra virgin olive oil
2 tablespoons chopped parsley
1 tablespoon chopped mint
2 tablespoons chopped watercress or rocket,
   spring onions or chives
1/2 tablespoon chopped basil or lemon balm
2 large or 4 small garlic cloves, crushed

Cook the spaghetti in lots of boiling salted water until al dente – this can range from 2–3 minutes for homemade pasta, to up to 20 minutes for dried pasta. Or use the 'Cheat's Method' above.

Meanwhile, make the herb butter. Melt the butter in a small pan and add all the herbs and the crushed garlic. Cook over a very low heat for 2 minutes, no longer.

Drain the spaghetti and place in a dish. Pour over the herb butter and toss well. Serve with the grated Parmesan. Sprinkle chive flowers and wild garlic over the top for extra excitement.

Variations
1 Add 225g (8oz) cooked, sliced, wild or cultivated mushrooms to the herb butter – chanterelles are great.
2 Add some halved cherry tomatoes to the herb butter.
3 Add 1 teaspoon chilli flakes to the herb butter.
4 Add 110–225g (4–8 oz) diced chorizo to the herb butter.

Linguini with Chilli, Crab and Coriander

SERVES 8   (P: 10 MINS/C: 15 MINS)

salt and freshly cracked pepper
450g (1lb) linguini or spaghetti
100ml (3½ fl oz) extra virgin olive oil
2 garlic cloves, crushed
1–2 red chillies, chopped
1 green chilli, chopped
2 tablespoons coarsely chopped flat parsley
2 tablespoons coarsely chopped coriander
   leaves, plus extra to garnish
grated zest and juice of 1 lemon
250g (9oz) white crab meat, freshly cooked
8 lime wedges to serve

Put 6 litres (10 pints) cold water into a large saucepan and bring to a fast, rolling boil. Add 2 tablespoons salt, then add the pasta and stir gently. Cover the saucepan and continue to boil for 2 minutes, then turn off the heat and allow the pasta to continue to cook in the covered saucepan for 8–10 minutes or until al dente (cooked but still just firm).

Meanwhile, heat the olive oil in a sauté pan, add the garlic, chilli, flat parsley and coriander. Cook for 1–2 minutes

Drain the pasta and return it to the pan. Add the crab to the herb and chilli oil, heat through for 1–2 minutes and pour over the pasta. Add the lemon zest and a good squeeze of juice and lots of cracked pepper. Toss well, taste and adjust the seasoning if needed.

Serve immediately, with coriander leaves scattered over the top and some lime wedges.

Pangrilled Fish with Flavoured Butter

SERVES 4   (P: 10 MINS/C: 5 MINS)

8 fillets of very fresh fish, such as mackerel,
   sea bass or grey sea mullet, skin attached,
   scales removed where necessary (allow
   175g (6oz) fish for main course, 75g (3oz)
   for a starter)
seasoned flour
small knob of butter
flavoured butter of your choice (see below,
   p156 and p231)
segments of lemon and parsley, to garnish

Heat the grill pan. Dip the fish fillets in the flour. Shake off the excess flour and then using a knife, spread a little butter on the flesh side, as though you were buttering a slice of bread rather meanly.

When the grill pan is quite hot but not smoking, place the fish fillets, butter side down, on the grill – the fish should sizzle as soon as it touches the pan. Turn down the heat slightly and let the fillets cook for 4–5 minutes, then turn them over. Continue to cook on the other side until crisp and golden. Serve on hot plates with a few slices of flavoured butter: it may be served directly on the fish or, if you have a pretty shell, serve the butter on the side in the shell. Garnish with segments of lemon and parsley.

Note: Fillets of any small fish are delicious pangrilled in this way. Fish under 900g (2lb), such as mackerel, herring and brown trout, can also be grilled whole on the pan. Fish over 900g (2lb) can be filleted first and then cut across into portions. Large fish of 2–2.5kg (4–5½lb) can also be grilled whole. Cook them for about 10–15 minutes on each side and then put in a hot oven (180°C/350°F/gas mark 4) for another 15 minutes or so to finish cooking.

Flavoured Butters

Mâitre d'Hotel Butter
110g (4oz) butter
2 tablespoons finely chopped parsley
few drops of freshly squeezed lemon juice

Cream the butter, add in the parsley and a few drops of lemon juice at a time. Roll into butter pats or form into a roll and wrap in greaseproof paper or foil screwing each end like a cracker. Refrigerate to harden.

Lemon Butter
Omit the parsley and add the rind of the lemon to the Mâitre d'Hotel Butter recipe.

Mustard and Parsley Butter
Add 1 tablespoon Dijon mustard to the Mâitre d'Hotel Butter recipe.

Cashel or Crozier Blue Cheese Butter
110g (4oz) unsalted butter
50g (2oz) Cashel Blue cheese
1 teaspoon freshly ground pepper
1 tablespoon chopped parsley, optional

Mix all the ingredients together in a bowl or better still, whizz in a food processor. Form into a roll in tin foil or pure cling film, tighten the ends. Chill or freeze until needed.

friends' supper party

A participation party, where the guests get involved in the cooking is one of the simplest and fun ways to entertain a group of people. Make up some pancake batter (see p106), lay out a range of fillings and then get your guests to cook their own pancake. Not only does this save on cooking time, it also means that the menu is really flexible and you can cater for all your friends' tastes and dietary choices. And if any of your guests have specific needs, they can bring their own fillings and still be involved in the preparation.

This is also a really good way to have a casual supper. If you are having good friends round you may not necessarily want the formality of sitting round a dining table. The food may also not be the focal point of the evening – you may have gathered to plan a wedding or reunion, to have a film night or TV marathon or a sewing or games evening – and this kind of dining allows you to combine food with other activities.

Once you have made your pancakes, you can curl up on sofas and cushions around the TV or get on with the evening's entertainment. People can get up and make more pancakes as they like and you just need to keep an eye on the batter and put out more fillings as required.

participation party

Omelettes (see p108) are perfect for participation parties, and are the quintessential 'quick and easy meal'. Tacos and fajitas (p109) can also be served in this fashion, but they will need a little more preparation. If you have more time, sushi (see p44–45) is also great fun to make together

Make sure you have a good salad and dessert (for the lemon meringue pie, see p265) for guests to help themselves to, although with a pancake party you can simply move onto sweet fillings.

Have some wine, beers and soft drinks on a table, together with the appropriate glasses and people can refill when their glasses are low.

You will need very little in the way of place settings or decoration as the food itself will provide plenty of colour and entertainment. Find lots of generous bowls or chunky plates to set the fillings out on – or use square white plates for a more graphic look.

If you are worried about your guests' culinary skills, provide aprons and don't use your best pancake pan. Don't forget to get everybody to help with clearing up!

A Pancake Party

MAKES 12–15 PANCAKES   (P: 15 MINS
+ 1 HOUR TO REST/C: 2 MINS + FILLING)

A kitchen party is the best fun. Get everybody involved in cooking their pancakes as well as their filling. Make large quantities of basic pancake batter, provide lots of fillings both sweet and savoury, a few non-stick pans and maybe a few aprons for the more flamboyant cooks. This kind of participation party is great for catering for special diets – you can even ask guests to bring a filling or two themselves.

For the pancake batter:
175g (6oz) plain white flour, preferably
   unbleached
good pinch of salt
2 large free-range, organic eggs,
   plus 1–2 egg yolks,
425ml (³/4 pint) milk or, for very crisp, light,
   delicate pancakes, milk and water mixed
2 tablespoons melted butter

For the sweet pancake batter:
As above, plus 1 tablespoon caster sugar (if
   the pancakes are to be served with sugar
   and lemon juice, use 2 tablespoons caster
   sugar and the finely grated zest of ¹/2 lemon)

filling of your choice (see right), to serve

Note: If you make both batters, be careful not to mix them up.

To make the batter, sift the flour, salt and sugar (if making sweet batter) into a bowl. Make a well in the centre and drop in the eggs and yolks. With a whisk or wooden spoon, starting in the centre, mix the eggs and gradually bring in the flour from the sides. Add the milk gradually, beating all the while, until the batter is covered with bubbles. Alternatively, just bung all the ingredients into a liquidiser and whizz – it works beautifully.

Let the batter stand in a cold place for 1 hour or so – longer will do no harm. Just before you cook the pancakes, stir in 2 tablespoons melted butter. This will make all the difference to the flavour and texture of the pancakes, and will make it possible to cook them without greasing the pan each time.

To cook the pancakes, heat a non-stick frying pan until very hot. Pour in just enough batter to cover the base when you tilt and swirl the pan. Put the pan back on the heat and loosen the pancake around the edge with a non-metal fish slice. Flip over and cook for a few seconds on the reverse side. Slide on to a plate. Repeat until all the batter has been used up. To fill the pancakes, lay some of your chosen filling on the pancake and roll into a cigar or fold into a parcel or a fan shape depending on the filling.

Pancakes can be made ahead and finished later. They will keep overnight, covered, in the fridge. They will peel apart easily, so there's no need to interleaf them with greaseproof paper. To reheat, cover with aluminium foil and put in an oven at 180°C/350°F/gas mark 4.

Suggested Fillings

Savoury
Creamed spinach
Mushroom à la Crème (see p241)
Tomato Fondue (see p240)
Piperonata (see p243)
Spicy chicken with almonds
Crispy chorizo
Grated cheese
Smoked mackerel flakes
Cream cheese mixed with lots of dill and freshly ground pepper
Lots of chopped herbs in little bowls, such as parsley
Thin slices of cooked ham and Gruyère cheese
Smoked salmon and dill
Marmite and sardines
Shrimps and spring onions

Sweet
Freshly squeezed lemon juice, melted butter and caster sugar
Toffee Sauce (see p28) and bananas
Chocolate fudge sauce and bananas
Green Gooseberry and Elderflower Compote (see p229)
Poached Apricots with Sweet Geranium Leaves (see p29)
A shake of icing sugar
A shake of cocoa powder
Chocolate spread
Chopped toasted hazelnuts, almonds, pecans or walnuts

30-second Classic French Omelette

SERVES 1   (P: 10 MINS/C: 30–45 SECONDS)

A classic French omelette has to be the quintessential easy entertaining recipe, so if a pal or several suddenly turn up and look as though they are not about to leave until they are fed you can always whizz up an omelette! They are also great for participation parties – as with the pancakes (see p106), prepare a huge batch of omelette batter and line up a ton of fillings. People can then create their own masterpieces.

As ever the quality of the eggs really matters. The key to a successful omelette is to get the pan hot enough and to use clarified butter if at all possible. Ordinary butter will burn if your pan is as hot as it ought to be. The best tender golden omelettes take no more than 30 seconds to cook – 45 seconds if you are adding a filling. Time yourself: you'll be amazed.

2 free-range, organic eggs
1 dessertspoon water or milk
salt and freshly ground pepper
filling of your choice (see right)
1 dessertspoon clarified butter or olive oil

Omelette pan, preferably non-stick, 23cm
  (9 in) diameter

Warm a plate in the oven. Whisk the eggs with the water or milk in a bowl with a fork or whisk, until thoroughly mixed but not too fluffy. Season with salt and freshly ground pepper. Put the warm plate beside the cooker. Have your chosen filling close to hand, hot, if necessary, with a spoon at the ready.

Heat the omelette pan over a high heat and when it is almost smoking add the clarified butter or the olive oil – it should sizzle immediately. Pour in the egg mixture. It will start to cook instantly, so quickly pull the edges of the omelette towards the centre with a plastic spoon or spatula, tilting the pan so that the uncooked egg runs to the sides. Continue until most of the egg is set and does not run when the pan is tilted; the centre will still be soft and uncooked at this point but will continue to cook on the plate. If you are using a filling, spoon the hot filling in a line across the centre of the omelette.

To fold the omelette, flip the edge just below the handle of the pan into the centre, then hold the pan almost perpendicular over the plate so that the omelette will flip over again, then half roll, half slide the omelette on to the plate so that it lands folded in three. Serve immediately.

Suggested Fillings
Tomato Fondue with or without pesto
Piperonata (see p243)
Mushroom à la Crème (see p241)
Crispy bacon, diced cooked ham or chorizo sausage
Goat's cheese, grated Cheddar, Gruyère or Parmesan cheese or a mixture and lots of fresh herbs
Fine herbs: add 1 teaspoon each of chopped parsley, chives, chervil and tarragon to the eggs
  just before cooking or scatter over the omelette just before folding
Smoked salmon or smoked mackerel: add about 25g (1oz) and perhaps a little finely
  chopped parsley or dill

How to Clarify Butter
Clarified butter is excellent for cooking because it can withstand a higher temperature as the salt and milk particles have been removed.

Melt 225g (8oz) butter gently in a saucepan or in the oven. Allow to stand for a few minutes, then skim the crusty white layer of salt particles from the top of the melted butter. Underneath this crust is a clear liquid butter – the clarified butter. The milky liquid at the bottom can be discarded or used in a white sauce. Cover and store. It will keep covered in the fridge for several weeks.

Beef Fajitas with Tomato and Coriander Salsa and Guacamole

SERVES 6–8   (**P:** 20 MINS + 1 HOUR MARINATING/**C:** 5 MINS)

This is another great recipe for a partici-pation party, although here you might want to prepare the beef and fillings before your guests arrive and then let them put their fajitas together themselves.

450 (1lb) rump steak, 2.5 cm (1in) thick, cut into steaks
12–16 flour tortillas
salt and freshly ground black pepper
handful of shredded lettuce, such as Iceberg or Cos
Tomato and Coriander Salsa (see p294)
Guacamole (see p294)
125ml (4fl oz) soured cream

For the marinade:
2 garlic cloves, crushed
1 chilli, deseeded and chopped, or
$1/2$ teaspoon chilli flakes
1 teaspoon ground cumin
1 tablespoon chopped marjoram
2 tablespoons Mexican beer or lager
2 tablespoons extra virgin olive oil

To make the marinade, put all the marinade ingredients in a pie dish and mix well. Add the steak and turn to coat well. Cover and refrigerate for 1 hour.

When ready to cook, heat a grill pan. When it is very hot, drain the steaks and cook to your taste. Transfer to a plate and leave to relax for 5 minutes.

Meanwhile, heat a frying pan and flip the tortillas over to heat through. When the meat has relaxed, carve it into 1cm ($1/2$in) thick slices.

To prepare the fajitas for serving, put the sliced steak on the warm tortillas. Sprinkle with salt and freshly ground pepper. Top with lettuce, Tomato and Coriander Salsa, Guacamole and soured cream. Roll up or fold over the tortillas and serve hot.

Alternatively, put a stack of warm tortillas on the table, set out the Tomato and Coriander Salsa, Guacamole, soured cream, lettuce and sliced steak, and let your guests have fun making up their own fajitas – a delicious interactive supper.

Taco Party

SERVES 20   (**P:** 10 MINS/**C:** 2–3 HOURS)

Another fun way to have a carefree party. Although the pork takes a couple of hours to cook, this recipe can be made in advance and it is easy to serve.

1 shoulder of pork, boned
2 onions, peeled and quartered
4 celery sticks, chopped
3 garlic cloves
6 black peppercorns
1 bouquet garni
sea salt
about 60 warm flour tortillas

For the accompaniments:
Refried Beans (see p21)
Tomato and Coriander Salsa (see p294)
soured cream
tomatilla salsa (optional; available in delis)
grated Cheddar cheese
lots of fresh coriander
lime segments for squeezing (optional)

Put the pork into a casserole just large enough to hold the meat and vegetables comfortably. Add the onions, celery, garlic, peppercorns and bouquet garni. Cover with cold water and bring to the boil. Reduce the heat to medium and simmer for $1 1/2$–2 hours or until the meat is soft and tender.

Transfer the pork to a plate, strain the liquid and discard the vegetables. Skim the fat off the liquid, return to the pan and cook over a medium heat until reduced to about 225ml (8fl oz).

Meanwhile, preheat the oven to 160°C/320°F/gas mark 3. Using two forks, pull the pork into shreds. Spread the shreds out on two baking trays and season with sea salt. Pour the reduced cooking liquid over the shredded pork and transfer to the oven. Cook until the edges of the meat start to brown and crisp, about 15 minutes. Taste and adjust the seasoning if needed. The dish may be prepared ahead to this point.

Set out the hot pork, preferably in an earthenware casserole, on the table with the accompaniments. Warm the tortillas or, if it's a casual kitchen party, have an iron or non-stick frying pan on a low heat so guests can warm their own.

To serve, take a warm tortilla, sprinkle a line of shredded pork down the centre, top with some Refried Beans, soured cream, salsa, grated cheese and coriander, and squeeze a little lime juice over the top if you fancy.

Ballycotton Prawns Whole in their Shells with Watercress and Dill Mayo

SERVES 8   (P: 10 MINS/C: 5 MINS)

Not cheap, but always a wow. If you can, buy the prawns already cooked from your fishmonger – great, but they are very simple to cook. Homemade mayo is a must to embellish beautiful fresh prawns.

40–48 large very fresh raw prawns
3.6 litres (6 pints) water
3 tablespoons salt

For the accompaniments:
4–8 tablespoons homemade dill mayonnaise
   (see p297)
lemon wedges
wild watercress leaves
crusty wholemeal soda bread (see p38)
butter

First cook the prawns. In a large saucepan, bring the water to the boil, add the salt and stir briefly to dissolve (the quantity given may sound a lot, but this is the secret of real flavour when cooking prawns or shrimps). Add a half or a third of the prawns and, as soon as the water returns to a rolling boil, test to see if the prawns are cooked – they should be firm and white, not opaque or mushy. Remove the cooked prawns immediately; very large ones may take a further 30 seconds–1 minute in the boiling water. Repeat in batches until all the prawns are cooked. Spread them in a single layer on a tray, uncurl the tails and allow to cool.

Put 5–6 cooled whole prawns on each plate. Spoon a tablespoon or two of dill mayonnaise into a little bowl or oyster shell on the side of the plate, and add a wedge of lemon. Garnish with some fresh wild watercress. Serve with crusty wholemeal soda bread and Irish butter.

Note: Do not be tempted to cook too many prawns together, otherwise they may overcook before the water even comes back to the boil. Cook them in 2–3 batches. Shrimp can be cooked in the same way, but take 2–3 minutes to cook.

Seared Fresh Salmon with Vine-ripened Tomatoes and Herbs

SERVES 8   (P: 5 MINS/C: 5 MINS)

900 (2lb) fillet of salmon, scales removed
salt, freshly ground pepper and sugar, to taste
125ml (4fl oz) extra virgin olive oil or clarified
   butter (see p108), plus extra for frying
8 very ripe vine tomatoes, coarsely chopped
4 tablespoons each chopped basil, marjoram
   and mint

Cut the salmon fillet into strips about 6cm (2½in) wide. Season well with salt and pepper.

Heat a little olive oil or clarified butter in a frying pan or grill-pan, and fry the fish carefully so the fish doesn't fall apart – about 3–4 minutes on each side. Transfer to a serving dish, skin side up.

In a bowl, mix the chopped tomatoes and the herbs, then add the olive oil or clarified butter and season with salt, pepper and sugar. Spoon over the fish. Serve warm or cold.

Other good things to serve with roast or seared salmon
Dill butter and Tomato Fondue (see p240)
Teriyaki sauce with new potatoes and bok choy
Rhubarb, cucumber and mint salsa

Great Beans and Sausages

SERVES 6   (P: 5 MINS/C: 10 MINS)

1 quantity well-seasoned Tomato Fondue
   (see p240)
2 tablespoons chopped rosemary
400g (14oz) tin cannellini or haricot beans,
   drained
450g (1lb) best pork sausages
flat parsley leaves, to garnish

Heat the Tomato Fondue in a sauté pan. Add the chopped rosemary and beans and bubble for 6–8 minutes.

Meanwhile, in a wide frying pan, cook the sausages until golden on all sides.

Taste the beans and adjust the seasoning if needed. Serve with the sausages and scatter with lots of flat parsley. Serve with crusty bread.

Pork with Rosemary and Tomatoes

SERVES 6   **(P:** 10 MINS**/C:** 30 MINS**)**

900g (2lb) trimmed pork fillet
35g (1¼oz) butter
2 shallots, finely chopped
450g (1lb) very ripe but firm tomatoes,
   skinned and cut into 1cm (½in) slices
salt, freshly ground pepper and sugar
250ml (9fl oz) cream
1 tablespoon chopped rosemary, plus whole
   sprigs to garnish
1 tablespoon extra virgin olive oil

Cut the trimmed pork fillet into slices about 2cm (¾in) thick.

Melt 25g (1oz) of the butter in a saucepan. When it foams add the shallots, cover with a butter wrapper and sweat gently for 5 minutes. Remove the butter wrapper, increase the heat slightly, add the tomatoes in a single layer, and season with salt, pepper and sugar. After 2 minutes turn the tomatoes and season on the other side, then add the cream and chopped rosemary. Simmer gently for 5 minutes. The sauce should not be too thick – just a light coating consistency. Check the seasoning.

Place the remaining butter and the olive oil in a sauté pan over a high heat. Season the pork, and when the butter and oil are quite hot, arrange the pork in the pan in a single layer. Allow the pork to turn a rich golden brown on the underside before turning the slices over. Reduce the temperature and finish cooking on the other side. The meat should feel slightly firm to the touch. Be careful not to overcook the pork or it will be dry and tasteless.

Add the pork to the sauce, taste and correct the seasoning. The dish may be prepared ahead to this point. Garnish with rosemary sprigs and serve immediately or reheat later.

Orzo or rice make a delicious accompaniment and will mop up the herby sauce. This recipe is also great with chicken breasts.

Lamb Chops with Cumin and Dill Tzatziki

SERVES 8   **(P:** 5 MINS**/C:** 30 MINS**)**

16 lamb chops, preferably side loin (the chops
   with the rib loin)
extra virgin olive oil, for brushing
3 tablespoons cumin seeds, toasted and
   ground
sea salt and freshly ground pepper
Dill Tzatziki (see p297)
roast cherry tomatoes (optional)

Trim the chops of excess fat and score the back fat. Lay the chops in a single layer on one or two flat dishes, brush with olive oil and season with the ground cumin seeds and pepper. Leave to sit for at least 15 minutes, better still an hour.

Heat a grill pan, season the chops with sea salt and cook in batches for a few minutes each side until crisp on the outside, but slightly pink and juicy on the inside. Make sure the fat is crisp, so that those who love a little sweet fat can enjoy it.

Serve 2 chops per person, with a little bowl of Dill Tzatziki on each plate; a branch of roast cherry tomatoes is a delicious addition if you have time.

Top Tip: If you'd rather not stand over a grill pan in your best frock, buy 2 racks of lamb. Score the skin in a diamond pattern, rub well with cumin seeds and drizzle with olive oil as above. Roast in the oven preheated to 200°C/400°F/gas mark 6 for 20–30 minutes depending on the size of the racks of lamb. Serve as above.

Spiced Chicken and Red Peppers with Orzo

SERVES 6–8   (P: 5 MINS/C: 30 MINS)

A simple recipe that works really well if cooking for a lot of people.

1 tablespoon coriander seeds
1 tablespoon cumin seeds
1/2 teaspoon ground turmeric
good pinch of cayenne pepper
2 teaspoons salt
1 teaspoon sugar
110g (4oz) onions, roughly chopped
2.5cm (1in) piece of fresh ginger, peeled and
  sliced
3 garlic cloves, crushed
25g (1oz) shelled almonds, blanched
350g (12oz) red peppers, deseeded and
  coarsely chopped
5 tablespoons sunflower oil

900g (2lb) boned chicken thighs, cut into
  finger-sized strips; alternatively use breast meat
150ml (1/4 pint) water
2 tablespoons lemon juice, plus extra to taste

In separate dry pans, toast the coriander and cumin seeds, ensuring the seeds do not burn. Grind them using a pestle and mortar. Transfer the ground seeds to a food processor and add the turmeric, cayenne, salt, sugar, chopped onions, ginger, garlic, almonds and peppers. Whizz to a smooth paste.

Heat the oil in a sauté pan, add the spice paste and cook for about 10 minutes until reduced. Add the chicken pieces, water and lemon juice and stir well. Taste and adjust the seasoning, adding a little more lemon juice if needed. Cover and cook on a low heat for 15–30 minutes or until the chicken is tender.

Serve with orzo or pilaff rice (see recipe below).

Note: If you like a hot curry, increase the amount of cayenne pepper to 1/2 teaspoon.

Orzo with Fresh Herbs

SERVES 4   (P: 5 MINS/C: 30 MINS)

Orzo looks like fat grains of rice but is in fact made from semolina.

2.4 litres (4 pints) water
200g (7oz) orzo
salt and freshly ground pepper
1 tablespoon chopped parsley
1 tablespoon snipped chives
1 tablespoon thyme
butter

Bring the water to a rolling boil and add 11/2 teaspoons salt. Sprinkle in the orzo and cook for 8–10 minutes or until just cooked. Drain, rinse under hot water and toss with the herbs and a little butter. Season with freshly ground pepper.

Orzo with peas
Add 200g (7oz) blanched peas to the orzo.

Pilaff Rice

SERVES 8   (P: 5 MINS/C: 30 MINS)

Although a risotto can be made in 20 minutes, it entails 20 minutes pretty constant stirring, which makes it feel laboursome. A pilaff on the other hand looks after itself once the initial cooking is under way. It is also versatile – serve it as a staple or add whatever tasty bits you have to hand. Ensure all additions are seasoned and balanced.

25g (1oz) butter
2 tablespoons finely chopped onion or shallot
400g (14oz) long-grain rice, preferably basmati
salt and freshly ground pepper
900ml (32fl oz) homemade chicken stock
  (see p295)
2 tablespoons chopped herbs such as
  parsley, thyme or chives (optional)

Melt the butter in a casserole, add the onion and sweat for 2–3 minutes. Add the rice and toss for a minute or two, just long enough for the grains to change colour. Season with salt and freshly ground pepper, add the chicken stock, cover and bring to the boil. Reduce the heat to a minimum and then simmer on top of the stove, or in the oven preheated to 160°C/320°F/gas mark 3, for about 10 minutes. By then the rice should be just cooked and all the water absorbed. Just before serving stir in the fresh herbs (if using).

Spicy Thai Fish Cakes with Cucumber Relish or Arjard

SERVES 4   (**P**: 10 MINS + 30 MINS
STANDING TIME/**C**: 5 MINS)

275g (10oz) cod or hake (redfish or red
  snapper fillets are used in Thailand)
2 tablespoons red or green curry paste
1 free-range, organic egg
3 tablespoons fish sauce (*nam pla*)
1 teaspoon sugar
5 kaffir lime leaves, stems removed and very
  finely shredded
50g (2oz) green beans, finely sliced across
sunflower or peanut oil, for deep-frying
coriander leaves and chilli powder, to garnish

For the Thai cucumber relish:
1 large cucumber
4 tablespoons rice vinegar
2–4 teaspoons sugar
1 teaspoon salt
1 small red chilli, deseeded and chopped
1 shallot, very thinly sliced

First make the cucumber relish. Peel the cucumber and cut in half lengthways. With a melon baller or sharp spoon, scoop out the seeds from the centre and discard them. Slice the cucumber diagonally into thin slices.

Mix the remainder of the relish ingredients in a glass bowl, add 2 tablespoons hot water and stir well to dissolve the sugar and salt. Add the cucumber slices and toss well. Allow the relish to stand for at least 30 minutes before serving.

Put the fish into a food processor, add the curry paste, egg, fish sauce and sugar, and blend well. Transfer to a medium bowl. Add the lime leaves and green beans and mix well. Shape the mixture into little discs 5cm (2in) in diameter and 6mm ($1/3$in) thick.

Heat the oil to deep-fry the fish cakes, then fry them for 4–5 minutes or until golden.

Serve the fish cakes with the cucumber relish, and garnish with fresh coriander and chilli powder.

Puff Pastry Tart with Tomato, Chorizo, Mozzarella and Basil Leaves

SERVES 4   (**P**: 5 MINS/**C**: 30 MINS)

**A piece of puff pastry is definitely an
invaluable standby to make a quick tart.**

225g (8oz) puff pastry
4–6 very ripe tomatoes or Tomato Fondue
  (see p240)
salt, freshly ground pepper and sugar, to taste
110g (4oz) chorizo, sliced
2 balls buffalo mozzarella cheese, thinly sliced
extra virgin olive oil, for drizzling
4 tablespoons pesto (see p297)
basil leaves, to garnish
green salad, to serve

Preheat the oven to 230ºC/450ºF/gas mark 8.

Roll out the puff pastry to a sheet about 5mm ($1/4$in) thick. Cut into a square or rectangle that will fit a baking tray, or stamp into four 13cm (5in) rounds. Transfer to a cold baking tray. Prick the base with a fork. Chill for a few minutes in a fridge.

Cut the tomatoes into 5mm ($1/4$in) thick slices. Arrange overlapping slices on the pastry base, or spread a thin layer of Tomato Fondue. Season with salt, freshly ground pepper and some sugar. Tuck in slices of chorizo here and there, and top with slices of mozzarella. Sprinkle on some pesto and drizzle over some olive oil. Bake for 10–20 minutes depending on size.

Drizzle with a little pesto, scatter over a few fresh basil leaves and serve immediately, with a good green salad.

Son-in-law's Eggs Khai Loog Kheoy

SERVES 6   (P: 15 MINS/C: 15 MINS)

Wasinee Beech, the lovely Thai cook, gave me this family recipe, which can be prepared ahead of time.

6 free-range, organic eggs
5 tablespoons extra virgin olive oil
3 garlic cloves, crushed and finely chopped
100g (3¹/₂oz) free-range organic minced pork
5 fresh shiitake mushrooms, sliced, or dried
   Chinese mushrooms, soaked for 20 minutes
   and sliced (reserve the water)
2 tablespoons palm sugar or soft brown sugar
2 tablepoons fish sauce (*nam pla*)
5 tablespoons tamarind water (see p126)
1 tablespoon lemon juice
3 spring onions, sliced into 1cm (¹/₂in) lengths
8 shallots, thinly sliced, and 2 dried red chillies,
   thinly sliced, both fried in a little oil or roast
   until fragrant but not burnt
plain boiled rice, to serve

For Wasinee's Arjard cucumber salad:
3–4 tablespoons sugar
4 tablespoons white wine vinegar
4 tablespoons water
¹/₂–1 teaspoon salt
1 cucumber, quartered lengthways and
   thinly sliced
2 shallots, finely sliced
1 red chilli, deseeded and sliced
1 green chilli, deseeded and sliced

To make Wasinee's Arjard cucumber salad, mix together the sugar, vinegar, water and salt in a small saucepan. Bring to the boil and simmer for 5 minutes. Leave to cool. Meanwhile, mix together in a bowl the cucumber, shallots and red and green chillies. When the sauce has cooled, pour it over the vegetables.

Cook the eggs gently in boiling salted water for 7 minutes to hard-boil them. Drain and cover with cold water. When cool, shell and set aside.

Heat 3 tablespoons of the olive oil in a wok, add the cooked and shelled eggs and fry until golden brown all around. Transfer to a serving dish. Cut each egg in half and arrange nicely.

Clean the wok and heat the remaining olive oil. Stir-fry the garlic until golden. Add the minced pork and mushrooms. Stir and fry until the pork is cooked. Add the palm or brown sugar, fish sauce, tamarind water and lemon juice. If more liquid is required, add a little bit of water from soaking the mushrooms, or some plain water.

Taste and adjust the seasoning if needed. Add the spring onions, give a quick stir and spoon the sauce over the arranged eggs. Top with the crispy shallots and chillies. Serve with plain boiled rice and Wasinee's Arjard cucumber salad.

Shermin's Lamajun (Turkish Lamb Pizza)

MAKES ABOUT 8–10   (P: 10 MINS/C: 5 MINS)

This little gem of a recipe was given to me by Shermin Mustafa, whose food I love. It's fantastic for an informal kitchen party or for a family supper.

275g (10oz) plain white flour, plus extra for
   dusting
225ml (8fl oz) natural yogurt
lemon wedges and lots of sprigs of flat parsley,
   to serve

For the topping:
1 tablespoon extra virgin olive oil or butter
1 large onion, finely chopped
225g (8oz) minced lamb
4 ripe tomatoes, finely diced
2 tablespoons chopped flat parsley
salt and freshly ground pepper

First make the topping. Heat the oil in a frying pan and cook the onion over a low heat until soft but not coloured. Allow to cool completely. Mix the onion with the remaining topping ingredients and season well with salt and pepper.

Preheat a heavy iron frying pan, preheat the grill and warm a baking sheet.

Mix the flour with the yogurt to form a soft dough. Divide into 8–10 pieces and roll each out until it's as thin as possible, using lots of flour to dust over the work surface and dough. Spread a few dessertspoons of the topping mixture on each round of dough as thinly and evenly as possible.

Fold the dough in half, then in quarters, slide your hand underneath, then transfer to the pan and open out gently; there is no need to oil the pan. Cook over a high heat for about 2 minutes or until golden on the bottom. Remove from the pan and slide on to the warm baking sheet, then place under the hot grill and cook for another 2–3 minutes or until the meat is cooked. Repeat with the remaining pizzas.

Serve with 3–4 lemon wedges and plenty of sprigs of flat parsley for each helping.

To eat the lamajun, squeeze lots of lemon juice over the surface. Pluck 4–5 parsley leaves and sprinkle over the top. Either eat flat like a pizza or rolled up like a tortilla.

Tortilla Pizza

SERVES 8   (P: 5 MINS/C: 5 MINS)

A cheat's version of a very-thin-crust pizza, but so easy and delicious. Keep a packet of corn or flour tortillas in your freezer or store cupboard, check what's in the fridge for suitable toppings, and have fun.

8 corn or flour tortillas

Suggested toppings:
Tomato Fondue (see p240) with mozzarella
   cheese and basil leaves
Piperonata (see p243) with crispy pancetta
   or chorizo sausage
Mushroom à la Crème (see p241) with lots of
   marjoram
Crumbled blue cheese with rosemary and
   caramelised onions
Pesto (see p297), mozzarella cheese and
   rocket leaves
Four-cheese pizza: Cheddar, mozzarella, Cashel
   Blue and Durrus cheese, and rocket leaves
Smoked salmon, cream cheese and crispy
   capers and chive blossoms

Preheat the grill. Pop the tortillas under the grill for 2–3 minutes per side. Top with your chosen topping, and pop back under the hot grill, or into a preheated oven at 230ºC/450ºF/gas mark 8, for 3–4 minutes. Scatter with fresh herbs or leaves as appropriate and serve immediately.

Frittata with Oven-roasted Tomatoes, Chorizo and Goat's Cheese

SERVES 6–8   (**P:** 10 MINS/**C:** 30 MINS)

A frittata is an Italian omelette. Along with 'kuku' and 'Spanish tortilla', it sounds much more exciting than a flat omelette, although that's basically what they all are. Unlike their soft and creamy French cousin, these omelettes are cooked slowly over a very low heat, during which time you can be whipping up a delicious salad to accompany them! A frittata is cooked on the stove and under the grill, then cut into wedges like a piece of cake. Omit the tomato and chorizo given here and you have a basic recipe flavoured with grated cheese and a generous sprinkling of herbs. As is the case of the omelette, though, you'll occasionally want to ring the changes. For a yummy vegetarian alternative, omit the chorizo and use 110g (4oz) grated Gruyère cheese to add extra zing. Other tasty morsels include spinach, ruby chard, calabrese or broccoli, asparagus, smoked mackerel… the list is endless, but be careful: don't use a frittata as a dustbin – think about the combination of flavours before you empty your fridge!

A frittata can also be cooked in a preheated oven at 160°C/320°F/gas mark 3. You could also bake mini versions in muffin tins (about 15 minutes in the oven) – perfect for taking on a picnic (see p220) as the tins will protect them on the journey.

450g (1lb) ripe or sun-blush tomatoes
salt and freshly ground black pepper
8 large free-range, organic eggs
2 tablespoons chopped parsley
4 teaspoons thyme leaves
1 tablespoon chopped basil, mint or marjoram
110–175g (4–6oz) chorizo, thickly sliced
  and each slice quartered
40g (1¹/₂oz) Parmesan cheese, grated
25g (1oz) butter
110g (4oz) soft goat's cheese
green salad and olives, to serve

If using fresh tomatoes, preheat the oven to 180°C/350°F/gas mark 4. (If using sun-blush tomatoes, there is no need to roast them.) Cut the fresh tomatoes in half around their equator, arrange them cut side up in a single layer in a non-stick roasting tin and season with salt and pepper. Roast for 10–15 minutes until almost soft and slightly crinkly. Remove from the oven and leave to cool.

Whisk the eggs in a bowl and add salt and pepper, the herbs, chorizo and grated cheese. Add the tomatoes and stir gently.

Melt the butter in a non-stick frying pan. When the butter starts to foam, tip in the egg mixture. Reduce the heat to as low as it will go. Divide the goat's cheese into walnut-sized pieces and drop gently into the frittata, spacing them regularly. Leave the frittata to cook on a heat-diffuser mat for 15 minutes, or until the underneath is set. The top should still be slightly runny. Meanwhile preheat the grill.

Pop the frittata under the grill for 1 minute to set and barely brown the surface. Slide the frittata on to a warm plate and serve cut into wedges, with a good green salad and a few olives.

Middle Eastern Mezze with Chilli and Coriander Flat Bread

SERVES 10   (P: 5 MINS/C: 30 MINS)

salad leaves and fresh herbs, tossed with a
  little vinaigrette
Aubergine Purée (see p119)
Hummous Bi Tahina (see recipe below)
feta cheese with walnut and mint
Tunisian Spicy Carrot Salad (see p119)
Roasted Red Peppers (see p298)
generous amount of pine nuts, toasted
1 teaspoon paprika, or to taste
2 tablespoons extra virgin olive oil
generous amount of chopped flat parsley
cooked chickpeas, to scatter
sprigs of mint
2 tablespoons olives, or to taste
chopped coriander, to garnish

For the accompaniment:
10 flour tortillas or other flat bread (see
  p40), and extra virgin olive oil, chopped chilli
  and sea salt
or Pitta Crisps (see p119)
or tortilla chips

Prepare and make all the mezze components.

Put some salad in the centre of each plate. Around the salad drop a dollop of Aubergine Purée, Hummus Bi Tahina, some feta with walnut and mint, and some Tunisian Spicy Carrot Salad.

Lay a strip or two of roasted red pepper on top of the aubergine and sprinkle with toasted pine nuts. Mix some paprika with the olive oil and drizzle over the top of the hummous. Sprinkle with chopped parsley and a few chickpeas. Drop a sprig of mint on the feta and scatter a few olives on the plate. Sprinkle coriander on the mezze.

To make the chilli and coriander flat bread, brush the flour tortillas or flat bread with olive oil, sprinkle with chopped chilli and sea salt, and warm through in the oven for about 5 minutes. Cut the bread into triangular portions.

Serve the mezze with the chilli and coriander flat bread, the Pitta Crisps or tortilla chips.

Hummous Bi Tahina

SERVES 4–8   (P: 10 MINS)

Hummous with tahini's rich, earthy taste has got quite a cult following. Strange to the palate on first encounter, this flavoured purée of chickpeas and sesame seed paste soon becomes addictive. It makes an excellent starter, served as a dip with pitta bread, but is also delicious with kebabs or as a salad with a main dish.

175g (6oz) dried chickpeas, cooked,
  (reserve the cooking water) or 400g (14oz)
  tin chickpeas, drained
juice of 2–3 lemons, or to taste
2–3 garlic cloves, crushed
150ml (1/4 pint) tahini (sesame seed paste,
  available from health-food shops and
  delicatessens)
1 teaspoon ground cumin
salt
2 tablespoons olive oil
1/4 teaspoon paprika
flat parsley, to garnish
pitta or any crusty white bread, to serve

Drain the chickpeas, retaining the cooking liquid. Put the chickpeas in a food processor, add the lemon juice and whizz to a thick paste. Add the garlic, tahini, cumin and salt, blending to a soft, creamy paste; add a little of the chickpea cooking liquid if needed. Taste and adjust the lemon juice and salt until you are happy with the flavour. Transfer to a serving bowl.

Mix the olive oil with the paprika and drizzle over the top of the hummous. Scatter with parsley and serve with pitta or other crusty bread.

Aubergine Purée with Olive Oil and Lemon

SERVES 6   (**P**: 10 MINS/**C**: 10 MINS)

This is one of my favourite ways to eat aubergine. It is served throughout the southern Mediterranean region, and there are many delicious variations.

4 large aubergines
4–5 tablespoons extra virgin olive oil
juice of 2 lemons, unwaxed
2 garlic cloves, crushed (optional)
salt and freshly ground pepper

Roast or grill the aubergines depending on the flavour you prefer. Allow to cool. Peel the aubergines, retaining every little morsel of flesh. Discard the skin and drain the flesh in a sieve or colander.

Transfer to a bowl and mash the aubergine flesh with a fork or chop with a knife depending on the texture you like. Add the olive oil and lemon juice, garlic (if using), and salt and freshly ground pepper to taste.

Other good things to add

1 In Turkey some thick Greek-style yogurt is often added. Reduce the olive oil in the recipe by half and add 5–6 tablespoons yogurt. This makes a delicious 'sauce' for pasta when mixed with ricotta (instead of the yogurt) and chopped fresh herbs, such as marjoram.

2 A spicier version from Morocco includes 1 teaspoon harissa, 1 teaspoon cumin seeds, toasted and ground, and 2 tablespoons coarsely chopped coriander leaves.

3 In Syria they add some pomegranate molasses – our new 'flavour of the month.' Use 3–4 tablespoons instead of the lemon juice.

4 *Julia's aubergine purée:* Roast or grill the aubergines as above, peel, drain and mash the flesh, and mix with 2 small garlic cloves, finely chopped, $1/2$–1 teaspoon ground roasted cumin seeds, 1–2 tablespoons chiffonade of mint (roll into a cigar shape and chop), the freshly squeezed juice of $1/2$–1 lemon, and some freshly ground pepper or chilli oil if you prefer. Mix well.

Tunisian Spicy Carrot Salad

SERVES 6   (**P**: 5 MINS/**C**: 30 MINS)

A delish salad to serve alone or as part of a mezze plate

700g (1$1/2$lb) carrots
3–4 tablespoons extra virgin olive oil
3 tablespoons white wine vinegar
2 garlic cloves, crushed
1 teaspoon harissa, or to taste, or 1 teaspoon
  paprika and a good pinch of chilli powder
1$1/2$ teaspoons freshly ground cumin seeds
salt
black olives (optional)

Peel the carrots and cut into large pieces. Cook them in a little boiling salted water until tender. Drain and mash them with a potato masher or fork. Mix in the olive oil, white wine vinegar, crushed garlic, harissa or paprika and chilli powder, cumin and some salt. Taste and adjust the seasoning if needed. Sprinkle with a few black olives if you like. Refrigerate until needed and serve cold or at room temperature.

Pitta Crisps

mini pitta breads, halved crossways
extra virgin olive oil, for brushing
cumin seeds, freshly ground and toasted
salt

Preheat the oven to 200C°/400°F/gas mark 6.

Cut the pitta into triangular wedges. Brush evenly with olive oil, and sprinkle with cumin and salt. Spread in a single layer on a baking tray and bake in the middle of the oven for 3 minutes or until crisp and golden. Serve immediately.

Chicken with Chorizo, Tomato and Chilli

SERVES 8–10   (**P:** 15 MINS/**C:** 20 MINS)

This works well for large numbers. Of course, it can be made ahead and reheated. When ready to eat, cook some pasta and serve.

25g (1oz) butter
1 tablespoon finely chopped rosemary
700g (1½lb) ripe tomatoes, skinned,
   deseeded and cut into 1cm (½in) dice, or
   1½ x 400g (14oz) tins tomatoes, chopped
salt, freshly ground pepper and sugar, to taste
8 free-range, organic chicken breasts,
   whole or sliced
175g (6oz) chorizo
pinch of chilli flakes
175ml (6fl oz) cream
2 tablespoons finely chopped flat parsley,
   plus extra, snipped, to garnish
450g (1lb) fresh noodles or fettuccini
4 tablespoons grated Parmesan cheese

Melt the butter in a large sauté pan and add the chopped rosemary and tomatoes. Season with salt, freshly ground pepper and some sugar to taste. Cook over a medium heat until the tomatoes have just begun to soften into a sauce, about 5 minutes. Add the chicken breasts.

Slice the chorizo into 5mm (½in) rounds and add them to the pan along with the crushed chilli flakes. Add the cream and chopped parsley and allow to bubble for 5–10 minutes, depending on the size of the chicken pieces, stirring frequently, until the chicken is cooked through. Remove the pan from the heat and set aside.

Cook the pasta in a large saucepan of boiling salted water (it should be al dente, or still just firm). Drain and toss with the sauce, then add the grated Parmesan. Toss again, and check and adjust the seasoning if needed. Sprinkle with lots of snipped flat parsley and serve at once.

Chicken Breasts with Honey and Mustard

SERVES 8   (**P:** 5 MINS/**C:** 30 MINS)

4 tablespoons honey
4 tablespoons Dijon mustard
8 free-range organic chicken breasts
extra virgin olive oil, for drizzling
salt and freshly ground pepper

To serve: green vegetables and potatoes,
   rice or orzo

Preheat the oven to 180°C/350°F/gas mark 4.

In a large bowl, mix together the honey and mustard. Toss the chicken in this mixture until well coated. Arrange in a single layer in a roasting tin. Drizzle with oil and season with salt and pepper. Bake for 20–30 minutes until the chicken is cooked through.

Serve with fresh green vegetables and potatoes, rice or orzo.

Phillippa's Magret de Canard with Port Sauce

SERVES 4   (**P:** 10 MINS/**C:** 35 MINS)

This is one of Phillippa Canning's favourite recipes for easy entertaining.

1 tablespoon extra virgin olive oil
110g (4oz) butter
2 medium onions, chopped
2 tablespoons brown sugar
125ml (4fl oz) port
200g (7oz) crème fraîche
3–4 duck breasts
salt and freshly ground pepper
sprigs of flat parsley, to garnish

First make the sauce. Pour the olive oil into a heavy-bottomed pan and add the butter, then heat gently until the butter has melted. Add the chopped onions and brown sugar, and cook for 15 minutes on a low heat until the onions are soft and slightly sticky.

Add the port, followed by the crème fraîche, and simmer very gently for about 10 minutes until the sauce has reduced a little and has thickened slightly. This can be made in advance and reheats very well later in the day.

Score the skin of the duck breasts and put skin-side down on a cold grill pan. Cook on a low heat for 15–20 minutes or until the skin is crisp and the fat has rendered out. Season with salt and freshly ground pepper. Turn the duck breasts on to the flesh side and cook for a further 5–10 minutes depending on size. Allow to rest for 10–15 minutes before serving. Meanwhile, reheat the sauce. Thinly slice the duck breasts and serve with a generous pool of sauce. Garnish with flat parsley sprigs.

Mexican Spiced Pork Chops with Pineapple, Chilli and Lime Salsa

SERVES 8   (**P**: 5 MINS + 2 HOURS/**C**: 20 MINS)

8 pork loin chops, preferably free-range, organic
  with a nice layer of fat (2.5cm/1in thick)
salt

For the marinade:
4 garlic cloves, crushed
1 teaspoon chopped marjoram
1 teaspoon ground cumin
1/2 teaspoon ground coriander
1/4 teaspoon ground cinnamon
2 tablespoons red wine vinegar
3 tablespoons orange juice
1 tablespoon runny honey
4 tablespoons extra virgin olive oil
freshly ground black pepper

In a bowl or jug, mix together all the marinade ingredients.

Put the chops in a large dish and pour the marinade mixture over, turning them several times to coat thoroughly. Cover and refrigerate for a couple of hours if you have time.

Season the chops with salt. Pangrill or barbecue over medium-hot coals until fully cooked but still juicy, 8–10 minutes per side. Season the chops with salt. Serve hot, with the Pineapple, Chilli and Lime Salsa.

Pineapple, Chilli and Lime Salsa

SERVES 8   (**P**: 5 MINS/**C**: 30 MINS)

1/2 pineapple, cored and finely diced
1 fresh red chilli, deseeded and finely chopped
1 red onion, finely chopped
2 tablespoons chopped coriander or mint
grated zest of 1 lime
3 tablespoons lime juice
salt and sugar

In a bowl, mix together the pineapple, chilli, onion, coriander or mint, lime zest and lime juice. Add salt and sugar to taste. Cover and let stand at room temperature for 30 minutes to allow the flavours to blend. Serve this at room temperature or chilled if you prefer.

Bubbly Pork Chops with Gruyère Cheese and Thyme Leaves

SERVES 8   (**P**: 5 MINS/**C**: 20 MINS)

extra virgin olive oil, for drizzling
8 pork chops, preferably free-range, organic
salt and freshly ground pepper
175g (6oz) Gruyère or Coolea cheese, grated
2 tablespoons Dijon mustard
4 tablespoons cream
1 teaspoon thyme leaves

To serve: new potatoes, Colcannon (see p236)
  or watercress mash

If you want to cook the meat in the oven, preheat the oven to 230°C/450°F/gas mark 8.

Heat a grill pan on a high heat. Drizzle a tiny drop of olive oil on the chops and season the chops with salt and pepper. Working in batches if necessary, place the meat on the grill pan (don't overcrowd the pan or the meat will stew) and seal on both sides. Transfer to the oven and cook for about 10 minutes until just cooked through; alternatively, reduce the stove-top heat to medium and continue to cook.

Meanwhile, mix the grated cheese with the mustard, cream and thyme leaves.

Transfer the pork chops to a wide, ovenproof serving dish. Spread a layer of the cheesy topping evenly over each pork chop. Return to the oven or pop under a preheated grill for a few minutes until the top is hot, bubbly and golden brown.

Serve with new potatoes or Colcannon or watercress mash.

Pork or Lamb Chops with Tapenade
Sauté the lamb chops in the usual way. Spread a little tapenade (see p75) over one side, sprinkle with grated cheese and pop under the grill for a couple of minutes until the cheese melts. Yummy!

Martha Rosenthal's Red Lentil Dahl

SERVES 6   (P: 15 MINS/C: 25 MINS)

This is the quickest dahl to cook – it takes only 20 minutes without using a pressure cooker. The orange/red colour of the lentils becomes pale yellow once they are cooked. The dahl keeps very well, so I usually double or triple this recipe.

The *Baghar* is an indispensable process in South Asian cooking – a lot of dishes, mostly dahls are finished with this process. It is used as a garnish to perfume a dish and is essentially seasoning in sizzling oil; i.e, the frying of spices in hot oil to release their fragrance and aromas, which is then added to the dish just before serving.

225g (8oz) orange/red lentils
450ml (16fl oz) tin coconut milk
1 teaspoon ground turmeric
1 tablespoon lemon juice
1 teaspoon Garam Masala (see recipe below)
1 teaspoon salt

For the Baghar:
1 tablespoon sunflower oil
1 teaspoon cumin seeds
1 teaspoon cayenne pepper
1 teaspoon ground coriander

For the garnish:
6 slices of onion, sautéed until golden
a few chopped coriander or mint leaves

For the accompaniments:
basmati rice
Tamarind Relish (see recipe below)

Put the lentils in a heavy-bottomed saucepan and add the coconut milk and turmeric. Bring to the boil and simmer for about 20 minutes, by which time the lentils will be soft, almost mushy. Turn off the heat, add the lemon juice, Garam Masala and salt.

To make the baghar, heat the oil, add the cumin seeds and fry for 2 minutes, then turn off the heat. Add the cayenne and coriander, stir and pour over the cooked lentils. Mix well and garnish with sauteed onion slices and chopped coriander or mint leaves.

Serve with basmati rice and Tamarind Relish.

Top Tip: Martha sometimes adds 2 ripe tomatoes, quartered, just before serving.

Garam Masala

What adds flavour to the simple dahl recipe (above) is to make your own garam masala. I usually make triple the quantity as it stores well.

20g (3/4oz) cumin seeds
40g (1 1/2oz) coriander seeds
1 1/2 teaspoons cardamom seeds
1 1/2 teaspoons black peppercorns
15 whole cloves
5cm (2in) piece of cinnamon stick
3 tablespoons fennel seeds
1 tablespoon brown mustard seeds
1/2 teaspoon red pepper flakes

Preheat a heavy frying pan over medium-low heat. Add all of the ingredients and dry-fry, stirring occasionally or, until they darken slightly, about 8–10 minutes. Transfer to a coffee grinder or blender and grind to a powder. Use while fresh or store in an airtight container for up to 1 month.

Tamarind Relish

2 teaspoons tamarind concentrate
200ml (7fl oz) boiling water
1 teaspoon peeled and grated fresh ginger
40g (1 1/2oz) chopped dates or raisins,
   or an equal combination of both
1/2 teaspoon dry-roasted cumin seeds,
   crushed
1/4–1/2 teaspoon cayenne pepper, or to taste
salt, to taste

Mix the tamarind paste with the boiling water until dissolved, then add the ginger. Stir and add the dates and/or raisins. Mix well, then add the cumin, cayenne and salt to taste.

This sauce keeps for 2–3 weeks.

Chilli, Salt and Pepper Squid with Frizzled Coriander

SERVES 4–6   (P: 20 MINS/C: 5 MINS)

Squid is divine, but can be a serious chew unless you have cooked it in a twinkle — otherwise it will toughen. You can substitute five-spice powder for the chilli, if you like.

700g (1¹/₂lb) whole squid (tiny ones are best but not easy to come by)
peanut or sunflower oil, for frying
8–12 sprigs of coriander
lemon segments, to garnish
Sweet Chilli Sauce (see p296), to serve

For the coating:
100g (3¹/₂oz) plain white flour
2 tablespoons sea salt
1 tablespoon freshly ground black pepper
1–2 teaspoons chilli powder

Clean and prepare the squid (see below), then cut into strips. Alternatively, ask your fishmonger to do it for you.

Mix the coating ingredients together in a bowl. In a deep-fryer, heat the oil to 180°C/350°F. Toss the squid in the coating mixture. Shake off any excess flour and drop the squid pieces one at a time into the hot oil, ensuring you do not overcrowd the basket or pan; if necessary, cook the squid in batches. Fry for 1–2 minutes, then remove and drain on kitchen paper.

If you wish you can put the coriander sprigs in the oil as well and cook for a few seconds until they frizzle up. This has a tendency to spit, so be careful. Drain on kitchen paper.

Divide the squid between 4 plates. Top with the crispy or uncooked coriander.

Garnish with a lemon segment and serve immediately with a little bowl of Sweet Chilli Sauce on each plate.

How to Prepare Squid
Cut off the tentacles just in front of the eyes. Pull the entrails out of the sac and discard. Remove the beak. Catch the tip of the quill and pull it out of the sac. Pull off the wings and scrape the purplish membrane off them and the sac. Cut the sac into 5mm (¹/₄in) rounds and cut the wings into 5mm (¹/₄in) slices. Trim the two long tentacles; leave the remaining light tentacles intact. Wash all the pieces under cold water. Drain.

Seared Chicken Breasts

SERVES 4   (P: 5 MINS/C: 15 MINS)

4 free-range, organic chicken breasts, skinless and boneless
extra virgin olive oil
salt and freshly ground pepper
accompaniment of your choice (see below right)

Heat a grill pan until quite hot. Brush each chicken breast with olive oil and season with salt and freshly ground pepper.

Put the chicken breasts on the pan for about 1 minute, then turn them round by 90° so that the grill pan sears criss-cross marks on the chicken. Turn the breasts over and repeat. If the chicken breasts are large, put in oven, preheated to 180°C/350°F/gas mark 4, for about 8–15 minutes, depending on size, until they are cooked through.

Serve with one of the good things below.

Ten Good Things to Serve with Seared Chicken Breasts
1 Tomato Fondue (see p240) with coriander. Add 1–2 tablespoons chopped coriander.
2 Mushroom à la Crème with Ginger Root (see recipe given on p241).
3 Sweet Chilli Sauce (see p296) mixed with lime juice. Drizzle this over the seared chicken and sprinkle with toasted sesame seeds and serve with a herb salad.
4 Honey, mustard and rosemary. For 4 chicken breasts, use 3 tablespoons honey, 2 teaspoons wholegrain mustard and 1 teaspoon finely chopped rosemary. Smear over both sides of the pangrilled chicken breasts and serve.
5 Spiced Aubergine Purée (see p119) and rocket leaves.
6 Brush the chicken breasts with harissa before pangrilling. Serve with cous cous, coarsely chopped sun-blush tomatoes, red onion, diced feta cheese and fresh mint leaves.
7 Satay sauce and Thai Cucumber Salad (see p115).
8 Combine 1 tablespoon soy sauce, 1 tablespoon French mustard and 2 tablespoons honey and marinate the chicken breasts for 30 minutes before pangrilling.
9 Banana and Cardamom Raita (p294) with Ballymaloe Relish or a good tomato relish and poppadoms.
10 Salmoriglio and rocket salad.

Monkfish with Coconut Milk

SERVES 4–6   (P: 15 MINS/C: 15 MINS)

This curry can be made in advance – it reheats beautifully as all the flavours have had time to rise to the occasion.

40ml (1¹/₂fl oz) coconut oil or sunflower oil
2 tablespoons chopped shallot
1 tablespoon peeled and grated fresh ginger
2 green chillies, split lengthways
³/₄ teaspoon ground turmeric
1 teaspoon sugar
³/₄ teaspoon chilli powder
1 teaspoon ground coriander
400ml (14fl oz) coconut milk (preferably fresh) or 400ml (14oz) tin condensed coconut milk
salt
700g (1¹/₂lb) well-trimmed monkfish, cut into 5cm (2in) pieces

For the tamarind water:
25g (1oz) tamarind paste
50ml (2fl oz) hot water

For the tempering:
1 tablespoon coconut oil
1 tablespoon fresh curry leaves
1 teaspoon black mustard seeds

For the accompaniments:
lots of fresh coriander leaves
rice
poppadoms

First make the tamarind water. Put the lump of tamarind paste into a small bowl and cover with the hot water. Leave to soak for 15–30 minutes. Squeeze with your fingers to loosen the seeds and fibre from the pulp. Press through a sieve and discard the seeds and fibre. Reserve the sieved tamarind water for use in the curry.

Heat the coconut or sunflower oil in a sauté pan. Add the chopped shallot, grated ginger and green chillies. Cook for about 5 minutes or until they start to turn golden.

Add the turmeric, sugar, chilli powder and ground coriander. Cook for a further 2 minutes. Add the coconut milk and tamarind water. Season with salt and add the fish. Cover and poach the fish until cooked, about 5–6 minutes.

Meanwhile, prepare the tempering. Heat the coconut oil in small pan and when it is smoking hot, add the curry leaves and mustard seeds (they will pop and crackle). When the mustard seeds finish crackling, pour the tempering over the curry.

Sprinkle with plenty of coriander leaves and serve with rice and poppadoms.

Shermin's Thai Green Chicken Curry

SERVES 4–6   (P: 10 MINS/C: 15 MINS)

350g (12oz) chicken thighs
400ml (14fl oz) tin coconut milk
1 tablespoon green curry paste
1 Thai green chilli, deseeded and pounded (optional – add if you like a hotter curry)
175ml (6fl oz) chicken stock (see p295)
2 aubergines, cut into 1cm (¹/₂in) cubes, or 20–24 pea aubergines
2 kaffir lime leaves
¹/₂ tablespoon palm sugar, or a little less soft brown sugar
2 tablespoons fish sauce (*nam pla*)
1 large red chilli, deseeded and pounded
20 basil leaves
1 tablespoon soy sauce

To serve: steamed rice

Remove the skin and bones from the chicken thighs, then cut the meat into thin strips.

Heat a wok on a low heat. Pour 125ml (4fl oz) of the coconut milk into the wok. Add the green curry paste and the pounded green chilli (if using), and mix well.

Add the chicken strips and increase the heat to medium. Cook until the chicken changes colour, then add the stock, the remainder of the coconut milk, the aubergine dice,* kaffir lime leaves, palm or brown sugar, fish sauce, pounded red chilli and half the basil leaves. Stir continuously until the curry boils and foams up. Reduce the heat and simmer, stirring continuously or the sauce may separate – it should be cooked in about 10 minutes.

Add the remainder of the basil leaves, taste and add soy sauce if necessary to perk it up. Serve hot, with steamed rice.

* If using pea aubergines, add them 1–2 minutes before the end of cooking.

making meals quick and easy

Always be prepared – make sure you have all the basic ingredients for two or three quick-and-easy recipes in your storecupboard. Frittatas and omelettes are easy to prepare and can be bolstered by a good selection of cold meats, olives and cheese from a deli. But your freezer should be your first port of call. Keep some buttermilk in the freezer so you can make up soda bread. The next time you make a lasagne, stew or curry (see the recipes in Prepare-Ahead Suppers), double the quantities and freeze the extra in small quantities. Then in times of need, you can just pull one out, defrost and hey presto, a ready meal you will really enjoy.

Don't forgot to have a couple of bottles of wine in your storecupboard too – have a look at Tom Doorley's wise words on p11.

Even if you don't have much notice, there are a few things you can do to spruce up a room. Quickly bundle papers, magazines and everyday clutter into the nearest cupboard or the back of your wardrobe. Then look around your house for decorative inspiration. Keep a selection of fabrics to use as tablecloths and a roll of coloured paper or cardboard that can quickly be turned into place mats. Use a colourful, chiffon scarf as a table runner or throw it over a lampshade (but never on a naked bulb) to soften the light. Dig out your collection of pebbles or sea shells and scatter them on the table – the shells will also make great salt and pepper holders. Strings of fairy lights add glamour to any evening and a stock of candles or tea lights will always be useful. A bowl of ripe peaches, cherries, greengages or apricots make an irresistible centrepiece which can double up as pudding.

Bright and breezy lunch
Bocconcini, Olive, Sun-blush Tomato and Pesto on Skewers (see p55)
Tortilla Pizza or Yufka (Turkish flat bread) (see p116 or p40)
Banana with Lime Syrup (p259)

To drink
Red wines don't come any brighter or breezier than the light and gulpable Bardolino from Italy's Veneto region, but it must be good. Choose a sound producer like the organically-minded Guerrieri-Rizzardi. Banana with lime syrup simply demands a Late Harvest Riesling from Australia.

Vegetarian option
Ciabatta Stuffed with Good Things (p68)
Spicy Omelette Sambo with Tomato and Red Onion Salsa (p98)
Poached Apricots with Sweet Geranium Leaves (p29)

To drink
Bardolino will work here too but vegetarian food often needs something a little more robust. Good Beaujolais or Beaujolais cru (such as Fleurie or Morgon) may not be the height of fashion but it is worth seeking out. Serve it cool but not quite chilled in order to emphasise the fruit. Cabernet Franc wines from the Loire, such as Chinon, can be treated the same way. The apricots provide one of the few occasions where a Muscat de Beaumes de Venise, served fairly cold, will taste really good.

Deceptively easy
Basmati Rice, Pea, Broad Bean and Dill Salad (p90)
Seared Fresh Salmon with Vine-ripened Tomato and Herbs (p110)
Chocolate Truffle Tree (p251)

To drink
The choice here is very straightforward: an unoaked or very lightly oaked New World Chardonnay will have the exuberant fruit that you need but without any danger of overpowering the food. Shaw & Smith of South Australia make several excellent examples. Try to find their M3 Chardonnay. Cool Banyuls from Provence will merge deliciously with the chocolate.

prepare-ahead suppers

Sometimes a little planning and preparation can make all the difference, especially if you are entertaining mid-week or if you have very little time on the night. All of these recipes can be made in advance and polished off or re-heated later. Then all you have to do on the night is cook up some vegetables or orzo perhaps, and add the finishing touches. In less than a blink of the eye, you will have a sensational meal on the table without any fuss. The good news is that rich stews and feisty curries improve with time as the flavours meld and intensify.

Beef Rendang

SERVES 8   (**P:** 30 MINS/**C:** 2 HOURS)

**Rendang is a wonderful slow-cooked dish
from Malaysia, Indonesia and Sumatra
usually served for feasts and celebrations.
It should be chunky and dry, yet succulent.**

1¹/₂kg (3lb) brisket, or good stewing steak
5 shallots, chopped
4 garlic cloves, chopped
3cm (1¹/₂in) root ginger, roughly chopped
4 red chillies, seeded and roughly chopped,
  or 2 teaspoons chilli powder
1 bay leaf
1 stalk fresh lemon grass, bruised
salt and freshly ground pepper
1 teaspoon turmeric
1.8 litre (3 pints) coconut milk
mint leaves (optional) and lime segments

Cut the meat into 4cm (1¹/₂in) cubes. Puree the shallots, garlic, ginger and chillies in a food processor. Put all these ingredients in a wide sauté pan or a wok, add the bay leaf, lemon grass, salt, turmeric and meat and cover with coconut milk. Stir and bring to the boil on a medium heat, uncovered. Reduce the heat and allow to bubble gently for 1¹/₂ hours, stirring from time to time. By this time the coconut milk should be quite thick. Continue to cook stirring frequently until the coconut milk starts to get oily. Keep stirring until the oil is reabsorbed by the meat. Taste and add more salt if necessary.

Serve hot with a bowl of fluffy rice. I like to serve some fresh mint leaves and segments of lime with the rendang.

Note: Rendang keeps well in the fridge, and reheats perfectly.

Lamb Korma with Fresh Spices, Basmati Rice, Mangoes and Lime, Tamarind and Banana Chutney, Ballymaloe Relish and Bread

SERVES 8   (P: 20 MINS/C: 90 MINS)

900g (2lb) boneless lamb (leg or shoulder)
1 tablespoon peeled, grated and pounded
   fresh ginger
salt
50g (2oz) clarified butter (see p108)
4 onions, sliced into rings
4 garlic cloves, crushed
1 teaspoon green cardamom pods
2 teaspoons coriander seeds
2 teaspoons black peppercorns
8 whole cloves
1 tablespoon ground turmeric
2 teaspoons sugar
freshly squeezed lime juice

For the nut milk:
110g (4oz) whole almonds
450ml (16fl oz) single cream

For the accompaniments:
basmati rice
Mangoes and Lime (see recipe below)
Tamarind and Banana Chutney (see below)
Ballymaloe Country Relish or mango chutney
paratha, naan bread or poppadoms

Trim the meat of the majority of the fat. Cut the meat into 2.5cm (1in) cubes and mix it with the ginger and a generous sprinkling of salt.

To make the nut milk, blanch, peel and coarsely chop the almonds (they should be the texture of nibbed almonds). Put into a small saucepan with the cream and simmer for 4–5 minutes. Turn off the heat and leave to infuse for 15 minutes.

Melt the butter in a flameproof casserole and cook the onion rings and crushed garlic over a gentle heat for 5 minutes.

Meanwhile, remove the seeds from the cardamom pods and measure 1/2 teaspoon. Discard the pods. Grind the seeds with the other whole spices in a clean spice or coffee grinder.

Add these to the onions and cook over a medium heat for 2–3 minutes. Remove the onions from the casserole and set aside, then add the meat to the casserole. Stir over a high heat until the meat changes colour.

Return the onions to the pot. Add the nut milk, turmeric and sugar and stir well. Cover and simmer gently on top of the stove, or better still in the oven, preheated to 160ºC/325ºF/gas mark 3, until the meat is cooked, about 1 hour. Finish by adding a few drops of lime juice to taste. This recipe can be prepared several days in advance up to this point and kept in the fridge.

Serve with basmati rice and other curry accompaniments which might include, apart from the suggestions listed, tomato chutney, mint chutney, raita, sliced bananas and chopped apples. A hot chilli sauce is also good and, of course, a selection of Indian breads – paratha, naan, poppadoms…

Mangoes and Lime

2 ripe mangoes
juice of 1 lime

Peel and dice the ripe mangoes and add the lime juice. Toss, taste, and add more lime juice if needed.

Tamarind and Banana Chutney

SERVES 4–6

A piece of tamarind, the size of a
   mandarin orange
1–2 tablespoons sugar
1 teaspoon salt
1 teaspoon freshly roasted ground
   cumin seed
1/2 teaspoon cayenne pepper (optional)
1 banana

Soak the tamarind overnight or at least 2 hours in 175ml (6fl oz) hot water in a small non-metallic bowl or cup (make sure the water should cover the tamarind).

Break the lump to make a thick uneven pulp. It is more effective to use hands for this, but you could use the back of a wooden spoon. Then push the tamarind pulp through a strainer, with the back of a spoon. Keep pressing until just the fibres and seeds are left in the strainer. Scrape all the strained pulp from the outside of the sieve. Use extra water, if necessary, to separate all the pulp from the fibres. Discard the seeds and fibre.

Mix the pulp with the sugar, salt, cumin and cayenne. Slice a peeled banana into 1cm (1/2in) slices and mix with tamarind pulp.

Taste and balance the flavours if necessary.

Portuguese Pork, Bean and Chorizo Stew

SERVES 10   (**P**: 30 MINS/**C**: 2¹/₂ HOURS)

Oh, I so love this big, gutsy stew inspired by the version I enjoy at one of my favourite London pubs, The Eagle, on Farringdon Road.

600g (1¹/₄lb) dried cannellini beans, haricot beans, butter beans or black beans

1.1kg (2¹/₂lb) streaky pork

700g (1¹/₂lb) streaky bacon or pancetta

450g (1lb) ham hock

4 tablespoons extra virgin olive oil

4 garlic cloves, sliced

450g (1lb) onions, roughly chopped

450g (1lb) carrots, sliced 8mm (¹/₃in) thick

2 green peppers, deseeded and chopped

1 sprig of thyme

1 bay leaf

450g (1lb) very ripe tomatoes, skinned and chopped, or 400g (14oz) tin tomatoes

450g (1lb) chorizo sausage, cut in 5mm (¹/₄in) slices

1 teaspoon hot or smoked paprika

freshly ground pepper

parsley stalks (optional)

generous amount of coarsely chopped coriander or parsley, to garnish

crusty bread, to serve

Soak the beans overnight in plenty of cold water.

When ready to cook, remove the pork and back rind and cut the meat into 2.5–4cm (1–1¹/₂in) chunks. Cut the ham hock into chunks also. Working in batches, heat a little oil in a frying pan and brown the pork, ham hock and bacon or pancetta on all sides. Transfer to a large casserole.

If you are going to cook the stew in the oven, preheat it to 160°C/320°F/gas mark 3.

Pour off excess fat from the frying pan but leave enough to fry off the garlic, onions, carrots and peppers with the sprig of thyme and bay leaf. Cook on a low heat, stirring every now and then, for 5–6 minutes.

Transfer the vegetables to the casserole and add the chopped tomatoes, chorizo, paprika, and some pepper. Add just enough water almost to cover the meat. Bring to the boil, put the lid on (add a big bunch of parsley stalks if you have them) and transfer to the oven for 2–2¹/₂ hours; alternatively, reduce the heat to low and simmer gently on top of the stove.

Meanwhile, drain the beans, place in a saucepan and cover with fresh cold water. Bring to the boil and simmer until cooked – about 40 minutes–1¹/₂ hours depending on the type of beans.

Add the cooked beans to the stew 15–20 minutes before the end of cooking. Taste and adjust the seasoning if needed – it's unlikely to need salt. This recipe can be prepared in advance up to this point.

Serve in deep, wide soup bowls, sprinkled with lots of coarsely chopped coriander or parsley. You'll need crusty bread to mop up the juices.

Italian Beef Stew with Polenta

SERVES 6–8   (**P**: 30 MINS/**C**: 3 HOURS)

A hearty stew that can be made in large quantities – it reheats and freezes brilliantly.

1.3kg (3lb) well-hung stewing beef or lean flank

4 tablespoons extra virgin olive oil

275g (10oz) onions, sliced

2 large carrots, cut into 1cm (¹/₂in) slices

150ml (¹/₄ pint) red wine

150ml (¹/₄ pint) beef or chicken stock (see p295)

225ml (8fl oz) tomato purée (see p294), or best-quality tinned tomatoes, puréed and sieved

1 heaped tablespoon white flour

salt and freshly ground pepper

175g (6oz) mushrooms, sliced

1 tablespoon chopped parsley

For the accompaniments:
Polenta (see p298), mashed potatoes or noodles, and green salad.

Preheat the oven to 160°C/320°F/gas mark 3.

Trim the meat of any excess fat and cut into 4cm (1¹/₂in) cubes. Heat 2 tablespoons of the olive oil in a flameproof casserole, then reduce the heat to very low, add the onions and carrots, cover and cook for 10 minutes.

Mix the wine, stock and tomato purée together in a bowl or jug. Heat the remaining olive oil in a frying pan until almost smoking. Sear the pieces of meat on all sides, then stir in the flour and cook for just 1 minute.

Transfer the meat to the casserole. Add the prepared wine and stock, mix, season with salt and pepper, and cover. Place in the oven and cook for 2¹/₂–3 hours until the meat is tender. About 30 minutes before the end of cooking, sauté the mushrooms and add them to the casserole along with the parsley.

Serve with polenta, mashed potatoes or noodles and a good green salad.

This recipe can be prepared a couple of days in advance, kept in the fridge and reheated when needed.

Pork and Ginger Stew

SERVES 10   (P: 20 MINS/C: 1 1/2 HOURS)

The quality of the pork is as ever crucially important for this rustic pork stew. Because we have free-range pigs, the children, grandchildren and all their friends love this dish. It is such a brilliantly easy way to feed lots of hungry people – one can, of course, halve the recipe. It can be prepared ahead and then heated up.

2.75kg (6lb) free-range, organic shoulder
  of pork
900g (2lb) carrots, cut into large chunks
  (leave new carrots whole and unpeeled)
10 onions, roots trimmed and cut in half
6 shallots
12 garlic cloves, barely crushed
60g (2 1/2oz) fresh ginger, peeled and sliced
salt and freshly ground black pepper
2–3 thyme stalks
2–3 parsley stalks
850ml (1 1/2 pints) chicken stock (see p295)
roux (optional; see p139)
snipped flat parsley, to garnish
baked jacket potatoes, to serve

Trim the fat off the pork and cut the meat into 4cm (1 1/2in) cubes. In a hot frying pan, render down some of the fat (the fat runs out of the meat) while you prepare the other ingredients.

Preheat the oven to 180°C/350°F/gas mark 4.

Working in batches, fry the pork and allow to brown well on all sides. Transfer to a large casserole. Build up the stew with a layer of pork, then a mixture of carrots, onions, shallots, garlic, sliced ginger and then another layer of pork. It's crucially important to season each layer well with salt and black pepper. Tuck a little bunch of thyme and parsley stalks into the centre (tie into a bouquet garni). Pour in the chicken stock. Bring to the boil over a medium heat, then cover and transfer to the oven for about 1 1/2 hours. Check after 1 hour to see how it is progressing. (The stew can be simmered gently on top of the stove, but we usually transfer it into the oven for ease of cooking and to free up the stove top.)

When the meat is tender and succulent, strain the cooking liquid into a saucepan. Skim the fat off, then bring to the boil, and whisk in just enough roux to thicken slightly if you wish.

Remove the bouquet garni from the casserole and discard. Pour the liquid back over the stew and bring back to the boil. Taste and adjust the seasoning if needed. This recipe can be prepared in advance up to this point.

Scatter lots of flat parsley over the top and serve. You could transfer the stew into serving bowls, but we just bring the casserole to the table and tuck in. Serve with lots of floury potatoes cooked in their jackets.

Tagine of Lamb with Medjool Dates

SERVES 6   (P: 10 MINS/C: 1 1/4 HOURS)

Tagines are brilliant for easy entertaining and although this takes a while to cook, it is remarkably easy to make and, if you multiply up the quantities, great for large numbers. The word 'tagine' refers both to the distinctive North African earthenware cooking pot, with its shallow base and conical top, and to a multitude of stew-like dishes cooked in it. This lamb tagine, which Emer Fitzgerald and I worked on together, has become our new favourite.

1.3kg (3lb) boned shoulder of lamb
1/2 tablespoon ground cinnamon
1 teaspoon peeled and grated fresh ginger
1/2 teaspoon paprika
1 teaspoon freshly ground black pepper
generous pinch of saffron strands
50g (2oz) butter
2 onions, chopped

2 garlic cloves, finely chopped
300ml (1/2 pint) tomato juice
salt
175g (6oz) Medjool dates
2 tablespoons chopped coriander

To serve: cous cous

For the garnish (optional):
1 tablespoon oil
50g (2oz) flaked almonds
coriander leaves

Trim the lamb, discarding excess fat, and cut into 4cm (1 1/2in) cubes. In a large bowl, mix together the cinnamon, ginger, paprika, pepper and saffron with 4 tablespoons water. Toss the lamb in this mixture. If you have time, leave to marinate in the fridge for up to 24 hours.

Melt the butter in a large, wide saucepan. Add the lamb, onions, garlic, tomato juice and some salt, and pour in enough water to come half way up the meat mixture. Bring to the boil, reduce the heat to bring to a gentle simmer, and cover. Cook for about 45 minutes, stirring occasionally, until the meat is meltingly tender. Add the dates and coriander. Continue to simmer, uncovered, for a further 30 minutes or so until the sauce is thick and unctuous. Taste and adjust the seasoning if needed. The dish can be prepared ahead to this stage. Serve with cous cous.

If you like, garnish the dish. Heat the oil and fry the flaked almonds until pale golden. Drain on kitchen paper, sprinkle over the dish and throw over a few coriander leaves before serving.

A Scrummy Chicken Pie

SERVES 6–8   (P: 30 MINS/C: 2¹/₂ HOURS)

This can be prepared ahead of time – refrigerate until required and increase the cooking time by a few minutes.

850ml (1¹/₂ pints) homemade chicken stock
  (see p295) or water
2 large carrots, cut into chunks
2 large unpeeled onions, quartered
2 celery sticks, cut into small chunks
6 black peppercorns
1 bouquet garni
1 large free-range, organic chicken or
  boiling fowl
1 sprig of tarragon (optional)
16 small flat mushrooms
25g (1oz) butter
salt and freshly ground black pepper
16 button onions, peeled
450g (1lb) streaky bacon in a piece, cooked
110g (4oz) peas – frozen are fine (optional)
500g (1lb 2oz) puff pastry
egg wash (1 egg beaten with 1 tablespoon milk)
green salad, to serve

For the sauce:
150ml (¹/₄ pint) dry white wine
110g (4oz) roux (see p139)
250ml (9fl oz) single cream

Preheat the oven to 180°C/350°F/gas mark 4.

In a heavy casserole, pour chicken stock or water to a depth of 5cm (2in) and add the vegetables, peppercorns and bouquet garni. Lay the chicken on top. Add a sprig of tarragon if available, and cover with a tightly fitting lid. Bring to the boil and then transfer to the oven. Cook for 1–1¹/₂ hours, depending on the size of the bird – when it is cooked, the leg joints should feel loose and there should be no trace of pink. Ensure that it does not boil dry – check from time to time and add more liquid as necessary. The cooking liquid should be deliciously rich and may be a little fatty.

Meanwhile, fry the mushrooms in a little of the butter in a hot pan and season with salt and pepper. Sweat the onions in butter in a small covered pan until soft. Cut the cooked bacon into cubes. Remove the chicken from the casserole on to a large platter, reserving the cooking liquid. Do not turn the oven off, but increase the temperature to 230°C/450°F/gas mark 8.

Carve the chicken flesh. Arrange the sliced chicken in layers in a deep pie dish (or in 6–8 small individual pie dishes), covering each layer with bacon, onions and mushrooms. Add the peas if using (no need to pre-cook).

Next make the sauce. Strain and degrease the cooking liquid. Put 600ml (1 pint) of the cooking liquid and the dry white wine into a saucepan and bring to the boil. Whisk in the roux. Cook until thick and smooth. Add the cream and bring to the boil again, then remove from the heat. Taste and adjust the seasoning if needed. Allow to cool.

Pour the cooled sauce over the chicken and vegetables in the pie dish and cover with puff pastry. Have fun decorating the top with the leftover puff pastry – we sometimes make funny faces, write messages such as 'yummy', 'scrummy' or 'yippee', or put a fine pastry cockerel on top!

Just before cooking, brush the top of the pastry with egg wash. Bake for 10 minutes, then reduce the temperature to 200°C/400°F/gas mark 6 and bake for a further 15–20 minutes or until golden brown. Serve with a good green salad.

Lamb Chilli con Carne

SERVES 6–8   (P: 10 MINS/C: 35 MINS)

4 tablespoons extra virgin olive oil
1 large onion, chopped
2 garlic cloves
1–2 chillies, deseeded and chopped
1 red pepper, deseeded and cut into
  5mm (¹/₄in) dice
1 teaspoon smoked or sweet paprika
1 teaspoon ground cumin
700g (1¹/₂lb) leg or shoulder of lamb,
  chopped into 5mm (¹/₄in)
2 x 400g (14oz) tins tomatoes, chopped
1 tablespoon tomato purée
grated zest of ¹/₂ unwaxed lemon
1 tablespoon chopped marjoram
1 teaspoon thyme leaves

1 teaspoon soft brown sugar
salt and freshly ground pepper
2 x 400g (14oz) tins red kidney beans or
  black beans, rinsed and drained

For the accompaniments:
basmati rice
soured cream
Tomato and Red Onion Salsa (see p294)
tortillas
fresh coriander leaves

Heat the oil in a heavy flameproof casserole, add the chopped onion, garlic and chillies and sweat on a medium heat for about 5 minutes. Add the diced red pepper, toss, and continue to cook for 1–2 minutes. Add the paprika and cumin and continue to cook

for a few minutes. Add the lamb and toss until it changes colour.

Add the chopped tomatoes and their juice, the tomato purée, lemon zest and herbs. Add the sugar and season with salt and pepper. Bring to the boil and cook for 30 minutes.

Add the beans and cook for a further 15 minutes. Taste and adjust the seasoning if needed. This dish can be prepared in advance up to this point.

Serve with basmati rice, soured cream, Tomato and Red Onion Salsa and lots of warm tortillas and fresh coriander. Beef or pork is also great in this recipe.

Vegetarian Lasagne

SERVES 12   (**P:** 1¹/₂HOURS/**C:** 30 MINS)

Lasagne is basically a formula – once I realised that simple fact, I started to play around and now we make many versions with meat, fish and vegetables. The end result needs to be bubbly and juicy with lots of filling.

450g (1lb) fresh spinach lasagne
  or 375g (13oz) dried plain spinach or lasagne
6 quantities Béchamel Sauce (not too
  thick; see recipe below)
1 quantity Piperonata (see p243)
225g (8oz) Parmesan or mature Cheddar
  cheese, grated or a mixture
1 quantity Buttered Spinach (see recipe below)
2 quantities Mushroom à la Crème (see p241)
salt and freshly ground pepper
green salad, to serve

1 large or 2 medium-sized lasagne dishes

First taste each component to make sure it is delicious and well seasoned.

Preheat the oven to 180°C/350°F/gas mark 4.

Blanch the lasagne pasta as directed on the packet – some of the 'easy cook' lasagne may be used without blanching. Spread a little Béchamel Sauce on the base of a large lasagne dish, then cover with strips of pasta and a layer of Piperonata. Top with another layer of pasta. Spread this with Béchamel Sauce, sprinkle with grated cheese and add a layer of Buttered Spinach. Cover with another layer of pasta, then the Mushroom à la Crème. Top with another layer of pasta. Carefully spread more Béchamel Sauce over the lot and finally sprinkle liberally with cheese. Make sure all the pasta is under the sauce.

Bake in the oven for 10–15 minutes for fresh pasta, or 30 minutes for dried pasta, or until bubbly and golden on top. If possible, leave to stand for 5–10 minutes before cutting to allow the layers to compact. Serve with a good green salad.

Other ideas for layers

Buttered Courgette with marjoram or basil, pangrilled aubergine, Roasted Red Pepper (see p298) and Pesto (see p297), Spiced Aubergine (see p243) with raisins.

Béchamel Sauce

This is a marvellous quick way of making Béchamel Sauce if you already have roux. Put the cold milk into a saucepan with the carrot, onion, peppercorns, thyme and parsley. Bring to the boil, simmer for 4–5 minutes, remove from the heat and leave to infuse for 10 minutes.

300ml (¹/₂ pint) milk
few slices of carrot
few slices of onion
3 peppercorns
1 small sprig of thyme
1 small sprig of parsley
40g (1¹/₂oz) roux (see p139)
salt and freshly ground pepper

Strain and discard the vegetables. Put the milk back in the pan and bring to the boil. Thicken with roux to a light coating consistency. Season with salt and freshly ground pepper, taste and correct the seasoning if necessary.

Buttered Spinach

SERVES 4–6

Here are three different basic methods of cooking spinach – a huge improvement on the watery mush that frozen spinach often unfortunately ends up as!

50–110g (2–4oz) butter
900g (2 lb) fresh spinach, with stalks removed
salt, freshly ground pepper
a little freshly grated nutmeg

Method 1: Melt a scrap of butter in a wide frying pan, toss in as much spinach as will fit easily, season with salt and freshly ground pepper. As soon as the spinach wilts and becomes tender, strain off all the liquid, increase the heat and add some butter and freshly grated nutmeg. Serve immediately.
Method 2: Wash the prepared spinach and drain. Put into a heavy saucepan on a very low heat, season and cover tightly. After a few minutes, stir and replace the lid. As soon as the spinach is cooked, about 5–8 minutes, strain off the copious amount of liquid that spinach releases and press between two plates until almost dry. Chop or purée in a food processor if you like a smooth texture. Increase the heat, add butter, correct the seasoning and add a little freshly grated nutmeg to taste.
Method 3: Cook the spinach uncovered in a large saucepan of boiling salted water until soft, about 4–5 minutes. Drain and press out all the water. Continue as in method 2. Method 3 produces a brighter-coloured spinach.

Chicken and Courgette Lasagne

SERVES 8   (**P:** 2 HOURS/**C:** 20 MINS)

1 quantity chicken and courgette gratin
  (see below)
8–9 sheets best-quality lasagne
salt
75g (3oz) Parmesan cheese, grated
green salad, to serve

Preheat the oven to 200°C/400°F/gas mark 6.

Cook the chicken and courgette, following the instructions for Gratin of Chicken with Courgette and Marjoram (see recipe below) up to the seasoning with salt and freshly ground pepper.

Bring a large saucepan of salted water (2 tablespoons salt to 6 litres/10 pints water) to the boil. Working in 2–3 batches, drop the lasagne sheets into the pan, return to the boil and blanch them. Refresh them under cold running water.

Spread a little sauce on the base of a lasagne dish. Cover first with a layer of pasta, then a layer of chicken, then sauce, and then a layer of courgettes. Repeat with another similar sequence of layers. Then cover with a layer of pasta, then a layer of chicken pieces only, then a final layer of pasta, and finally a layer of chicken sauce. The disk may be prepared ahead to this point.

Sprinkle grated Parmesan over the top and pop into the oven for 15–20 minutes or until bubbling and golden. Allow to rest for 5 minutes. Serve with a good green salad.

Variations
Chicken and Piperonata Lasagne – replace the courgette with Piperonata (see p243).
Chicken and Tomato Fondue lasagne – replace the courgette with Tomato Fondue (see p 240).

Gratin of Chicken with Courgette and Marjoram

SERVES 4–6

1.5kg (3¹/₂lb) free-range, organic chicken
2 onions, sliced
2 carrots, sliced
sprig each of thyme and tarragon
a few peppercorns
600ml (1 pint) homemade Chicken Stock
  (see p295)
225g (8oz) mushrooms, sliced
350ml (12fl oz) milk
2–3 tablespoon annual marjoram
roux (see p139)
knob of butter
900g (2lb) courgettes, green and
  golden, cooked
50g (2oz) Buttered Crumbs (see p142)
50–110g (2–4oz) grated mature Cheddar
  cheese

2 x lasagne dish 25.5 x 20.5cm (10 x 8 in)

Put the chicken into a saucepan or casserole with the onions and carrots, add a sprig of thyme, tarragon and a few peppercorns. Pour in the stock, bring to the boil, cover and simmer for 1–1¹/₄ hours or until the chicken is tender.

Sauté the mushrooms in the butter on a hot pan, season with salt and freshly ground pepper and keep aside also.

When the chicken is cooked, remove the meat and carve into bite-sized pieces.

Strain and degrease the cooking liquid, add the milk, bring to the boil and add the annual marjoram. Simmer for a few minutes, thicken to a light coating consistency with roux, then add the chicken to the sauce. Season with salt and freshly ground pepper.

Butter an ovenproof lasagne dish, put a layer of courgette on the base, scatter the mushrooms on top and cover with the creamy chicken mixture.

Mix the Buttered Crumbs with the grated cheese and sprinkle over the surface. Reheat in a moderate oven 180°C/350°F/gas mark 4 for 15–20 minutes and flash under the grill until the top is crunchy and golden. Serve immediately.

Gratin of Chicken with Broccoli
Substitute 900g (2lb) broccoli florets cooked al dente for the courgettes.

Gratin of Chicken with Cauliflower
Substitute cauliflower florets for broccoli in the above recipe and substitute tarragon for marjoram.

Classic Daube of Beef Provençale with Melted Leek Champ

SERVES 8   (P: 30 MINS/C: 2 HOURS)

This stew has a rich, robust flavour. It's classic French country winter food at its most comforting. It reheats perfectly and can also be made ahead and frozen. The meat should be cut and served in large chunks.

1.3kg (3lb) lean well-hung stewing beef
  (topside or chuck)
extra virgin olive oil
450g (1lb) streaky bacon, cut into
  1cm (½in) lardons
400g (14oz) tomatoes, chopped
150ml (¼pint) beef stock
175g (6oz) mushrooms, sliced
2 tablespoons olive oil
10 tinned anchovy fillets
2 tablespoons capers
2 tablespoons chopped parsley
2 garlic cloves, crushed
3 tablespoons wine vinegar
roux (optional, see p139)
chopped parsley, to garnish

For the marinade:
2 tablespoons extra virgin olive oil
300ml (½ pint) dry white or red wine
1 teaspoon chopped thyme, sage or
  annual marjoram
1 bay leaf
2 garlic cloves, crushed
1 large carrot, thinly sliced
1 large onion, thinly sliced
1 teaspoon salt
plenty of freshly ground pepper

For the accompaniment:
Melted Leek Champ (see p139) or fluffy
  mashed potatoes

Cut the beef into large chunks, around 7.5cm (3in) wide. In a large bowl, mix together the marinade ingredients. Add the meat, cover and marinate in the fridge or a cool larder overnight.

The next day, drain on a wire rack over a roasting tin to collect the marinade. Strain the marinade, and reserve the vegetables and marinade separately .

Heat the oil in a heavy frying pan, cook the bacon lardons until crisp, then transfer to a casserole. Dry the beef with kitchen paper. Add to the hot pan and cook briefly, stirring, to seal on all sides. Add to the bacon in the casserole, along with the marinated vegetables and the tomatoes.

Skim the fat from the juices in the frying pan. Place over a high heat, pour in the marinade and the beef stock and stir to deglaze, then add to the casserole. Bring to the boil and simmer very gently on top of the stove (or transfer to a preheated oven at 160°C/320°F/gas mark 3) for 1½–2 hours.

Meanwhile, sauté the mushrooms in the olive oil in a hot pan and set aside.

When the meat is soft and tender, liquidise the anchovies with the capers, parsley, garlic and wine vinegar. Add to the casserole with the mushrooms. Simmer gently for 8–10 minutes to combine the flavours. Taste and adjust the seasoning if needed. Skim off the fat and, if necessary, thicken the boiling liquid by whisking in a little roux. Sprinkle with chopped parsley and serve with Melted Leek Champ or fluffy mashed potatoes.

Melted Leek Champ

SERVES 6   (**P**: 15 MINS/**C**: 15 MINS)

We cook the potatoes in their jackets – this means much more flavour and much less waste.

4 organic medium leeks, total weight around
   1.3kg (3lb)
110–175g (4–6oz) butter
salt and freshly ground pepper
6–8 unpeeled main-crop potatoes, such as
   Golden Wonder or Kerr's Pink
300–350ml (¹/₂ pint–12fl oz) milk
1 tablespoon chopped chives

Trim off the dark green leaves from the top of the leeks (wash and add to the stock pot or use for making green leek soup). Slit the leeks about half way down the centre and wash well under cold running water. Slice into 5mm (¹/₄in) rounds.

Melt 50g (2oz) of the butter in a heavy saucepan or casserole. Once it foams add the sliced leeks and toss gently to coat. Season with salt and pepper. Cover with a paper lid and then with a close-fitting pan lid. Reduce the heat and cook very gently for 8–10 minutes, or until almost soft and moist. Turn off the heat and leave to continue cooking in the residual heat of the casserole.

Scrub the potatoes and boil them in their jackets. Meanwhile, bring the milk and chives to the boil, simmer for about 3–4 minutes, turn off the heat and leave to infuse.

Drain the potatoes well. Peel the potatoes while hot, mash immediately and mix with most of the infused milk. Add the drained leeks and beat in 50g (2oz) of the butter. Add the remaining milk for a softer consistency if wished. Season to taste with salt and pepper. Serve in 1 large or 6 individual bowls, with a knob of butter melting in the centre.

Melted Leek Champ may be set aside and reheated later in the oven, preheated to 180°C/350°F/gas mark 4. Cover with aluminium foil while it reheats so that it doesn't get a skin.

Roux

Brilliantly useful stuff to have in your fridge. Use it to thicken sauces or gravies.

110g (4oz) salted butter
110g (4oz) plain flour

Melt the butter in a small saucepan over a low heat, add the flour and cook for 2 minutes, stirring occasionally.

Roux can be stored in a cool place and used as required, or made up on the spot if preferred. It will keep at least a fortnight in the fridge.

Gravadlax with Sweet Mustard and Dill Mayonnaise

SERVES 12–16 AS A STARTER
    (P: 20 MINS + 25 HOURS TO MARINATE)

This is a simply brilliant standby, miles more impressive than smoked salmon. We use it for canapés, starter salads and as a main course for a light summer lunch, accompanied by pickled cucumber, deliciously runny semi-hard-boiled eggs and salad leaves. It keeps for up to 1 week. Fresh dill is essential but we also have fun with black peppercorns, coriander seeds, whole grain mustard, vodka…

700–900g (1½–2lb) tail piece of fresh
  wild salmon
1 heaped tablespoon sea salt
1 heaped tablespoon sugar
1 teaspoon freshly ground black pepper
2 tablespoons finely chopped dill, plus whole
  sprigs to garnish
Sweet Mustard and Dill Mayonnaise (see below)
bread and butter, to serve

Fillet the salmon and remove all the bones with a tweezer. In a bowl, mix together the salt, sugar, pepper and dill. Place the fish on a piece of clingfilm and scatter the mixture over the surface of the fish. Wrap tightly with clingfilm and refrigerate for a minimum of 24 hours. If you have 2 pieces of fish, place one on top of the other, flesh side together.

To serve, wipe the dill mixture off the salmon and slice thinly, cutting straight down to the skin. Arrange a few slices on a white plate (square for preference) with a zig-zag of Mustard and Dill Mayonnaise over the top.

Alternatively, arrange in a rosette shape and fill the centre of the rosette with Sweet Mustard and Dill Mayonnaise. Garnish with fresh dill.

Serve with brown bread and butter – Brown Yeast Bread (see p35) or pumpernickel works particularly well.

Sweet Mustard and Dill Mayonnaise

1 large free-range, organic egg yolk
2 tablespoons French mustard
1 tablespoon caster sugar
150ml (¼ pint) groundnut or sunflower oil
1 tablespoon white wine vinegar
1 tablespoon finely chopped dill
salt and freshly ground white pepper

In a bowl, whisk the egg yolk with the mustard and sugar.

Add the oil drop by drop, whisking all the time, then add the vinegar and dill and season to taste.

Gravadlax with Cucumber Ribbon Salad and Mustard and Dill Mayonnaise

SERVES 8   (P: 15 MINS)

225–350g (8–12oz) gravadlax (see recipe
  above)
Mustard and Dill Mayonnaise (see recipe
  above)
brown bread, to serve

For the pickled cucumber strips:
1 cucumber
2 teaspoons salt
110g (4oz) sugar
75ml (3fl oz) cider vinegar

For the garnish:
sprigs of dill
chive or wild garlic flowers
freshly cracked black pepper

Prepare the gravadlax 2–3 days before serving.

The cucumber ribbon salad should be prepared on the day. Cut the cucumber in half, then cut into strips using a potato peeler. Put the cucumber strips into a deep bowl and add the salt, sugar and cider vinegar. Toss gently and leave to macerate for at least 30 minutes.

To assemble, unwrap the gravadlax and, using a thin, sharp knife, carefully cut down to the skin in thin slices.

Drain the cucumber strips. Arrange the cucumber strips and gravadlax in a haphazard way on each serving plate. Drizzle with Mustard and Dill Mayonnaise. Garnish with tiny sprigs of dill and chive or wild garlic flowers.

Finally sprinkle a little freshly cracked black pepper over each serving. Serve with Brown Yeast Bread (see p35).

Haddock with Dijon Mustard Sauce

SERVES 6   (**P**: 15 MINS/**C**: 15 MINS)

This is a brilliant recipe for easy entertaining. Virtually any round fish may be used in this recipe – for instance cod, hake, ling, grey sea mullet and pollock.

50g (2oz) butter
225g (8oz) onions, chopped
900g (2lb) haddock fillets
salt and freshly ground pepper
600ml (1 pint) milk
50ml (2fl oz) cream
25g (1oz) white flour
2 tablespoons Dijon mustard
2 tablespoons wholegrain mustard
1 tablespoon chopped parsley
800g (1³⁄₄lb) mashed potato (optional)

Melt the butter in a saucepan and sweat the onions, covered, until golden brown.

Meanwhile, skin the haddock and cut into 6 portions. Season with salt and pepper. Put the fish into a wide sauté pan, cover with the milk and cream, bring to the boil and simmer gently for 4–6 minutes, depending on the thickness of the fish. Remove the fish carefully to a serving dish with a slotted spoon, reserving the cooking liquid.

Add the flour to the onions, stir and cook for 2 minutes. Add the reserved hot cooking liquid and bring back to the boil, then simmer for 3–4 minutes. Add the mustard and chopped parsley, taste and adjust the seasoning if needed, then pour over the fish and serve.

For a retro version, mashed potato may be piped around the dish. It can also be prepared in advance: allow to cool, refrigerate and reheat later in the oven, preheated to 180°C/350°F/gas mark 4, for about 20 minutes.

Variations
1 Sprinkle 110–175g (4–6oz) sliced sautéed mushrooms over or under the fish before saucing.
2 Sweat 450g (1lb) finely sliced leeks in 25g (1oz) butter in a covered casserole over a gentle heat and use instead of the mushrooms in Variation 1.
3 Peel pieces of cucumber and sweat in 10–25g (¹⁄₂–1oz) butter with 1 dessertspoon chopped dill in a covered casserole over a gentle heat. Use instead of the mushrooms in Variation 1, and omit mustard from the sauce.

Hake with Gruyère Cheese and Buttered Crumbs

SERVES 6–8   (**P**: 10 MINS/**C**: 35 MINS)

This is a sort of 'basic' recipe, which like the recipe above, can be used for almost any round fish such as pollock, ling, haddock or grey sea mullet. It is a perfect recipe for entertaining because it can be prepared ahead, refrigerated and reheated later. Cheddar or Parmesan cheese, or a combination of the two, may also be used.

1kg (2¹⁄₄lb) hake fillets
salt and freshly ground pepper
10g (¹⁄₂oz) butter
600ml (1 pint) milk
50g (2oz) roux (see p139)
¹⁄₄ teaspoon mustard, preferably Dijon
175g (6oz) Gruyère cheese, grated
900g (2lb) fluffy mashed potato or
  Scallion Champ (optional; see p237) to serve

For the buttered crumbs:
25g (1oz) butter
50g (2oz) soft white breadcrumbs

Skin the fish and cut into 6–8 portions. Season with salt and pepper.

Lay the pieces of fish in a lightly buttered sauté pan and cover with the cold milk. Bring to the boil and simmer for 4–5 minutes, or until the fish has changed colour. With a slotted spoon, remove the fish to a serving dish or dishes, reserving the milk.

Bring the milk back to the boil and thicken with roux to a light coating consistency. Add the mustard and two thirds of the grated cheese; set aside the remainder of the cheese. Season with salt and pepper, taste and correct the seasoning if necessary.

Preheat the oven to 180°C/350°F/gas mark 4.

Next make the buttered crumbs. Melt the butter in a pan and stir in the breadcrumbs. Remove from the heat immediately and leave to cool.

Coat the fish with the sauce. Mix the remaining grated cheese with the buttered crumbs and sprinkle over the top. For a more substantial dish, pipe a ruff of fluffy mashed potato or champ around the edge. The recipe can be prepared in advance up to this point.

Bake for 15–20 minutes or until the fish and sauce are heated through and the top is golden brown and crisp. If necessary, place under the grill for a minute or two before serving, to brown the edge of the potato.

Note: This dish may be served in individual dishes; scallop shells are fun, completely ovenproof, and can be used over and over again.

preparing ahead

If you have very little time on the day of the event, preparation is everything. You will need to shop and cook in advance, leaving only the finishing touches just before the guests arrive. Choose the recipes several days in advance and make two shopping lists – one for the food to be prepared in advance, and the second for what must be bought at the last minute – herbs and salad ingredients, for example. Take the time to read each recipe and work out when you need to make each stage. Most important of all, check if you need to marinate meat or allow batter or pastry to rest and plan this time into your schedule.

On the day, take the prepared meal out to defrost if you need to, and organise what you have to do for the accompanying dishes. Bear in mind that salad dressings are best made at the last minute. While the food is heating, you will have time to get yourself and the room ready and be ready to welcome your guests without any fuss or flapping!

To avoid last-minute rushing around, set out the number of plates, cutlery, glasses and napkins you need in the morning. Pick up some flowers with your last-minute shopping. Or, the weekend before, hunt out dried flowers or tiny cacti potted in colourful containers (look for cacti with eye-catching shapes, smouldering colours or stripy succulents) for the table. A pile of glass beads can be used to great effect and stuffing fairy lights into a glass vase is one of the simplest ways to illuminate and decorate a side table or mantelpiece.

A taste of India
Mini Poppadoms with Spicy Chicken, Banana and Cardamom Raita (p54)
Rogan Josh (p130)
Indian Paratha Bread (p39)
Yogurt and Cardamom Cream with Apricot and Saffron Syrup (p266)

To drink
Don't serve just any old lager with this Indian menu. It deserves the best and many of the world's best lagers come from the Czech Republic. Pilsener Urquell, Staropramen or Budvar all have real character and style. The yogurt and cardamom cream cries out for a vendage tardive Gewurztraminer from Alsace which will be expensive. Cheaper dessert wines from the same grape come from South Africa.

Veggie delight
Fougasse (p38)
Salad of Goat's Cheese with Rocket, Figs and Pomegranate Seeds (p68)
Vegetarian Lasagne (p136)
A Seasonal Green Salad (p94)
Molten Chocolate Puddings (p246)

To drink
To be geographically correct with the fougasse you need to look to Provence. A red Bandol will deliver plenty of fruit with a herby edge, while a white Bandol will be good with the salad. Domaine Tempier is a brilliant producer. Goat's cheese, on the other hand, is always best with a Sauvignon Blanc, even a basic one from Chile or Touraine. Chocolate pudding would defeat most wines, even sweet ones, but a good LBV Port from Taylor's, Fonseca or Noval is well up to the job.

The healthy choice
Gravadlax (p140)
Hake with Gruyère Cheese in Buttered Crumbs (p142)
Carrigeen Moss Pudding with Gooseberry and Elderflower Compote (p232)

To drink
Hake always suggests a Spanish white, especially the fashionable wines made from Albarinho. The most fashionable and most expensive ones come from Rias-Baixas, but they are still quite affordable. These crisp, slightly sea-scented whites will deal equally well with the gravadlax where the dill flavour would knock many other wines for six. The pudding, because of the heady elderflower scent, will work best with a sweet Muscat. Brown Brother's Late Picked Muscat is fresh, aromatic, ripe and still delicate.

slow food

The Slow Food Movement, which started in Italy in 1986, has taken the world by storm – it now has in excess of 80,000 international members who respond to its concerns about the standardising effects of fast food and the frenetic pace of life in the fast lane. Slow Food is not just about long, slow cooking, although it can be. It celebrates differences in flavours, artisanal food production and small-scale agriculture. It is about using products that are produced in a time-honoured, sustainable, usually non-intensive way. Slow Food links ethics and pleasure. In a word, eco-gastronomy. Food with a feel-good factor.

Slow-cooked Lamb Shanks with Haricot Beans and Tomatoes with Lots of Fresh Herbs

SERVES 8   (**P:** 20 MINS/**C:** 3 HOURS)

Lamb shanks can be from the back leg or the shoulder. Choose one or the other so they cook evenly – the shoulder takes much longer to cook. Gutsy herbs like rosemary or thyme are a brilliant accompaniment, as are beans, lentils or a robust mash with added root vegetables or kale.

8 lamb shanks
8 small sprigs of rosemary or thyme
8 slivers of garlic
salt and freshly ground black pepper
3–4 tablespoons extra virgin olive oil or
   25g (1oz) goose or duck fat
2 carrots, roughly chopped
2 celery sticks, roughly chopped
1 leek, roughly chopped
1 onion, roughly chopped
4 garlic cloves, bruised
150ml (1/4 pint) good red wine
150ml (1/4 pint) chicken stock (see p295)
   or lamb stock
1 sprig of thyme
2 sprigs of rosemary
2 bay leaves
2 strips of dried orange peel

For the haricot beans and tomatoes:
25ml (1fl oz) olive oil
225g (8oz) streaky bacon, cut into lardons
   and blanched
2 quantities Tomato Fondue (see p240)
2 x 400g (14oz) tins haricot beans, drained

To garnish:
Lots of flat parsley, coriander, mint and chives

Preheat the oven to 150°C/300°F/gas mark 2.

Make an incision in each lamb shank and insert a small sprig of rosemary or thyme and a sliver of garlic. Season the meat with salt and freshly ground black pepper. Heat the olive oil or fat in a heavy sauté pan or flameproof casserole and sauté the meat in it until well browned on all sides.

Remove the meat from the pan. Add the carrots, celery, leek, onion and bruised garlic and cook over a high heat until it starts to brown. Pour the red wine into the pan, bring to the boil and bubble for a minute or two. Add the stock, herbs and orange peel to the pan, then arrange the lamb shanks on top, bones pointing upwards. Bring to the boil. Cover and cook in the oven for 1½–2½ hours depending on size – the meat should be almost falling off the bones.

Meanwhile, for the haricot beans and tomatoes, heat the olive oil in a saucepan and brown the bacon in it until golden and fully cooked. Add the Tomato Fondue and haricot beans. Cover and simmer for 5–10 minutes.

When the lamb has finished cooking, remove the lamb shanks to a deep, wide serving dish. Strain the liquid and press to extract all the delicious juices. Discard the vegetables, which have by now contributed all their flavour. Return the juices to the pan and cook to reduce and concentrate the flavour if necessary. Meanwhile, reheat the beans and tomatoes. Add the concentrated juices. Taste and correct the seasoning. Spoon the beans over the lamb shanks and scatter with a fistful of roughly chopped herbs.

Other Good Things to Serve with Lamb Shanks
Root Vegetable Mash (see p236), Colcannon (see p236) or Parsnip Mash (see p151)
Chickpeas with Tomato Fondue (see p240) and cumin
Lentils or cous cous

Paella

SERVES 10–12   (**P:** 20 MINS/**C:** 40 MINS)

Paella is a fantastic dish to make for large numbers of people. In Spain you can buy a gas ring especially for cooking paella on a picnic – how wonderful is that?

6 tablespoons extra virgin olive oil

225g (8oz) streaky pork, preferably organic, cut into 2.5cm (1in) cubes

2 large onions, chopped

8 garlic cloves, sliced

1 each large green and red pepper, deseeded and cut into 1cm (1/2in) cubes

1 free-range organic chicken, jointed and cut into smallish pieces

salt and freshly ground pepper

1 chorizo sausage, thickly sliced

1 teaspoon saffron strands

1.8–2.4 litres (3–4 pints) homemade chicken stock (see p295)

1kg (21/4lb) paella rice

450g (1lb) frozen peas

450g (1lb) mussels, in their shells

12 prawns, in their shells

To garnish:

4 very ripe tomatoes, chopped

sprigs of flat parsley and coarsely chopped chives

Paella pan, about 46cm (18in)

Warm the olive oil in the paella pan. Add the pork and cook for a few minutes until the fat begins to run.

Add the onions, garlic and peppers and cook for 4–5 minutes. Add the chicken and season with salt and freshly ground pepper, then add the sliced chorizo. Cook, stirring regularly, for 15 minutes. Meanwhile, soak the saffron strands in a cup of warm chicken stock.

Add the saffron and its soaking liquid to the pan, then stir in the uncooked rice. Add stock almost to cover and stir to blend. Add the peas and then don't stir again unless absolutely necessary. Bring to the boil, reduce the heat and simmer very gently uncovered for about 20 minutes until the meat is fully cooked through. About 5 minutes from the end of cooking, add the mussels and prawns in their shells. Continue to cook, stirring occasionally, until the mussels open and the prawns are cooked; discard any mussels that do not open.

Bring the paella pan to the table. Scatter with chopped tomatoes, lots of flat parsley sprigs and some chives. Serve immediately, directly from the pan.

Slow-roasted Shoulder of Lamb with Cumin Seeds

SERVES 8–10 (P: 20 MINS/C: UP TO 7 HOURS)

A shoulder of lamb is much trickier to carve than a leg, but it's so sweet and juicy that it is certainly worth the struggle. I sometimes put this dish into the low oven of our 4-door Aga in the morning. By 7.30pm, it is cooked – how easy is that! The cumin seeds give a delicious flavour to the meat.

2 tablespoons cumin seeds
1 whole shoulder of lamb on the bone,
  3.3–3.6kg (7–8lb)
salt and freshly ground pepper
extra virgin olive oil, for drizzling

For the cumin gravy:
600ml (1 pint) homemade lamb or chicken
  stock (see p295)
1–2 teaspoons cumin seeds, toasted and ground
roux (optional; see p139)

To serve: roast potatoes

Preheat the oven to 130°C/275°F/gas mark 1.

Warm the cumin seeds slightly in a pan, then crush them using a pestle and mortar. Score the skin of the meat in a diamond pattern with a sharp knife. Transfer to a roasting tin. Sprinkle the meat with salt, pepper and the ground cumin seeds, and drizzle with olive oil.

Roast for 6–7 hours – this gives a delicious, juicy, succulent texture. (Alternatively preheat the oven to 160°C/320°F/gas mark 3 and roast for 2–2½ hours.) Transfer to a serving dish and leave in a warm place while you make the gravy.

To make the cumin gravy, spoon the fat off the roasting tin. Add the stock to the remaining cooking juice. Boil for a few minutes on top of the stove, stirring and scraping the tin well to dissolve the caramelised meat juices (I find a small whisk is ideal for this). Add the ground toasted cumin. Thicken with a very little roux if you like. Taste and add salt and pepper if needed. Pass through a sieve and transfer to a gravy boat.

Carve the meat into thick slices so that everybody gets some crushed cumin seeds. Serve with the cumin gravy, and crusty roast potatoes.

Lamb Roast with Coriander
Substitute coriander seeds for the cumin seeds, both for roasting the lamb and flavouring the gravy. Alternatively use a mix of cumin and coriander seeds.

Cocido

Spain's national lunchtime stew epitomises easy entertaining. You can reduce the temperature and allow it to cook for 6–7 hours or speed it up by semi-cooking the chickpeas first. This robust dish has the added advantage of producing two courses in one – soup and a main dish.

SERVES 8   (P: 30 MINS/C: 4 HOURS)

450g (1lb) dried chickpeas
generous pinch of saffron strands
4 litres (7 pints) light chicken stock (see p295),
  or water
4 free-range organic chicken thighs and
  4 drumsticks
310g (11oz) chorizo
450g (1lb) belly of pork, cut into large chunks
8 shallots
8 garlic cloves
6 sprigs of rosemary
3 sprigs of thyme
salt and freshly ground pepper
250g (9oz) little pasta shapes, such as stellini
  (stars), orzo or medolinne (melon seed)
4–6 tablespoons chopped flat parsley
110g (4oz) Parmesan or Manchego cheese

Put the chickpeas in a bowl, cover with plenty of water and leave to soak overnight. Next day, preheat the oven to 150°C/300°F/gas mark 2.

Put the saffron into a little bowl and cover with 3–4 tablespoons boiling stock or water. Soak the saffron while preparing the other ingredients.

Drain the chickpeas and put them into a large casserole or, better still, an earthenware pot. Add the chicken, chorizo, pork, shallots, garlic, rosemary and thyme. Add the saffron, its soaking liquid and the remainder of the stock or water. Season well with salt and pepper. Bring to the boil over a medium heat on top of the stove, then cover and pop into the oven. Cook for 3–4 hours or until the chickpeas and meat are completely tender.

When the casserole has cooked, cook the pasta in boiling salted water for 8–10 minutes depending on size. Drain and divide between 8 soup bowls. Add some chopped parsley and a ladleful of casserole broth to each bowl. Eat the pasta soup with some grated Parmesan or Manchego and lots of crusty country bread.

Put the casserole in the centre of the table and serve the cocido as the main course. Follow with a good green salad and some seasonal fresh fruit.

Beef and Oxtail Stew with Parsnip Mash

SERVES 8   (P: 1 HOUR/C: 3 HOURS)

Oxtail makes an extraordinarily rich and flavoursome winter stew, considering how cheap it is. The stew is best cooked ahead and reheated, and is so comforting and yummy eaten with champ, colcannon or parsnip mash.

25g (1oz) beef dripping or 2 tablespoons
   extra virgin olive oil
110g (4oz) streaky bacon, cut into
   2.5cm (1in) cubes
225g (8oz) onions, finely chopped
225g (8oz) carrots, cut into 2cm (³/₄in) cubes
50g (2oz) celery, chopped
450g (1lb) stewing beef, cut into 4cm
   (1¹/₂in) cubes
2 oxtails, cut into joints
150ml (¹/₄ pint) red wine
450ml (16fl oz) beef stock
1 bay leaf
1 sprig of thyme
parsley stalks, plus 2 tablespoons chopped
   parsley to garnish
1 tablespoon tomato purée
salt and freshly ground pepper
butter, for frying
175g (6oz) mushrooms, sliced
10g (¹/₂oz) roux (see p139)

To serve:
Parsnip Mash (see p151)
If you want to cook the stew in the oven,

preheat the oven to 160ºC/320ºF/gas mark 3.

Heat the dripping or olive oil in a frying pan, add the bacon and sauté for 1–2 minutes until the fat runs. Add the onions, carrots and celery and continue to cook for 2–3 minutes, stirring occasionally. Transfer to a casserole.

Put the beef and oxtail pieces in the frying pan, a few at a time, and cook until the meat is beginning to brown. Add to the casserole. Pour the wine and 150ml (¹/₄ pint) of the stock into the pan. Bring to the boil and use a whisk to dissolve the caramelised meat juices, then return to the boil. Add to the casserole and mix in the bay leaf, thyme and parsley stalks, the remainder of the stock and the tomato purée. Season with salt and pepper. Cover and cook in the oven, or over a low heat on top of the stove, for 2–3 hours or until the beef, oxtail and vegetables are very tender. The meat should be falling off the bones.

Meanwhile, melt a little butter in a frying pan and cook the sliced mushrooms for 2–3 minutes. Season with salt and pepper. About 5 minutes before the stew is fully cooked, stir in the mushrooms.

Transfer the meat and vegetables to a hot serving dish and keep warm. Remove and discard the bay leaf, thyme and parsley stalks. Bring the liquid back to the boil. Whisk in a little roux and cook until slightly thickened. Return the meat and vegetables to the pan and add the chopped parsley. Bring to the boil, taste and adust the seasoning. Serve with Parsnip Mash.

Parsnip Mash

SERVES 8   (P: 15 MINS/C: 20 MINS)

700g (1¹/₂lb) parsnips
700g (1¹/₂lb) fluffy mashed potatoes
50–75g (2–3oz) butter
salt and freshly ground pepper
chopped parsley

Peel the parsnips thinly. Cut off the tops and tails and cut the parsnips into wedges. If the inner core seems to be at all woody, remove it. Divide the wedges into 2cm (³/₄in) cubes. Cook them in boiling salted water for 15–20 minutes until quite soft.

Drain and mash the parsnips. Mix in the mashed potato and a nice bit of butter, and season well with salt and pepper. The texture should not be too smooth. Scatter with chopped parsley.

Steamed Sultana Pudding

SERVES 4   P: 30 MINS/C: 2 HOURS)

Oh, my goodness, does this bring back memories or what? Serve a steamed pud for an autumn or winter dinner party and everyone of a certain age will dissolve into a sepia tinted haze of nostalgia!

10g (¹/₂oz) butter, melted, plus 110g (4oz)
    butter, at room temperature
50–75g (2–3oz) sultanas or 75g (3oz) stoned
    and split Lexia or Muscatel raisins
110g (4oz) caster sugar
grated zest of ¹/₂ unwaxed organic lemon
2 free-range, organic eggs
175g (6oz) plain white flour
¹/₂ teaspoon baking powder
1–2 tablespoons milk

For the homemade custard:
¹/₂ vanilla pod or a few drops of vanilla extract
300ml (¹/₂ pint) rich milk
2 free-range, organic egg yolks
1 tablespoon caster sugar

12.5cm (5in) pudding bowl

Brush the pudding bowl with the melted butter. Press some of the sultanas or stoned and split raisins around the sides. Cream the remaining butter, add the sugar and lemon zest and beat until light and fluffy. Gradually add the eggs, beating well after each addition. Stir in the flour and baking powder and enough milk to make the mixture just loose enough to drop from a spoon, then add the remainder of the fruit. Spoon into the pudding bowl.

Cover with a tight-fitting lid, pleated piece of double greaseproof paper or aluminium foil and tie down. (The paper is pleated to allow for expansion.) Bring a saucepan of water to the boil and put in the pudding bowl – the water should come half way up the sides. Cover and steam for 2 hours.

Meanwhile, make the custard. Put the vanilla pod (if using) into the cold milk and bring slowly to the boil. Whisk the egg yolks with the sugar in a bowl. Remove the vanilla pod from the milk and pour the milk on to the egg mixture, whisking all the time. At this point add the pure vanilla extract (if using). Return the mixture to the saucepan and stir over a gentle heat until it thickens just enough to coat the back of a spoon – be careful not to boil it. Pour into a cold bowl and stir occasionally as it cools.

Turn out the pudding and serve with the custard.

Raspberry Jam Pudding
Another children's favourite. Substitute 4–6 tablespoons raspberry jam for the raisins, spreading it over the sides and base of the pudding bowl. Serve with a warm raspberry jam sauce (thin the jam with a little water) and lots of lightly whipped cream.

Jellied Ham Hock and Parsley Terrine

SERVES 12–16   (**P:** 1 HOUR/**C:** 2¹/₂ HOURS)

Jambon persillé **is a classic in French charcuteries. When I first looked up recipes for it they would always go into a long palaver about making a clear jelly with calves' feet. I tried it once and was exhausted by the effort, and forgot about it until recently when I ate a delicious version at a friend's house. I was wildly impressed – my goodness, he must have spent days, I said. Nonsense, he replied, just use gelatine! So now it's child's play and makes a super dish for a summer lunch. It can be prepared several days ahead; it's also a terrific way to use up leftover ham or bacon.**

4kg (9lb) ham hocks, or 2.75kg (6lb) piece of
  dry-cured ham (bacon or oyster cut is good)
dash of dry white wine
2 onions, each stuck with 1 clove
2 carrots
1 celery stick
1 small bay leaf
few sprigs of thyme
10 black peppercorns
4 rounded teaspoons powdered gelatine
50g (2oz) parsley, finely chopped
  (stalks reserved)

To serve:
Tomato and Mint or Basil Salad (see p89)
spring onions
gherkins
green salad

If the ham is salty, soak it in cold water for a few hours, preferably overnight. Discard the soaking water. Put the ham in a large saucepan, cover with fresh water and bring to the boil; as soon as it boils, discard the water, cover with fresh water and bring to the boil again. Repeat two or three times depending on how salty the ham is.

Finally cover with fresh water and a dash of white wine. Add all the remaining ingredients except the gelatine and chopped parsley, but do include the parsley stalks. Bring to the boil, cover and reduce the heat, then simmer for 2–2¹/₂hours – a skewer should go through easily. Remove the ham and strain the cooking liquid through a fine sieve or one lined with muslin into a shallow dish. Skim the fat off the liquid and allow to cool.

Remove the rind from the ham and cut the meat into 2.5cm (1in) cubes.

Measure the cooking liquid – you won't need much more than 600ml (1 pint). Put 4 tablespoons of the cooking liquid into a small bowl, sprinkle on 4 rounded teaspoons gelatine per 600ml (1 pint) and allow to soak for a few minutes. Meanwhile, bring a small saucepan of water to the boil. Put the bowl into the simmering water to dissolve the gelatine. When the gelatine is clear, add a little of the measured liquid, stir well and then mix with the remainder, finally stirring in the chopped parsley. Mix well. Put the cubed ham into an oiled bowl or terrine (it should be about 10cm/4in deep) and pour the liquid over. Try to flatten the top so it does not wiggle around too much when you take it out. (In France it is traditionally made in a round-bottomed bowl.) Cover and refrigerate overnight.

Serve in slices with summer salads.

Slow-roasted Belly of Pork with Crackling and Spiced Aubergine

SERVES 6–8   (**P:** 30 MINS/**C:** 2 HOURS)

2.25kg (5lb) belly of free-range organic pork
  with the rind intact. (You will most certainly
  need to order the joint ahead to ensure that
  the rind is still on – no rind, no crackling!)
sea salt and cracked black pepper

To serve:
Spiced Aubergine (see p243)
rocket leaves

Score the pork rind at 5mm (¹/₄in) intervals running with the grain – let your butcher do this if possible because the skin, particularly of free-range pork, can be quite tough. This is to give you really good crackling and make it easier to carve later.

Preheat the oven to 160°C/320°F/gas mark 3. Put the pork, skin side up, on a chopping board and season with salt and pepper. Pour 1cm (¹/₂in) water into a roasting tin and roast the joint on a wire rack in the roasting tin. Allow 30–35 minutes per 450g (1lb). Baste with the rendered pork fat every now and then.

Just before the end of the cooking time remove the pork to another roasting tin. Return to the oven and increase the temperature to 230°C/450°F/gas mark 8, to crisp the crackling further, for 10–15 minutes. When the joint is cooked the juices should run clear. Allow to rest for 10–15 minutes in a low oven before carving.

Degrease the cooking juices and reduce to a few tablespoons. Serve the pork sprinkled with some flakes of sea salt with the juices, the Spiced Aubergine and rocket. Rustic roast potatoes and a good green salad would also be great.

why slow cook?

Slow food requires time and patience, but the results are well worth it and it is something that I am passionate about. How does this fit into a book on easy entertaining? Well, most of these recipes require no more preparation than any other, but can be left to cook happily by themselves for several hours.

Moreover, if you love to cook, then you will find these recipes all the more rewarding because the resultant taste makes it all worth while. The meat will be so juicy and succulent, full of flavour and coaxed into such tenderness that your guests will talk about it for weeks. These recipes are perfect for when you have a whole day or weekend to prepare, or if you have house guests for a lazy weekend – you can start in the morning and check on it every so often. As with all recipes, read them carefully and work out when you will need to get started on each stage

Another joy is that you can spend the cooking time getting ready for the party. Why not make your own cordials or lemonade, fruit ice cubes for drinks and whip up a divine dessert to finish off. With 2–3 hours to spare, you also have plenty of time to set the house to rights and you can really go to town on the decoration. If you are the least bit artistic, take the time to create some simple table settings and placemats using wrapping paper, cardboard or tissue paper and pinking shears for a funky finish. Or edge the cardboard with matching ribbon. Then devote some time to yourself – a long bath or a home manicure, all the while sipping some bubbly – what better way to prepare for a party.

Traditional

A Plate of Cured Meats
Beef and Oxtail Stew with Parsnip Mash (p150)
Steamed Sultana Pudding (p151)

To drink

Cured meats go best with red wines that are big on fruit but low on tannin. Beaujolais or Sancerre Rouge are ideal and they are best served quite cool, especially if the weather is warm. By contrast, fino or manzanilla sherry, the classic partner of tapas, will do the same job but in a very different way. The stew requires something much more gutsy and full-bodied. A southern Rhone red, such as Gigondas or Vacqueyras, has the concentration for the job. Really intense New World reds, especially Californian Zinfandel or Hunter Valley Shiraz, which are often a bit overpowering with food, will meet their match here. There are two ideal wines for steamed sultana pudding: the treacly Liqueur Muscats of Victoria and the sweetest of them all, Pedro Ximenez from Jerez.

Take it slow

Salmon Rillette with Piquillo Peppers (p74)
White Yeast Bread (p34)
Cocido (p149)
A Great Lemon Meringue Pie (p265)

To drink

The white wines of Spain's cool climate Rueda region, often using Sauvignon Blanc, can tackle the combination of richness and smokiness that the rillettes present. Alternatively, a straight Sauvignon Blanc from Chile will do the job, or even a Muscadet, provided it's from a really good source. Cocido is quite a contrast, requiring a Spanish red with oodles of fruit, brawny structure and some vanilla-scented oak. Think in terms of Rioja, Ribera del Duero or Bierzo. An Australian GSM (e.g. Grenache, Shiraz, Mourvedre) blend is a good substitute.

formal suppers

A formal dinner party is the ultimate challenge. The first place to start is with pen and paper – think of it as you would a military operation. Make lots of lists – the guests, shopping list for ingredients, wine list. Consider drawing up a schedule of works – it may sound a bit like hard work, but it does avoid a mad dash before your guests arrive (remember to leave yourself at least half an hour to get yourself ready for dinner). There are lots of elegant suppers in this chapter that will wow your guests, and they can easily be complimented by recipes from earlier chapters. And take a look at Sweet Things and A Cheese Course for the finishing touches. My final tip – if you have time, have a practice run with the recipes, so you will be full of confidence on the night.

Grey Sea Mullet or Sea Bass in a Salt Crust with Fresh Herb Butter

SERVES 2–4   (**P:** 15 MINS/**C:** 30 MINS)

Preheat the oven to 220°C/425°F/gas mark 7.

So easy and so elegant.

1 sea mullet or sea bass, 700–900g (1½–2lb)
1 free-range, organic egg white, lightly beaten
  (optional)
1kg (2¼lb) sea salt

To serve:
Herb Butter (see below)
tiny new potatoes
oven-roasted cherry tomatoes

1 large oval dish, preferably cast iron, large
  enough to hold the fish, cook the fish and
  bring to the table

Gut the fish and wash out the inside well to remove any trace of blood (I often use a clean washing-up brush). Do not remove the head. Use strong kitchen scissors to cut away the dorsal fin. Remove the scales, if needed, by holding the fish by the tail and pushing against the scales with the back of a knife from the tail to the head on both sides. (Grey sea mullet has scales as large as a thumbnail; other fish, such as sea bass or bream, need not necessarily be scaled.)

If you want a harder crust, mix the egg white with the salt. Spread one third of the sea salt evenly over the bottom of a large cast-iron dish. Lay the fish on top. Cover completely with the remainder of the sea salt. Bake for 18–20 minutes.

Meanwhile, make the herb butter (see below). Don't do this too far in advance or it will lose its fresh flavour and green colour.

When the fish is cooked, bring the dish to the table, crack the hard crust on top. Remove the top crust to a plate and peel the skin off the fish. Lift the fillets off on to individual serving plates and spoon over a little herb butter.

A few tiny new potatoes and maybe a branch of sweet oven-roasted cherry tomatoes on the side would be delicious with this.

Herb Butter

110g (4oz) butter
4 teaspoons finely chopped mixed herbs,
  such parsley, chives, fennel and thyme

Melt the butter in a small saucepan and stir in the herbs. Remove from the heat.

Fish in Fresh Fig Leaves with Nasturtium and Parsley Butter

SERVES 8   (**P:** 15 MINS/**C:** 15MINS)

Preheat the oven to 200°C/400°F/gas mark 6.

8 large fresh fig leaves
8 portions of fresh fish, such as sea bass, wild
  salmon, about 1.1kg (2½lb)
extra virgin olive oil
salt and freshly ground pepper

To garnish:
flat parsley and nasturtium flowers

For the nasturtium and parsley butter:
110g (4oz) butter
freshly squeezed lemon juice
zest from 1 unwaxed lemon
1 tablespoon chopped parsley
1 teaspoon chopped chives
30 fresh nasturtium flowers, coarsely chopped

First make the nasturtium and parsley butter. Cream the butter and beat in the lemon juice bit by bit. Add the lemon zest and chopped parsley, chives and nasturtium flowers. Form into a roll and wrap in greaseproof paper, twist the ends like a cracker and chill in the fridge.

Wash the fig leaves in cold water. Dry gently. Skin the fish and dip each portion in extra virgin olive oil. Season well on both sides with salt and freshly ground pepper. Wrap each piece of fish individually in a fig leaf – it may not be perfectly enclosed but that's fine. Roast on a baking tray in the oven for 8–10 minutes depending on the thickness of the fish.

Serve on hot plates. Open the fig-leaf packages and put a slice of nasturtium and parsley butter on top of the fish. Garnish with a sprig of flat parsley and a nasturtium flower. Serve immediately as the butter melts over the fish.

Pacific Oysters with Asian Vinaigrette

SERVES 8 AS A STARTER   (P: 40 MINS)

Even though Pacific oysters are available all year round, they are best in winter (see the photograph on p172).

32–40 Pacific oysters

For the Asian vinaigrette:
1/2–1 teaspoon peeled and finely grated fresh ginger
4 tablespoons rice wine vinegar
1 teaspoon caster sugar
1 teaspoon soy sauce
6 tablespoons sunflower oil
2 tablespoons extra virgin olive oil
1/2 tablespoon lemon juice

To garnish:
fresh seaweed, if available
chives or coriander sprigs

To make the Asian vinaigrette, mix all the ingredients in a glass jar, seal and shake well.

If you can get some, place a little fresh seaweed on each plate. Arrange 4–5 oysters per person on top and spoon a little vinaigrette over each one.

Sprinkle the oysters with the finely chopped chives, or a criss-cross of 2 longer chives, or a sprig of coriander.

Top Tip: If you can find some fresh seaweed, such as bladder wrack, dip the fronds into boiling water for a second or two and it will turn bright green. Drop it straight into a bowl of iced water to prevent it cooking and to set the colour. It will make an attractive garnish, which you could eat if you were very hungry but it doesn't taste delicious! Use it soon otherwise it will go slimy.

Salad of Smoked Mackerel with Beetroot, Watercress and Horseradish Sauce

SERVES 8   (P: 10 MINS)

4–6 fillets of smoked mackerel, skin on
Pickled Beetroot (see p86)
generous amount of watercress and baby salad leaves
sprigs of dill, to garnish

To serve:
Ballymaloe Brown Yeast Bread (see p35)
Horseradish Sauce (see below)

Cut the smoked mackerel into 2.5cm (1in) pieces and the pickled beetroot into 1cm (1/2in) dice.

Strew the base of each plate with a mixture of watercress and baby salad leaves. Put 5–6 pieces of mackerel on top. Scatter with some diced beetroot and top with a few little dollops of horseradish sauce. A few sprigs of dill add to the deliciousness. Serve with Ballymaloe Brown Yeast Bread.

Horseradish sauce

SERVES 8–10   (P: 20 MINS/C: 3 HOURS)

Horseradish is widely available in greengrocers nowadays, but it also grows wild in many parts of Ireland. It looks like giant dock leaves. If you can't find it near you, plant some in your garden. It is very prolific and the root, which is the part you grate, can be dug up at any time of the year. Serve horseradish sauce with roast beef, smoked venison or smoked mackerel.

This is a fairly mild horseradish sauce. If you want to really 'clear the sinuses', increase the amount of horseradish.

enough horseradish root to make 1 1/2–3 tablespoons grated horseradish
2 teaspoons white wine vinegar
1 teaspoon lemon juice
1/4 teaspoon Dijon mustard
1/4 teaspoon salt
pinch of freshly ground pepper
1 teaspoon sugar
250ml (9fl oz) lightly whipped cream

Scrub and rinse the horseradish root well, peel and grate. Put the grated horseradish into a bowl and mix in the vinegar, lemon juice, mustard, salt, freshly ground pepper and sugar. Fold in the lightly whipped cream – do not overmix or the sauce will curdle.

Covered, the sauce will keep in the fridge for 2–3 days.

Chickpeas with Fresh Spices

SERVES 8–10

(**P**: 10 MINS IF USING TINNED CHICKPEAS,
70 MINS IF DRIED/**C**: 15 MINS)

A few little jars of fresh spices are a crucial part of any storecupboard, they will add terrific zest and an exotic flavour to your food.

450g (1lb) dried chickpeas, soaked overnight
  in cold water, or 2 x 400g (14oz) tins
  chickpeas
2 fresh green chillies
5cm (2in) piece of fresh ginger, peeled and
  roughly chopped
4 garlic cloves
4 tablespoons extra virgin olive oil
225g (8oz) onions, finely chopped
1 teaspoon cumin seeds, crushed
2 teaspoons coriander seeds, crushed
8 very ripe tomatoes, skinned and chopped,
  or 1¹/₂ x 400g (14oz) tins tomatoes
225g (8oz) spinach leaves
salt and freshly ground pepper
2 tablespoons chopped coriander
1 tablespoon chopped mint

To serve:
yogurt, crème fraîche, fresh coriander and
  mint leaves
or
boiled rice and Tomato and Red Onion Salsa
(see p294)

Drain the soaked chickpeas (if using) into a saucepan, cover with fresh water and cook until tender; this can take 30–60 minutes depending on the quality. Drain and reserve the cooking liquid.

Meanwhile, remove the seeds from the chillies. Using a pestle and mortar or food processor, grind together the chillies, ginger and garlic to a paste.

Heat the oil in a heavy-bottomed sauté pan and sweat the onions over a low heat until soft but not coloured. Add the chilli paste, the crushed cumin and coriander seeds and cook for a minute or two. Add the tomatoes, the drained chickpeas and a little of their cooking liquid (save the rest for soup). If using tinned chickpeas, add them at this point. Simmer gently for about 10 minutes until the flavours have mingled.

Add the spinach leaves, tossing gently until they wilt. Add salt and pepper to taste and sprinkle with chopped coriander and mint. Serve immediately with plain boiled rice and Tomato and Red Onion Salsa (see p294), or allow to cool and serve cold with yogurt, crème fraîche and lots of fresh coriander and mint leaves.

Goat's Cheese, Spring Onion, 'Pink Fir Apple' Potato, Chorizo and Thyme Leaf Tart

SERVES 6   (P: 30 MINS/C: 1 HOUR)

If you don't have access to these intensely flavoured Pink Fir Apple potatoes use some small new potatoes.

10g (¹/₂oz) butter
1 tablespoon extra virgin olive oil
110g (4oz) spring onions (white and green parts), finely chopped
salt and freshly ground pepper
50g (2oz) chorizo, diced (optional)
3 free-range, organic eggs, plus extra beaten egg for brushing
3 tablespoons thyme leaves
175ml (6fl oz) cream
4–6 Pink Fir Apple potatoes, cooked and sliced or cut into chunks
110g (4oz) soft goat's cheese
thyme flowers, to garnish (optional)

To serve:
green salad

For the shortcrust pastry:
150g (5oz) white flour
60g (2½oz) butter
1 free-range, organic egg

1x 20cm (8in) tart tin or flan ring
dried beans or baking beans

First make the shortcrust pastry. Sift the flour into a bowl and rub in the butter until the mixture resembles coarse breadcrumbs. Mix the egg with 2 tablespoons water, and mix in just enough to bind the pastry, being careful not to make it too sticky. Chill for 15 minutes.

Roll out the pastry to a thickness of about 3mm (¹/₈in) and use to line the quiche tin. Line the pastry with greaseproof paper and fill to the top with dried beans or baking beans. Leave to rest for 15 minutes.

Preheat the oven to 180°C/350°F/gas mark 4.

Bake the tart case for 20 minutes, then remove from the oven but do not turn off the oven.

Remove the beans and paper, brush the pastry base with beaten egg and return to the oven for a minute or two. This seals the pastry and helps to avoid a 'soggy bottom'.

To make the filling, melt the butter in a frying pan. Add the olive oil and spring onions, sprinkle on some salt and cook over a low heat for a few minutes until the onions are soft but not coloured. Add the chorizo (if using). Leave to cool.

Whisk the eggs and the thyme leaves in a bowl, add the cream, the softened onions and chorizo and cooked potatoes. Season well with salt and freshly ground pepper and pour into the pastry case. Scatter pieces of goat's cheese into the tart. Bake for 40–45 minutes, or until just set in the centre.

Sprinkle thyme flowers over the top if available. Serve with a good green salad.

Glazed Baby Onion or Shallot Tarte Tatin

SERVES 6   (P: 30 MINS/C: 1 HOUR)

50g (2oz) butter
600g (1¹/₄lb) baby onions or shallots
12 garlic cloves
300ml (¹/₂ pint) homemade chicken or vegetable stock (see p295)
200g (7oz) puff pastry
2 tablespoons sugar
1 tablespoon balsamic vinegar
2 teaspoons thyme leaves
salt and freshly ground black pepper

To serve:
fresh rocket leaves

23cm (9in) non-stick frying pan with a metal handle.

Heat a heavy frying or sauté pan. Melt half the butter in the pan, add the onions and fry gently for about 10 minutes, tossing occasionally until golden. After about 5 minutes add the garlic cloves. Pour in the stock, cover and simmer for 5–10 minutes, depending on the size of the onions – they should be tender when pierced with a sharp knife but still hold their shape. Remove the onions and garlic to a plate with a slotted spoon, drain well and pat dry with kitchen paper (save the remaining stock for sauces or soup). Allow to cool completely.

Roll out the pastry to a 25cm (10in) circle. Chill for at least 30 minutes to allow the pastry to rest. Preheat the oven to 200°C/400°F/gas mark 6.

Melt the remaining butter in a 23cm (9in) ovenproof, preferably non-stick, frying pan. Sprinkle the sugar over the base of the pan and cook until caramelised. Sprinkle the balsamic vinegar over the top, add the onions, toss until well coated – about 3 minutes – and remove from the heat. Tuck the garlic cloves in between the shallots. Sprinkle with the thyme leaves.

Season with salt and pepper. Lay the pastry on top, tucking the edges down around the inside of the pan, and prick all over with a fork. Bake for about 30 minutes or until the pastry has risen and is golden brown. Leave to rest for a few minutes, then loosen the sides with a knife and invert on to a flat serving plate. Serve warm or cold, with a rocket salad.

Tofu and Vegetable Stir-fry

SERVES 6   (P: 15 MINS, PLUS 2 HOURS TO
MARINATE (OPTIONAL)/C: 15 MINS)

Tofu is made from soya milk which is heated
and stirred with coagulants. It solidifies into
curds which are pressed to make blocks of
tofu. It can be soft and silky or very firm.
Chinese-style tofu is firm in texture and
looks coarse but becomes smoother when
cooked. It can be marinated for a longer
period and is also good fried or grilled, or
used for brochettes. It comes packed in
water in a sealed plastic container, either in
slabs or slices, and can be frozen. Always
check the use-by date and keep refrigerated.
Tofu should smell mild, sweet and vaguely
nutty. Once it begins to smell sour, it is not
good to eat.

2 tablespoons soy sauce
2 tablespoons rice wine vinegar
1 tablespoon brown sugar
1 teaspoon peeled and grated fresh ginger
1 chilli, chopped, or 1 teaspoon chilli flakes
2 teaspoons Chinese five-spice powder
350g (12oz) firm tofu, drained
2 tablespoons extra virgin olive oil
200g (7oz) mushrooms, sliced
salt and freshly ground pepper
1 large red pepper, quartered, deseeded and
    sliced at an angle
1 large yellow pepper, quartered, deseeded
    and sliced at an angle
200g (7oz) small broccoli or cauliflower florets,
    blanched and refreshed
1 tablespoon sesame oil
2–4 spring onions, chopped
1 tablespoon toasted sesame seeds

To serve:
Steamed Thai fragrant rice

Mix the soy sauce, vinegar, sugar, ginger,
chilli and five-spice powder together. Cut the
tofu into 2.5cm (1in) dice, place it in a small
pie dish, cover with the spicy mixture and
leave to marinate for 1–2 hours if possible.

Drain the tofu, reserving the marinade. Heat
a wok or frying pan and add the olive oil.
Cook the tofu in batches for 3–4 minutes
until golden and transfer to a plate. Increase
the heat. Add a little more oil if needed, toss
in the mushrooms and season with salt and
freshly ground pepper. Toss until fully
cooked through. Add the peppers, stir and
fry for a minute or two, then add the
broccoli or cauliflower florets.

Drizzle with the sesame oil and stir-fry for
2–3 minutes. Add the tofu, chopped spring
onions and the reserved marinade. Bubble
up, taste and correct the seasoning. Scatter
with sesame seeds and serve immediately
with Thai fragrant rice.

Warm Salad of Pigeon Breast with Spiced Pears and Mushrooms

SERVES 12   (P: 20 MINS/C: 15 MINS)

6 ripe pears, such as Conference or Doyenné
    de Comice
2.5cm (1in) piece of cinnamon stick
1/2 teaspoon allspice berries
1 teaspoon coriander seeds
1/4 teaspoon black peppercorns
1 star anise
1 tablespoon sugar
grated zest of 1 orange
225g (8oz) flat mushrooms, sliced
25g (1oz) butter
extra virgin olive oil, for frying
salt and freshly ground black pepper
12 pigeon breasts, skinned
flat parsley leaves, to garnish
enough salad leaves for 12 helpings

For the dressing:
1 tablespoon verjuice (see p95)
1 tablespoon lemon juice
6 tablespoons extra virgin olive oil
1/2 teaspoon Dijon mustard
1 teaspoon honey

Peel the pears and cut them into quarters.

Put the cinnamon stick in a spice grinder, add the allspice berries, coriander seeds,
peppercorns, star anise and sugar, and whizz to a powder. Transfer to a bowl. Add the grated
orange zest. Toss the pears in the spice mixture.

Make the dressing by whisking all the ingredients together in a bowl.

Heat the butter in a sauté pan, add the pears, toss and cook on a low heat until the pears
are tender. Keep warm.

Heat a little olive oil in a frying pan and sauté the mushrooms over a high heat. Season with
a little salt and pepper and keep warm.

Clean the frying pan and heat a little more olive oil on a very high heat. Season the pigeon
breasts and fry very quickly – they should be sealed on the outside but still pink otherwise
they will be tough. Remove to a plate to rest while you dress the salad leaves.

Toss the leaves in the dressing and divide between 12 plates. Divide the warm pears and
mushrooms between the plates. Quickly slice the pigeon breasts and add to the plates.
Scatter with flat parsley and serve immediately.

Fettucine with Asparagus

SERVES 4   (**P:** 15 MINS/**C:** 15 MINS)

You can use this as a basic creamy pasta sauce and add all manner of good things.

Don't make this recipe with out-of-season asparagus that has been flown halfway around the globe. In Ireland and Britain the asparagus season comes in May and June.

225g (8oz) fettucine or noodles
sea salt and freshly ground pepper
16 spears of fresh asparagus, trimmed
225ml (8fl oz) cream
40g (1¹/₂oz) butter, diced
75g (3oz) Parmesan cheese, grated, plus extra
  to serve

First cook the pasta. Bring 6 litres (10 pints) water to the boil, add 2 tablespoons salt and tip the pasta in all at once. Stir well to ensure the strands are separate, cover the pan just long enough to bring the water back to the boil. Cook, uncovered, until al dente, cooked but still firm to the bite – about 1–2 minutes for fresh pasta; for dried pasta follow the instructions on packet, but test 2–3 minutes before the suggested time. Drain the pasta as soon as it is cooked, but don't overdrain: fresh pasta and all long pasta should still be wet and slippery.

Meanwhile, cook the asparagus in very little water for 4–5 minutes or until almost soft or when the tip of a knife pierces the root end easily. Drain and set aside.

Next make the sauce. Heat the cream in a wide saucepan or sauté pan, add the butter and simmer over a medium heat for a minute or two until the cream and butter are incorporated and slightly thickened. Add the Parmesan and lots of pepper. Taste and add salt if needed. Toss in the drained pasta.

Slice the still-warm asparagus at an angle, keeping the tip intact. Scatter over the top of the pasta, toss gently and serve immediately in hot pasta bowls.

Have an extra bowl of grated Parmesan for guests to sprinkle over the pasta at the table.

Other Good Additions
1 Instead of the asparagus, add 110g (4oz) freshly cooked broad beans and lots of coarsely chopped flat parsley to the sauce.
2 To the basic sauce, add thin strips of freshly roasted and peeled sweet red pepper or piquillo (2 large ones should be enough) instead of the asparagus. Top with fresh rocket leaves.
3 Add some diced roasted pumpkin, toasted pine nuts and rocket leaves to the sauce instead of the asparagus.

Involtini di Melanzane alla Mozzarella

SERVES 6   (**P:** 40 MINS/**C:** 10 MINS)

1 very large aubergine, about 400–500g
  (14oz–1lb), or 2 small ones
salt and freshly ground black pepper
extra virgin olive oil, for frying
250g (9oz) buffalo mozzarella cheese
12 basil leaves
freshly ground pepper

To serve:
Tomato Fondue (see p240)
green salad (see p94)

Slice the aubergine thinly, sprinkle with salt and leave to drain for 30 minutes. Rinse and pat dry. Brush with olive oil and pangrill until tender and slightly browned. Drain on kitchen paper.

Heat the grill until it is really hot.

Cut the mozzarella into thin slices, place 2 basil leaves on each slice and sprinkle with freshly ground pepper. Roll an aubergine slice around each piece of cheese and arrange in a single layer on an ovenproof plate.

Grill until the cheese melts. Serve at once with Tomato Fondue and a mixed green salad.

Spiced Vegetable Pie

SERVES 6   (P: 1 HOUR/C: 1 HOUR)

250g (9oz) onions, chopped
225g (8oz) potatoes, chopped
250g (9oz) carrots, chopped
225g (8oz) celeriac, chopped
110g (4oz) parsnips, chopped, and/or
   110g (4oz) mushrooms, sliced and sautéed
2 tablespoons extra virgin olive oil
salt and freshly ground pepper
2 teaspoons cumin seeds
3 teaspoons coriander seeds
1/2 teaspoon cardamom seeds
2 tablespoons flour
1 teaspoon ground turmeric
pinch of sugar
300ml (1/2 pint) vegetable stock (see p295)
egg wash
green salad, to serve

For the hot water pastry crust:
450g (1lb) flour
pinch of salt
250g (9oz) butter
175ml (6fl oz) water

1 tin, 20cm (8in) in diameter, 4cm
   (11/2in) deep

Cut the vegetables into uniform-sized cubes of about 1cm (1/2in). Heat the olive oil in a wide sauté pan, add the onions, potatoes, carrots, celeriac and parsnips. Season with salt and pepper, toss in the oil, cover the pot and sweat on a gentle heat for 4–5 minutes.

Meanwhile, heat the cumin, coriander and cardamom seeds in a pan until they smell aromatic – just a few seconds. Crush lightly, add to the vegetables and cook for 1–2 minutes. Take off the heat, sprinkle over the flour, turmeric and sugar and stir well.

Put back on the heat and add the vegetable stock, stirring all the time. Cover the pot and simmer for 20–30 minutes or until the vegetables are almost tender but not mushy.

Meanwhile make the pastry. Sift the flour and salt into a mixing bowl and make a well in the centre. Dice the butter, put it into a saucepan with the water and bring to the boil. Pour the liquid all at once into the flour and mix together quickly; beat until smooth. At first the pastry will be too soft to handle, but as it cools, roll out until it is 3–5mm (1/8–1/2in) thick and use two-thirds of it to line a tin. The pastry may be made into individual pies if you prefer. Keep back one-third of the pastry to make the lid.

Preheat the oven to 230ºC/450ºF/gas mark 8.

Fill the pastry-lined tin with the vegetable mixture, including the sautéed mushrooms (if using); the vegetables should be almost, but not quite, cooked and cooled a little. Brush the edges of the pastry with the egg wash and put on the pastry lid, pinching the edges tightly together. Roll out the trimmings to make pastry leaves or twirls to decorate the top of the pie. We sometimes make a smiley face. Make a hole in the centre, then egg-wash the lid and the decoration also.

Bake the pie for about 30 minutes. Serve with a good green salad.

Jeannie's Roast Lamb with Chocolate

SERVES 7–8   (P: 30 MINS/C: 11/2 HOURS)

This bizarre-sounding but utterly delicious recipe was given to me by the lovely bubbly Scottish cook Jeannie Chesterton, who with her husband Sam owns one of my favourite getaways in the whole world – Finca Buenvino at Los Marines in Andalucia.

1 leg of free-range organic lamb
salt and freshly ground pepper
1 head of garlic
extra virgin olive oil, for drizzling
450–600ml (16fl oz–1 pint) cold coffee or
   tea, strained
25–50g (1–2oz) good-quality dark chocolate,
   chopped, plus extra if needed

To serve:
new potatoes

Preheat the oven to 180ºC/350ºF/gas mark 4.

Score the skin of the lamb and sprinkle with salt and pepper. Peel the garlic cloves and put into a roasting tin. Lay the leg of lamb on top of the garlic and drizzle with a little olive oil.

Pour the coffee or tea into the roasting tin – it should come about 1cm (1/2in) up the side of the tin. Roast for 8 minutes per kg (15 minutes per lb), about 11/4–11/2 hours depending on the size of the joint.

When the meat is cooked, transfer it to a serving dish to rest.

Meanwhile, skim the fat off the juices in the roasting tin. Put the tin over a low heat, add the chocolate and whisk to emulsify; the sauce will thicken slightly and become darker brown in colour. Taste and adjust the seasoning and chocolate if needed.

Carve succulent slices of lamb and serve with the sauce and perhaps a few new potatoes. Surprisingly delicious!

Debbie's Thai Green Vegetable Curry

SERVES 6–8   (**P:** 30 MINS/**C:** 45 MINS)

This is the yummiest vegetable curry. The recipe was given to me by Debbie Shaw, who originally came to the school as a student and is now a teacher. Her curry is great for everyone, including vegetarians who don't mind a drop of fish sauce!

3 tablespoons sunflower oil

4 medium courgettes, cut into 2.5cm (1in) cubes

salt and ground white pepper

350–400g (12–14oz) mushrooms, quartered

3 tablespoons extra virgin olive oil

2 medium aubergines, cut into 2.5cm (1in) cubes

1/2 head large cauliflower (about 450g/1lb), broken into large florets

1 large shallot or small onion (about 50g/2oz), finely chopped

2 large garlic cloves, finely chopped

2.5cm (1in) piece of fresh galangal or ginger, peeled and finely chopped

2 green chillies, finely chopped

1 tablespoon Thai green curry paste (add a bit more if you like it hot!)

2 x 400ml (14fl oz) tins coconut milk

2 tablespoons fish sauce (*nam pla*)

1 tablespoon sugar

juice of 1 lime

3 tablespoons roughly torn Thai basil leaves, or other basil

8 kaffir lime leaves

350–400ml (12–14fl oz) homemade vegetable stock (see p295)

175g (6oz) frozen peas

To serve:

basmati rice or Thai noodles

herby green salad

Heat 1 tablespoon of the sunflower oil in a frying pan over a medium heat and add the courgettes. Season lightly with salt and sauté until cooked and slightly browned. Set aside in a bowl. In the same pan, sauté the mushrooms in the same way; add them to the courgettes when cooked.

Heat 2 tablespoons of the olive oil over a medium heat and fry the aubergines until cooked through and slightly brown. Season with a pinch of salt and white pepper. Remove from the heat and add to the bowl.

Cook the cauliflower florets in boiling salted water for 4–5 minutes or until cooked but still slightly crunchy. Add to the other vegetables.

Heat the remaining sunflower oil in a frying pan over a medium heat. Fry the shallot or onion, garlic, chillies and galangal or ginger for 2–3 minutes or until the shallot is cooked, but do not allow it to burn. Add the curry paste and continue to cook for a further 3 minutes.

Add the coconut milk and simmer for 5–6 minutes, stirring, until the sauce thickens.

Add the fish sauce, sugar, half the lime juice, half the basil and all the kaffir lime leaves. Stir in 350ml (12fl oz) vegetable stock; if the sauce is too thick, add a little more stock. Bring to the boil and add the frozen peas. Reduce the heat and continue to cook for a further 4 minutes, stirring occasionally.

Add all the cooked vegetables and the remaining basil and lime juice. Taste and adjust the seasoning if needed.

Serve on warm dishes, with boiled basmati rice or Thai noodles and a green salad with lots of fresh herbs.

Note: Debbie stressed that when curry paste is newly opened, it is very hot, but will gradually become milder, so adjust the quantity accordingly.

Roast Pheasant with a Salad of Rocket, Pomegranate and Game Chips

SERVES 2–3　　(**P**: 30 MINS/**C**: 1¹/₄ HOURS)

A roast pheasant makes the perfect romantic dinner for two, and you'll probably have a little left over that may be eaten cold for a picnic the next day. This slightly unorthodox way of cooking the pheasant produces a moist, juicy bird. Guinea fowl is also wonderful cooked and served in this way.

1 young plump pheasant
25g (1oz) butter
300ml (¹/₂ pint) game or chicken stock
　(see p295)

For the stuffing:
40g (1¹/₂oz) butter
75g (3oz) onions, chopped
60g (2¹/₂oz) breadcrumbs
1 tablespoon chopped mixed herbs,
　such as parsley, thyme, chives and marjoram
salt and freshly ground pepper

To serve:
Salad of Rocket, Pomegranate and Game Chips
　(see below)

Gut the pheasant if necessary and remove the crop, which is at the neck end; wash all over and dry well.

Preheat the oven to 190°C/375°F/gas mark 5.

To make the stuffing, melt the butter in a small pan and sweat the onions over a low heat until soft but not coloured. Remove from the heat and stir in the breadcrumbs and herbs, then season with salt and pepper to taste. If you are cooking the bird right away, the stuffing can be used warm; otherwise allow the stuffing to get quite cold before you use it.

Season the pheasant cavity with salt and pepper and fill loosely with the stuffing. Sprinkle some more salt and pepper over the top of the bird. In a small saucepan, melt the butter and soak a piece of clean muslin or J-cloth in it. Wrap the pheasant completely in the cloth. Alternatively, smear the breast and legs generously with butter.

Roast for about 45 minutes–1 hour, depending on size. Test by pricking the thigh at the thickest point: the juices should run clear when the bird is cooked. Remove the cloth and keep the pheasant warm on a serving dish while you make the gravy.

Spoon off any surplus fat from the roasting tin (keep it for roasting or sautéing potatoes later). Put the roasting tin over a high heat and pour in the game or chicken stock to deglaze. Bring to the boil, and use a whisk to dislodge the crusty caramelised juices so they can dissolve into the gravy. Boil for a minute or two and adjust the seasoning to taste. Pour into a hot gravy boat.

Carve the pheasant and serve with some stuffing, gravy and the Salad of Rocket, Pomegranate and Game Chips.

Top Tip: This stuffing is also delicious for a chicken or a traditional roast turkey – multiply quantity by four.

Salad of Rocket, Pomegranate and Game Chips

Game Chips (see p167)
Generous amount of rocket leaves, or a
　mixture of rocket and other little leaves,
　such as misuna, mibuna, bok choi, daytonia,
　mache (lamb's lettuce) and buckler leaf sorrel
¹/₂ pomegranate
Pomegranate Molasses Salad Dressing
　(see p167)

Make the Game Chips and drain on kitchen paper.

To prepare the salad, wash and dry the leaves and keep refrigerated.

Extract the pomegranate seeds by holding the pomegranate cut-side down over a bowl. Tap firmly with the bowl of a wooden spoon to loosen the seeds. Keep refrigerated.

Just before serving, assemble the salad. Remove the salad leaves from the fridge and place in a deep bowl. Sprinkle some Pomegranate Molasses Salad Dressing over the green salad leaves and toss gently to coat the leaves. Add the pomegranate seeds and the Game Chips and toss gently again. Turn out on to a flat serving dish and serve with the roast pheasant.

Game Chips

SERVES 4   (**P**: 15 MINS/**C**: 15 MINS)

Game chips are traditionally served with roast pheasant, but they are also very good with guinea fowl or just as a snack with a drink.

450g (1lb) large even-sized potatoes
olive oil, for deep-frying
salt

Wash and peel the potatoes. For even-sized chips, trim each potato with a swivel-top peeler until smooth. Slice them very finely, preferably on a mandolin. Soak in cold water to remove the excess starch (this will also prevent them from discolouring or sticking together). Drain off the water and dry well.

Heat the olive oil to 180°C/350°F. Working in batches of a few dry slices of potato at a time, drop them in the oil and fry until golden and completely crisp. Drain on kitchen paper and sprinkle lightly with salt. Repeat until they are all cooked.

If they are not to be served immediately, they may be stored in a tin box and reheated in a low oven just before serving.

Other Good Things to Do with Game Chips:
Use to scoop up a warm, melting Camembert or Brie cheese.
Pour sizzling garlic butter over a bowl of homemade crisps and nibble immediately.

Pomegranate Molasses Salad Dressing

This versatile dressing is delicious with salad leaves, but also with grilled fish, grilled chicken and grilled vegetables.

Pomegranate molasses is made by reducing the juice of sour pomegranates to a thick, dark brown syrup that has a distinctive sweet and sour flavour. It's available from Asian shops and good delicatessens.

2 garlic cloves, crushed
1/4 teaspoon ground cumin
1/2 teaspoon sugar, plus extra if needed
4 tablespoons pomegranate molasses
2 tablespoons lemon juice
8 tablespoons extra virgin olive oil
salt and freshly ground black pepper

In a bowl, mix the garlic, ground cumin, sugar, pomegranate molasses and lemon juice. Whisk in the olive oil. Season to taste with salt and pepper, and add a little extra sugar if you think it's a bit too sharp.

It will keep for several weeks and there is no need to store it in the fridge.

Roast Rack of Lamb with Rosemary and Membrillo Aioli and Rustic Roast Potatoes

SERVES 8   (**P:** 20 MINS/**C:** 3 HOURS)

I love this recipe. My good friend the Australian cook Maggie Beer, from the Barossa Valley, made this membrillo aioli when she taught a class at the Cookery School a few years ago. Membrillo, or quince paste, is available from delicatessens and many good cheese shops, and brings a delicious, fruity flavour to the dish.

4 racks of lamb, or 1 leg of spring lamb
3 tiny sprigs of rosemary and 1–2 garlic cloves
  (optional)
salt and freshly ground pepper
sprigs of rosemary, to garnish

To serve:
Rustic Roast Potatoes (see p237)

For the rosemary and membrillo aioli:
2 teaspoons finely chopped rosemary
225ml (8fl oz) oil (sunflower, peanut or olive
  oil, or a mixture; we use 6 parts sunflower oil
  and 2 parts extra virgin olive oil)
2 free-range, organic egg yolks
$1/4$ teaspoon salt
dab of English mustard or $1/4$ teaspoon
  French mustard
1 dessertspoon white wine vinegar
1 garlic clove, crushed
40–50g ($1^1/2$–2oz) membrillo (quince paste)

Preheat the oven to 220ºC/425ºF/gas mark 7. Score the skin of the lamb; you may like to insert a few tiny sprigs of rosemary and slivers of garlic here and there on the skin side. Season with salt and pepper.

Roast for 25–30 minutes for a rack or $1^1/4$–$1^1/2$ hours for a leg, depending on the age of the lamb and how well done you like it.

Meanwhile, make the aioli. Put the chopped rosemary into a little saucepan with 3 tablespoons of the oil and warm gently for 2–3 minutes, ensuring you do not burn the herb. Set aside.

Put the egg yolks into a bowl with the salt, mustard, white wine vinegar and crushed garlic. Put the oil into a measuring jug. Take a whisk in one hand and the oil in the other, and drip the oil on to the egg yolks drop by drop, whisking at the same time. Within a minute you will notice that the mixture is beginning to thicken. When this happens you can add the oil a little faster, but not too fast or it will suddenly curdle – the egg yolks can absorb the oil only at a certain pace. Taste and add a little more seasoning and vinegar if needed.

(If the aioli curdles it will suddenly become quite thin, and if it is left sitting the oil will start to float to the top of the sauce. If this happens you can quite easily rectify the situation: put another egg yolk or 1–2 tablespoons boiling water into a clean bowl, then whisk in the curdled aioli $1/2$ teaspoon at a time until it emulsifies again.)

Chop the membrillo and warm gently in a little saucepan until it melts, then leave to cool. When it is cold, add it to the aioli with the infused rosemary oil and chopped rosemary. Taste and adust the seasoning if necessary, then store in the fridge until needed.

When the lamb is cooked, remove from the oven and allow to rest for 5–10 minutes. Carve, allowing 2–3 cutlets per person if using rack of lamb. Garnish with a sprig of rosemary and serve with the rosemary and membrillo aioli and Rustic Roast Potatoes.

Guard of Honour

A guard of honour looks mightily impressive for a dinner party. It is made up simply of two interlinked racks of lamb, tied in one or two places to secure while cooking. Add 5–10 minutes extra cooking time on top of the above recipe.

Other Good Things to Serve with a Rack of Lamb, Guard of Honour or Pangrilled Lamb Chops
1 Sauce Paloise (see Béarnaise Sauce, p295).
2 Spiced Aubergine (see p243).
3 Roast cumin and tzatziki.
4 Three sauces: Sauce Soubise (see p296), Mint Sauce (see p176) and redcurrant jelly.

Pangrilled Steak with Chipotle Chilli Butter

SERVES 8   (P: 20 MINS/C: 3 HOURS)

Chipotle in adobo is one of my favourite flavours. You can buy it in small tins from specialist food shops.

8 sirloin or fillet steaks, about 225g (8oz) each
1 garlic clove
salt and freshly ground pepper
extra virgin olive oil, for drizzling
watercress or rocket leaves

To garnish:
chopped parsley

For the chipotle chilli butter:
75g (3oz) butter
2 tablespoons chipotle chilli in adobo sauce
2 tablespoons chopped parsley

First make the chipotle butter. Cream the butter in a bowl and mix in the chipotle and chopped parsley. Shape into a roll, wrap in greaseproof paper, twist the ends like a Christmas cracker and refrigerate until needed.

About 1 hour before cooking, prepare the steaks. If using sirloin steaks, score the fat at 2.5cm (1in) intervals. Cut the garlic clove in half and rub both sides of each steak with the cut sides. Grind some pepper over the steaks and sprinkle on a few drops of olive oil. Turn the steaks in the oil and set aside for about an hour.

Heat the grill pan, season the steaks with a little salt and put them down on to the pan. For the weight given (see left), the approximate cooking time for each side of the steaks is:

	Sirloin	**Fillet**
Rare	2 minutes	5 minutes
Medium rare	3 minutes	6 minutes
Medium	4 minutes	7 minutes
Well done	5 minutes	8–9 minutes

If using sirloin steaks, once they are cooked turn them over on to the fat and cook for 3–4 minutes or until the fat becomes crisp.

Put the steaks on to a plate and leave them to rest for a few minutes in a warm place. Transfer to individual serving plates, with a slice of chipotle butter melting on top and some watercress or rocket leaves on the side. Sprinkle over some chopped parsley.

Other Good Things to Serve with a Steak
1 Mushroom à la Crème (see p241).
2 Béarnaise Sauce (see p295) and frites.

Roast Fillet of Beef with Béarnaise Sauce, Twice-cooked Roasted Potatoes with Shallots and Thyme Leaves

SERVES 8–10   (P: 20 MINS/C: 3 HOURS)

Caul fat is light, lacy fat which melts and bastes the meat during cooking.

1 whole fillet of well-hung dried aged beef, about 2.75kg (6lb), trimmed
1–2 garlic cloves
sea salt and freshly cracked pepper
pork caul fat (if available), or extra virgin olive oil, for drizzling
2–3 sprigs of thyme

To serve:
Twice-cooked Roast Potatoes with Shallots and Thyme Leaves (see p237)
flat mushrooms
Béarnaise Sauce (see p295)

Double over the fillet at the tapered end and tie it securely with fine butcher's cotton twine. Alternatively, ask your butcher to do the 'butchering' for you.

Preheat the oven to 230°C/450°F/gas mark 8.

Cut the garlic cloves in half and rub the fillet all over with the cut sides. Season well with lots of pepper and wrap loosely in caul fat (if using), then season well with sea salt; if you have no caul fat, season the fillet well with salt and pepper and drizzle with olive oil.

Heat a cast-iron grill-pan to very hot. Sear the beef until nicely browned on all sides.

Transfer it to a roasting tin and tuck a couple of sprigs of thyme underneath. Roast for 25–30 minutes. If you have a meat thermometer, the internal temperature should read 118°C/245°F. Alternatively, the meat should feel springy to the touch and when it is pierced with a skewer, the juices should be pale pink.

Transfer to a carving dish. Cover loosely with aluminium foil and allow to rest for 15–20 minutes, by which time the juices will have redistributed themselves and the beef will be uniformly medium rare. Serve cut in 5mm (¼in) thick slices, with Twice-cooked Roast Potatoes with Shallots and Thyme Leaves, flat mushrooms (sautéed whole for 5–8 minutes depending on size) and Béarnaise Sauce.

dinner for two

Dinner for two, what could be more romantic? In fact many of the principles for a successful dinner à deux can be applied to any formal dinner party.

This is an occasion when you want to make an impression so give yourself plenty of time to prepare. Firstly, check whether your guest has any dietary restrictions. Also, be clear about what time you want them to arrive – 7.30 for 8pm, for example. This will not only ensure that you are not caught in mid-preparation, but that you can time everything perfectly. For formal invitations the guest's name is always hand written in ink as is the envelope. For more informal and fun invitations you might fill the envelope with glitter or confetti or paper cut-outs.

Choose at least one recipe that can be prepared ahead or easily, 'cheat's recipes' I call them. Think about the presentation – if a goat's cheese salad calls for balsamic vinegar, serve it on a white plate with little drizzles. Likewise, a dusting of icing sugar is stunning on dark china. Herb butter balls look gorgeous in oyster shells.

If you are having a large party, see if you can get some help – teenage children or students may be up for some extra cash in return for clearing the table and washing up between courses and at the end of the meal. If you are planning a romantic evening, warn any flatmates or family and get them out of the way – bribe them with cinema tickets if necessary, but make sure they know to be discreet.

arranging a formal supper

Creating an atmosphere is vital. Lighting should be your first consideration. Candles do a beautiful job – dot the room with stately church candles, pretty tea lights or stylish candelabras. Paper lampshades are cheap but incredibly effective, for example, red Chinese lanterns can bring a soft-coloured hue to your table. Find some glass beads and thread colourful strings around the table to catch the candlelight. Velvet or satin ribbon can be used to tie bundles of breadsticks, napkins and cutlery. Line the breadbasket with a square of satin fabric.

Flowers are essential. For a romantic evening, go for luscious peonies, antique papery roses, frilly parrot tulips or gerberas with dark centres. For a formal dinner, aurum lilies or orchids are stunning, or ask your florist to create a centrepiece for your table.

Seating plans are helpful for large numbers. Not only do they avoid awkward dances round the table, but they are are a great way of introducing people. Even if you don't write it down, do give it thought.

Epicurean (see p170–172)
Pacific Oysters (see p158)
Roast Pheasant with a Pomegranate Salad and Game Chips (see p166–167)
Molten Chocolate Puds (see p246)
A Plate of Farmhouse Cheddar

To drink
You can't go wrong with oysters and Champagne but there are other possibilities such as Guinness or Guinness combined with Champagne to make Black Velvet. Good Chablis, too, is, as they say, no hardship to drink with oysters. Roast pheasant with gamey red Burgundy is a classic combination but the sweetness of the pomegranate seeds complicates matters. A New Zealand Pinot Noir will have some Burgundy character but often with a touch

more ripeness to counteract the sweetness. Châteauneuf-du-Pape is another possibility. Banyuls, the Provençal red dessert wine, has a great affinity with chocolate, as does port.

Cheat's dinner
Salad of Goat's Cheese with Rocket, Figs, Pomegranate Seeds (p67)
Bowl of Warm Mussels with Homemade Mayonnaise (see p98)
Brioche with Sugared Strawberries and Mascarpone (see p254)
Piece of Local Cheese with Turkish Figs or Medjool Dates

To drink
In keeping with the ease and simplicity of the menu, you can serve a Sancerre or Pouilly-Fumé (or any other dry, fresh Sauvignon Blanc, perhaps from New Zealand or the Cape) with both starter and main course. A light dessert Muscat will go with the brioche without overpowering it and provide an unusual accompaniment to the cheese, especially if it happens to be blue.

Vegetarian
Peach, Gorgonzola and Watercress salad (see p67)
Goat's Cheese, Spring Onion and Thyme Leaf Tart (see p160)
A Good Green Salad (see p94)
Frosted Blackcurrant Parfait with Blackcurrant Coulis (see p252)
Homemade Cottage Cheese with Fresh Herbs and Crackers (p274)

To drink
Once again, a Sancerre or Pouilly-Fumé will be perfect with both starter or main course, or you may prefer to try a Sauvignon Blanc from elsewhere. Such wines will enhance the fresh, clean flavours of the cottage cheese. If you want a red, keep it light: basic Bordeaux would be good.

Exotic
Moroccan Harira Soup (see p54)
Seared Fresh Salmon with Tomatoes and Herbs (see p110)
A Good Green Salad (see p94)
Summerberry Tart with Rose Water Cream (see p173)

To drink
In keeping with the exotic theme, why not choose an off-beat white? Perhaps a Viognier or a white Crozes-Hermitage, a Verdelho from Western Australia, a Roero Arneis from Piedmont or even an Assyrtiko from Greece. The rosewater cream needs a dessert Muscat or Gewürztraminer.

festive meals

Easter, Hallowe'en, Thanksgiving, Christmas – these are times to celebrate and party with friends and family. This chapter contains some of my favourite festive recipes, many of them with a clever twist. If you have served up the traditional turkey one too many times, you will love my spicy version. There is also spring lamb for Easter, Bacon and Cabbage for St Patrick's Day and pumpkin for Thanksgiving, not forgetting some boozy plum puddings for Christmas.

Roast Leg of Spring Lamb with Sea Salt, Mint Sauce and Glazed Baby Carrots

SERVES 6–8   (**P**: 15 MINS/**C**: UP TO 1³/4 HOURS)

Young spring lamb is sweet and succulent and needs absolutely no embellishment, apart from a dusting of salt and pepper and a little fresh mint sauce – made from the first tender sprigs of mint from the cold frame in the kitchen garden. Follow it with rhubarb tart made with the first pink spears of the season. For me this is the quintessential taste of Easter.

1 leg of milk-and-grass-fed spring lamb
sea salt (preferably Halen Mon or Maldon)
  and freshly ground pepper

For the gravy:
600ml (1 pint) lamb or chicken stock
  (see p295)
a little roux (see p139)

To serve:
Glazed Baby Carrots (see p238)
Roast Onions (see p236)
Rustic Roast Potatoes (see p237)
Mint Sauce (see recipe below)

If possible ask your butcher to remove the aitchbone (or rump bone) from the top of the leg of lamb so that it will be easier to carve later, then trim the knuckle end of the leg.

Preheat the oven to 180°C/350°F/gas mark 4.

Season the skin of the meat with sea salt and freshly ground pepper. Put the lamb into a roasting tin and roast – the time will depend on size and cooking preference. For rare, roast for 1–1¹/4 hours; for medium, 1¹/4–1¹/2 hours; or for well done, 1¹/2–1³/4 hours. When the lamb is cooked to your taste, remove the joint to a carving dish. Rest the meat for 10 minutes before carving.

Meanwhile, make the gravy. Skim the fat off the juices in the roasting tin and add the stock. Bring to the boil and whisk in a little roux to thicken slightly. Taste and allow to bubble up and reduce until the flavour is concentrated enough. Adjust the seasoning if needed and serve hot with the lamb, Glazed Baby Carrots, Roast Onions, lots of Rustic Roast Potatoes and Mint Sauce.

Mint Sauce

MAKES ABOUT 175ML (6FL OZ)   (**P**: 15 MINS)

Traditional mint sauce, made with tender young shoots of mint, takes only minutes to make. It's the perfect accompaniment to spring lamb, but for those who are expecting a bright green jelly, the slightly dull colour and watery texture comes as a surprise. That's how it ought to be – try it.

2 tablespoons finely chopped fresh mint
2 tablespoons sugar
6–8 tablespoons boiling water
2 tablespoons white wine vinegar or
  lemon juice

Put the chopped mint and the sugar into a bowl or sauce boat. Add the boiling water and vinegar or lemon juice.

Allow to infuse for 5–10 minutes before serving.

Easter Egg Nests

MAKES ABOUT 24   (**P:** 15 MINS/**C:** 15 MINS)

These nests are irresistible to kids of all ages, and grown-ups too!

175g (6oz) good-quality dark chocolate
   roughly chopped
110g (4oz) Rice Krispies
72 mini chocolate eggs

cupcake papers or ring moulds

Melt the chocolate in a heatproof bowl over a saucepan of hot water. Bring the water just to the boil, turn off the heat and allow the chocolate to melt in the bowl. Stir in the Rice Krispies.

Spoon the mixture into cupcake cases. Flatten a little and make a well in the centre. Fill each one with three speckled mini chocolate eggs. Allow to set and hide from the grown-ups.

Spicy Roast Turkey with Banana and Cardamom Raita

SERVES 10–15   (**P:** 15 MINS + 3³/₄ HOURS MARINATING/**C:** 3 HOURS)

1 free-range, organic turkey, 4.5–5.4kg (10–12lb)
extra virgin olive oil, for brushing
425ml (³/₄ pint) turkey or chicken stock (see p295)
175ml (6fl oz) cream
roux (optional; see p139)

For the spice paste:
2 tablespoons cumin seeds, toasted and ground
2 tablespoons paprika
2 teaspoons cayenne pepper
2 tablespoons ground turmeric
2 teaspoons sugar
2 teaspoons freshly ground pepper
1 tablespoon salt
4 garlic cloves, crushed
juice of 2 lemons
4 tablespoons extra virgin olive oil or
  vegetable oil

To serve:
Ballymaloe Country Relish or Mango Chutney
Banana and Cardamom Raita (see p294)
jewelled rice
sprigs of coriander

To make the spice paste, mix all the ingredients together in a bowl. Set aside 1–2 tablespoons for the sauce.

If you are cooking the turkey whole, put it into a roasting tin. Spread the spice paste all over the skin – breast, legs, wings – and tuck a little under the breast skin if possible. Alternatively, remove the breasts and legs. Bone the legs (retain the carcass and giblets to make a turkey stock). Spread the spice paste all over the surface of the turkey pieces and put them into a roasting tin. Cover and leave in the fridge for 3 hours, or better still overnight, to absorb the spicy flavours.

Preheat the oven to 180°C/350°F/gas mark 4. Brush the turkey with a little oil and roast for 3–3¹/₂ hours.* Check from time to time that the skin is not burning – you may need to cover loosely with aluminium foil about halfway through cooking.

Remove the turkey to a hot serving dish. Add the retained 1–2 tablespoons spice paste to the juices in the roasting tin. Stir and cook over a low heat for 3–4 minutes. Spoon off any excess fat. Add the stock and cream to the tin and bring to the boil. Whisk in a little roux if necessary. Taste and adjust the seasoning if needed.

Carve the turkey, or serve the turkey pieces. Spoon a little spicy sauce over each helping. Serve with Ballymaloe Country Relish or Mango Chutney, Banana and Cardamom Raita, jewelled rice and a green salad, with some sprigs of coriander to garnish.

* Note: When roasting turkey, allow about 15 minutes per 450g (1lb) plus an extra 15 minutes.

Zanne Stewart's Pumpkin Pie

SERVES 8   (**P:** 15 MINS/**C:** 1 HOUR)

My quest for a pumpkin pie started and ended with my friend Zanne Stewart, food editor of *Gourmet* magazine. Zanne suggested I use the terrific Eagle brand recipe. We've baked the pastry case first. I serve the pumpkin pie topped with whipped cream and drizzle honey over the top as Zanne's grandmother did.

425g (15oz) tin pumpkin purée
400ml (14fl oz) tin sweetened
  condensed milk
2 free-range, organic eggs
1 teaspoon ground cinnamon
¹/₂ teaspoon ground ginger
¹/₂ teaspoon freshly grated nutmeg
¹/₂ teaspoon salt

23cm (9in) shortcrust pastry case,
  baked blind, (see recipe on p247)
whipped cream and honey, to serve

Preheat the oven to 220°C/425°F/gas mark 7.

Whisk the pumpkin, condensed milk, eggs, spices and salt in a bowl until smooth. Pour into the pastry case and bake for 15 minutes. Protect the edges of the pastry if necessary. Reduce the temperature to 180°C/350°F/gas mark 4 and continue to bake for 35–40 minutes or until a knife inserted 2.5cm (1in) from the crust comes out clean. Allow to cool.

Serve topped with whipped cream and a drizzle of honey. Store any leftover pie in the fridge.

Other Yummy Toppings
1 Soured cream topping:
Mix 175ml (6fl oz) soured cream, 2 tablespoons sugar and 1 teaspoon vanilla extract in a medium bowl. After the pie has been baked for 30 minutes at 180°C/350°F/gas mark 4, spread evenly over the top and bake for another 10 minutes.
2 Streusel topping:
Mix 100g (3¹/₂oz) brown sugar and 75g (3oz) plain white flour in a bowl and rub in 50g (2oz) cold butter until crumbly. Add a generous 25g (1oz) chopped almonds, pecans or walnuts. After the pie has baked for 30 minutes at 180°C/350°F/gas mark 4, sprinkle the streusel evenly over the top and continue to bake for 10 minutes.
3 Chocolate glaze:
In a small saucepan over a low heat, melt 110g (4oz) chocolate chips and 1 teaspoon butter. Drizzle or spread over the top of the baked pumpkin pie.

Teeny Weeny Plum Puddings with Boozy Ice Cream

SERVES 8–10, IN TINY PUDDING BOWLS OR ESPRESSO CUPS   (P: 2 DAYS/C: 1¼ HOURS)

It has always been the tradition in our house to eat the year's first plum pudding on the evening it is made. As children we could hardly contain ourselves with excitement – somehow that plum pudding seemed all the more delicious because it was our first taste of Christmas. It was usually made in mid-November and everyone in the family had to stir so we could make a wish – I now know that it helped to mix it properly. It's fun to put silver plum pudding charms in the pudding destined to be eaten on Christmas Day.

175g (6oz) Muscatel raisins
175g (6oz) sultanas
175g (6oz) currants
175g (6oz) brown sugar
175g (6oz) white breadcrumbs
175g (6oz) organic beef suet, finely chopped
50g (2oz) good-quality candied peel
1 Bramley cooking apple, diced or grated
grated zest of 1 lemon
2 cloves, pounded
3 free-range, organic eggs
50ml (2fl oz) Jamaica rum
25g (1oz) shelled almonds, chopped
25g (1oz) shelled hazelnuts, chopped
pinch of salt

To serve:
Irish whiskey or brandy, for flaming brandy
  butter, rum or whiskey cream or Boozy Ice
  Cream (see recipe below)

In a large bowl, mix all the ingredients together very thoroughly and leave overnight; don't forget – everyone in the family must stir and make a wish!

Next day, stir again for good measure. Fill into tiny bowls or espresso cups, then cover with aluminium foil or a double thickness of greaseproof paper. Tie tightly under the rims with cotton twine, making a twine handle also for ease of lifting.

Pour a little boiling water in a wide pan or baking tray, and place the bowls or cups at the bottom – the water should come halfway up the side of the bowls or cups. Cover with a lid or aluminium foil and steam over a medium heat for 1¼ hours. Check regularly and top up with boiling water if needed.

Allow to cool completely and re-cover each pudding with fresh greaseproof paper. Store in a cool, dry place until needed. It will keep for months.

On Christmas Day or whenever you wish to serve the plum puddings, steam as above for a further 30 minutes.

Turn the plum puddings out on to very hot serving plates, pour over some Irish whiskey or brandy and ignite. Serve immediately on very hot plates, with brandy butter, rum or whiskey cream, or Boozy Ice Cream.

This recipe will also make 1 large or 2 medium puddings. The large size will serve 5–6 people, the medium 3–4. Cook for 6 hours on first day, re-cover and store in a cool place. Steam for 2 hours in a covered saucepan on the day of serving.

Boozy Ice Cream with Nuts and Raisins

SERVES 20   (P: 20 MINS + 3 HOURS FREEZING)

A gorgeous, rich ice cream with a scoopable texture. Serve it in small helpings.

110g (4oz) butter
225g (8oz) dark soft brown Barbados sugar
1 free-range, organic egg
65ml (2½fl oz) medium sherry
65ml (2½fl oz) port
1.3–1.5 litres (2¼–2½ pints) cream, lightly
  whipped

For the nuts and raisins:
110g (4oz) Muscatel raisins
65ml (2½fl oz) rum
65ml (2½fl oz) sherry
50g (2oz) fresh walnuts, chopped

x2 13 x 20cm (5 x 8in) loaf tins or plastic box

Melt the butter, stir in the sugar and allow to cool slightly. Whisk the egg and add to the butter and sugar with the sherry and port. Cool. Add the lightly whipped cream. Put into a plastic box, cover and freeze. Alternatively line two loaf tins with clingfilm, cover and freeze.

Meanwhile, put the raisins into a bowl, cover with a mixture of rum and sherry and allow to plump up. Chop the walnuts coarsely and add to the raisins just before serving.

Cut the ice cream in slices or serve in little glasses scattered with a few of the boozy raisins and some chopped walnuts. Sliced banana is also delicious with this combination.

Roast Bramley Apples with Amaretto Cream

SERVES 8   (**P**: 15 MINS/**C**: 45 MINS)

8 large Bramley apples
50g (2oz) butter, softened
50g (2oz) caster sugar
finely grated zest of 1 lemon
2 tablespoons golden sultanas
150ml (¼ pint) cream
1–2 tablespoons amaretto almond liqueur

Preheat the oven to 180°C/350°F/gas mark 4.

First core the apples and score the skin around the equator. Mix the butter with the sugar, lemon zest and sultanas. Stuff the butter mixture into the coring holes. Stand the apples in an ovenproof dish and pour about 150ml (¼ pint) water into the base of the dish.

Roast for 30–45 minutes. The apples should be beginning to burst – this is vital, so hold your nerve; they should look fat and squishy.

Meanwhile, whip the cream and add amaretto to taste. Serve the apples straight from the oven, with the amaretto cream.

Top Tip: Stuff the apples with mincemeat or cinnamon sugar (see p207).

Thanksgiving Turkey with Fresh Herb Stuffing, Spiced Cranberry Sauce and Bread Sauce

SERVES 10–12   (**P**: 30 MINS/**C**: 3¼ HOURS)

This is my favourite roast stuffed turkey recipe. Cook a chicken in exactly the same way but use one-quarter of the stuffing quantity given.

For the fresh herb stuffing:
350g (12oz) onions, chopped
175g (6oz) butter
400–450g (14oz–1lb) soft breadcrumbs
50g (2oz) chopped herbs such as parsley,
    thyme, chives, marjoram, savory, lemon balm
salt and freshly ground pepper

5 5.4kg (10–12lb) free-range, organic turkey,
    with neck and giblets
225g (8oz) butter
roux (optional; see recipe on p139)
1.2 litres (2 pints) turkey or chicken stock
sprigs of parsley, watercress or a sprig of holly
    to garnish

Large square of muslin (optional)

For the spiced cranberry sauce:
450g (1lb) sugar
125ml (4fl oz) wine vinegar
½ stick cinnamon, 1 star anise, 6 cloves and a
    5cm (2in) piece of fresh ginger, peeled and
    sliced, 1 chilli, split and seeded, all tied in a
    muslin bag
450g (1lb) cranberries
freshly squeezed lemon juice

To make the fresh herb stuffing, sweat the onions gently in the butter until soft, for about 10 minutes, then stir in the crumbs, herbs and a little salt and pepper to taste. Allow it to get quite cold. If necessary, wash and dry the cavity of the bird, then season and half-fill with cold stuffing. Put the remainder of the stuffing into the crop at the neck end.

Preheat the oven to 180°C/350°F/gas mark 4. Weigh the turkey and calculate the cooking time. Allow 15 minutes per 450g (1lb), plus an additional 15 minutes.

Melt 2 dessertspoons of the butter and, if you have a large piece of good-quality muslin, soak it in the melted butter, cover the turkey completely with the muslin, place in a roasting tin and roast for 3–3½ hours. The turkey browns beautifully, but if you like it even browner, remove the muslin 10 minutes before the end of the cooking time. Alternatively, smear the breast, legs and crop well with soft butter, and season with salt and freshly ground pepper. If the turkey is not covered with butter-soaked muslin, it is a good idea to cover the whole roasting tin with aluminium foil. However, your turkey will then be semi-steamed, not roasted in the traditional sense of the word.

The turkey is cooked when the juices run clear. To test, prick the thickest part at the base of the thigh and examine the juices – they should be clear. Remove the turkey to a carving dish, keep it warm and allow it to rest while you make the gravy.

To make the gravy, spoon off the surplus fat from the roasting tin. Deglaze the tin juices with the stock. Using a whisk, stir and scrape well to dissolve the caramelised meat juices from the roasting tin. Boil it up well, season and thicken with a little roux if you like. Taste and correct the seasoning. Serve in a hot gravy boat.

To make the spiced cranberry sauce, place the sugar, 225ml (8fl oz) water, the vinegar, spice bag and chilli in a non-reactive saucepan and bring to the boil. Add the cranberries and simmer very gently until they become tender. Some will burst, but that's OK. Add a little lemon juice to taste.

Serve with the turkey garnished with parsley, watercress or holly, roast potatoes (see recipe on p237), along with the spiced cranberry sauce, the bread sauce and the gravy.

Witches' Bread with Chocolate and Raisins

MAKES 1 LOAF or 8–10 MINI LOAVES
(**P:** 15 MINS/**C:** 45 MINS)

450g (1lb) plain flour, preferably unbleached
1 teaspoon bicarbonate of soda, sifted
1 teaspoon salt
2 teaspoons sugar
50g (2oz) good-quality dark chocolate,
  roughly chopped
50g (2oz) raisins
400ml (14fl oz) buttermilk, or 350ml (12fl oz)
  buttermilk beaten with 1 free-range, organic egg
butter, to serve

Preheat the oven to 230°C/425°F/gas mark 7.

In a large bowl, sift the flour and bicarbonate of soda, then add the salt, sugar, chocolate and raisins. Make a well in the centre and pour all the buttermilk in at once. Using one hand, mix in the flour from the side of the bowl to make a softish, but not too wet and sticky dough. When it all comes together, turn out the dough on to a floured work surface. Wash and dry your hands.

With floured fingers, tidy up the dough gently, flip it over, and tuck it in underneath. Pat the dough into a round about 4cm (1½in) deep. Cut a deep cross in the top with a sharp knife and prick in the centre of the four segments (to 'let the fairies out').

Bake for 10 minutes, then turn the oven down to 200°C/400°F/gas mark 6 and continue baking for a further 35 minutes or until cooked. If you are in doubt, tap the bottom of the loaf: it should sound hollow. Cool on a wire rack. Serve freshly baked, cut into thick slices and smeared with butter.

Hallowe'en Weeny Witches: make 8–10 mini loaves – don't forget to cut a cross in these too.

Lana Pringle's Barm Brack

MAKES 2 LOAVES   (**P:** 25 MINS + OVERNIGHT
SOAKING/**C:** 1 HOUR)

Halloween is a terrific time to have a party. In Ireland a barm brack is a must for this. The word 'barm' comes from the old English 'beorma', meaning yeasted fermented liquor. 'Brack' comes from the Irish 'brac', meaning speckled – which the cake is, with dried fruit and candied peel. Halloween has always been associated with fortune telling and divination, so various objects are wrapped up and hidden in the cake mixture – a wedding ring, a coin, or a thimble (signifying spinsterhood). I treasure this recipe, which was given to me by Lana Pringle. Her breads and cakes are legendary among her friends. Lana dislikes the din of food processors, so all her cakes are creamed, beaten and whisked by hand and baked in the Aga.

400g (14oz) mixed raisins and sultanas
450ml (15fl oz) strong tea
50g (2oz) glacé cherries, halved
50g (2oz) good-quality candied peel, chopped
110g (4oz) soft brown sugar
110g (4oz) granulated sugar
1 free-range, organic egg
400g (14oz) plain white flour
⅓ teaspoon baking powder
melted butter, for greasing

x2 13 x 20cm (5 x 8in) 6cm (2½in) deep tins

Put the raisins and sultanas into a bowl, cover with the tea (Lana occasionally uses a mixture of Indian and Lapsang Souchong, but any good strong tea will do) and leave overnight to allow the fruit to plump up.

Next day add the cherries, candied peel, sugars and egg and mix well. Sift the flour and baking powder and stir in thoroughly. The mixture should be softish, so add a little more tea if necessary.

Preheat the oven to 180°C/350F/gas mark 4. Grease the tins with melted butter (Lana uses old tins, heavier-gauge than are available nowadays; light, modern tins may need to be lined with silicone paper for extra protection.)

Divide the mixture between the tins and bake for 1 hour or until the bread is cooked. Lana bakes her barm bracks in the Aga, and after 1 hour she turns the tins around and gives them a further 10 minutes. Leave in the tins for about 10 minutes and then remove and cool on a wire rack.

Traditional Irish Bacon, Buttered Cabbage, Parsley Sauce and Scallion Champ

SERVES 12–15   (P: 10 MINS/C: 2 HOURS)

The Irish national dish of bacon and cabbage is real comfort food. When I serve this delicious peasant food for a dinner party everyone really tucks in and loves it to bits.

1.8–2.25kg (4–5lb) loin of bacon, smoked or
   unsmoked, with the rind on and a nice
   covering of fat
Buttered Cabbage (see recipe below)
Parsley Sauce (see recipe below)
Scallion Champ (see p237)

Put the bacon in a large saucepan, cover in cold water and bring to the boil over a medium heat. If the bacon is very salty there will be a white froth on top of the water, in which case it is preferable to discard the water and start again. Depending on how salty the bacon is, it may be necessary to change the water several times. Finally cover with hot water and simmer until fully cooked; allow 20 minutes for each 450g (1lb). It is cooked when a skewer will come out easily and the rind will peel off easily.

Remove the rind and serve with Buttered Cabbage, Parsley Sauce and Scallion Champ.

Parsley Sauce

SERVES 8–10   (P: 5 MINS/C: 15 MINS)

600ml (1 pint) milk
salt and freshly ground pepper
50g (2oz) roux (see p139)
30–50g (1–2oz) chopped parsley
a few slices of carrot (optional)
a few slices of onion (optional)
1 bouquet garni (optional)

If you are not using the vegetables or bouquet garni, bring the milk to simmering point. Season with salt and pepper and simmer for 4–5 minutes. Whisk in the roux until the sauce reaches a light coating consistency and season. Add the chopped parsley and simmer on a very low heat for 4–5 minutes. Serve hot.

If using vegetables and a bouquet garni, put them in a saucepan, add the cold milk and bring to simmering point. Season with salt and pepper and simmer for 4–5 minutes. Strain out the vegetables and bouquet garni and bring the milk back to the boil. Whisk in the roux until the sauce reaches a light coating consistency and season. Add the chopped parsley and simmer on a very low heat for 4–5 minutes. Serve hot.

Buttered Cabbage

SERVES 4–6   (P: 10 MINS/C: 5 MINS)

This method takes only a few minutes to cook, but first the cabbage must be sliced into fine shreds. It should be served the moment it is cooked.

450g (1lb) Savoy cabbage
25–50g (1–2oz) butter, plus extra to serve
salt and freshly ground pepper

Remove the tough outer leaves from the cabbage and discard. Divide the cabbage into four. Cut out the core and then cut the cabbage crossways into fine shreds. Put 2–3 tablespoons water into a wide saucepan and add the butter and a pinch of salt. Bring to the boil, add the cabbage and toss continuously over a high heat for 3–4 minutes then set aside, covered, for a few minutes. Toss again and adjust the seasoning to taste. Add a knob of butter and serve.

Buttered Cabbage with Caraway Seeds
Add 1–2 tablespoons caraway seeds to the cabbage at the start of cooking, and continue as per the above recipe.

Buttered Cabbage with Ginger
Add 2–3 teaspoons peeled and grated fresh ginger to the butter in the pan, and continue as per the above recipe.

Buttered Cabbage with Smoky Bacon
Heat 1 tablespoon extra virgin olive oil in a frying pan. Add 110g (4oz) smoked bacon lardons and cook until crisp. Add to the cooked cabbage, along with 50ml (2fl oz) cream, and allow to bubble for 2–3 minutes. Scatter with chopped parsley and serve.

Buttered Cabbage with Chorizo
Substitute chorizo for the smoked bacon in the above recipe, and omit the cream.

fabulous festivities

Let the occasion be your inspiration. Easter is a time for eggs, so why not hard-boil some eggs and paint them in bright colours. Hallowe'en is an excuse to play all sorts of old-fashioned games and to indulge in divination. Make some Witches' Bread or a Barm Brack and hide a ring, pea, stick and rag inside so your guests can predict their fortune. Colcannon is another traditional Hallowe'en dish — don't forget to put a little bowl on the windowsill for the fairies and to ward off evil spirits. To get everyone in the spirit of things, drape twists of black and orange crepe paper all over doors and windowframes. Weave cobwebby tangles of grey wool and make broomsticks from autumnal twigs and leaves. At Christmas, make old-fashioned orange pomanders (stud oranges with cloves) or mini puddings for your guests and leave brightly wrapped and beribboned gifts as place settings. Wrap the table in tinsel and long strands of ivy and the bases of thick church candles in coloured foil. Less is not more at this time of year.

Christmas dinner

Campari and Blood Orange Granita (see p66)
Spicy Roast Turkey (p178)
Rustic Roast Potatoes (see p237)
Spiced Aubergine (see p243)
Rocket or Watercress Salad
Teeny Weeny Plum Puddings with Boozy Ice Cream (see p179)

To drink

The ideal match with the turkey is a wine that many people feel poses difficulties for food: a ripe, buttery, oaky Chardonnay from the New World. Turkey cries out for it. There are lots of candidates but one of the best, because it's elegant and stylish as well as big and buttery, is the organic Bonterra Chardonnay from California. If you must have red try the Zinfandel from the same stable, or even the Sangiovese. Otherwise, any luscious red wine, such as Chilean Pinot Noir or an Argentinian Bonarda. The dark-brown, sugary Pedro Ximenez from Jerez is simply too sweet to drink on its own but with boozy ice cream and plum pudding it's magic. You can even pour some over this dessert and drink the rest!

St Patrick's Day

A Dozen Oysters and a Pint of Murphys (see p74)
Colcannon (see p236)
Traditional Irish Bacon, Cabbage, Parsley Sauce and Scallion Champ (see p184)
Irish Rhubarb Tart (see p271)

To drink

Murphys is what goes with oysters in Cork. If you want a bit more bite and bitterness, Guinness is the right partner. Alternatively, good Chablis, but this may seem curiously out of place for this day. Bacon and cabbage, strange as it may seem, are stunning with a Riesling Kabinett, which has the gentle sweetness and crisp backbone of a Granny Smith apple. Any good one will do, but ideally it should come from the Mosel. Ernst Loosen and von Kesselstatt are names to bear in mind. Rhubarb tart is very good, odd as it may seem, with a sweet Oloroso Sherry from a top producer like Lustau or Valdespino.

Thanksgiving dinner

Thanksgiving Turkey with Fresh Herb Stuffing, Spiced Cranberry Sauce and Bread Sauce (see p181)
Twice-cooked Roast Potatoes with Shallots and Thyme Leaves (see p237)
Zanne Stewart's Pumpkin Pie (see p178)

To drink

Cranberries and turkey are a terrific combination. Unfortunately wine and cranberries are a bit of a nightmare, so we must tread cautiously. This is not the time to open cherished old bottles of fine claret; you need something cheap, cheerful and pretty robust. Australian Merlot, Chilean Carmanere, Argentinian Bonarda or Bonarda/Shiraz all stand a good chance of fighting their way through the cranberries. In keeping with the American theme it might be an idea to try Bonny Doon's Big House Red or Cardinal Zin. Fetzer Merlot is another candidate. Pumpkin pie will need a dessert wine with a citrus character and one of the tastiest comes from California: Quady's Essencia Orange Muscat.

children's food

Children's parties should be bright and colourful, with food to match. This is a time for treats and indulgence, but sneak in healthy vegetables in wraps and sandwiches and use nutritious fruit and milk to make lurid-coloured smoothies. Give the recipes exciting names – crispy potato skins can become 'dragon's skin' and soured cream 'dinosaur milk.'

Icky Sticky Sausage Wraps

MAKES 10   (**P:** 15 MINS/**C:** 15 MINS)

1 tablespoon extra virgin olive oil, for frying
10 good-quality juicy pork sausages
4 tablespoons Sweet Chilli Sauce (see p296)
4 tablespoons soy sauce
2 tablespoons sesame seeds, for sprinkling
1–2 avocados, peeled and cut into wedges
10 small flour tortillas
some curly lettuce, we love Little Gem

If you want to cook the sausages in the oven, preheat it to 220°C/425°F/gas mark 7.

Heat the oil in a roasting tin or, if you prefer to fry the sausages, in a frying pan. Cook the sausages in the oven or the frying pan until golden on all sides.

In a bowl, mix the Sweet Chilli Sauce with the soy sauce. Slip in the sausages and toss until all are well coated with the sweet sticky glaze. Sprinkle with sesame seeds and toss again.

To assemble, peel the avocados and cut into thick slices. Heat a frying pan and heat a tortilla on both sides. Put a sausage, a wedge or two of avocado and some curly lettuce on to the tortilla. Turn up the end and roll over to make an open-ended wrap. Prepare 9 more wraps in the same way. Serve immediately.

Lunch Wraps

Wraps were inspired by the Mexican burrito – originally invented as a convenient way for cowboys and farmers to carry a packed lunch! For years Americans have been eating burritos filled with Mexican ingredients such as refried beans, salsa and coriander, but more recently they have acquired a new name and are now stuffed with a multitude of fillings inspired by cuisines from all over the world. They are the perfect easy casual food for breakfast, lunch or dinner. Have fun with the fillings!

flour tortillas
your choice of fillings

Heat a wide frying pan on a medium heat, lay a tortilla on the pan, warm on one side for about 15–30 seconds, then turn over to warm the other side. This makes it soft and pliable.

Lay the warm tortilla on a chopping board and arrange the filling, in a rectangle roughly 5 x 12.5cm (2 x 5in) in size, on the bottom half of the tortilla. Fold in the right and left edges, then fold the bottom edges over the filling and gently but firmly roll the tortilla over until the filling is completely enclosed.

Wraps can be made ahead, covered in clingfilm or aluminium foil and refrigerated. Depending on the filling they can also be reheated.

Open Wraps
Proceed as above but fold only in one side initially, and continue to roll until the filling is wrapped.

Fun Fillings
1 Lots of crunchy lettuce, goat's cheese, Roasted Red Peppers (see p298), Pesto (see p297) and crispy bacon or prosciutto.
2 Lots of crunchy lettuce, smoked salmon, cream cheese and dill, cucumber strips, freshly cracked pepper and a few crispy capers.
3 Lots of crunchy lettuce and rocket leaves, rare roast beef, Garlic Mayonnaise (see p296) and crispy French fried onions.
4 Lots of crunchy lettuce, roast chicken, fresh herb stuffing, Tarragon Mayonnaise (see p218) and sun-dried tomatoes.
5 Lots of crunchy lettuce, spicy chicken, crème fraîche, Cucumber Pickle (see p73) and coriander leaves.
6 Lots of crunchy lettuce, strips of Cheddar cheese, Cucumber Pickle (see p73), Ballymaloe Country Relish or mango chutney and spring onion.

children's birthday party

Birthday parties are a great opportunity to have as much fun as the children. Remove all the vases, ornaments and fragile objects from the rooms and prepare for an invasion.

The food should be as simple as possible. Consider making lots of cup cakes instead of one big confection – they are much easier for young kids to eat. Use different-coloured icings, rainbow sprinkles and sweeties to decorate. Ice each cake with letters from the alphabet to spell out the birthday name, or make meringue initials so that children can spell out their own.

Make kiddie-friendly sandwiches using pastry cutters to cut out stars and circles, with mustard and cress and slices of mini radishes to decorate – how grown up! Ice creams are a great treat and you can make them a bit special by decorating the cones with gingham ribbon. If you are a DIY whizz, you could make an ice-cream holder box out of MDF or perspex with holes cut out to fit the cones.

Make lots of fruit juice or smoothies instead of fizzy drinks so that they don't get too hyperactive, but serve them in fun plastic glasses with curly straws. Cut fresh fruit up into small chunks – if you make funny faces with banana and raisin eyes, berry noses and a big strawberry mouth, children might think they are sweeties and be persuaded to eat them.

Goodie bags are a must – make them up from leftover pieces of fabric or sheets of tissue paper. Fill them with small toys, crayons and sherbet. Tie them closed with ribbon and decorate them with big butterflies, cut from craft-shop stencils.

balloons and sparklers

This is a time for a riot of colour, pattern and exuberance. Put away your best china and buy lots of rainbow-coloured paper plates – plain, patterned or with popular cartoon characters. Use lots of lacy doilies to decorate plates and protect the table, and blow up as many balloons as you can – the children will have a lot of fun catching and popping them. A sweet idea is to write each child's name on a balloon and tie it to a chair as place settings. Hang cut-out birds and butterflies and deck the room with bunting – craft and gift shops will have lots of paper creations.

Adorn the cup cakes with stripy candles and little sparklers, but keep a close eye on the children when they are lit. Party poppers and streamers will fill the table with colour. If you can find squares of origami paper, you can make little boxes for chocolate eggs.

Provide glamorous headgear – sailor and clown hats, tiaras and play jewellery – and get the children to act out their costumes. And don't forget the old favourite games such as 'pass the parcel' and 'musical chairs'.

Remember to organise lots of crowd control – make sure a couple of other parents stay to help you. Children tire quickly, so don't let the party go on for too long or you run the risk of tears and tantrums from all the excitement.

Party time

Something for lunch

Penny's Cup Cakes

MAKES 36   (**P**: 15 MINS/**C**: 20 MINS)

My daughter-in-law is famous for her yummy cakes. Depending on how the cup cakes are decorated, they can fit any occasion – a wedding, christening, anniversary, children's party (see pp190–195).

450g (1lb) butter, at room temperature
450g (1lb) caster sugar
450g (1lb) self-raising flour
6 large free-range, organic eggs
1¹/₂ teaspoons vanilla extract
6 tablespoons milk

Icing: see recipes below
Decorations: dolly mixture, crystallised flowers, chocolate buttons, fondant hearts or stars, Smarties, streamers, tiny crackers, sparklers…

3 muffin trays, each lined with 12 muffin cases

Preheat the oven to 190ºC/375ºF/gas mark 5.

Put all the cup-cake ingredients except the milk into a food processor and whizz until smooth. Scrape down the sides, then add the milk and whizz again.

Divide the mixture between the muffin cases in 3 muffin trays (you may need to make the cup cakes in 3 separate batches), and bake for 15–20 minutes until the cakes have risen and are golden. Remove from the trays and cool on a wire rack.

Make one or several icings and smear over the tops of the cup cakes, then decorate with a selection of little items.

Arrange in a pyramid on 2–3 cup-cake stands or on a Perspex cake stand.

Lemon Icing

MAKES ENOUGH FOR 12 CUP CAKES (**P**: 5 MINS)

110g (4oz) icing sugar
finely grated zest of ¹/₂ unwaxed, organic lemon
1–2 tablespoons lemon juice

Sift the icing sugar into a bowl. Mix in the lemon rind and enough lemon juice to make a softish icing.

Dark Chocolate Icing

MAKES ENOUGH FOR 12 CUP CAKES
          (**P**: 15 MINS/**C**: 5 MINS)

175g (6oz) icing sugar
50g (2oz) cocoa powder
75g (3oz) butter
75ml (3fl oz) water
110g (4oz) caster sugar

Sift the icing sugar and cocoa powder into a mixing bowl. Put the butter, water and caster sugar into a saucepan. Set over a low heat and stir until the sugar has dissolved and the butter is melted. Bring just to the boil, then remove from the heat and pour at once into the sifted ingredients. Beat with a wooden spoon until the mixture is smooth and glossy. It will thicken as it cools.

Coffee Icing

MAKES ENOUGH FOR 12 CUP CAKES
          (**P**: 5 MINS)

225g (8oz) icing sugar
scant 1 tablespoon Irel coffee essence
about 2 tablespoons boiling water

Sift the icing sugar into a bowl. Add the coffee essence and enough boiling water to make icing the consistency of thick cream.

Chicken Goujons with Sweet Chilli Dip

SERVES 6–8   (**P:** 10 MINS/**C:** 10 MINS)

This is a clever, quick and delicious way to make a little chicken go a long way and tempting enough to wean kids off processed chicken nuggets.

good-quality oil, for deep frying
3 free-range, organic chicken breasts,
  skinned and boned
salt and freshly ground pepper
seasoned flour
beaten egg
fine white breadcrumbs

For the Sweet Chilli Dip:
125ml (4fl oz) Sweet Chilli Sauce (see p296)
freshly squeezed juice of ¹/₂–1 lime

Heat some oil in a deep-fryer. Cut the chicken breasts diagonally into 1cm (¹/₂in) strips. Season with salt and pepper. Turn the pieces in the seasoned flour, the egg and the breadcrumbs, or simply in some milk and seasoned flour.

Drop pieces individually into the hot oil and fry for 2–3 minutes or until crisp and golden. Drain on kitchen paper.

Serve immediately, with a bowl of Sweet Chilli Sauce mixed with lime juice, to taste.

Other Good Things to Serve with Goujons:

Garlic Mayonnaise

To 1 quantity of Homemade Mayonnaise (see p296), add 2 tablespoons of crushed garlic and 2 tablespoons of chopped parsley.

Chilli and Parsley Mayonnaise

To 1 quantity of Homemade Mayonnaise, add 1 roasted, peeled, deseeded and chopped fresh chilli and 2 tablespoons of chopped parsley.

Pesto Mayonnaise

Into 1 quantity of Homemade Mayonnaise, stir 3 generous teaspoons of Pesto (see p297).

Garlic and Sun-dried Tomato Mayo

Add 4–5 chopped sun-dried tomatoes to the Garlic Mayonnaise.

Spicy Tomato Mayo

Add 2 tablespoons of Ballymaloe Country Relish or a good tomato chutney into 1 quantity of Homemade Mayo (see p297).

197

Crispy Potato Skins with Dips

SERVES 4   (**P**: 15 MINS/**C**: 1¹/₄ HOURS)

8 large 'old' potatoes, such as Golden Wonders
melted butter or extra virgin olive oil, for brushing
salt and freshly ground pepper

Preheat the oven to 200ºC/400ºF/gas mark 6.

Prick the potatoes once or twice. Bake for
45–60 minutes depending on size. When
they are cooked, remove from the oven and
turn the oven up to 230ºC/450ºF/gas mark 8.

Slice the potatoes in half lengthways. Scoop out the flesh, set aside in a bowl and use later
for mashed potato or potato fish cakes.

Cut the skins into 3–4 pieces and arrange in a single layer in a roasting tin. Brush well with
melted butter or olive oil and season with salt and pepper. Bake for 10–15 minutes or until
crisp and delicious. Serve with a selection of dips.

Dips
Sweet Chilli Sauce (see p296)
soured cream
tuna mayonnaise and cucumber
melted cheese and chorizo

Hot Chocolate with Churros for Dunking

SERVES 4　　　　　　　(P: 5 MINS/C: 5 MINS)

100–110g (3¹/₂–4oz) good-quality dark chocolate
65ml (2¹/₂fl oz) water
600ml (1 pint) whole milk
1–2 teaspoons sugar
4 large teaspoons whipped cream
churros (Spanish fried sponge fingers) or
　ladyfingers, for dunking

Put the chocolate and water into a heavy-bottomed saucepan and melt over a very low heat. Meanwhile, in a separate saucepan, heat the milk until it just shivers before boiling. When the chocolate has melted, pour the milk into it, whisking all the time; the drink should be smooth and frothy. Taste and add some sugar if needed, and pour into warmed cups. Dunk the churros in the hot chocolate and enjoy!

Hot Chocolate with Marshmallows
Pop a fat marshmallow on to the top of the hot chocolate – luscious!

Chocolate Butterfly Buns

MAKES 24　　　　　　(P: 25 MINS/C: 20 MINS)

225g (8oz) butter, cut into dice and at
　room temperature, plus extra for greasing
275g (10oz) plain white flour,
　plus extra for dusting
225g (8oz) caster sugar
50g (2oz) cocoa powder
4 free-range, organic eggs
2 teaspoons baking powder
¹/₂ teaspoon vanilla extract

300ml (¹/₂ pint) whipped cream
icing sugar, sprinkles and/or praline for dusting

Dark Chocolate Icing (see p196)
2 bun trays

Preheat the oven to 220°C/425°F/gas mark 7. Grease the bun trays and sprinkle with flour.

Put the butter dice into a food processor, add the sugar, cocoa powder, flour, eggs, baking powder and vanilla extract and whizz for about 30 seconds. Clear the sides down with a spatula and whizz again until the consistency is nice and creamy, about 30 seconds more.

Spoon the mixture into the bun trays and transfer to the oven. As soon as the buns begin to rise (about 10 minutes), reduce the temperature to 190°C/375°F/gas mark 5. Bake for 20 minutes in total. Cool on a wire rack.

Meanwhile make the icing.

To assemble, cut the top off each bun, cut the top in half and set aside. Spread a layer of chocolate icing on the bottom part of the bun. Pipe a ruff of whipped cream across the centre and replace the two little top pieces, arranging them like wings. Dredge with icing sugar, and scatter with sprinkles and/or praline.

Top Tip: Bake in a conventional rather than fan-assisted oven if you can – this applies to all cakes and biscuits, but meringues benefit from fan-assisted ovens.

Strawberry Gelato in Sugar Cones

SERVES 6–8 (P: 20 MINS/C: 3 HOURS FREEZING)

This gelato is also yummy served alone on chilled plates with fresh strawberry sauce.

225g (8oz) caster sugar
300ml (¹/₂ pint) water
900g (2lb) very ripe strawberries
juice of ¹/₂ orange
juice of ¹/₂ lemon
700ml (1¹/₄ pints) whipped cream

6–8 sugar cones or ice-cream cones
fresh mint leaves, to garnish

For the strawberry sauce:
400g (14oz) strawberries
50g (2oz) icing sugar
freshly squeezed lemon juice (optional)

In a small saucepan, dissolve the sugar in the water over a medium heat and boil for 7–10 minutes. Set aside to cool.

Purée the strawberries in a food processor or blender, then sieve the purée into a bowl. When the sugar syrup is cold, mix in the orange and lemon juice. Stir the flavoured syrup into the strawberry purée and fold in the whipped cream.

Freeze immediately, preferably in a sorbetière, but if you don't have one, just stir once or twice during the freezing process. Store in the freezer, and transfer to the fridge 15–20 minutes before serving. Scoop the ice cream into balls and fill into the cones.

To make the strawberry sauce, clean and hull the strawberries and transfer to a blender. Add the icing sugar and blend until smooth. Sieve into a bowl, taste and add lemon juice if you like.

Pour the sauce over scoops of strawberry gelato and garnish with some fresh mint leaves.

Mini Sponges with Raspberry Jam and Cream

MAKES 12   (**P**: 30 MINS/**C**: 15 MINS)

A really terrific sponge recipe. If you'd rather make a cake, divide the mixture between two 18cm (7in) sponge cake tins.

125g (4¹/₂oz) butter, softened, plus extra
   for greasing
175g (6oz) plain white flour, plus extra for
   dusting
175g (6oz) caster sugar
3 free-range, organic eggs
1 teaspoon baking powder
1 tablespoon milk

icing sugar, for dusting

For the filling:
110g (4oz) homemade raspberry jam
300ml (¹/₂ pint) whipped cream

2 x 12-hole sloping cupcake tins

Preheat the oven to 180°C/350°F/gas mark 4. Grease and flour the tins well.

In a large bowl, cream the butter and gradually add the caster sugar, beating until soft, light and quite pale in colour. Add the eggs one at a time, beating well between each addition. (If the butter and sugar are not creamed properly and if you add the eggs too fast, the mixture will curdle, resulting in a cake with a heavier texture.)

Sift the flour and baking powder and stir in gradually. Mix all together lightly and add the milk to moisten.

Divide the mixture evenly between the tins. Bake for 10–15 minutes or until golden and firm to the touch. Turn out on to a wire rack and allow to cool.

Sandwich the cup cakes together in pairs with raspberry jam and cream. Dust with icing sugar.

Other Good Fillings for Mini Sponges
Kumquat Compote (see p267) and cream
Blackberry jam and cream
Green Gooseberry and Elderflower Compote (see p229)
Mango and passion fruit
Chocolate spread and cream
Lemon curd and cream

Meringue Initials

MAKES 20–30   (**P**: 45 MINS/**C**: 2 HOURS)

2 free-range, organic egg whites
110g (4oz) caster sugar
edible food colouring (optional)

To decorate: hundred and thousands,
   silver dragées, cocoa powder, or crystallised
   violets or rose petals
whipped cream, to sandwich or Chocolate
   Ganache, see p247 (optional)
sparklers (optional)

piping bag and small star nozzle (1cm/¹/₄in)

Preheat the oven to 110°C/225°F/gas mark ¹/₄ (a fan-assisted oven is good for meringues).

Whisk the egg whites until stiff but not yet dry. Fold in half the sugar and whisk again until the mixture will stand in a firm, dry peak. Carefully fold in the remainder of the sugar. Add a few drops of food colouring to create your desired effect. Transfer to a piping bag.

Line several baking trays with silicone paper. Pipe the required initials on to the paper – do two of each if you would like to sandwich them together with cream. The letters can be sprinkled with hundred and thousands, silver dragées or cocoa powder, but don't get too carried away. Bake in the oven for 2 hours or until the meringue shapes will lift easily off the paper. Turn off the oven and allow to cool in the oven.

When the meringues are cold, sandwich them together with cream or Chocolate Ganache (see p247).

It's fun to spell out children's names or write 'happy birthday' or a funny message. A few sparklers here and there on the final assembly add to the impact and excitement. (We sometimes scatter crystallised violets or rose petals over the meringues for a more grown-up version.)

portable food

Food for picnics and barbecues needs to be robust enough to travel well and be easy to serve. Many of these recipes can be cooked on a barbecue or camp fire or else eaten cold. Some of my favourite meals have been eaten outside, so I hope you will pack up a hamper, crank up the barbie and enjoy these recipes al fresco.

Paillarde of Chicken with Cucumber, Mango and Spearmint Salsa

SERVES 8   (P: 20 MINS/C: 10 MINS)

Butterflying chicken is a brilliant way to ensure that it cooks faster and more evenly on a barbecue. This recipe is easy-peasy and so delicious!

8 free-range, organic chicken breasts
4 tablespoons extra virgin olive oil
2 tablespoons chopped rosemary or marjoram
salt and freshly ground pepper

To serve:
rocket leaves
Cucumber, Mango and Spearmint Salsa
  (see below)

First prepare the chicken paillarde. Remove the skin, and inner fillet from each chicken breast if it is still attached, and retain for use in another recipe. Slice the chicken breast from top to bottom, keeping it attached along one side – you should be able to open it like a book.

Flatten each breast with the palm of your hand to ensure that it is of an even thickness. In a shallow dish, mix the olive oil and chopped rosemary or majoram. Season the chicken with salt and pepper and coat evenly with the rosemary oil. Allow to marinate until ready to cook.

Prepare the Cucumber, Mango and Spearmint Salsa.

Cook the chicken on a barbecue or preheated grill pan for 3–4 minutes each side, turning to give a criss-cross effect. Serve on a bed of rocket leaves with the Salsa.

Other Good Things to Serve with Chicken Paillarde:
1   Sweet Chilli Sauce (see p296)
2   Banana and Cardamom Raita (see p294)
3   Roast summer vegetables with Tapenade Oil (see p75)

Cucumber, Mango and Spearmint Salsa

SERVES 8   (P: 15 MINS)

1 small cucumber, cut into 5mm (1/4in) dice
salt
1 mango, peeled and cut into 5mm (1/4in) dice
3 tablespoons coarsely chopped spearmint
3 tablespoons coarsely chopped coriander
3 tablespoons shelled peanuts, roasted and
  coarsely chopped

For the dressing:
25g (1oz) soft brown sugar
1 tablespoon fish sauce (*nam pla*)
juice of 2 limes
1/2–1 chilli, deseeded and chopped

Put the diced cucumber in a sieve over a bowl. Sprinkle with salt and allow to release its juice.

To prepare the dressing, mix all the ingredients together.

Put the mango into a bowl, add the herbs, roasted nuts and the cucumber dice, and spoon over some dressing. Toss well and taste. Add more dressing if needed.

Wire-rack Salmon with Dill Butter and Roast Tomatoes

SERVES 10–20   (P: 15 MINS/C: 15 MINS)

Fish cooks brilliantly on the barbecue, provided you put it in a 'fish cage' for ease of turning. However, you can do a perfectly good job using two wire cake racks (see p210).

1–2 sides of fresh wild salmon, unskinned
extra virgin olive oil or melted butter
sea salt and freshly ground pepper

For the dill butter:
110–225g (4–8oz) butter
4–8 tablespoons chopped dill

For the roast tomatoes:
10–20 branches of cherry tomatoes on the vine
extra virgin olive oil, for drizzling

Up to 1 hour before cooking, sprinkle the salmon generously with sea salt. Chill until needed.

Light the grill or barbecue. When ready, lay the salmon fillets skin-side down on one of the wire racks. Brush the flesh with oil or melted butter and sprinkle with pepper. Put the other wire rack on top. Lay on the barbecue, 15–20cm (6–8in) from the heat, and cook for 10–15 minutes. Turn the entire cage over and cook for a further 5–6 minutes or until just cooked through – the time will depend on the thickness of the fish. Transfer to a serving plate.

Roast Cherry Tomatoes
Drizzle a little olive oil over the tomatoes and season with salt and freshly ground pepper. Cook on the barbecue for 5–6 minutes until they are warm through and just beginning to burst.

Meanwhile, make the dill butter. Melt the butter and stir in the dill. Spoon a little dill butter over the salmon and serve with the Roast Cherry Tomatoes.

Camilla Plum's Spatchcock Chicken with Roasted Fennel and Pickled Lemon

SERVES 6–8   (**P:** 20 MINS/**C:** 40 MINS)

1 free-range, organic chicken
salt and freshly ground pepper
chopped rosemary or thyme leaves
extra virgin olive oil, for drizzling
a few garlic cloves
4 fennel bulbs
4 pickled lemons (see p298)
8–24 potatoes, depending on size
seeds from 4 cardamom pods, crushed
1 teaspoon saffron strands
600ml (1 pint) natural yogurt

Preheat the oven to 180°C/350°F/gas mark 4 or heat the barbecue. Insert a heavy chopping knife into the top of the chicken, from the back end to the neck. Press down sharply to cut through the backbone. Or use poultry shears to cut along the outer length of the backbone as close to the centre as possible. Open the bird out as much as possible. Season with salt and freshly ground pepper, sprinkle with rosemary or thyme, and drizzle over a bit of olive oil.

Transfer to a roasting tin, skin-side upwards, and tuck the whole garlic cloves underneath. Roast in the oven for 40 minutes or until cooked through and golden. Alternatively barbecue about 15cm (6in) away from the coals for about 40 minutes. Allow to rest for 5–10 minutes.

Meanwhile cut the fennel bulbs into quarters through the root. Cut the lemons in half. If the potatoes are large, cut into chunks. Arrange all the vegetables on a roasting tray, drizzle with olive oil and season. Add the cardamom and a good pinch of saffron to the yogurt. Mix well and pour over the vegetables. Roast under the spatchcock chicken for 30–45 minutes. Serve.

Sticky Chicken Thighs with Soy and Ginger Sauce

SERVES 10   (P: 10 MINS + MARINATING/
                    C: 40 MINS)

10 free-range, organic chicken thighs
salt and freshly ground pepper

For the marinade:
225ml (8fl oz) soy sauce
3 tablespoons sunflower oil
3 tablespoons honey
3 tablespoons rice wine or dry sherry
1 tablespoon peeled and grated fresh ginger
2 garlic cloves, crushed
1–2 chillies, deseeded and finely chopped

To serve:
cucumber and lime wedges
Spicy Green Salad (see p91)
Sweet Chilli Sauce (see p296)

Mix all the ingredients for the marinade in a bowl. Score the skin of the chicken thighs. Put them into a large dish, cover with the marinade and turn well to coat. Cover and keep refrigerated for at least 1 hour, or even overnight.

Preheat the oven to 180°C/350°F/gas mark 4 or heat the barbecue.

Drain the chicken pieces, retaining the marinade for basting. Arrange the chicken skin-side up in a roasting tin or on the barbecue. Season with salt and pepper. Roast or barbecue for about 30 minutes, then baste every 10 minutes or so with some of the reserved marinade. Continue to cook until the chicken is cooked through and there is no pink.

Serve with cucumber wedges, lime wedges, some Spicy Green Salad and a bowl of Sweet Chilli Sauce for dipping.

Oriental Marinated Chicken Wings

SERVES 4   (P: 20 MINS + MARINATING/
                    C: 75 MINS)

20 chicken wings (see photograph on p209)
lime wedges

For the marinade:
2 garlic cloves, crushed
2 teaspoons peeled and grated fresh ginger
110g (4oz) onions, finely chopped
1 red chilli, deseeded
2 tablespoons dark soy sauce
2 tablespoons oyster sauce

For the dipping sauce:
6 tablespoons plum sauce
2 tablespoons Sweet Chilli Sauce (see p296)
1 tablespoon dark soy sauce
1 tablespoon rice vinegar, or to taste

Divide the chicken wings into 3 joints and retain the 2 joints closest to the body – save the wing tips for a stockpot.

To make the marinade, mix all the ingredients together in a medium bowl. Add the retained chicken wing pieces and toss well. Cover and leave to marinate in the fridge for at least 1 hour, better still for several hours or overnight.

Preheat the oven to 180°C/350°F/gas mark 4. To cook in the oven, transfer the chicken pieces to a deep roasting tin, cover with a lid or aluminium foil and cook for 15 minutes, then remove the cover and turn over the chicken pieces. Continue to cook, uncovered, for a further 35–45 minutes until fully cooked through, adding a splash of water during cooking if the chicken becomes too dry.

Meanwhile, make the dipping sauce by mixing all the ingredients together.

Serve the sticky chicken wings with the dipping sauce and some wedges of lime, and eat with your fingers – you will need lots of napkins and a finger bowl.

Roast Bananas with Chocolate and Roasted Hazelnuts

SERVES 6   (P: 5 MINS/C: 15 MINS)

6 ripe bananas
75–110g (3–4oz) good-quality dark chocolate,
  chopped
50g (2oz) roasted hazelnuts (or walnuts),
  chopped

To serve: crème fraîche or whipped cream

Cook the bananas, unpeeled, on the barbecue until black on all sides. Transfer to serving plates. Split the skin on one side and sprinkle some chopped chocolate and roasted nuts over the hot banana flesh. Serve immediately, with a dollop of crème fraîche or lightly whipped cream. Alternatively cook in the oven preheated to 180°C/350°F/gas mark 4.

Other Good Things to Serve with Roast Bananas
1 Cinnamon sugar – combine 110g (4oz) caster sugar and 1–2 teaspoons ground cinnamon.
2 A mixture of rum-soaked raisins and chopped walnuts.
3 Toffee sauce and chopped pecans.

a summer barbecue

Barbecues are relaxed occasions where the food is a bit hit or miss, but the sunshine makes up for that. The key to a successful barbie is, like every other kind of entertaining, preparation. The best place to start is with top-quality meat and fish. If you have a gorgeous steak, all you need to go with it is some extra virgin olive oil, sea salt, black pepper and fresh herbs. A good marinade works wonders on chicken wings and juicy prawns. You will also need lots of dips and sauces, as well as plenty of fresh bread – the Tear and Share bread (see p211 and p34) is perfect for grabbing hunks to wrap around sausages and mop up plates.

Roast corn on the cob and jacket potatoes can be cooked in aluminium foil, but put tomatoes on the vine straight onto the grill. A big green salad is also essential as well as a good flow of fresh fruit juice or lemonade. Pimms with lots of fruit and cucumber or a big bowl of punch is a good thing and stash bottles of white wine or champagne in a cool place – under the shade of a tree or in a bucket full of ice.

For dessert, wrap a banana in aluminium foil, bake in its skin and serve with chunks of chocolate or chopped nuts. It's an old classic but a real crowd pleaser.

The best thing about a barbecue is that normally reluctant cooks will often suddenly take charge of all the cooking, but do give them a break every so often. Or, as they do in Australia, everybody brings something to put on the barbie and cooks it themselves.

alfresco dining

Before your guests arrive, make sure you have room for everybody to sit comfortably – bring out chairs, stools and deckchairs and beg and borrow outdoor seating from neighbours and guests. Put lots of cushions on brick or stone walls, so people can perch on them and spread out rugs on grass.

Get hold of thick American-style tumblers for both soft drinks and wine – wine glasses are too difficult in the open air. You can buy drink holders on spikes that you push into the ground as well as silly foam beer holders.

For an evening meal, put candles in terracotta flowerpots filled with sand or find some of those big outdoor candles on sticks. Hang jam jars with tea lights from branches or place them on paths to light the way back to the house. Outdoor fairy lights are enchanting strung on trees, over bushes or draped around the structure of the house.

A note of warning – be careful where you position the barbecue – don't put it under hanging branches or close to shrubs and avoid smoking out your neighbours – or just invite them to the party too!

Periwinkles with Homemade Mayonnaise

We love to forage along the seashore. We've got lots of secret places where we gather cockles and mussels and razor claws – just enough for supper, and I always throw one of them back for good karma. Periwinkles are widely available: they nestle under stones and cling to the harbour walls. Not everyone finds the idea of eating wiggly little sea snails appetising; I love them now, but as a child the thought completely repulsed me. I used to watch in fascination as my Dad devoured them with relish out of a newspaper cornet on holidays in County Clare. Now our grandchildren giggle with delight as they help us to collect periwinkles and shrimps. When we picnic by the beach we light a fire in a small circle of stones so we can cook our little feast. (See photographs on p221.)

fresh live periwinkles *or* shrimps

To serve:
Homemade Mayonnaise or Garlic Mayonnaise
  (see p296)
vinegar (optional)
freshly baked brown bread
lemon wedges
wild watercress

To cook the periwinkles, bring plenty of salted water to the boil – you need 2–4 tablespoons salt to every 2.4 litres (4 pints) water. Add the periwinkles, then cook for 3–4 minutes, strain off the water and allow to cool.

When cold, serve with Homemade Mayonnaise or Garlic Mayonnaise. Some people love to dip them in vinegar. Either way you will need to supply a large pin for each person to extract the winkles from the shells.

Shrimps with Homemade Mayo
Shrimps are cooked in much the same way, but need slightly less cooking time. Bring the salted water to the boil. Toss in the shrimps – they will change colour from grey to pink almost instantly. Bring the water back to the boil and cook for 2–3 minutes; the shrimps are cooked when there is no trace of black at the back of the head. Drain immediately and spread out on a large serving plate to cool.

Serve with Homemade Mayonnaise and freshly baked brown bread, and perhaps a wedge of lemon and some watercress. Let the picnickers peel their own shrimps! (To peel, first remove the head, pinch the end of the tail and tug it, it will pull off half the shell. Remove the remainder of the shell with your fingers. Shrimps are much easier on the fingers than Dublin Bay prawns!)

Cruditées with Garlic Mayonnaise in Spotted Plastic Beakers

Cruditées with garlic mayonnaise or aioli are among my favourite starters. They fulfil all my criteria for a first course: small helpings of very crisp vegetables with a good garlicky homemade mayonnaise. The cruditées can be either very funky or frumpy, depending on the presentation. Serve them in spotted plastic beakers or shot glasses or on simple white plates – it's your call!

Another great plus for this recipe, I've discovered, is that children love cruditées. They even love aioli, provided they don't hear some grown-up saying how much they dislike garlic, and you can feel happy to see your children polishing off plates of raw vegetables for their supper. It's really quick to prepare and full of wonderful vitamins and minerals.

Cruditées are a perfect first course for winter or summer, but for them to be really delicious one must choose very crisp and fresh vegetables. Cut the vegetables into bite-sized bits so they can be picked up easily. You don't need knives and forks because they are usually eaten with fingers. Use as many of the following vegetables as are in season.

ripe tomatoes, quartered, or whole with the calyx on if they are freshly picked
purple-sprouting broccoli, broken (not cut) into florets
calabrese (green sprouting broccoli), broken into florets
cauliflower, broken into florets
french beans or mangetout
baby carrots, or larger carrots cut into sticks about 5cm (2in) long
cucumber, cut into sticks about 5cm (2in) long
tiny spring onions, trimmed
red cabbage, cut into strips
tender celery, cut into sticks about 5cm (2in) long
chicory leaves
red, green or yellow peppers, deseeded and cut into sticks about 5cm (2in) long
very fresh Brussels sprouts, halved or quartered
whole radishes, with green tops left on
fennel bulbs, cut into wedges
young asparagus
sugar peas, sugar snaps or fresh peas in the pod
parsley, finely chopped
thyme, finely chopped
chives, finely chopped
sprigs of watercress

To serve:
Garlic Mayonnaise (see p297)

A typical plate of cruditées might include the following: 4 sticks of carrot, 2–3 sticks of red and green pepper, 2–3 sticks of celery, 2–3 sticks of cucumber, 1 whole radish with a little green leaf left on, 1 tiny tomato or 2 quarters, 1 Brussels sprout, cut in quarters, and a little pile of chopped fresh herbs.

Wash and prepare the vegetables. Arrange them on individual white side plates with contrasting colours next to each other, with a little bowl of Garlic Mayonnaise in the centre. Alternatively, do a large dish or basket for the centre of the table. Arrange little heaps of each vegetable in contrasting colours. Put a bowl of Garlic Mayonnaise in the centre and then guests can help themselves.

Instead of serving the Garlic Mayonnaise in a bowl, you could make an edible container by cutting a slice off the top of a tomato and hollowing out the seeds. Alternatively, cut a 4cm (1½in) round of cucumber and hollow out the centre with a melon baller or a teaspoon. Then fill or pipe the mayonnaise into the tomato or cucumber and place in the centre of the plate of cruditées.

Other Good Things to Serve with Cruditées
1 Tapenade (see p75)
2 Dukkah (see p75)
3 Hummous bi tahina (see p118)

Ballymaloe Irish Stew in a Haybox

SERVES 4–6　(**P:** 45 MINS/**C:** UP TO 2 HOURS)

**Irish stew is a brilliant one-pot meal, a
wonderfully comforting traditional dish, and
great for entertaining. It's best made in early
summer when the lamb is still young and
sweet and the new-season onions and
carrots are small and tender.**

1.3kg (3lb) lamb chops or hogget (gigot or
　rack chops), not less than 2.5cm (1in) thick
6 medium onions or 12 baby onions
6 medium carrots or 12 baby carrots
salt and freshly ground pepper
1 litre (1³/₄ pints) lamb stock, chicken stock
　(see p295) or water
8–12 potatoes, or more if you like (Golden
　Wonder or Kerrs Pink are excellent)
sprig of thyme
1 tablespoon roux (optional; see p139)
2 tablespoons chopped parsley
1 tablespoon chopped chives

If you intend to cook the stew in the oven, preheat the oven to 180°C/350°F/gas mark 4.

Cut the chops into 50g (2oz) pieces and trim off some of the excess fat. Set aside. Render down the fat over a low heat in a heavy pan (discard the rendered-down pieces).

Meanwhile, peel the onions and, if they are large, cut them into chunks; if they are small, they are best left whole; and if young, leave some of the green stalks on. Scrape or thinly peel the carrots and, if they are large, cut them into large chunks; if young, leave them whole and leave some of the green stalks on.

Toss the meat in the hot fat until it is slightly brown. Transfer the meat to a casserole and season with salt and pepper, then briefly toss the onions and carrots in the fat in the pan. Add them to the casserole and season again. Deglaze the pan with a little lamb or chicken stock, pour into the casserole and add the rest of the stock.

Peel the potatoes and lay them whole on top of the casserole, so they will steam while the stew cooks. Season the potatoes. Add a sprig of thyme and bring to the boil on top of the stove. Cover and transfer to the oven, and cook for 1–2 hours depending on whether the stew is being made with tender lamb or tougher mutton; alternatively, simmer on top of the stove.

When the stew is cooked, pour off the cooking liquid, degrease it and reheat in another saucepan. If you like, thicken it slightly with a little roux. Taste and adjust the seasoning if needed, then add chopped parsley and chives and pour the liquid back over the stew. Bring it back up to boiling point and serve direct from the pot or in a large pottery dish.

Irish Stew with Pearl Barley
Add 2 tablespoons pearl barley to the stew with the vegetables. Increase the liquid to 1.2 litres (2 pints), as the pearl barley absorbs a considerable amount of liquid.

The Essential Picnic Haybox
No home should be without a haybox. It's a brilliant invention that certainly dates back to wartime and possibly long before. The idea is to make an insulated box that can be transported in the back of the car to your picnic spot. Stew is the poshest nosh for an autumn or winter race meeting, point-to-point or chilly boat ride. I always get a brilliant response when I whip off the lid and produce a piping-hot stew hours after it was made!

Start with a timber case with a separate lid. If you're handy, a couple of posh wine boxes can be adapted to make a haybox. Don't forget to add rope handles. Layer the bottom and sides with soft hay to a thickness of at least 6–8cm (2¹/₂–3in). When the casserole or earthenware pot of bubbling stew is ready, tuck it into the haybox, tightly pack more hay in around the sides and cover with another thick layer of hay and then the timber lid.

The haybox was initially invented to save fuel in wartime, as the food continues to cook by retained heat. My husband's family have very warm memories of a haybox, because his mother Myrtle used it to transport a delicious stew when they were at boarding school. How cool an idea is that?

Chest of Sandwiches with a Selection of Fillings Surrounded by Watercress

SERVES 8 (MAKES 24 SANDWICHES)

I was totally enchanted when my mother-in-law Myrtle Allen taught me how to make this chest of sandwiches soon after I arrived in Ballymaloe. It has been a delightful tradition in the family for several generations.

900g (2lb) loaf or round country loaf
50g (2oz) butter, at room temperature
salt and freshly ground pepper

Sandwich fillings might include:
scrambled egg and chives
Gravadlax with Sweet Mustard and Dill Mayo
 (see p140)
Roasted Peppers (see p298), mozzarella
 cheese and Pesto (see p297)
mature Cheddar cheese with Ballymaloe
 Country Relish or mango chutney and
 Cucumber Pickle (see p73)
roast chicken with Roasted Red Pepper
 Mayonnaise (see p297) and sunflower
 sprouts
tomato, buffalo mozzarella cheese, Tapenade
 (see p75) and basil leaves

To garnish:
salad leaves
watercress
flat parsley
cherry tomatoes
spring onions

You will need a long, sharp knife with a pointed tip. Insert the knife at the side of the loaf just over the bottom crust, just inside one end of the loaf. Push it through until it reaches, but does not go through, the crust on the far side. Without enlarging the cut through which the knife was inserted, work the knife in a fan shape as far forward as possible, then pull it out. Do the same from the opposite corner at the other end of the loaf. You should now be able to cut the bread away from the bottom crust inside without a noticeable mark on the exterior of the loaf.

Next cut through the top of the loaf to make a lid, carefully leaving one long side uncut, as a hinge.

Finally, with the lid open, cut the bread away from the sides. Ease it out carefully: it should turn out in a solid brick or a round, leaving an empty case behind.

Cut the bread into slices – long horizontal ones, square vertical ones or rounds, depending on the shape of the loaf. Carefully stack them, butter them and fill them with your chosen filling or fillings in the order in which they were cut. Don't forget to season each sandwich.

Press the sandwiches together firmly and cut into fingers (I usually cut each into 6). Fill them back, still in order, into the loaf.

For a picnic, close the top of the case – it will gape slightly because of the extra bulk of delicious filling. Cover with clingfilm – the sandwiches will stay very fresh.

For a party, leave the lid slightly open. Decorate inside and out with lettuce and watercress leaves, small ripe cherry tomatoes, spring onions and so on, so that the loaf looks like a little hamper overflowing with fruit and vegetables.

Cherry Tomatoes on the Branch, and Tiny Spring Onions and Radishes

very ripe cherry tomatoes on the branch
tiny spring onions, roots trimmed
lots of radishes, roots trimmed
unsalted butter
sea salt

Fill 1–3 separate little baskets with cherry tomatoes, spring onions and radishes. Picnickers can pick and nibble as they choose. We love to eat radishes as the French do, with unsalted butter and sea salt.

Rum and Raisin Cake

(**P**: 35 MINS/**C**: 60 MINS)

A favourite picnic cake (see opposite).

175g (6oz) raisins
6 tablespoons Jamaica rum
275g (10oz) butter, softened
175g (6oz) golden caster sugar
4 free-range, organic eggs
50ml (2fl oz) milk
1½ teaspoons vanilla extract
275g (10oz) plain white flour
1 tablespoon baking powder
50g (2oz) shelled walnuts, hazelnuts or
  pecans, chopped
1½ tablespoons Barbados sugar

23cm (9in) round tin with a spring form base,
  buttered and floured

Soak the raisins in the rum for 30 minutes. Drain and reserve the rum, and set aside the raisins.

Preheat the oven to 180°C/350°F/gas mark 4.

Cream the butter, add the caster sugar and beat until light and fluffy. Separate the eggs and set the whites aside. Add the egg yolks, one at a time, to the creamed butter, beating well between each addition. Mix in the retained rum, the milk and the vanilla extract.

Mix together the flour and baking powder and fold in, a little at a time, to the base mixture.

Whisk the egg whites until stiff and fluffy. Working in batches of a third of the beaten egg whites at a time, fold into the cake mixture; with the final third, add the raisins and chopped nuts.

Pour into the prepared tin, sprinkle with the Barbados sugar and cook for 45 minutes–1 hour, until the top is golden and the centre set and firm. Allow the cake to cool a little in the tin. Then invert and remove from the tin, invert again and finish cooling on a wire rack.

Gâteau Pithivier with Gruyère and Ham

SERVES 8   (**P**: 30 MINS/**C**: 50 MINS)

So yummy for a picnic (see photograph on p222), but also delicious for a summer lunch at home with a salad of organic leaves.

450g (1lb) puff pastry

For the filling:
350g (12oz) cooked ham, thinly sliced
350g (12oz) Gruyère or Emmental cheese,
  very thinly sliced
3 tablespoons Dijon mustard
egg wash, to glaze

Preheat the oven to 230°C/450°F/gas mark 8.

Divide the pastry in half and roll out each half to just under 5mm (¼in) thick. Cut each into a circle about 25cm (10in) in diameter. Sprinkle some water over a baking tray and put one of the pastry circles on it; put the other on a plate and chill both.

To assemble, you will need to divide the ham and cheese into 5 layers each. Lay some ham on the pastry in the baking sheet, top with a layer of cheese and repeat until all are used. Dab the layers with a little Dijon mustard every now and then. Slightly dome the stack in the centre, leaving a rim of about 2.5cm (1in) free around the pastry edge.

Brush the rim with egg wash or water. Place the other circle of puff pastry over the top and press it down well around the edges. Flute the edges with a knife. Make a small hole in the centre, brush the top with egg wash and leave for 5 minutes in the fridge.

With the back of a knife, nick the edge of the pastry 12 times at regular intervals to form a scalloped edge with a rose-petal effect. Mark long, curving lines from the central hole outwards to designate formal petals. Ensure you do not cut through the pastry – just score it.

Bake for 20 minutes, then reduce the oven temperature to 200°C/400°F/gas mark 6 and bake for a further 30 minutes. This is best eaten warm, but it also reheats remarkably well.

Hard-boiled Eggs and Dips

Hard-boiled eggs (or semi hard-boiled eggs) with dips are a must-have for a picnic. Easy, munchable food – no fuss and very moreish!

10–12 free-range, organic eggs
dips of your choice

Bring a pan of water to the boil. Gently slide in the eggs, bring the water back to the boil and simmer for 10–12 minutes.

Choose 3–5 dips: Tomato and Red Onion Salsa (see p294), Spicy Mayonnaise (see below), Tarragon Mayonnaise (see below), Tapenade (see p75), Anchovy and Flat Parsley Mayonnaise (see below), Dukkah (see p75).

Sausages with Dips

450g (1lb) best-quality pork sausages

Cook the sausages in the usual way and serve with 1 or more of the following dips.

Barbecue Sauce

MAKES ABOUT 225ML (8FL OZ)

This is yummy as a dip or sauce and can also be used to marinate the sausages, or pork, lamb or chicken.

4 tablespoons extra virgin olive oil
2 garlic cloves, crushed
110g (4oz) onions, finely chopped
400g (14oz) tin tomatoes, chopped
salt and freshly ground pepper
7 tablespoons tomato purée (see p294)
7 tablespoons red or white wine vinegar
4 tablespoons honey
4 tablespoons Worcestershire sauce
2 tablespoons Dijon mustard

Heat the oil in a frying pan, add the garlic and onions and cook over a low heat for 4–5 minutes. Add the tomatoes and their juice and cook for a further 4–5 minutes. Season with salt and freshly ground pepper. Purée in a liquidiser or food processor. Return to the heat, mix in the remainder of the ingredients and bring to the boil, then simmer for 4–5 minutes.

Anchovy and Flat Parsley Mayonnaise

To 300ml (1/2 pint) Homemade Mayonnaise, (see p296), add 6 mashed tinned anchovies and 2 tablespoons chopped flat parsley.

Honey Grainy Mustard and Rosemary Dip

4 tablespoons honey
4 tablespoons grainy mustard
1–2 teaspoons finely chopped rosemary

Mix all the ingredients together and put into a deep bowl ready for dipping.

Sweet Chilli Sauce Mixed with Lime Juice

4 tablespoons Sweet Chilli Sauce (see p296)
3–4 tablespoons freshly squeezed lime juice

Mix together to taste (see photograph on p223).

Tuna Mayonnaise

1 tin of tuna
2 tinned anchovies, crushed
2 tablespoons chopped parsley
300ml (1/2 pint) Homemade Mayonnaise, (see p296)

Mix all the ingredients together to taste.

Tarragon Mayonnaise

To 300 ml (1/2 pint) Homemade Mayonnaise (see p296), add 2 tablespoons chopped tarragon.

Thai Green or Red Curry Mayonnaise

1 tablespoon Thai green or red curry paste
4 tablespoons coconut milk
300ml (1/2 pint) Homemade Mayonnaise, (see p296)
2 tablespoons chopped coriander leaves
1–2 tablespoons apricot jam (optional)

Cook the curry paste in a wok or heavy frying pan for 3–4 minutes. Add the coconut milk and allow to bubble for a minute or two, then remove from the heat and leave to cool. Mix together with some mayonnaise and the chopped coriander. A bit of apricot jam is a delicious addition.

tips on portable food

Portable food is all about the packaging. Collect lots of plastic containers with lids – old takeaway boxes, for example, and big yogurt pots. A picnic hamper will help – many now come with straps and small compartments to hold cutlery and glasses, but you can improvise using an old small suitcase. If your destination is some hours away, don't take anything that will melt or lose its shape easily.

For barbecues, do try to marinate meat and make lots of dips and sauces. Set the barbecue up as near to the kitchen as possible, or keep a clear path. Be realistic: if you have a small kettle barbecue, don't try to cook a whole chicken or rack of ribs – stick to breasts and fillets. Fish will cook easily and quickly. Half-cook jacket potatoes in the oven first, then transfer them to the barbecue, otherwise you will be waiting for hours. Remember not to leave uncooked meat in the open for too long and keep a bucket of water nearby, just in case.

Best barbecued (see p208–211)
Pasta, Bocconcini and Tomato Salad (see p89)
Dukkah (see p75) with Fougasse (see p38)
Tear and Share Bread (see p34)
Edamame with Sea Salt (see p62)
Dill Mayo (see p297)
Cherry Tomatoes on the Branch (see p217)
Wire-rack Salmon with Dill Butter (see p204)
Oriental Marinated Chicken Wings (see p207)
Marinated Olives (see p62)
Roast Bananas (see p207)

To drink
The ideal wine here is one that will work with all the elements in the meal. While there are plenty of white wines, such as Viognier or New World Marsanne or Rousanne, which will work well, most people seem to prefer a red. The salmon will need a Pinot Noir or, perhaps, a Chinon, Bourgeuil or Saumur from the Loire, all of which will work well with the chicken too. An unusual but effective choice might be a straight red Bordeaux or Bordeaux Supérieur. If you want a wine for the bananas, consider a Late Harvest Sauvignon Blanc from Chile or Torcolato from Italy.

An old-fashioned picnic (see p220–223)
Frittata with Oven-Roasted Tomatoes, Chorizo and Goat's Cheese (see p117)
Periwinkles with Homemade Mayonnaise (see p212)
Sausages with Dips (see p218)
Gâteau Pithivier with Gruyère and Ham (see p217)
Marinated Olives (see p62)
White Soda Bread (see p36)
Rum and Raisin Cake (see p217)
Homemade Lemonade (see p288).

To drink
Pink wines really come into their own in the open air and for picnics they have the added bonus of going with virtually every savoury dish you care to mention. A good rosé – emphatically not Rosé d'Anjou or Blush Zinfandel, which are too flabby and sweet – has a lovely colour, a crisp backbone of acidity and a bone-dry finish. It may come from virtually anywhere in the wine world, but most often from the south of France or from Spain. You may want a red to accompany the sausages and the Pithivier, in which case a fruity Côtes du Rhone will do nicely. And for the rum and raisin cake you might like to chill a bottle of tawny port in a nearby stream.

Party picnic
Buttermilk Bread (see p36)
Bloody Mary Jellies (see p66)
Temari Sushi (see p45)
Alicia's No-Cook Chorizo (see p56)
Middle Eastern Mezze (see p118–119)
Sticky Chicken Thighs (see p207)
Belgian Chocolate Biscuit Cake (see p248)

To drink
As this is a party, kick off with some sparkling wine or even champagne if it's a very special occasion. This will serve as an aperitif and take you through to the sushi. The mezze and sticky chicken thighs won't object to decent fizz, but a chunky red wine will be better. Think in terms of ripe fruit: Malbec from Argentina, Grenache from Australia or Tempranillo from Spain. Or be really adventurous with an Agiorghitiko from Greece.

picnic on the beach

Before you set out, make sure you have packed the food carefully. Everything needs to be well secured for the journey, so the simplest thing is to transport food in the dishes they were cooked, for example, make individual frittata in muffin tins, keep the cake in its baking tin and wrap it in a collar of baking parchment to protect it. The next priority is to keep food cool. Carry salad greens in a bucket of water to keep them fresh. If you freeze a couple of bottles of water or juice (don't fill the bottles completely or else they will explode when they freeze), not only will you have cold drinks on the picnic, but they will also keep neighbouring food cool on the journey.

Don't forget plates, cutlery, napkins and a corkscrew as well as condiments – salt, pepper, oil and vinegar – plus plenty of paper napkins and a big rubbish bag to take the remnants home with you.

out in the open

Pies, especially the gâteau pithivier (see centre photograph and p217) are robust enough to survive a journey. Fat, juicy sandwiches and hard-boiled eggs are a picnic staple and cold sticky chicken wings are also a winner.

Part of the pleasure of eating outside is campfire cooking, so rather than bring everything fully prepared, see if you can build a small fire in a circle of stones to cook sausages or toast bread or marshmallows.

Choose a wine that does not need to be chilled. Rosé is great for the outdoors, but I have to say that there is nothing quite like champagne, drunk under the skies in plastic beakers.

Freezable wine sleeves are handy to have as are padded coolbags. You will also need a good rug or two – plastic backed to protect against damp ground – plus cushions to sit on, if you have room in the car. Director's chairs are cheap and fold up easily.

Simple food, a view to die for and a friendly dog to eat up the leftovers, what could be better?

foraging

I love foraging and I particularly love to combine foraging with entertaining. How wild and free it feels to organise a blackberry or cockle-picking expedition or a mushroom hunt and then head back to the kitchen to cook the spoils. And how much will you enjoy the meal knowing that you have searched for and picked the ingredients!

Wild Mushroom Soup

SERVES 8–9   (P: 15 MINS/C: 20 MINS)

Some years not a single mushroom pops up in the fields; other years they are so abundant that we are frantically making sauces, soups and so on to use them up. In fact, the soup base of this recipe, without the stock, is a perfect way to preserve field mushrooms for another time. If wild mushrooms are unavailable, flat mushrooms also make a delicious soup.

110g (4oz) onions
25g (1oz) butter
600ml (1 pint) Homemade Chicken Stock
  (see p295)
450g (1lb) wild mushrooms, such as *Agaricus
  campestris*
25g (1oz) white flour
salt and freshly ground pepper
600ml (1 pint) milk
cream (optional)
sprig of flat parsley, to garnish

Chop the onions finely. Melt the butter in a saucepan on a low heat. Toss the onions in it, cover and sweat until soft and completely cooked, about 7–10 minutes.

Meanwhile, heat the chicken stock to boiling point. Chop the mushrooms very finely, add to the onions and cook on a high heat for 3–4 minutes. Stir in the flour, reduce the heat to low and cook for 2–3 minutes. Season with salt and pepper, then gradually add the hot stock and the milk, stirring all the time. Increase the heat and bring to the boil. Taste, adjust the seasoning if needed and add a dash of cream if you like. Serve right away or reheat later.

Top Tip: If you can't be bothered to chop the mushrooms finely, just slice them. When the soup is cooked, whizz in a liquidiser for a few seconds.

Spring Nettle Soup

SERVES 6   (P: 15 MINS/C: 20 MINS)

This is now a 'cool' soup for spring dinner parties. Nettles grow in profusion throughout the Irish countryside – go foraging in spring when they are young and tender. You'll need gloves when you are gathering them so as not to sting yourself! Nettles are high in iron and other minerals and trace elements. Traditionally, Irish people ate a feed of nettles during the month of May to clear the blood after winter, and to keep away 'the rheumatics' for the coming year.

40g (1¹/₂oz) butter
275g (10oz) potatoes, chopped
110g (4oz) onions, chopped
110g (4oz) leeks, chopped
salt and freshly ground pepper
1 litre (1³/₄ pints) Homemade Chicken Stock
  (see p295)
150g (5oz) young nettle leaves
150ml (¹/₄ pint) cream or creamy milk,
  plus extra, to serve

Melt the butter in a heavy saucepan. When it foams add the potatoes, onions and leeks and toss them until well coated. Sprinkle with salt and freshly ground pepper. Cover with a paper lid (to keep in the steam) and the saucepan lid, and sweat on a low heat for 10 minutes or until the vegetables are soft but not coloured.

Discard the paper lid, add the stock, bring to the boil and boil until the vegetables are just cooked, about 10 minutes. Add the chopped nettles. Simmer, uncovered, for just a few minutes. Do not overcook or the vegetables will lose their flavour.

Add the cream or creamy milk and liquidise. Taste and adjust the seasoning if needed. Serve hot, with a swirl of cream on top.

Roast Rabbit with Potatoes, Onions and Thyme Leaves

SERVES 8   (**P:** 30 MINS/**C:** 1 HOUR)

Preheat the oven to 200°C/400°F/gas mark 6.

Bring the roasting tin to the table and serve this dish family-style. Chicken is also delicious cooked in this rustic way.

Joint the rabbits into 6 or 8 pieces each. Peel the potatoes if necessary (new potatoes may not need it) and cut into halves or quarters depending on size – they should be large chunks. Peel the onions, carefully trimming the root end so they keep intact during cooking; if the onions are large, cut in quarters through the root.

2 rabbits
8–16 potatoes, depending on size
8–16 shallots or baby onions
salt and freshly ground pepper
dry white wine, for drizzling
extra virgin olive oil, for drizzling
4 teaspoons thyme leaves
green salad, to serve

Transfer the rabbit, potatoes and onions to 1–2 roasting tins. Season well with salt and pepper. Drizzle generously with white wine and olive oil. Sprinkle with the thyme leaves and toss well.

Roast for 45 minutes–1 hour or until the rabbit is cooked and everything looks golden and slightly crispy at the edges. Serve with a good green salad.

A Salad of Rabbit (or Chicken) Livers with Apples, Hazelnuts and Wild Garlic Flowers

SERVES 4   (**P:** 15 MINS/**C:** 5 MINS)

First make the hazelnut oil dressing by whisking all the ingredients together.

1 sweet crisp dessert apple, such as
  Cox's Orange Pippin or Egremont Russet
2 tablespoons chopped hazelnuts
1 teaspoon butter
1 tablespoon extra virgin olive oil
4 rabbit or chicken livers
a selection of salad leaves, such as
  butterhead and oak leaf lettuce, frisée,
  wild sorrel, radicchio, rocket, salad burnet
  and golden marjoram
wild garlic flowers or chive flowers, to garnish

Cut the apple into thin julienne strips. Transfer to a bowl and mix with the hazelnuts and 1 tablespoon of the hazelnut oil dressing.

Heat the butter with the oil in a frying pan and cook the livers gently until just cooked (about 2–3 minutes, a little more if you prefer no trace of pink).

Meanwhile, toss the salad leaves in enough dressing to make them just glisten, and divide between the serving plates.

Place a quarter of the apple and nuts on each salad, and then set the warm livers on top. Sprinkle with wild garlic flowers or chive flowers and serve immediately.

For the hazelnut oil dressing:
6 tablespoons hazelnut oil
2 tablespoons white wine vinegar
1/2 teaspoon Dijon mustard
salt, freshly ground pepper and sugar to taste

Pasta with Chanterelles, Tapenade and Flat Parsley

SERVES 4–6   (**P:** 10 MINS/**C:** 20 MINS)

Bring the water to a fast rolling boil in a large saucepan, then add the salt and the pasta. Stir and cook until *al dente*, or just cooked but still slightly firm, about 10 minutes.

4.5 litres (8 pints) water
1 1/2 tablespoons salt
225g (8oz) penne, conchiglie or farfalle pasta
225–450g (8oz–1lb) chanterelle mushrooms,
  or a mix of different types of wild mushrooms
25g (1oz) butter
salt and freshly ground pepper
125ml (4fl oz) double cream
2–3 tablespoons Tapenade (see p75)
4 tablespoons chopped flat parsley

Meanwhile, gently wash the mushrooms under cold running water. Trim the stalks and discard. Slice the mushrooms thickly.

Melt the butter in a frying pan over a high heat. When it foams add the mushrooms and season with salt and pepper. Cook on a high heat – the juice will exude at first, but continue to cook until the mushrooms reabsorb it. Add the cream and allow to bubble for a few minutes. Stir in the Tapenade and remove from the heat.

Drain the pasta well, then put it back into the saucepan and add the sauce. Sprinkle on the flat parsley and toss gently. Turn into a hot bowl and serve immediately.

Elderflower Fritters with Gooseberry and Elderflower Compote

SERVES 8   (P: 20 MINS/C: 5 MINS)

Elderflowers are in full bloom in hedgerows all over the Irish countryside in late May and June. Make cordials, elderflower champagne, syrups, compote and fritters, and partner with gooseberries to impart a divine Muscat flavour. Elderflower vinegar is also delicious.

110g (4oz) plain white flour
pinch of salt
1 free-range, organic egg
150ml (1/4 pint) lukewarm water
extra virgin olive oil or sunflower oil
8–16 elderflower heads
caster sugar, for coating
Green Gooseberry and Elderflower Compote
  (see recipe below), to serve

Sift the flour and salt into a bowl. Make a well in the centre and drop in the egg. Using a whisk, gradually bring in the flour from the edges, adding the water at the same time.

Heat the oil in a deep-fryer to 180°C/350°F. Hold the flowers by the stalks and dip into the batter. Fry until golden brown, about 1 minute. Drain the fritters on kitchen paper, toss in caster sugar and serve immediately, with Green Gooseberry and Elderflower Compote.

Green Gooseberry and Elderflower Compote

SERVES 6–8   (P: 10 MINS/C: 15 MINS)

900g (2lb) green gooseberries
2–3 elderflower heads, plus extra to decorate
450g (1lb) sugar
600ml (1 pint) cold water

Top and tail the gooseberries.

Tie the elderflower heads in a little square of muslin, put them in a stainless-steel or enamelled saucepan, add the sugar and cover with the water. Bring to the boil over a medium heat and continue to boil for 2 minutes. Add the gooseberries and simmer until the fruit begin to burst, about 5–6 minutes.

Allow to cool. Serve in a pretty bowl and decorate with fresh elderflowers. This compote is also delicious with Yogurt and Cardamom Cream (see p266), Carrigeen Moss Pudding (see p232) or vanilla ice cream.

Compote of Blackberries and Apples with Sweet Geranium Leaves

SERVES 6   (P: 20 MINS/C: 10 MINS)

A delicious autumn dessert.

225g (8oz) sugar
450ml (16fl oz) water
8 large sweet geranium leaves
  (Pelargonium graveolens)
4 large dessert apples, such as
  Worcester Permain or Cox's Orange Pippin
275g (10oz) blackberries
shortbread biscuits, to serve

Put the sugar in a saucepan and add the water and sweet geranium leaves. Bring to the boil, stirring occasionally to dissolve the sugar, and boil for 1–2 minutes.

Peel the apples thinly, keeping a good round shape. Cut them into quarters, remove the core and trim the ends. Cut into segments 5mm (1/4in) thick. Add to the syrup, bring to the boil, reduce the heat to low and cover with a paper lid and then the saucepan lid. Poach until translucent but not broken, about 8–10 minutes. About 3–5 minutes before they have finished cooking, add the blackberries and simmer together so that they are both cooked at the same time. Allow to cool and chill in the fridge. Serve chilled, with little shortbread biscuits.

Compote of Cranberries and Apples
Substitute 175g (6oz) fresh cranberries for the blackberries in the above recipe.

Yogurt with Honey and Toasted Wild Hazelnuts

Delicious for either dessert or breakfast

best-quality natural Greek-style yogurt
strongly flavoured local honey
toasted wild hazelnuts, sliced

Serve a portion of chilled natural yogurt per person. Just before serving drizzle generously with really good honey and sprinkle with toasted hazelnuts.

Yogurt with dates, bananas and honey
Add some chopped dates and sliced banana to the yogurt and drizzle with honey.

Brown Trout with Marsh Samphire

SERVES 4   (P: 20 MINS/C: 15 MINS)

**A fat brown trout is a rare treat nowadays; if
you cannot get hold of any, rainbow trout
are available at virtually every fishmonger's.
Marsh samphire or sea asparagus grows in
the salt marshes along the coast. It is in
season from July to August and is so easy to
cook and delicious as a vegetable and
garnish. This combination is surprisingly
delicious and very quick to make.**

4 fresh trout, preferably brown
seasoned flour, for coating
butter
salt and freshly ground pepper
225–275g (8–10oz) marsh samphire
chopped parsley, to garnish
lemon wedges, to serve

For the parsley butter:
50g (2oz) butter
2–4 teaspoons finely chopped parsley
few drops of lemon juice

First make the parsley butter. Cream the butter, stir in the parsley and a few drops of lemon juice. Roll into butter pats or form into a roll and wrap in greaseproof paper or aluminium foil, screwing each end so that it looks like a cracker. Refrigerate to harden.

Gut the trout and fillet carefully, then wash and dry well. Put some seasoned flour in a shallow dish and coat the fillets. Shake off the excess flour and then spread a little butter on the flesh side, as if you were buttering a slice of bread rather meanly. Season with salt and freshly ground pepper.

Wash the marsh samphire well. Bring a large saucepan of unsalted water to the boil, add the marsh samphire and return to the boil for 3–4 minutes. Drain and toss in a little butter. Keep warm.

Heat a grill pan over a medium-high heat. When it is quite hot but not smoking, lay the fish fillets, buttered side down; the fish should sizzle as soon as they touch the pan. Reduce the heat slightly and cook for 3–4 minutes on the buttered side, then turn them over and continue to cook until crisp and golden, about 2–3 minutes. Serve immediately on hot plates with the marsh samphire, wedges of lemon and some parsley butter melting over the top, and sprinkle with chopped parsley.

Insalata di Campo

**A salad of wild leaves and flowers from the
woods and hedgerows is always a delight. It
might include any of the leaves and flowers
suggested below.**

For the leaves:
watercress
dandelion leaves
wood and field sorrel
salad burnet
red and green orach
chickweed
wild garlic leaves
lamb's tongue sorrel
wild thyme
bishop weed
samphire
daisy courgette

For the flowers:
primroses
violets
wild garlic flowers
borage, blue and white

dressing of your choice (see pp94–95)

Wash and carefully dry the leaves. Choose a dressing, such as Wholegrain Mustard and Honey, and toss the leaves in just enough of it to make them glisten. Scatter the flowers over the top and enjoy!

Carrigeen Moss Pudding

SERVES 6   (P: 20 MINS/C: 2 HOURS)

We find that visitors to Ireland are fascinated by the idea of a dessert made with seaweed, and carrigeen moss just bursts with goodness. But if too much carrigeen is used in this dish it will be stiff and really unpalatable. This recipe is from my mum-in-law, Myrtle Allen. It's the best and most delicious recipe I know for carrigeen.

Fred Dawes taught me how to forage for and harvest carrigeen moss. The word 'carrigeen' means 'little rock' in Gaelic, and Fred picks it off the rocks in the small cove of Ballyandreen in East Cork, after the spring tides. He then spreads it out on the grass on the cliffs, where it is washed by the rain and bleached by the sun. He turns it over every few days, and when it's ready he stores it in a paper or plastic bag in a dry cupboard. Carrigeen keeps almost indefinitely and is one of the most valuable of all our wild foods; it's loaded with vitamins, minerals and trace elements, particularly iodine. Another 'cool food' with a story – it helps our metabolism to work to its optimum and so breaks down fats while giving us lots of strength and energy.

semi-closed fistful of cleaned, well-dried carrigeen moss (about 7g/¹/₄oz)
850ml (1¹/₂ pints) whole milk
1 vanilla pod or ¹/₂ teaspoon vanilla extract
1 free-range, organic egg
1 tablespoon caster sugar

For the accompaniments:
compote of fruit in season (see p29 or p229), or soft brown sugar and lightly whipped cream

Soak the carrigeen in a little bowl of tepid water for 10 minutes. It will swell and increase in size.

Strain off the water and put the carrigeen into a saucepan. Add the milk and vanilla pod (if using; if using vanilla extract, do not add it now). Bring to the boil, then reduce the heat and simmer very gently, covered, for 20 minutes.

At this point and not before, separate the egg and put the yolk into a bowl. Add the sugar and vanilla extract (if using) and whisk together for a few seconds.

Pour the hot milk and carrigeen moss through a sieve on to the egg-yolk mixture, whisking all the time. The carrigeen will now be swollen and exuding jelly. Rub all this jelly through the sieve and beat it into the milky egg mixture. Test for a set on a chilled plate as you would with gelatine – a drop should set to a wobbly consistency within minutes. If it is too stiff, add a little more milk; if too runny, dip the sieve into the infused milk and push the carrigeen through again.

Whisk the egg white stiffly. Fold it gently into the carrigeen mixture. It will rise to make a fluffy top. Allow to cool completely, then chill.

Serve chilled with a fruit compote, such as poached rhubarb or Green Gooseberry and Elderflower (see p229), or with soft brown sugar and whipped cream.

Wild Damson Jam

MAKES ABOUT 4–4.5KG/9–10LB
          (P: 10 MINS/C: 30 MINS)

Damsons, bullaces or wild plums grow wild in many parts of Ireland, ripening towards the end of September. We love collecting them, and eat lots freshly picked; the surplus we make into damson pies, compotes and jam. The fruit also make a delicious sauce to accompany roast pork with crackling, and freeze perfectly. The new cultivated varieties of damson are much sweeter than the wild; if using cultivated fruit you would need to reduce the sugar to 1.8kg (4lb) for 2.75kg (6lb) fruit.

2.75kg (6lb) damsons
butter
850ml (1¹/₂ pints) water
2.75kg (6lb) sugar

Stainless steel preserving pan
Hot sterilised jars

Preheat the oven to 160°C/320°F/gas mark 3.

Pick over the fruit carefully, discard any damaged damsons, and wash and drain well. Grease a stainless-steel preserving pan with butter to prevent the damsons from sticking to the bottom and put in the fruit and water. Stew them over a low heat until the skins break, about 8–10 minutes, stirring regularly.

Meanwhile, put the sugar in an ovenproof dish and pop it into the oven to warm. Add it to the fruit and stir over a low heat until the sugar is dissolved. Increase the heat and boil steadily, stirring frequently. Skim off the stones and scum as they rise to the top. After 15 minutes boiling, test for a set – it should register 220°C/100°F on a sugar thermometer. Alternatively, put a little jam on a cold plate, allow to cool for 1–2 minutes. If it trembles when pressed with the tip of your finger, the jam is set.

Pour into hot sterilised jars and cover. Store in a cool dry place.

food from the wild

If you know what to look for, you can make a wonderful feast after a day in the wild. Wild food adds a whole new dimension to your menu and is a much welcome seasonal change from the familiar supermarket offerings. Cooked fresh, herbs, plants, mushrooms, fruit and fish will taste better than anything bought in a supermarket. And foraging is not limited to autumn, when there is such an abundance of wild food. Once you get in tune with your local area, you will find delicious treasures from the fields, woods and seashore to incorporate into menus all year round: carrigeen moss, periwinkles, field sorrel, marsh samphire, watercress, elderflowers, crab apples, blackberries, sloes, damsons, hazelnuts, rosehips and a myriad of shellfish along the shores if you live close to the sea. Go with an experienced forager the first few times – someone who knows one end of a mushroom from the other if you do not, or get a good book on the subject – and take a walk on the wild side.

A good day's work

Wild mushroom soup (see p226)
Roast rabbit with potato, onion and thyme leaves (see p228)
Insalata di Campo green salad (see p231)
Compote of blackberry and apples with sweet geranium leaves (see p229)

To drink

Soup and wine generally don't strike up much of a relationship, but a small glass of dry – and it has to be dry – Amontillado Sherry makes each taste more intensely of itself. Roast rabbit with the scent of thyme is an easy match for any number of medium-bodied red wines, but Barbera d'Asti from Piedmont in north-west Italy is quite simply perfect. And if the budget allows you could trade up to a Barolo to similar effect. The compote is more difficult but a 20-year-old Tawny Port will be no hardship to drink with it.

veg and spuds

The all-important side dishes. Here are some fantastic vegetable and potato dishes to accompany your meals. Many of the recipes in the previous chapters will have led you here, but feel free to pick and choose to suit your menu. Tomato Fondue, Mushroom à la Crème, Piperonata and Cucumber Neopolitana are all brilliant examples of versatile vegetable dishes that can be cooked ahead, reheated and frozen.

Root Vegetable Mash 1

SERVES 6 (**P:** 15 MINS/**C:** 45 MINS)

225g (8oz) parsnips, cooked and mashed
225g (8oz) Jerusalem artichokes, braised and
 mashed
110g (4oz) celeriac, mashed
110g (4oz) potatoes, cooked and mashed
1–2 tablespoons chopped parsley (optional)
25–50g (1–2oz) butter
salt and freshly ground pepper

Mix all the mashed root vegetables and the
parsley together, beat in the butter and
season well.

Root Vegetable Mash 2

SERVES 6 (**P:** 15 MINS/**C:** 45 MINS)

110g (4oz) swede, cooked and mashed
225g (8oz) carrots, cooked and mashed
350g (12oz) parsnips, cooked and mashed
1–2 tablespoons chopped parsley (optional)
25–50g (1–2oz) butter
salt and freshly ground pepper

Mix all the mashed root vegetables and the
parsley together, beat in the butter and
season well.

Colcannon

SERVES 8 (**P:** 15 MINS/**C:** 30 MINS)

**Songs have been sung and poems have been
written about colcannon. It's one of Ireland's
most famous potato dishes: comfort food at
its very best and terrific for a party.**

Did you ever eat colcannon
When 'twas made with yellow cream
And the kale and praties blended
Like a picture in a dream?
Did you ever scoop a hole on top
To hold the melting lake
Of the clover-flavoured butter
Which your mother used to make?

1.3kg (3lb) 'old' potatoes, such as Golden
 Wonder or Kerrs Pink, unpeeled
salt and freshly ground pepper
450g (1lb) Savoy cabbage or spring cabbage,
 or kale
225ml (8fl oz) milk
25g (1oz) spring onion, finely chopped
 (optional)
50g (2oz) butter

Scrub the potatoes, put them in a saucepan of cold water, add a good pinch of salt, cover and bring to the boil. When the potatoes are half cooked – about 15 minutes for 'old' potatoes – strain off two thirds of the water. Replace the lid on the saucepan, put on a low heat and allow the potatoes to steam until they are cooked.

Meanwhile, remove the dark outer leaves from the cabbage and discard; wash the cabbage and cut into quarters, then remove the core and slice crossways (if using kale, remove the central rib). Put a little water in a large saucepan and bring to the boil. Add the cabbage or kale and cook until soft. Drain, season with salt and pepper and add a little butter.

When the potatoes are just cooked, put the milk in a saucepan, add the spring onion (if using) and bring to the boil. Pull the skin off the potatoes and discard. Mash quickly while they are still warm and beat in enough boiling milk to make a fluffy purée (if you like, put the potatoes in the bowl of a food mixer and beat with the spade). Stir in the cooked cabbage and adjust the seasoning to taste.

For perfection, serve immediately in a hot dish, with a lump of butter melting in the centre.

Colcannon can also be made ahead and reheated later: cover the dish so it doesn't get too crusty on top, pop it in an oven preheated to 180°C/350°F/gas mark 4, and warm through for 20–25 minutes.

Roast Onions

SERVES 6–8 (**P:** 5 MINS/**C:** 30 MINS)

**Just pop the onions into the hot oven – they
don't even need to be peeled. The flesh
becomes soft and melting. I'm always
surprised that so few people cook onions in
this ultra-simple way.**

450g (1lb) small or medium onions, unpeeled
butter or extra virgin olive oil
sea salt

Preheat the oven to 200°C/ 400°F/gas mark 6.

Cook the onions on a baking tray until soft – this can take anything from 10 to 30 minutes depending on size. Serve in their jackets. To eat, cut off the root, squeeze out the onion and enjoy with butter or olive oil and salt.

Scallion Champ

SERVES 4–6   (P: 10 MINS/C: 30 MINS)

A bowl of mashed potatoes, flecked with green spring onions and with a blob of butter melting in the centre, is 'comfort food' at its best.

1.3kg (3lb) 'old' potatoes, such as Golden Wonders or Kerrs Pink, unpeeled
salt and freshly ground pepper
110g (4oz) spring onions, chopped (use both the bulb and the green stem), or 50g (2oz) chives, chopped
300–350ml (1/2 pint–12fl oz) milk
50–110g (2–4oz) butter

Scrub the potatoes and cook them in their skins in boiling salted water.

Put the chopped spring onions or chives in a saucepan and cover with the milk. Bring slowly to the boil and simmer for 3–4 minutes, turn off the heat and leave to infuse.

Peel and mash the freshly boiled potatoes and, while they are hot, mix in the hot milk and onions or chives, then beat in the butter. Season to taste. Serve in a large serving dish, or in individual bowls, with a knob of butter melting in the centre.

Scallion champ may be put aside and reheated later, covered, in an oven preheated to 180°C/350°F/gas mark 4 for 20–25 minutes.

Scallion and Potato Cakes
Shape leftover Scallion Champ into potato cakes. Heat some butter, clarified butter (see p108) or oil in a frying pan and cook the cakes on both sides. Serve piping hot.

Wild Garlic Mash
Add 50–75g (2–3oz) roughly chopped wild garlic leaves to the milk just as it comes to the boil. Continue as above.

Rustic Roast Potatoes

SERVES 4–6   (P: 10 MINS/C: 45 MINS)

So quick and easy. Just scrub the spuds well, and don't bother to peel them.

6 large 'old' potatoes, such as Golden Wonder or Kerrs Pink
extra virgin olive oil, beef dripping, or duck or goose fat, for drizzling
sea salt

Preheat the oven to 230°C/450°F/gas mark 8.

Scrub the potatoes well. Cut into quarters lengthways, or into rounds about 2cm (3/4in) thick. Put into a roasting tin, drizzle with olive oil (or heat the fat or dripping in the oven until sizzling and toss in the potatoes) and toss so they are just coated. Roast for 30–45 minutes depending on size. Sprinkle with sea salt and serve in a hot terracotta dish.

Rustic Roast Potatoes with Rosemary
Mix 6–8 sprigs of rosemary or some coarsely chopped rosemary with the olive oil and cook as above. Serve garnished with fresh sprigs of rosemary.

Rustic Roast Potatoes with Cumin
Mix 1–2 teaspoons roasted and ground cumin seeds with the olive oil and cook as above.

Twice-cooked Roast Potatoes with Shallots and Thyme Leaves

SERVES 8–10   (P: 15 MINS/C: 40 MINS)

I love to cook potatoes and shallots (or baby onions) in the roasting tin after I've roasted a duck. The duck fat and juices soak into the vegetables and give them a sublime flavour.

8–10 large potatoes, boiled in their skins
24–30 shallots
3–4 tablespoons duck or goose fat, or extra virgin olive oil
sea salt and freshly ground pepper
2–3 tablespoons thyme leaves

Preheat the oven to 230°C/450°F/gas mark 8.

Peel the potatoes (no need if they are new potatoes) and cut in 2cm (3/4in) slices. Peel the shallots and cut in half if large.

In 1 or 2 roasting tins, heat the fat or oil. Put in the potato slices and shallots, season and add the thyme leaves. Toss gently to coat in the fat or oil. Roast for 30–40 minutes, turning regularly, until the outsides are all crisp and golden.

Mary Jo McMillin's Gratin Dauphinoise

SERVES 6–8   (**P**: 10 MINS/**C**: 30–45 MINS)

Everyone loves this rich potato dish, and it is so easy; put it in the oven alongside a roasting chicken or leg of lamb.

2 garlic cloves, crushed
salt and freshly ground white pepper
225ml (8fl oz) milk, warmed
125ml (4fl oz) cream
40g (1^1/$_2$oz) butter, sliced
1kg (2^1/$_4$lb) even-sized potatoes (we use
   Golden Wonder or Kerrs Pink)
40–50g (1^1/$_2$–2oz) Gruyère cheese or Cheddar
   cheese, grated

Preheat the oven to 200°C/400°F/gas mark 6.

In a 2.4 litre (4 pint) baking dish, sprinkle the garlic, salt and pepper. Add the milk, cream and slices of butter and place the dish in the oven to heat.

Meanwhile, peel and thinly slice the potatoes. When the milk is bubbling at the edges, remove the dish from the oven but do not turn off the oven. Strew sliced potatoes into the dish and sprinkle with the cheese. Return to the oven and bake for 30–45 minutes or until the potatoes are tender and the top is golden brown.

Glazed Carrots

SERVES 4–6   (**P**: 10 MINS/**C**: 10 MINS)

You might like to try this method of cooking carrots; admittedly it takes a little vigilance, but the resulting flavour is a revelation to many people.

450g (1lb) organic carrots (Early Nantes and
   Autumn King have particularly good flavour)
10g (^{1}/$_2$oz) butter
125ml (4fl oz) water
salt and sugar, to taste
chopped parsley or mint, to garnish

Cut off the tops and tips of the carrots, scrub and peel thinly if necessary. Leave very young carrots whole, cut others into even slices 1cm (^{1}/$_2$in) thick, either straight across or diagonally.

Put them in a saucepan with the butter, water and some salt and sugar. Bring to the boil, cover and cook over a low heat until tender, by which time the liquid should have all been absorbed; if not, remove the lid and increase the heat until all the water has evaporated.

Taste and adjust the seasoning if needed. Shake the saucepan so the carrots become coated with the buttery glaze. Serve in a hot vegetable dish, sprinkled with chopped parsley or mint. Freshly roasted and ground cumin or coriander are also delicious.

Note: It is really important to cut the carrots to the same thickness, otherwise they will cook unevenly.

Baby Carrots
Scrub the carrots with a brush, but don't peel. Trim the tails, but if the tops are really fresh, leave a little of the stalks attached. Cook and glaze as above.

Melted Leeks

SERVES 6–8   (**P**: 10 MINS/**C**: 20 MINS)

8 medium leeks
50g (2oz) butter
salt and freshly ground pepper
chopped parsley or chervil, to garnish

Cut off the dark green leaves from the top of the leeks. Slit the leeks from the top until about half way down the centre and wash well under cold running water. Slice into 6mm (^{1}/$_3$in) rounds.

Melt the butter in a heavy flameproof casserole dish; when it foams, add the leeks and toss gently to coat with butter. Season with salt and pepper. Cover with a paper lid and then a close-fitting lid. Reduce the heat to very low and cook for 8–10 minutes, stirring every now and then, until semi soft and moist. Turn off the heat and allow to continue to cook in the heat for 4–5 minutes. Serve on a warm dish, sprinkled with chopped parsley or chervil.

Melted leeks with rosemary: before tossing, add 1–2 tablespoons of freshly chopped rosemary to the leeks.

Melted leeks with ginger: Add 2 teaspoons freshly grated ginger to the foaming butter before adding the leeks.

Tomato Fondue

SERVES 6　　　　(P: 10 MINS/C: 25 MINS)

Tomato Fondue has a myriad of uses – we serve it as a vegetable dish, as a sauce for pasta, a filling for omelettes, and topping for pizza or a base for bean stew.

1 tablespoon extra virgin olive oil
110g (4oz) onions, sliced
1 garlic clove, crushed
900g (2lb) very ripe tomatoes, skinned, or
　2$^{1}/_{2}$ x 400g (14oz) tins tomatoes
salt, freshly ground pepper and sugar, to taste
1 tablespoon of one or a mix of any of these
　chopped herbs, such as mint, thyme, parsley,
　lemon balm, marjoram or basil
few drops of balsamic vinegar

Heat the olive oil in a flameproof casserole dish or non-reactive saucepan. Add the sliced onions and garlic, toss to coat them well in oil, cover and sweat on a low heat until soft but not coloured. It is vital for the success of this dish that the onions are completely soft before the tomatoes are added.

Slice the tomatoes and add with all their juice to the onions. Season with salt, pepper and some sugar (tinned tomatoes need lots of sugar because of their high acidity). Add a generous sprinkling of herbs. Cook, covered, for 10 minutes, then remove the lid and continue to cook until the tomatoes soften (cook fresh tomatoes for a shorter time than tinned, in order to preserve the lively fresh flavour). Just before the end of cooking, sprinkle in a few drops of balsamic vinegar to enhance the flavour.

Tomato Fondue with Chilli

While the onions are sweating, add 1–2 chopped fresh chillies or 4 sliced Hungarian wax chillies.

Tomato Fondue with Chilli and Coriander

While the onions are sweating, add 1–2 chopped fresh chillies and 4 tablespoons coriander leaves.

Tomato Fondue with Kabanossi

Five minutes before the end of cooking, add 1–2 sliced kabanossi sausages – great with pasta.

Tomato Fondue with Chorizo

Ten minutes before the end of cooking, add 1 sliced chorizo.

Tomato Fondue with Chorizo and Black-eyed or Cannellini Beans

Add 400g (14oz) of black-eyed or cannellini beans to the recipe above, just before the end of the cooking time, and heat through.

Tomato Fondue with Green Olives and Marjoram

Add 110g (4oz) green olives and 2 tablespoons of marjoram to the above recipe 5 minutes before the end of cooking. Serve with meatballs or hamburgers.

Cucumber Neapolitana

SERVES 6　　　　(P: 10 MINS/C: 25 MINS)

A terrifically versatile vegetable dish that may be made ahead and reheats well. It is also delicious served with rice or pasta and makes a great stuffing for tomatoes. It is particularly good with roast lamb.

10g ($^{1}/_{2}$oz) butter
1 medium onion, sliced
1 large, organic cucumber
4 very ripe tomatoes
salt, freshly ground pepper and sugar
65ml (2$^{1}/_{2}$fl oz) cream
1 dessertspoon freshly chopped mint
Roux (optional; see p139)

Melt the butter in a heavy-bottomed saucepan. When it foams add the onion, then cover and sweat for about 5 minutes until the onion is soft but not coloured.

Meanwhile, peel the cucumber and cut into 1cm ($^{1}/_{2}$in) cubes. Add to the onion, toss well and continue to cook.

Scald the tomatoes with boiling water for 10 seconds. Skin the tomatoes and slice into the pan, then season with salt, freshly ground pepper and a pinch of sugar. Cover the pan and cook for a few minutes until the cucumber is tender and the tomatoes have softened, then add the cream and bring back to the boil. Add the chopped mint. If the liquid is very thin, thicken it by carefully whisking in a little roux.

Cucumber Neapolitana keeps for several days and may be reheated.

Variation
Use 450g (1lb) courgettes or patty pan squash instead of the cucumber.

Mushroom à la Crème

SERVES 8   (P: 10 MINS/C: 20 MINS)

Like Tomato Fondue and Piperonata (see p243), Mushroom à la Crème is another of our great convertibles. If you keep some in your fridge or freezer you can use it in a myriad of ways. It can be served as a vegetable, or as a filling for vol au vents, bouchées or pancakes, or as a sauce for pasta, steak or hamburgers. It may be used to enrich casseroles and stews or, by adding a little more cream or stock, it may be served as a sauce with beef, lamb, chicken, veal or fish. A crushed clove of garlic or a teaspoon of freshly grated ginger can be added while the onions are sweating.

25g (1oz) butter
175g (6oz) onions, finely chopped
450g (1lb) mushrooms, sliced
squeeze of fresh lemon juice
225ml (8fl oz) cream
1 tablespoon freshly chopped parsley
1 tablespoon freshly chopped chives
  or marjoram (optional)
salt and freshly ground pepper

Melt half the butter in a heavy saucepan until it foams. Add the chopped onions, cover and sweat on a low heat for 5–10 minutes or until quite soft but not coloured. Set aside.

Meanwhile, melt the rest of the butter in a frying pan and cook the sliced mushrooms, in batches if necessary. Season each batch with salt, pepper and a tiny squeeze of lemon juice. Add the mushrooms to the onions in the saucepan over a medium heat, then add the cream and herbs and allow to bubble for a few minutes. Taste and adjust the seasoning.

Mushroom à la Crème keeps well in the fridge for 4–5 days and also freezes perfectly.

Wild Mushroom à la Crème
For the mushrooms in the recipe above, substitute wild field mushrooms or a mixture of mushrooms, such as oyster, enoki, shiitake, nameko, girolle or chanterelle.

Mushroom à la Crème with Ginger
To the sweated onions add 1–2 teaspoons of grated fresh ginger – delicious with chicken breast, pasta or a hamburger.

Buttered Courgettes with Marjoram

SERVES 4   (P: 5 MINS/C: 10 MINS)

450g (1lb) courgettes, no longer than
  13cm (5in)
25g (1oz) butter
dash of extra virgin olive oil
2–3 tablespoons chopped marjoram
salt and freshly ground pepper

Top and tail the courgettes and cut them into 5mm (¼in) slices. In a large frying pan, melt the butter over a medium heat and add a dash of olive oil. Toss in the courgettes, coating them evenly in the butter and oil. Cook, tossing occasionally, for 4–5 minutes or until tender. Sprinkle in the chopped marjoram and season to taste. Turn into a hot serving dish and serve immediately.

Note: it is important to undercook the courgettes slightly as they continue to cook after they have been removed from the heat.

Broccoli with Anchovy Butter

SERVES 4   (P: 15 MINS/C: 15 MINS)

450g (1lb) broccoli
freshly ground pepper
50g (2oz) butter
4 tinned anchovy fillets, chopped

First cook the broccoli in boiling, salted water (use 3 teaspoons salt to 1.2 litres/2 pints of water). Drain well.

Melt the butter in a small frying pan, add the anchovy fillets and allow to sizzle for just a minute. Add the broccoli, sprinkle on some pepper, toss and taste. Adust the seasoning if needed.

Piperonata

SERVES 8–10   (P: 10 MINS/C: 40 MINS)

Another brilliant easy entertaining basic. We use this not only as a vegetable dish but also as a topping for pizzas, as a sauce for pasta, grilled fish or meat, and as a filling for omelettes and pancakes.

2 tablespoons extra virgin olive oil
1 garlic clove, crushed
1 onion, sliced
2 red peppers
2 green peppers
6 large very ripe tomatoes
salt, freshly ground pepper and sugar, to taste
few basil leaves

Heat the olive oil in a flameproof casserole dish, add the garlic and cook for a few seconds, then mix in the sliced onion and allow to soften over a low heat, covered, for 5–10 minutes.

Meanwhile, prepare the peppers: cut them in half, remove the seeds, cut into quarters and then into crossways strips. Add to the onion and toss in the oil; replace the lid and continue to cook.

Skin the tomatoes (cover in boiling water for 10 seconds, then pour off the water and peel immediately). Slice the tomatoes and add them to the casserole. Season to taste with salt, pepper, some sugar and a few leaves of basil. Cook until the vegetables are just soft, about 30 minutes.

Piperonata, Bean and Chorizo Stew
Add a tin of rinsed haricot beans, black-eyed beans or chick peas to the Piperonata, with 110g (4oz) sliced chorizo sausage. Continue to cook for about 10 minutes or until the chorizo is fully cooked.

Spiced Aubergine

SERVES 6   (P: 15 MINS/C: 20 MINS)

This is another of our favourite recipes and is completely delicious served with a rack of lamb or a few lamb chops. It is also great with pork and divine partnered with soft goat's cheese and a few rocket leaves as a starter. It keeps well in the fridge for 4–5 days.

800g (1³/₄lb) aubergines
225ml (8fl oz) vegetable oil
2.5cm (1in) cube of fresh ginger, peeled and
    coarsely chopped
6 large garlic cloves, coarsely crushed
50ml (2fl oz) water
1 teaspoon whole fennel seeds
2 teaspoons whole cumin seeds
350g (12oz) very ripe tomatoes, skinned and
    finely chopped, or 400g (14oz) tin tomatoes
    and 1 teaspoon sugar
1 tablespoon freshly ground coriander seeds
¹/₄ teaspoon ground turmeric
¹/₄ teaspoon cayenne pepper (more if you like)
sea salt
50g (2oz) raisins

Cut the aubergines into 2cm (³/₄in) thick slices. Heat 175ml (6fl oz) of the oil in a deep 25–30cm (10–12in) frying pan. When it is almost smoking, add a few aubergine slices and cook until golden and tender on both sides. Remove and drain on a wire rack over a baking sheet. Repeat with the remainder of the aubergine slices, adding more oil if necessary.

Put the ginger, garlic and water into a blender. Blend until fairly smooth.

Heat 3 tablespoons of the oil in the frying pan. When it is hot, add the fennel and cumin seeds and stir for just a few seconds (careful not to let them burn). Add the tomatoes (and sugar if using tinned tomatoes) the ginger/garlic mixture, coriander, turmeric, cayenne and salt. Taste and correct the seasoning. Simmer, stirring occasionally until the spice mixture thickens slightly, about 5–6 minutes.

Add the fried aubergine slices and raisins, and coat gently with the spicy sauce. Cover the pan, turn the heat to very low and cook for another 3–4 minutes. Serve warm.

The spiced aubergine mixture is also good served cold or at room temperature as an accompaniment to hot or cold lamb or pork.

sweet things

The best part of the meal. A good dessert will simply seduce you, making your mouth water even before you take a spoon to it. And once you have – well, one is never enough. Light or heavy, chocolatey or fruit-based, creamy or spicy, these will have your guests humming with happiness. And don't forget, desserts can also be a meal in themselves – time for tea, anyone?

Molten Chocolate Puds

MAKES 6–8   (P: 45 MINS/C: 10 MINS)

These are the most delectable little puds (see photograph on p171) and a cinch to make provided you find the right mould and time it correctly. The mixture can be made ahead, refrigerated overnight, or frozen.

110g (4oz) butter, plus extra for greasing
2 teaspoons flour, plus extra for sprinkling
110g (4oz) good-quality bittersweet dark
  chocolate, chopped
2 free-range, organic eggs, plus 2 egg yolks
50g (2oz) caster sugar

To serve: lightly whipped cream or crème fraîche
icing sugar

6–8 moulds — we use aluminium foil moulds measuring 8.5cm (3^1/$_4$in) across at the top, 5.5cm (2^1/$_4$in) deep, 150ml (5fl oz) capacity

If the puddings are to be baked immediately, preheat the oven to 230°C/450°F/gas mark 8, and place a baking tray in the oven to heat.

Generously butter and flour the moulds, then tap the moulds on the worktop to shake off the excess flour. Base line the moulds with baking parchment.

Put the chocolate with the measured butter in a heat-resistant glass bowl and place the bowl over a saucepan of hot water. Bring to the boil, turn off the heat and allow to sit until the chocolate is melted. Meanwhile whisk the eggs and egg yolks with the sugar until thick and pale and doubled in volume. Add the melted chocolate and butter while still warm and mix gently but thoroughly. Sift the measured flour over the mixture and work in with a spatula until it is just combined. Spoon the mousse into the well buttered moulds until each is about two-thirds full.

If baking immediately, set the moulds on the heated baking tray and bake for 6–7 minutes. Alternatively, the puddings may be covered lightly with clingfilm, kept at room temperature and baked later. They can also be refrigerated, but they must be brought to room temperature before baking.

When they come out of the oven, invert each pudding onto a warmed dessert plate, wait for 10 seconds, then lift off moulds. Dust with icing sugar and serve with a dollop of whipped cream or crème fraîche. They are also delicious with a homemade vanilla ice cream.

Chocolate Tart with Fresh Raspberries

SERVES 8   (P: 20 MINS/C: 10 MINS)

1 x 24cm (9^1/$_2$in) Sweet Shortcrust Pastry
  (see recipe opposite)

For the filling:
200g (7oz) good-quality dark chocolate,
  chopped
150g (5oz) butter, preferably unsalted
2 free-range, organic eggs, plus 3 egg yolks
35g (1^1/$_2$oz) caster sugar

To serve: 700g (1lb 8oz) raspberries

To garnish: mint leaves
icing sugar

Preheat the oven to 190°C/375°F/gas mark 5.

Begin by making the filling. Melt the chocolate and butter together in a heat-resistant glass bowl set over hot but not simmering water. Whisk together the eggs, egg yolks and caster sugar in an electric mixer until pale and thick (about 5 minutes). Fold in the melted chocolate and mix carefully to amalgamate.

Pour the filling into the blind-baked pastry case and bake for 8 minutes; the mixture should still be slightly molten — it cooks a little more as it cools. Allow to cool slightly, then cut into slices and serve with the fresh raspberries. Garnish each slice with a sprig of mint and a little icing sugar.

Chocolate Meringue Layer Cake

SERVES 10–12   (P: 45 MINS/C: 45 MINS)

A luscious cake, very naughty and very nice (see photographs on pp262–263).

For the meringue:
4 free-range, organic egg whites
260g (9¹/₂oz) icing sugar
4 rounded teaspoons cocoa powder

For the chocolate wafers:
110g (3¹/₂oz) good-quality dark chocolate, chopped

For the chocolate and rum cream:
75g (3oz) good-quality dark chocolate, chopped
2 tablespoons Jamaica rum
2 tablespoons cream
600ml (1 pint) lightly whipped cream

Sparklers (optional)

Preheat the oven to 150°C/300°F/gas mark 2 and set out 3 baking trays. Mark three 23cm (9in) diameter circles on silicone paper and place a circle on each of three baking trays.

Put the egg whites into a bowl that is free from grease and is dry and spotlessly clean, add 225g (8oz) of the icing sugar all at once, and whisk until the mixture forms stiff, dry peaks – this will take about 10 minutes.

Sift the cocoa powder and the remaining icing sugar together and fold very gently into the whisked egg whites. Spread the mixture on the three silicone paper rounds with a palette knife.

Bake immediately for 45 minutes or until just crisp. Turn off the oven and leave to cool completely in the oven. When cold, peel off the paper.

Meanwhile, make the chocolate wafers. Put the chocolate in a heat-resistant glass bowl over simmering water. Bring the water to the boil, turn off the heat immediately and allow the chocolate to melt, sitting over the hot water. Stir until quite smooth.

Spread the chocolate on a flat piece of heavy, white notepaper, silicone paper or light card. Leave in the fridge until stiff enough to peel off and cut into square or diamond shapes.

Meanwhile, make the chocolate and rum cream. Very gently melt the chocolate with the rum in a heat-resistant glass bowl over hot water as before, and add the cream. Cool and then fold in the lightly whipped cream (do not stir too much, as this may make it curdle).

Sandwich the three meringue discs together with chocolate and rum cream and decorate with chocolate wafers and sparklers – perfect for a celebration.

Alison Henderson's Sweet Shortcrust Pastry

MAKES ENOUGH TO LINE 2 X 24CM (9¹/₂IN) OR 3 X 18CM (7IN) TART TINS
                 (P: 45 MINS/C: 20 MINS)

175g (6oz) cold butter, cut into cubes
50g (2oz) caster sugar
25g (1oz) icing sugar
290g (10¹/₂oz) plain white flour, plus extra for dusting
1 free-range, organic egg beaten, plus one beaten egg for egg wash.

Put the butter into a food processor, add the caster sugar, icing sugar and flour and pulse to give a coarse, 'flat' breadcrumb texture. Add the egg and pulse again until the pastry comes together. Tip on to a sheet of clingfilm, form into a roll and refrigerate for at least 30 minutes. Meanwhile preheat the oven to 180°C/350°F/gas mark 4.

Divide the pastry between the number of tart tins. Roll each out on a floured work surface, under a sheet of clingfilm. Slip the base of the tart tin under the pastry, lift the pastry and base into the tin and mould it around the sides of the tin. Cover with clingfilm and leave in the fridge to rest for 30 minutes, or freeze until needed. Remove the clingfilm from the pastry, line the pastry case with baking parchment and fill with dried beans or baking beans, and bake blind for about 15 minutes. Remove from the oven and brush with egg wash. Return to the oven for 2–3 minutes to dry off and seal. Let the pastry case cool, then patch any cracks with egg wash.

Mary Risley's Chocolate and Raspberry Truffles

MAKES ABOUT 24   (P: 45 MINS)

This recipe comes from my friend Mary Risley's terrific cookery book, *The Tante Marie's Cooking School Cookbook*. They are rather fiddly and a seriously messy job to make – but so worth it, because they taste divine.

225g (8oz) good-quality dark chocolate,
  chopped
75g (3oz) unsalted butter
125ml (4fl oz) raspberry jam, melted and sieved
2 tablespoons raspberry liqueur (framboise)
  or kirsch
3 tablespoons cocoa powder, unsweetened
24 raspberries
24 tiny paper cup cake cases

Put the chocolate and the butter in a heat-resistant glass bowl over a saucepan of hot water, without allowing the water to touch the bottom of the bowl. Bring slowly to the boil, then turn off the heat and allow the chocolate to melt, stirring gently until smooth. Let the chocolate cool for a few minutes, then stir in the sieved raspberry jam and the framboise or kirsch. Cover the bowl and leave to chill in the fridge until firm.

To shape the truffles, sift the cocoa powder onto a plate. Scoop out a teaspoonful of the truffle mixture, press it gently around a fresh raspberry, then lift it with your fingertips and drop it into the cocoa. Roll the truffle around in the cocoa, then lift it with a fork to transfer it to a little case. Repeat with the remaining raspberries. Place each truffle in its case on a tray and leave the tray in the fridge for an hour or two or until the mixture sets and firms up.

Chocolate and Rosemary Mousse with Pouring Cream

SERVES 8   (P: 10 MINS/C: 30 MINS)

The legendary British cookery writer, Jane Grigson gave me this recipe when she came to teach at the cookery school in 1989.

225g (8oz) caster sugar
225ml (8fl oz) dry white wine
juice of 1/2 lemon
600ml (1 pint) double cream
1 long rosemary branch
175g (6oz) good-quality dark chocolate,
  chopped

To serve: pouring cream and rosemary sprigs

In a stainless steel saucepan over a low heat, mix together the sugar, white wine and lemon juice, stirring until the sugar is dissolved. Add the cream and bring to the boil; the mixture will thicken somewhat. Add the rosemary branch and chocolate. Stir, bring to the boil, then reduce the heat and allow the mixture to simmer very gently for 20 minutes, stirring occasionally. It should be the consistency of thick cream.

Leave to cool, tasting occasionally to see if the rosemary flavour is intense enough. Pour through a sieve into 8 ramekins or little shot glasses. Cover with clingfilm and refrigerate until needed.

Serve with pouring cream and a sprig of rosemary.

Belgian Chocolate Biscuit Cake

SERVES 8–10   (P: 30 MINS)

225g (8oz) good-quality dark chocolate,
chopped
2 free-range, organic eggs
1 dessertspoon caster sugar
225g (8oz) unsalted butter
2 tablespoons raisins, soaked in boiling water
1/2 teaspoon vanilla extract
225g (8oz) plain biscuits, broken
25g (1oz) walnuts or toasted almonds, chopped

To serve: lightly whipped cream (optional)
raspberry coulis (optional)

Line a 13 x 20cm (5 x 8in) loaf tin with non-PVC clingfilm.

Melt the chocolate in a heat-proof bowl placed over a bowl of hot, but not simmering water, or in a very cool oven.

Whisk the eggs and sugar together until light and fluffy. Melt the butter and while it is still hot whisk it into the egg and sugar mixture. The mixture should thicken slightly. Next stir in the melted chocolate, drained raisins and vanilla extract and finally the broken biscuits.

Press into the prepared loaf tin. Sprinkle with the chopped nuts and allow to set in a cold place for a couple of hours or until firm enough to cut.

Cut into slices and serve with lightly whipped cream and/or a raspberry coulis.

Kara's Chocolate Boxes

MAKES 1 BOX   (**P:** 1 HOUR + 1 HOUR TO SET)

50–75g (2–3oz) good-quality dark chocolate,
   chopped

For the box frame:
1 empty 1 litre (1¹/4 pint) milk or
   buttermilk carton
small palette knife

To serve: chocolate mousse
Homemade Ice Cream (see p270)
fresh raspberries

Wash and dry the carton carefully. Cut the sides to the desired height – 5cm (2in) works well. Carefully cut down along all four corners. Align the edges and tape the sides together again with sellotape or masking tape.

Melt three-quarters of the chocolate in your preferred manner (using a double boiler or microwave). Pour the melted chocolate into the box and quickly spread the chocolate with the aid of a palette knife so that it evenly coats the sides and base and all the corners. Turn upside down on a wire rack set over a baking tray and leave to set for 1–2 hours.

When solid carefully peel off the tape. Gently pull back the sides of the carton then pop the base of the box. If necessary, smooth the top edges of the chocolate box by dipping a palette knife in warm water and using it to smooth each edge.

To make the top, melt the remaining chocolate and pour 2–3 tablespoons of melted chocolate into the empty carton, enough to cover the base. Make sure the entire surface is covered and leave to cool. Pop out when solid.

There is a lovely X pattern on the lid from the folding pattern at the bottom of the carton itself. Fill with mousse, ice cream or a filling of your choice.

White Chocolate Mousse with Fresh Strawberry Sauce

SERVES 8–12   (**P:** 30 MINS + 3 HOURS TO SET)

2 teaspoons powdered gelatine
250g (9oz) good-quality white chocolate
5 free-range, organic egg yolks
400ml (14fl oz) lightly whipped cream
Fresh Strawberry Sauce (see below)

Place the gelatine and 2 tablespoons cold water in a cup and leave to swell for a few minutes. Place the cup carefully in a saucepan of simmering water and leave until the gelatine has dissolved.

Bring a saucepan of water to the boil. Break up the white chocolate and put into a glass bowl. Place the bowl over the saucepan of boiling water and turn off the heat. Stir the chocolate until it dissolves completely.

Remove the bowl from the heat and add the egg yolks. Stir with a wooden spoon – the mixture may suddenly block at this stage, but if you stir like mad it will be fine.

Put a little of the chocolate mixture into the gelatine, stir well and then mix this carefully into the rest of the chocolate. Fold in the lightly whipped cream immediately. Pour into a serving dish, cover and refrigerate for at least 3 hours before serving. Alternatively fill espresso cups, shot glasses or chocolate boxes (see above). Cover and leave to set in the fridge.

Fresh Strawberry Sauce

450g (1lb) fresh strawberries
75g (3oz) icing sugar
lemon juice, to taste

Clean and hull the strawberries, place in the bowl of a blender along with the sugar and whizz to a purée. Strain, taste and add lemon juice as necessary. Cover and store in the fridge. It will keep for a day or two.

White Chocolate Mousse with Dark Chocolate Sauce

50g (2oz) dark chocolate
25g (1oz) unsweetened chocolate
About 175ml (6fl oz) Stock Syrup (see recipe
   on p252)
¹/2 teaspoon rum or vanilla extract (optional)

Follow the recipe for White Chocolate Mousse (see recipe above) and, after folding in the whipped cream, pour the mixture into shot glasses. When set, pour some Dark Chocolate Sauce over the top –- divine.

To make the sauce, melt the chocolate in a bowl over simmering water or in a low heat oven. Gradually stir in the syrup. Flavour with rum or vanilla extract.

Boozy Chocolate Mousse

SERVES 8   (P: 20 MINS + TIME TO SET)

300ml (1/2 pint) cream
200g (7oz) good-quality chocolate, chopped
2 free-range, organic large egg yolks
3 tablespoons brandy or 2 tablespoons
  Jamaica rum
25g (1oz) unsalted butter

To serve: pouring cream

In a heavy-based saucepan, heat the cream until it shivers – almost boiling. Remove from the heat and leave for about 1 minute. Add the chocolate and whisk until fully smooth. Beat in the egg yolks and brandy or rum. Finally add the butter and whisk until smooth and silky.

Pour into individual serving pots, espresso cups or chocolate boxes (see left). Cover well and leave to set for 1–3 hours, depending on the size of the serving pots, in the fridge. Serve with a jug of pouring cream.

Variations
You can use orange zest and orange liqueur instead of brandy.
For a lighter mousse fold in 2 stiffly beaten egg whites before pouring into pots.

Chocolate and Peanut Butter Pie

SERVES 8   (P: 45 MINS + 5 HOURS TO SET)

This is an all-American flavour and it's always a wow for a party.

110g (4oz) unsalted butter
110g (4oz) good-quality dark chocolate,
  chopped
2 tablespoons strong coffee (preferably
  espresso)
1 x 25cm (10in) Sweet Shortcrust Pastry,
  (see p247)
110g (4oz) cream cheese
75g (3oz) icing sugar
215g (71/2oz) smooth peanut butter
75ml (3fl oz) milk
350ml (12fl oz) cream

Melt the butter and chocolate together in a heatproof bowl over a saucepan of hot, but not simmering water or in a microwave. Whisk in the coffee and leave to set for a while. When the chocolate is beginning to set pour the chocolate mixture into the blind-baked pastry case and refrigerate while you make the rest of the filling.

Put the cream cheese, icing sugar, peanut butter and milk into a food processor and whizz for a few seconds or until smooth. Whip the cream until soft peaks form. Tip the peanut butter mixture into a mixing bowl and fold the cream into the mixture. Pour into the pastry case, smooth the top and leave to set completely in a cool place, about 4–5 hours.

Chocolate Truffle Tree

MAKES 30   (P: 30 MINS + 5 HOURS TO SET)

A really indulgent centrepiece for a dinner party. Produce this at the end of the meal, accompanied by strong espresso coffee.

1 polystyrene or oasis cone
30–90 chocolate truffles (see below)
  depending on the size of the truffle tree
30–90 cocktail sticks
gold or silver foil

For the chocolate truffles:
350g (12oz) good-quality dark chocolate,
  chopped
75g (3oz) caster sugar
250g (9oz) unsalted butter
3 free-range, organic egg yolks

For the coatings:
white chocolate and coconut
white chocolate and flaked, toasted, roughly
  chopped, skin-on almonds
dark chocolate
cocoa powder
very fine praline powder
chopped pistachio nuts

To make the truffles, put the chocolate, sugar and butter into a heavy saucepan, add 1 tablespoon cold water and melt on the lowest possible heat. Cool slightly and whisk in the egg yolks. Leave in a cool place to set and solidify for 4–5 hours.

When solidified, shape the truffles into balls (larger than a hazelnut, smaller than a walnut) and roll in whichever coatings you choose. Leave to set.

Cover the cone neatly with aluminium foil and place on a glass or china cake stand. You might like to use a golden doiley and place the foil-covered cone in the centre.

Use cocktail sticks to attach the truffles to the mould. Build up in layers with one single truffle on top. It's fun to stick a few long sparklers into the top and light them just as you bring the truffle tree to the table.

Blackcurrant Fool

SERVES 10   (P: 30 MINS + CHILLING TIME)

350g (12oz) fresh or frozen blackcurrants
425ml (³/4 pint) Stock Syrup (see below)
425ml (³/4 pint) lightly whipped double cream
cream, for drizzling

To serve: shortbread biscuits

Cover the blackcurrants with the Stock Syrup. Bring to the boil and cook for about 4–5 minutes, or until the fruit bursts. Liquidise the fruit and syrup mixture, then sieve or purée it, measure and leave to cool. Set a little purée aside for garnish.

When the purée has cooled, add up to an equal quantity of the whipped cream, according to taste. The resulting blackcurrant fool should not be very stiff, more like the texture of lightly whipped cream. If it is too stiff, stir in a little milk rather than more cream. Taste; it may need a little more sugar. Serve chilled, with shortbread biscuits.

Alternatively, spoon 50ml (2fl oz) of the blackcurrant fool into the base of each sundae glass, then a layer of lightly whipped cream, follow with another layer of blackcurrant fool and top with a little cream. Drizzle a little thin blackcurrant purée over the top and chill.

Stock Syrup

450g (1lb) granulated sugar
600ml (1 pint) water

To make the stock syrup, dissolve the sugar in the water over a low heat, stirring often, and bring to the boil. Boil for 2 minutes, then allow the syrup to cool. Store in the fridge until needed – it will keep for weeks.

Blackcurrant Coulis

225g (8oz) blackcurrants
225ml (8fl oz) Stock Syrup (see left)
120–150ml (4–5fl oz) water

Put the blackcurrants into a saucepan, pour over 225ml (8fl oz) syrup, bring to the boil and cook for 3–5 minutes until the blackcurrants burst. Liquidise and press through a nylon sieve. Allow to cool, then add 120–150ml (4–5fl oz) water.

Frosted Blackcurrant Parfait with Blackcurrant Coulis

This is a really swanky name for a dessert I discovered by accident when I froze some leftover blackcurrant fool. I serve this parfait regularly at dinner parties. It is so easy.

Pour the Blackcurrant Fool (see above) into a loaf tin lined with clingfilm. Cover and freeze. Serve cut in slices with Blackcurrant Coulis (see above) drizzled over the top (see photograph opposite).

Olive Oil Ice Cream with Blood Orange Segments

SERVES 6–8   (P: 15 MINS + FREEZING TIME)

Jeannie Chesterton gave me this recipe when we spent a few blissful days at her tiny guest house, Finca Buenvino, in the middle of the chestnut forests near Aracena in Andalucia.

200g (7oz) caster sugar
125ml (4fl oz) water
4 free-range, organic eggs
200ml (7fl oz) pale light extra virgin olive oil
pinch of salt
225ml (8fl oz) milk

To serve: 200g (7oz) blood orange segments
sea salt flakes, such as Maldon Sea Salt

Pour the sugar and the water into a saucepan, place on a low heat and stir to dissolve the sugar before the water comes to the boil. Continue to boil for about 5 minutes or until the syrup reaches the thread stage (see p270), then remove from the heat and leave to cool.

Whizz the eggs in a food processor and add the oil gradually while the machine is still running. Next add the cooled syrup in a very thin stream. Finally, add the salt and the milk. This ice cream is best frozen in a sorbetière; otherwise, just freeze in a covered plastic box.

Serve with blood orange segments and a few sea salt flakes.

Brioche with Sugared Strawberries and Mascarpone

SERVES 8   (P: 15 MINS)

A delicious pudding but also divine for brunch.

1 loaf of brioche
450–700g (1lb–1¹/₂lb) fresh organic
  strawberries
caster sugar, to taste
freshly squeezed lemon juice, to taste
225g (8oz) mascarpone or crème fraîche
a little milk

To garnish:
sprig of mint (optional)
icing sugar (optional)

Slice the brioche into generous 1cm (¹/₂in) slices. Clean and hull the strawberries and slice lengthways into a shallow bowl. Sprinkle with caster sugar and squeeze some lemon juice over them. Toss gently, then taste – they should be quite sweet, so add extra sugar as needed.

Whip the mascarpone or crème fraîche, adding a little milk to soften if necessary. Taste and add a little sugar if it seems too tart. Keep refrigerated until ready to serve.

Just before serving, put the plates in the oven to heat and toast the brioche slices. Put a slice of toasted brioche on each plate and pile some sugared strawberries on top. Top with a dollop of mascarpone or crème fraîche. Garnish with a sprig of fresh mint and a shake of icing sugar – these are not essential but they make the dish look more elegant.

The brioche may be cut in triangles and arranged in an upright position to give a little more height. Individual brioches may also be used – they look and taste delicious.

Crème Brulée

SERVES 4 (P: 15 MINS + OVERNIGHT TO CHILL)

The ultimate custard and a universally favourite pudding. I like to eat it with a compote of fruit – perhaps poached apricots with sweet geranium leaves.

2 free-range, organic large egg yolks
1/2 tablespoon sugar
300ml (1/2 pint) double cream
1/2 vanilla pod (optional)

For the caramel topping:
110g (4oz) sugar
75ml (3fl oz) water
125ml (4fl oz) whipped cream (optional)
  or 110g (4oz) caster sugar for blowtorch method

Start the recipe at least 12 hours in advance of serving.

Mix egg yolks with the sugar. Heat the cream with the vanilla pod (if using) until it just shivers but do not allow to boil. Pour it slowly onto the yolks, whisking all the time. Return to the saucepan and cook over a medium heat, stirring until the custard is thick enough to coat the back of a spoon. It must not boil. Remove the vanilla pod, pour the custard into a serving dish and chill overnight. Be careful not to break the skin or the caramel may sink later.

Next day make the caramel. In a small pan over a medium heat, dissolve the sugar in the water. Bring to the boil and cook until it caramelises to a chestnut-brown colour. Remove from the heat and immediately spoon a thin layer of caramel over the top of the custard. (Alternatively sprinkle the top of the custard with a layer of white caster sugar or pale demerara sugar, spray with a film of cold water, then caramelise with a blowtorch).

Leave to cool and pipe a line of whipped cream around the edge to seal the join where the caramel meets the side of the dish. Serve within 12 hours, or the caramel will melt.

To serve, crack the top by knocking sharply with the back of the serving spoon.

Note: Using 2 yolks only just sets the cream. Be sure to use large eggs and measure the cream slightly short of 300ml (1/2 pint). The cream takes some time to thicken and usually does so just under boiling point. It the custard is not properly set, or if the skin that forms on top while cooking is accidentally broken, the caramel will sink to the bottom of the dish. If you notice either of these problems, freeze the pudding for 1–2 hours before spooning on the hot caramel.

Bumble's Ginger Roulade

SERVES 8–10   (P: 30 MINS/C: 15 MINS)

I spent a fun weekend at Strathgarry House in Scotland, teaching a cookery class with Bumble and her sisters, where she gave me this delightful recipe.

110g (4oz) butter
225g (8oz) golden syrup or treacle
50g (2oz) caster sugar
150ml (1/4 pint) hot water
110g (4oz) plain flour
1 teaspoon baking powder
1 teaspoon ground ginger
1 free-range, organic egg
icing sugar
300ml (1/2 pint) lightly whipped cream
50g (2oz) crystallised ginger, chopped (optional)

large Swiss roll tin – 25.5 x 38cm (10 x 15in)
silicone paper

Preheat the oven to 180°C/350°F/gas mark 4. Line the Swiss roll tin with silicone paper.

Put the butter, golden syrup or treacle and caster sugar with the hot water in a saucepan and warm over a low heat until the ingredients begin to melt.

Mix the flour, baking powder and ginger together in a bowl. When the liquids have cooled, stir in the flour, baking powder and ginger mixture. Separate the egg and add the yolk to the saucepan.

Whisk the egg white until it forms stiff peaks and fold gently into the mixture. Pour into the lined Swiss roll tin and bake for 12–15 minutes. Remove from the oven, cover with a damp cloth and leave to cool.

Meanwhile, dredge a sheet of silicone paper with icing sugar. Turn out the cooled roulade on to the silicone sheet, then fill with lightly whipped cream and crystallised ginger (if using) and roll up. Transfer to a serving plate, and decorate with rosettes of whipped cream and crystallised ginger.

Top Tip: Bumble discovered quite by accident that this ginger roulade freezes really well. You can pull it out when required, cut it into thick slices, put it into a gratin dish, sprinkle with demerera sugar and heat it through in a very hot oven (230°C/450°F/gas mark 8) for 8–10 minutes. Apparently it is delicious.

Fluffy Lemon Mousse with Crystallised Lemon Peel

SERVES 6–8   (P: 45 MINS)

3 free-range, organic large eggs
225g (8oz) caster sugar
juice and finely grated zest of 3 lemons,
   unwaxed
300ml (1/2 pint) double cream
3 teaspoons powdered gelatine
3 tablespoons cold water

For the decoration:
150ml (1/4 pint) whipped cream (optional)
tiny sprigs of lemon balm or sweet
   geranium leaves
Crystallised Lemon Peel (see recipe below) or
   funky sprinkles

Separate the eggs. Put the yolks into a mixing bowl and add the caster sugar and lemon zest. Using an electric food mixer if possible, whisk until thick and fluffy. Strain and heat the lemon juice until warmed through, add to the egg mixture and continue to whisk until the mousse reaches the 'ribbon' stage (if you lift the whisk out of the bowl and trace a figure of 8 on top, it should hold its shape for 30 seconds) – about 15 minutes.

Lightly whip the cream and fold it into the mixture. Put the gelatine and the water into a small bowl and leave the gelatine to swell for 5 minutes. Place the bowl into a saucepan of simmering water until the gelatine has dissolved completely. Add some of the lemon mixture to the gelatine and then carefully fold both mixtures together. Set the soufflé mixture on ice or chill in the fridge. Check it regularly.

Just as the mixture begins to thicken around the edge of the bowl, whisk the egg whites until they form stiff peaks and fold gently into the soufflé base. Pour into individual square, oval or round bowls, glasses or espresso cups.

Decorate the top with tiny sprigs of lemon balm or sweet geranium leaves and Crystallised Lemon Peel (see below) or funky sprinkles.

Crystallised Lemon Peel

We always try to have crystallised lemon, orange and lime peel in a jar to decorate tarts, scatter on mousses or just to nibble.

2 unwaxed lemons
450ml (16fl oz) cold water
Stock Syrup (see p252)
caster sugar

Peel the lemons very thinly with a swivel-top peeler, taking care not to include any white pith. Cut the strips into fine juliennes. Put into a saucepan with the cold water and simmer for 5 minutes. Drain, refresh in cold water, cover with fresh water, drain and refresh again.

Put the julienne strips of peel into a saucepan, add the Stock Syrup and heat gently until the lemon juliennes look translucent. Remove with a slotted spoon and leave to cool on silicone paper or a cake rack. When cold toss in caster sugar and leave to dry in a cool, airy place.

The dried crystallised peel can be stored in a jar or airtight tin for weeks, and perhaps months.

Fresh Apricot Cobbler

SERVES 6–8   (P: 30 MINS/C: 45 MINS)

Cobblers, which are similar to crumbles, always inspire cries of nostalgia. They are so easy to make – use whatever fruit you have in season.

700g (1 1/2lb) fresh apricots, or peaches or
   nectarines, or a mixture, stoned and cut
   into wedges
5 tablespoons granulated sugar
1 tablespoon plain white flour or cornflour
juice and grated zest (optional) of 1/2 lemon

For the cobbler topping:
110g (4oz) white flour
3/4 teaspoon baking powder
1/4 teaspoon bicarbonate of soda
1 tablespoon caster sugar
25g (1oz) butter, cut into cubes
125ml (4fl oz) buttermilk
1 tablespoon granulated sugar

1.2 litre (2 pints) pie dish

Preheat the oven to 200°C/400°F/gas mark 6.

Put the sliced fruit in a bowl, add the sugar and flour, a tablespoon of lemon juice and the grated zest if using, toss well and transfer to a pie dish.

To make the topping, sift the flour, baking powder and bicarbonate of soda into a bowl and add 1 tablespoon of caster sugar. Rub in the butter and mix gently with the buttermilk until it just comes together.

Drop tablespoons of the topping over the filling. It doesn't matter if there are spaces, the dough will expand as it cooks. Sprinkle with the granulated sugar. Bake for 30–45 minutes or until puffed and golden. Serve warm with crème fraîche or lightly whipped cream.

Normandy Pear or Apple Tart

SERVES 8–10   (P: 2 HOURS/C: 45 MINS)

This is certainly one of the most impressive of French tarts. It is wonderful served warm but is also very good cold and keeps for several days. Splash in a little kirsch if you are using pears, or calvados if you are using dessert apples.

4–5 ripe Poached Pears or apples (see below)

For the shortcrust pastry:
200g (7oz) plain white flour
pinch of salt
110g (4oz) cold butter
1 free-range, organic egg yolk

For the frangipane:
100g (3¹/₂oz) butter
100g (3¹/₂oz) caster sugar
1 free-range, organic egg, plus 1 egg yolk
110g (4oz) whole blanched almonds, ground,
  or a mix of ¹/₂ ready-ground almonds and
  ¹/₂ blanched and ground
25g (1oz) plain white flour
2 tablespoons kirsch if using pears,
  or calvados if using apples
150ml (¹/₄ pint) Apricot Glaze (see below)

To serve: lightly whipped cream

23cm (9in) diameter flan ring, or tart tin with a removable base

First make the shortcrust pastry. Sift the flour and salt into a bowl, cut the butter into cubes and rub into the flour using your fingertips. Keep everything as cool as possible; if the butter is allowed to melt the finished pastry may be tough. When the mixture resembles coarse breadcrumbs, stop. Whisk in the egg yolk and add 3–4 tablespoons cold water. Take a fork or knife (whichever you feel more comfortable using) and bring the pastry together, then collect the pastry into a ball with your hands. This way you can judge more accurately if you need a few more drops of liquid. Although slightly damp pastry is easier to handle and roll out, the resulting crust can be tough and may well shrink out of shape as the water evaporates in the oven. A drier and more difficult-to-handle pastry will give a crisper, shorter crust. Cover the pastry with clingfilm and leave to rest in the fridge for at least 15 minutes, preferably 30 minutes. This will make the pastry much less elastic and easier to roll.

Preheat the oven to 180°C/350°F/gas mark 4.

Roll out the pastry. Line the tart tin with it, prick lightly with a fork, flute the edges and chill again until firm. Bake blind for 15–20 minutes. Remove from the oven and increase the heat to 200°C/400°F/gas mark 6.

To make the frangipane, cream the butter, beat in the sugar and continue beating until the mixture is light and soft. Gradually add the egg and yolk, beating well after each addition. Stir in the ground almonds and flour and then add the kirsch or calvados. Pour the frangipane into the pastry case, spreading it evenly.

Drain the pears or apples well and cut them crosswise into very thin slices, then lift the sliced fruit halves intact and arrange them around the tart on the frangipane, pointed ends towards the centre. Arrange a final half pear or apple in the centre.

Bake the tart for 10–15 minutes until the pastry is beginning to brown. Reduce the oven temperature to 180C°/350F°/gas mark 4 and continue baking for 15–20 minutes or until the fruit is tender and the frangipane is set in the centre and nicely golden.

Meanwhile make the Apricot Glaze (see recipe below). When the tart is fully cooked, paint generously with the glaze, remove from the tin and serve warm or cold with a bowl of lightly whipped cream.

Poached Pears or Apples

225g (¹/₂lb) sugar
600ml (1 pint) water
2 strips of lemon zest and the
  juice of ¹/₂ lemon
6 pears or apples

Bring the sugar and water to the boil with the strips of lemon zest in a non-reactive saucepan. Meanwhile peel the fruit thinly, cut in half and core carefully with a melon baller or a teaspoon, keeping a good shape. Put the fruit halves into the syrup, cut side uppermost, add the lemon juice, and cover with a paper lid and then the pan lid. Bring to the boil and simmer until the fruit are just soft – the tip of a knife or skewer should go through without resistance. Remove from the heat and cool before use.

Apricot Glaze

Apricot glaze is invaluable to have ready made up in your fridge. It is used to glaze tarts that contain green, orange or white fruit, e.g. kiwi fruit, peaches, oranges or pears.

In a small saucepan (not aluminium), melt 350g (12oz) apricot jam with the juice of ¹/₄ lemon and just enough water to make a glaze that can be poured. Push the hot jam through a nylon sieve and store in an airtight jar. Reheat the glaze to melt it before using. The quantities given above make a generous 300ml (¹/₂ pint) glaze.

Frosted Lemon and Rosemary Squares with Crème Fraîche

MAKES 24   (**P:** 3 MINS/**C:** 25 MINS)

250g (9oz) butter, softened, plus extra
  for greasing
250g (9oz) caster sugar
3 free-range, organic eggs
250g (9oz) self-raising flour

For the frosting:
grated zest and juice of 2 unwaxed lemons
175g (6oz) caster sugar
2 tablespoons chopped rosemary

To garnish:
crème fraîche and sprigs of rosemary

Swiss roll tin 25 x 18cm (10 x 7in)

Preheat the oven to 180ºC/350ºF/gas mark 4. Grease the Swiss roll tin well.

Put the butter into a food processor, add the caster sugar, eggs and flour, and whizz for a few seconds to amalgamate. Spread evenly in the Swiss roll tin. Bake for 20–25 minutes, or until golden brown and well risen.

Meanwhile, make the frosting. Mix the grated lemon zest and juice with the caster sugar and chopped rosemary. As soon as the cake mixture is cooked, pour the glaze over the top and leave to cool.

Cut the cake into squares and garnish each square with a dollop of crème fraîche and a sprig of rosemary before serving. (See photograph on p263.)

Frosted Tangerines

SERVES 10–12
              (**P:** 1 HOUR + 3 HOURS TO CHILL)

This clean, fresh ice tastes like a superior ice lolly. To halve the work involved, pour it into ice-lolly moulds. Clementines, mandarins and satsumas may be substituted for tangerines in this recipe. Citrus fruit are at their best and most varied in the winter, when they are in season.

For the syrup:
250g (9oz) sugar
juice of 1/4 lemon
150ml (1/4 pint) water

20–28 tangerines
finely grated zest and juice of 1/2 lemon
icing sugar (optional)

To garnish:
vine leaves or bay leaves

First make the syrup. Put the sugar, lemon juice and water into a saucepan over a low heat and stir until the sugar dissolves. Bring to the boil, then boil for 2–3 minutes. Remove from the heat and leave to cool.

Meanwhile, grate the zest from 10 of the tangerines, then cut each one in half and squeeze out the juice.

Cut the top off each of the remaining tangerines to make a lid for each one. With a small spoon, scoop the segments out of the main part of the fruit. Press the segments through a nylon sieve into a measuring jug (alternatively, you could liquidise the pulp and then strain it). You should end up with 750ml (just over 1 1/4 pints) of juice. Put the tangerine shells in the fridge or freezer to chill. Add the grated lemon zest to the tangerine juice, and add the lemon juice and the syrup to taste – add icing sugar or extra lemon juice if more sweetness or sharpness is required. The juice should taste sweeter than you would like it to be, because it will lose some of its sweetness when it freezes. Freeze until firm in one of the ways suggested below.

Finally, fill the chilled tangerine shells with scoops of the frozen sorbet. Replace the lids and store the frosted tangerines in the freezer. If you do not intend to serve them on the day you make them, cover them with clingfilm. Serve the frosted tangerines on a white plate decorated with vine leaves or bay leaves, or on colourful plates for a children's party.

Make the sorbet in one of the following ways
1 Pour into the drum of an ice-cream maker or sorbetière and freeze for 20–25 minutes. Scoop out and serve immediately, or store in a covered bowl in the freezer until needed.

2 Pour the juice into a stainless steel or plastic container and put into the freezing compartment of a refrigerator. After 4–5 hours, when the sorbet is semi-frozen, remove from the freezer and whisk until smooth, then return to the freezer. Whisk again when almost frozen and fold in one stiffly beaten egg white. Keep in the freezer until needed.

Californian Three-stone Pie

SERVES 8–12   (P: 1¼ HOURS/C: 1 HOUR)

This pastry is made by the creaming method, so people who are convinced that they suffer from 'hot hands' don't have to worry about rubbing in the butter.

For the break-all-the-rules pastry:
350g (12oz) butter
75g (3oz) caster sugar
3 free-range, organic eggs
500g (1lb 2oz) white flour, preferably
  unbleached

For the filling:
1kg (2¼lb) apricots, peaches and nectarines
225g (8oz) sugar
3 tablespoons plain flour or cornflour
egg wash

To serve:
lightly whipped cream or crème fraîche
caster sugar

25 x 30 x 1cm (10 x 12 x ½in) or
  round pie dish

Preheat the oven to 180°C/350°F/gas mark 4.

Cream the butter and sugar together by hand or in a food mixer (do not overcream). Add the eggs and beat for a minute or two. Reduce the speed to the lowest setting and mix in the flour. Turn out onto a piece of floured greaseproof paper, flatten into a round, wrap and chill. This pastry needs to be chilled for at least 1 hour otherwise it is difficult to handle.

Stone and slice the fruit into a bowl, sprinkle with the sugar and flour and toss well.

Roll out the pastry to a thickness of about 4mm (¹⁄₆in), and use about two-thirds of it to line a suitable pie dish. Spoon the sugared fruit into the pastry base. Cover with a lid of pastry rolled out to the same thickness and seal the edges by pressing together. Decorate with peach shapes and pastry leaves cut out from the pastry trimmings. Brush with egg wash and bake until the fruit is tender and juicy and starts to ooze through, about 45–60 minutes.

Sprinkle lightly with caster sugar and serve with lightly whipped cream or crème fraîche.

Bananas in Lime Syrup

SERVES 4
(P: 15 MINS/C: 5 MINS + 1 HOUR TO MACERATE)

This is my number one standby pud when there is nothing in the house and all else fails. It is so delicious and refreshing that it's a must in anybody's easy entertaining repertoire.

110g (4oz) sugar
125ml (4fl oz) water
4 bananas
juice and zest of 1 lime

Put the sugar and water into a saucepan and stir over a gentle heat until the sugar dissolves. Bring to the boil, simmer for 2 minutes and allow to cool.

Peel the bananas and cut into slices. Put the slices into a bowl and cover with the cold syrup. Add the lime zest and juice to the syrup and leave to macerate for at least 1 hour. Serve chilled.

Mangoes in Lime Syrup

Use 2 ripe mangoes instead of bananas in the above recipe. Peel the mango, slice quite thinly down to the stone and continue as above.

Mango, Banana and Passion Fruit in Lime Syrup

Add the juice and seeds of 1 passion fruit to 1 ripe mango and 2 bananas and continue as above.

time for tea

Tea time is redolent of a more leisurely age, of Edwardian tea gowns, grand hotels and elegant gardens. For some, it was a time for planning social events and gossiping over a pot of imported tea and dainty sandwiches and cakes. For others, it was seen as an essential snack, needed to get them through to dinner.

Either way, it is a meal we should find more time for. Invite friends and family over for a lazy afternoon, to catch up on the week's happenings over a fragrant pot of tea or coffee. It is also a great opportunity to entertain people with children as it is the one meal where kids can join in and play around you.

Spend a couple of hours baking a cake or biscuits — ideally one centrepiece cake, for example a chocolate meringue layer cake (see p247), as well as some savoury coffee walnut biscuits (see p274) or lemon and rosemary squares (see p258). Some sandwiches are always welcome, though I leave it up to you whether to trim the crusts. Why not try a fruit bread or Barm Brack, which can be made a day in advance and stored in an air-tight container? Remember the old tradition of always having something in the tin in case someone drops in?

To drink, offer some homemade lemonade and freshly brewed coffee and tea (leaves give a much better flavour than tea bags). Green tea is now often served for tea and it is a good idea to provide some caffeine-free alternatives such as fruit and herbal teas. They should all be served in elegant china cups and saucers.

coffee and cake

This is a time for pretty elegance, not modern minimalism. Indulge your girly side and flood it with warm pinks, patterns and pastels. Use swathes of beautiful fabric as a tablecloth and don't worry about matching colour schemes or clashing patterns. Choose bright plates, stripy place mats and frilly glass cake stands. Pile chairs with tasselled cushions and bring out exotic trinkets from trips abroad – bangles from India, beads from Morocco. Ask your guests to dress for the occasion – no jeans or trainers – and just by doing that, you will create a special afternoon.

For the food, presentation is everything. A tea set or coffee set is essential (no mugs please), but it doesn't have to match. Nowadays you can buy individual pieces, old and new, and they also make fantastic presents, so hint madly near your birthday. A cake stand will show your efforts in the best light, but you could also buy squares of white lace to give your everyday plates a touch of glamour.

Use herbs and flowers to adorn the cakes and petals in tea cups. Then lean back, sip your tea and while away the time.

Tira Misu or Frosted Tira Misu with Irish Coffee Sauce

SERVES 8   (P: 1 HOUR)

250ml (9fl oz) strong espresso coffee
  (if your freshly made coffee is not strong
  enough, add 1 teaspoon instant coffee)
2 tablespoons brandy
2 tablespoons Jamaica rum
75g (3oz) good-quality dark chocolate
3 free-range, organic eggs, separated
4 tablespoons caster sugar
250g (9oz) mascarpone cheese
38–40 Boudoir biscuits (lady fingers)
unsweetened cocoa powder, to dredge

To serve: Irish Coffee Sauce (optional – see
  below)

450g (1lb) loaf tin, 20 x 10cm (8 x 4in),
  lined with clingfilm

Mix the coffee with the brandy and rum. Roughly grate the chocolate (we do it in the food processor, using the pulse button). Whisk the egg yolks with the sugar until the mixture reaches the 'ribbon' stage (if you lift the whisk out of the bowl and trace a figure of 8 on top, it should hold its shape for 30 seconds) and is light and fluffy, then fold in the mascarpone cheese a tablespoon at a time.

Whisk the egg whites stiffly and fold gently into the cheese mixture. Now assemble the tiramisu. Dip each side of the biscuits one at a time into the coffee mixture and arrange half of them side by side in the base of the loaf tin. Spread half the mascarpone mixture gently over the biscuits, sprinkle half the grated chocolate over the top, then another layer of soaked biscuits and finally the rest of the mascarpone.

Cover the loaf tin carefully with clingfilm or better still slide it into a plastic bag and twist the end. Refrigerate. Just before serving scatter the remainder of the chocolate over the top and dredge with unsweetened cocoa. Serve with Irish Coffee Sauce, if you like.

Frosted Tira Misu with Irish Coffee Sauce
Freeze for at least 6 hours. Cut the frosted tiramisu into thick slices and serve with Irish Coffee Sauce, if you like.

Teeny Weeny Tira Misu
Make the tira misu in little glasses – they can be eaten within 1 hour.

Irish Coffee Sauce

This sauce keeps indefinitely so make up a batch for ice cream, pancakes, mousses.

225g (8oz) sugar
75ml (3fl oz) water
250ml (9fl oz) strong coffee
1 tablespoon Irish whiskey

Put the sugar and water in a heavy-based saucepan and heat. Stir until the sugar dissolves and the water comes to the boil. Remove the spoon and do not stir again until the syrup turns a pale golden caramel. Draw the saucepan off the heat, add the hot coffee (beware it may froth up) and return to the heat to dissolve the caramel in the coffee. Leave to cool before adding the whiskey.

A Great Lemon Meringue Pie

SERVES 6   (P: 1¹/₂ HOURS/C: 1¹/₂ HOURS)

This is real retro food and this version always gets a rousing response (see photograph on p105).

For the pastry:
110g (4oz) plain white flour
50–75g (2–3oz) butter
1 free-range, organic egg yolk
1 free-range, organic, egg white, lightly beaten

For the lemon curd:
50g (2oz) butter
110g (4oz) caster sugar
finely grated zest and juice of 2 large
  unwaxed lemons
2 free-range, organic eggs, plus 1 egg yolk,
  well beaten

For the meringue:
2 free-range, organic egg whites
110g (4oz) caster sugar

18cm (7in) round tin, preferably with a
  pop-up base

First make the pastry as per the method for Normandy Pear or Apple Tart (see p257).

Use the pastry to line the flan ring and chill again for 15–20 minutes. Meanwhile preheat the oven to 180°C/350°F/gas mark 4. Line the chilled pastry case with silicone paper and fill it with dried beans or baking beans. Bake for 25 minutes or until the pastry case is fully cooked. Remove the paper and beans, paint the pastry case with a little lightly beaten egg white and put it back in the oven to seal for about 2–3 minutes.

Now make the lemon curd. Melt the butter in a saucepan over a very low heat, add the caster sugar, lemon juice and zest, then stir in the eggs. Stir over a very low heat until the mixture coats the back of a spoon. Take the saucepan off the heat and pour the mixture into a bowl. It will thicken further as it cools. Fill the pastry case with the lemon curd mixture.

Now make the meringue: first, turn down the oven temperature to a cool 120°C/250°F/gas mark ¹/₂. Whisk the egg whites in a perfectly clean, dry bowl until they begin to get fluffy, then add 50g (2oz) caster sugar and continue to whisk until the egg whites form stiff peaks. Fold in the remainder of the caster sugar and then either pipe or spread the whisked egg whites over the lemon mixture with a spoon. Note: do not whip the egg whites until you are ready to use it, since if it sits around it loses volume. Bake the lemon meringue pie for about 1 hour until the meringue is crisp on the outside. Serve warm or cold. Alternatively cook in an oven preheated to 210°C/400°F/gas mark 6 for just 7 minutes – this will result in a meringue that is slightly coloured, crisp on the outside and soft underneath. Serve warm or cold.

Lemon Petit Fours
Preheat the oven to 240°C/475°F/gas mark 9. Fill tiny petit four pastry cases with a dollop of lemon curd and pipe a rosette of meringue on top. Bake the petits fours for 60 seconds.

Mile-high lemon Meringue Pie
Double the quantity of meringue in the recipe and pile it into a cone or pyramid on top of the lemon mixture in the tart.

Sticky Toffee Pudding with Butterscotch and Pecan Nut Sauce

SERVES 6–8   (P: 1 HOUR/C: 1¹⁄₄ HOURS)

225g (8oz) chopped dates
300ml (¹/₂ pint) hot tea
oil, for greasing
110g (4oz) unsalted butter
175g (6oz) caster sugar
3 free-range, organic eggs
225g (8oz) self-raising flour, sifted
1 teaspoon bicarbonate of soda, sifted
1 teaspoon vanilla extract
1 teaspoon espresso coffee powder

For the butterscotch pecan sauce:
110g (4oz) butter
175g (6oz) dark soft brown Barbados sugar
110g (4oz) granulated sugar
275g (10oz) golden syrup
225ml (8fl oz) double cream
¹/₂ teaspoon vanilla extract
50g (2oz) chopped pecans

Preheat the oven to 180°C/350°F/gas mark 4.

Soak the dates in the tea for 15 minutes. Brush a 20cm (8in) spring form cake tin with oil and place oiled greaseproof paper on the base.

Cream together the butter and sugar until light and fluffy. Beat in the eggs, one at a time, and then fold in the flour. Add the bicarbonate of soda, vanilla and coffee to the dates and tea and stir this into the pudding mixture. Turn into the tin and cook for 1–1¹/₂ hours or until a skewer inserted in the centre comes out clean.

To make the butterscotch pecan sauce, put the butter, sugars and golden syrup into a heavy-based saucepan and melt gently over a low heat. Simmer for about 5 minutes. Remove from the heat and gradually stir in the cream, the vanilla and the pecans. Return to the heat and stir for 2–3 minutes until all the sugar is dissolved and the sauce is absolutely smooth.

Pour some hot sauce onto a serving plate, spoon the sticky toffee pudding on top, and pour a generous quantity of the sauce over the pudding. Serve with lightly whipped cream. Put the remainder of the sauce in a bowl, and pass round for extras.

Sticky Toffee Pudding reheats very well.

Meringue Roulade with Pomegranate Seeds and Rose Water

SERVES 6–8   (**P**: 45 MINS/**C**: 30 MINS)

sunflower oil, for greasing
4 free-range, organic egg whites
225g (8oz) caster sugar
300ml (¹/₂ pint) whipped cream, plus
    150ml (¹/₄ pint) for rosettes

For the filling:
1–2 pomegranates
1–2 teaspoons rose water

To garnish:
pomegranate seeds
rose petals if available (ensure before picking
    that the rose hasn't been sprayed)

For Christmas:
sprigs of holly with berries

Swiss roll tin 30 x 20cm (12 x 8in)

Preheat the oven to 180°C/350°F/gas mark 4. Line the Swiss roll tin with aluminium foil, and brush the foil lightly with oil.

Put the egg whites in a spotlessly clean food mixer bowl. Break them up with the whisk, then add all the caster sugar at once. Whisk at full speed for 4–5 minutes, or until the egg whites hold a stiff peak when the whisk is lifted.

Spread the meringue gently over the tin with a palette knife. Bake for 15–20 minutes. When cooked, the meringue ought to be quite thick and bouncy, crisp on the outside but still soft in the centre. Allow to cool.

Meanwhile, cut the pomegranates in half around their 'equator' and flick the seeds out into a bowl. Sprinkle with a few drops of rose water. Taste and add more if needed. Keep some seeds on one side to decorate the roulade.

To assemble, put a sheet of aluminium foil on the work surface and turn the meringue out on to it. Remove the base foil. Spread the 300ml (¹/₂ pint) whipped cream and pomegranate seeds over the meringue. Roll up the meringue from the long side and carefully ease it on to a serving plate. Pipe 6–8 rosettes of cream along the top of the roulade, and decorate with the reserved pomegranate seeds and rose petals if available. An alternative for Christmas is to surround the roulade with berried holly and dredge it with icing sugar. Serve the roulade cut into slices about 2.5cm (1in) thick.

Yogurt and Cardamom Cream with Apricots and Saffron Syrup

SERVES 8–10
          (**P**: 30 MINS + 4–5 HOURS TO CHILL)

225ml (8fl oz) milk
200ml (7fl oz) double cream
200g (7oz) caster sugar
¹/₂ teaspoon ground green cardamom seeds
3 rounded teaspoons powdered gelatine
4 tablespoons cold water
425ml (³/₄ pint) natural yogurt

Poached Apricots in Saffron Syrup (see below)

Put the milk, cream and sugar into a stainless steel saucepan and add the ground cardamom. Stir over a low heat until the sugar has dissolved and the mixture is warm to the touch. Remove from the heat and leave to infuse while you dissolve the gelatine.

Put the gelatine into a small bowl with the cold water. Leave the gelatine to swell for 4–5 minutes. Put the bowl into a saucepan of simmering water until the gelatine has melted and is completely clear.

Add a little of the infused milk mixture to the gelatine and stir well, then mix this into the rest of the milk. Whisk the yogurt lightly until smooth and creamy and stir it into the milk mixture.

Pour into a bowl or 8–10 individual moulds or shot glasses. Leave to set in a refrigerator for several hours. Serve with Apricot and Saffron Syrup. Yogurt and Cardamom Cream is also great with sugared strawberries or Gooseberry and Elderflower Compote (see p229).

Poached Apricots in Saffron Syrup

SERVES 8   (**P**: 5 MINS/**C**: 10 MINS)

450g (1lb) sugar (reduce the quantity of
    sugar if the apricots are very sweet)
500ml (18fl oz) cold water
¹/₂–1 teaspoon saffron strands
900g (2 lb) fresh apricots
juice of 2 lemons

Put the sugar and water into a saucepan, add the saffron and bring to the boil. Add the apricots whole or, if you prefer, cut them in half and remove the stones. Cover the saucepan and simmer until the apricots are soft. Add the lemon juice, turn into a bowl and chill before serving.

Almond Meringue with Kumquats

SERVES 6   (**P**: 45 MINS/**C**: 45 MINS)

**This meringue may break a few of the rules
of dieting, but it is one of our best and
favourite puddings. We fill it with any
suitable fruit in season – strawberries,
raspberries, loganberries, boysenberries,
tayberries, raspberries, peaches – and
combinations such as nectarine, mango and
passion fruit, green gooseberry and
elderflower, or rhubarb and strawberry…
This recipe uses egg whites, so save the yolks
for homemade Mayonnaise, (see p296).**

For the meringue:
35g (1¹/₂oz) almonds
125g (4¹/₂oz) icing sugar
2 free-range, organic egg whites

For the filling:
300ml (10fl oz) whipped cream
225g (8oz) Kumquat Compote (see below)

To garnish:
whipped cream
wafers of chocolate (optional – see p274)

silicone paper or prepared baking sheet

Preheat the oven to 150°C/300°F/gas mark 2.

Drop the almonds into boiling water and return to the boil for a minute or two to blanch them. When cool enough to handle, skin the almonds, then grind them or chop them up. They should not be ground to a fine powder but should be left slightly coarse and gritty. At a pinch, nibbed almonds could be used, but they won't taste quite so good.

Mark two 19cm (7¹/₂in) diameter circles on silicone paper or a prepared baking sheet.

In a bowl that is free from any grease and is dry and spotlessly clean, mix all the icing sugar with the egg whites and whisk until the mixture forms stiff, dry peaks. Fold in the ground almonds. Divide the mixture between the two circles and spread it evenly with a palette knife. Bake the meringues immediately for 45 minutes or until set crisp and just brown on top. Allow to cool.

To assemble, sandwich the meringues together with the whipped cream and drained Kumquat Compote. Chill for some hours before serving. Decorate with piped rosettes of whipped cream and wafers of chocolate.

For a celebration, mould the meringue into a star or heart shape, or the numerals '2' and '1' for a 21st-birthday party, for instance.

This recipe can be multiplied easily, but don't whisk more than 4 egg whites at a time otherwise you will lose volume.

Kumquat Compote

225g (8oz) kumquats
150ml (5fl oz) water
150g (5oz) sugar

Cut each kumquat into 4 slices and remove the pips. Put the kumquats in a saucepan with the water and sugar and let them cook very gently, uncovered, for 30 minutes. Allow to cool and drain off the excess juice before using as a filling for the meringue.

**Top Tip: Kumquat Frizzle
Use the kumquat syrup – the excess juice from the Kumquat Compote – to make a
Kumquat Frizzle. Put 1 tablespoon of the syrup into a champagne flute. Top with
Prosecco or another sparkling wine.**

Affrogata

Put a scoop of Homemade Vanilla Ice Cream (see p270) into an espresso cup, top with a shot of espresso and serve immediately. Yummeee!

Adorable Baby Banoffis

MAKES 8–12   (**P**: 15 MINS/**C**: 3 HOURS)

Have a few tins of toffee ready in your larder so you can make this yummy pud in minutes.

1 x 400g (14oz) tin condensed milk
8–12 digestive biscuits
3 bananas
freshly squeezed juice of 1 lemon
225ml (8fl oz) whipped cream
toasted flaked almonds
chocolate curls made from about 175g (6oz)
   chocolate

8–12 individual glasses or bowls

To make the toffee put the unopened tin of condensed milk into a saucepan and cover with hot water. Bring to the boil, cover and simmer for 3 hours by which time the condensed milk will have turned into a thick unctuous toffee.

Break a biscuit into each glass or bowl. Peel and slice the bananas and toss in the lemon juice and add to the bowls. Top with a little toffee. Put a blob of lightly whipped cream on top. Sprinkle with flaked almonds and decorate with a few chocolate curls.

Bread and Butter Pudding

SERVES 6–8   (**P**: 30 MINS + 1 HOUR
                  OR OVERNIGHT TO CHILL/**C**: 1 HOUR)

This irresistible pudding is a must for an easy-entertaining repertoire. This version will reheat perfectly. Note that cinnamon or mixed spice may be used instead of nutmeg to give an exotic flavour. It is also great served in a cappucino cup.

50g (2oz) butter, softened, plus extra
   for greasing
12 slices good-quality white bread,
   crusts removed
½ teaspoon grated nutmeg
200g (7oz) plump raisins or sultanas
450ml (16fl oz) double cream
225ml (8fl oz) milk
4 free-range, organic large eggs, lightly beaten
1 teaspoon vanilla extract
175g (6oz) sugar
pinch of salt
1 tablespoon granulated sugar, for sprinkling

To serve:
lightly whipped cream or crème fraîche

1 x 8in (20.5cm) square pottery or china dish

Butter the pottery or china dish.

Butter the bread and arrange 4 slices, buttered side down, in 1 layer in the dish. Sprinkle the bread with half the grated nutmeg and half the raisins and arrange another layer of bread, buttered side down, over the raisins. Sprinkle the remaining nutmeg and raisins on top. Cover the raisins with the remaining bread, buttered side down.

In a bowl whisk together the cream, milk, eggs, vanilla extract, sugar and a pinch of salt. Pour the mixture through a fine sieve over the bread in the dish. Sprinkle the granulated sugar over the top and let the mixture stand, covered loosely, at room temperature for at least 1 hour, or chill overnight.

Preheat the oven to 180°C/350°F/gas mark 4.

Bake the pudding in a bain-marie (a larger oven-proof bowl or tin filled with hot water) – the water should be halfway up the sides of the baking dish. Bake for about 1 hour, or until the top is crisp and golden. Serve warm with some lightly whipped cream or crème fraîche.

Delicious Bread and Butter Puddings can be made using:
Barm Brack (see p182) as a base. Add mixed spice or cinnamon.
Panettone as a base – proceed as in recipe above.
Brioche as a base – proceed as in recipe above, or use apricot jam and lace with apricot brandy.
Rhubarb, gooseberry and elderflower compote or spiced apple purée.
Cheese to make a savoury bread and butter pudding.
Marmalade – spread the slices of buttered bread generously with marmalade. Include or omit the raisins or sultanas as you fancy.

Homemade Vanilla Ice-cream

SERVES 12–16
(P: 30 MINS + 5–6 HOURS FREEZING TIME)

This is my favourite homemade ice cream, very rich and very delicious. It is made with an egg mousse base, with lightly whipped cream and flavourings added. Ice creams made in this way have a smooth texture, and do not need further whisking during the freezing period or a sorbetière. They should not be served frozen hard, so remove from the freezer at least 10 minutes before serving. Only the egg yolks are used in the egg mousse base, so save the whites to make the meringues on pp266–267.

4 free-range, organic egg yolks
110g (4oz) sugar
225ml (8fl oz) water
1 teaspoon vanilla extract
1.2 litres (2 pints) lightly whipped cream

Put the egg yolks in a bowl and whisk until light and fluffy.

Combine the sugar and water in a small heavy-bottomed saucepan, stir over a low heat until the sugar is completely dissolved, then remove the spoon and boil the syrup until it reaches the 'thread' stage, i.e., it will look thick and syrupy, and when a metal spoon is dipped in, the last drops of syrup will form thin threads.

Pour this boiling syrup in a steady stream onto the egg yolks, whisking all the time. Add the vanilla extract and continue to whisk until it becomes a thick, creamy white mousse. Fold the lightly whipped cream into the mousse, pour into a bowl, cover and freeze.

Here are some ideas for serving the ice cream:

Ice Cream Sandwich
Individual sandwiches of ice cream between two chocolate chip and hazelnut cookies.

Fudge Ripple Ice Cream
Swirl toffee sauce through soft frozen ice cream.

Ice Cream Parfait with coffee, chocolate and praline, strawberry, vanilla and blackcurrant, or mango, passion fruit and vanilla. Line a loaf tin and fill it with 3 various ice creams in layers. Serve the parfait in slices with a complementary sauce. Alternatively, fill the lined loaf tin with three alternate layers of vanilla ice cream and crushed praline powder. Serve cut into slices, sprinkled with extra crushed praline and perhaps a toffee sauce

Vanilla Ice Cream on a Stick
Spoon the ice cream into plastic ice-lolly moulds, cover and pop into the freezer. When the ice cream is partially frozen, insert ice cream sticks into the centre of each one. Remove from the moulds just before serving. For choc-ices, dip the unmoulded ice creams into cool melted chocolate and enjoy!

Sweet Geranium Cake with Blackberries

SERVES 8–10   (P: 30 MINS/C: 1 HOUR)

350g (12oz) butter, softened, plus extra for
  greasing
350g (12oz) caster sugar
4 free-range, organic eggs
350g (12oz) self-raising flour

For the sweet geranium syrup:
50g (2oz) caster sugar
150ml (1/4 pint) water
4–6 sweet geranium leaves (Pelargonium
  graveolens)
zest and juice of 1 unwaxed lemon

To serve:
900g (2lb) fresh blackberries
a little icing sugar
lightly whipped cream
rose petals (optional)

Preheat the oven to 180°C/350°F/gas mark 4. Grease a 23cm (9in) round cake tin

Put the butter into the bowl of a food processor and add the sugar, eggs and flour. Whizz for a few seconds to amalgamate. Spread evenly in the cake tin. Bake for about 1 hour or until golden brown and well risen.

Meanwhile make the syrup. Put the sugar, water and geranium leaves into a saucepan over a medium heat. Stir until the sugar dissolves, bring to the boil and simmer for 2–3 minutes. Remove from the heat and add the lemon zest and juice. Set aside to cool, then strain.

As soon as the cake is cooked, prick the surface, pour all the syrup over the top and leave to cool.

Remove the cake from the tin and serve with the blackberries, dusted with a little icing sugar, and lightly whipped cream. A few rose petals scattered over the top look divine.

A slice of cake on its own with a cup of tea is also delicious.

Irish Rhubarb Tart

SERVES 8–12   (**P:** 45 MINS/**C:** 1 HOUR)

This is such a terrific pastry. If I'm in a mad rush I make it in a food processor. It's easier to handle if chilled before rolling out, but works fine even if you use it right away and have to patch it up a bit. It's fun to trace a funny face or print a message on the tart.

For the pastry:
225g (8oz) butter, softened
50g (2oz) caster sugar
2 free-range, organic eggs, plus 1 egg beaten
  with a little milk, to glaze
350g (12oz) plain white flour

For the filling:
450g (1lb) red rhubarb
175g (6oz) sugar

To serve:
caster sugar
lightly whipped cream
Barbados sugar

1 x 23cm (9in) tin with 4cm (1½in) sides

First make the pastry. In a mixer, cream the butter and sugar together. Add the eggs and beat for several minutes.

Reduce the speed and add the flour a little at a time, to form a stiff dough. Turn out onto a floured work surface and flatten into a round. Transfer to a plate, cover with clingfilm and chill for at least 1 hour; this makes the pastry much easier to handle.

Preheat the oven to 180°C/350°F/gas mark 4. Roll out half the pastry to about 3mm (⅛in) thick and line a cake tin.

Slice the rhubarb into 1cm (½in) rounds. Put them into the pastry-lined tart tin and sprinkle with the sugar. Roll out the remaining pastry. Cover the rhubarb and trim and seal the edges. Use the pastry trimmings to make pastry leaves and decorate the pie. Brush with egg wash and bake for 45–60 minutes until the tart is golden and the rhubarb is soft.

Sprinkle lightly with caster sugar and serve with lightly whipped cream and Barbados sugar.

Note: This tart can also be filled with Bramley apples, gooseberries and elderflower, damsons, plums, blackberries and apples, peaches and raspberries, rhubarb and strawberries.

Dutch Apple Cake with Cinnamon Sugar

SERVES 8   (**P:** 45 MINS/**C:** 35 MINS)

2 free-range, organic large eggs
225g (8oz) caster sugar
110g (4oz) butter, plus extra for greasing
150ml (5fl oz) creamy milk
185g (6¹/₂oz) plain flour, plus extra for sprinkling
3 teaspoons baking powder
3–4 Bramley cooking apples
25g (1oz) sugar
lightly whipped cream, to serve

For the cinnamon sugar:
25g (1oz) caster sugar
1 teaspoon ground cinnamon

Preheat the oven to 200°C/400°F/gas mark 6. Grease and flour a 20 x 30cm (8 x 12in) roasting tin or lasagne dish.

Whisk the eggs and the caster sugar together in a bowl until the mixture is really thick and fluffy.

Put the butter and milk in a saucepan, bring to the boil and stir, still boiling, into the egg and sugar mixture. Sift the flour and baking powder and fold into the batter carefully, so that there are no lumps of flour. Pour the mixture into the roasting tin or lasagne dish.

Peel and core the apples, cut them into thin slices and arrange them, overlapping each other, on top of the batter. Sprinkle with the remaining sugar. Bake for 10 minutes, then reduce the heat to 180°C/350°F/gas mark 4 and continue baking for 20–25 minutes or until the apple cake is well risen and golden brown. Mix the cinnamon and sugar and sprinkle on top. Cut into slices and serve with lightly whipped cream.

Pear and Chocolate Chip Crumble

SERVES 6–8   (**P**: 30 MINS/**C**: 45 MINS)

Crumbles are year-round comfort food – vary the fruit according to the season.

700g (1¹/₂lb) pears
25g (1oz) sugar
50g (2oz) best quality chocolate chips
1 teaspoon fresh ginger, peeled and grated
  (optional)

For the crumble topping:
50g (2oz) cold butter
110g (4oz) white flour
50g (2oz) caster sugar
25g (1oz) chopped almonds or hazelnuts
  (optional)

1.2 litre (2pint) capacity pie dish

Preheat the oven to 180°C/350°F/gas mark 4.

Peel the pears, cut into quarters, remove the core and cut into large cubes. Turn into a pie dish, add the chocolate chips and ginger, (if using), and sprinkle with the sugar.

Rub the butter into the flour just until the mixture resembles really coarse breadcrumbs. Add the sugar and chopped nuts if using. Sprinkle this mixture over the pears. Bake for 40–45 minutes or until the topping is cooked and golden. Serve with whipped cream.

Bramley Apple Crumble
Substitute 700g (1¹/₂lb) Bramley Seedling apples for the pears, omit the chocolate. A good addition to the crumble topping is ¹/₂ teaspoon of ground cinnamon.

Blackberry and Apple Crumble
Use three parts apple to one part fresh or frozen blackberries and proceed as with the apple crumble.

Rhubarb Crumble
Partially stew 700g (1¹/₂lb) rhubarb with 225g (8oz) sugar until half cooked and proceed as with the basic recipe.

Rhubarb and Strawberry Crumble
Partially stew 450g (1lb) rhubarb with 225g (8oz) sugar, stir in 225g (8oz) strawberries and proceed as with Rhubarb Crumble.

Plum or Apricot
Partially stew 675g (1¹/₂lb) plums or apricots and 75g (3oz) sugar and proceed as with the basic recipe.

Variations on the Crumble Topping:
1 25g (1oz) oatflakes can be added to the topping instead of chopped nuts.
2 1 teaspoon ground cinnamon or mixed spice is also a delicious addition.

Coffee and Walnut Biscuits

MAKES 9–10   (**P:** 30 MINS/**C:** 10 MINS)

For the biscuit mixture:
175g (6oz) plain white flour, plus extra
  for dusting
75g (3oz) butter, cut into small cubes
50g (2oz) caster sugar
1 free-range, organic egg

For the coffee filling:
25g (1oz) butter, softened
50g (2oz) icing sugar, sifted
1 teaspoon coffee essence

For the coffee icing:
110g (4oz) icing sugar, sifted
scant ¹/₂ tablespoon coffee essence

To garnish:
fresh walnut halves

Preheat the oven to 180°C/350°F/gas mark 4.

First make the biscuits. Sift the flour into a bowl. Rub in the butter, then add the sugar and mix well. Beat the egg, then mix into the dry ingredients to form a stiff dough. Turn out onto a floured board and roll out to a scant 3mm (¹/₈in) thickness. Cut into 8cm (3¹/₄in) rounds. Bake for about 8 minutes until golden brown. Transfer the biscuits to a wire rack and leave until cold.

Meanwhile, make the coffee filling. Cream the butter and add the sifted icing sugar and the coffee essence. Continue to beat until light and fluffy, then set aside.

Next make the icing. Sift the icing sugar into a bowl. Add the coffee essence and about 1 tablespoon boiling water – just enough to mix to the consistency of a very thick cream. Beat until smooth and glossy.

When the biscuits are cold, sandwich them together with the coffee filling and spread a little thick coffee icing on top. Decorate each biscuit with half a walnut. Great for a picnic.

Summerberry Tart with Rose Water Cream

SERVES 8–12   (**P:** 1 HOUR/**C:** 15 MINS)

1 x 25cm (10in) Sweet Shortcrust Pastry
  (see p246)
redcurrant jelly, to glaze, heated gently to soften
450g (1lb) mixed summer fruit, such as
  raspberries, loganberries, blueberries,
  small strawberries, blackcurrants…

For the rose water cream:
300ml (¹/₂ pint) lightly whipped cream
1 tablespoon icing sugar
1–2 teaspoon rose water

Brush the base of the blind-baked pastry case with redcurrant jelly. Arrange the fruit in the case in concentric circles, or for a more haphazard look, just scatter them into the shell. Brush generously with more redcurrant jelly.

In a bowl, mix together the lightly whipped cream with the icing sugar and rose water. Taste and adjust the flavourings if needed. Serve with the Summerberry Tart.

Summerberry Tart with Cassis Cream
Substitute crème de cassis (blackcurrant syrup) for rose water in the above recipe.

don't forget dessert

Cakes, tarts, fools and ice cream – it should not be a problem to find something to match your menu. Give your guests a sneaky preview so that they leave room for dessert, no matter how tempting the previous courses. Always serve dessert at the table – it is often the best-looking of all courses, so show it off before you hack it to pieces.

This is a good opportunity to move from the table to more comfortable chairs, or to move guests around if you remain at the table. Giving your guests someone new to talk to can often give your dinner party a new lease of life. As the last course, dessert is also the most relaxed – let your guests linger over it. What's more – you can relax too – all that is left is coffee and cheese.

Time for tea (see p260–263)
Sweet Geranium Cake with Blackberries (see p270)
Chocolate Meringue Layer Cake (see p247)
Frosted Lemon and Rosemary Squares (see (p258)
Coffee and Walnut Biscuits (see p274)
Lana Pringle's Barm Brack (see p182)

A savoury tea
Wraps (see p188)
Witches' Bread with Chocolate and Raisins (see p182)
Mary Risley's Chocolate and Raspberry Truffles (see p258)
Bumbles Ginger Roulade (see p255)

What to drink
Tea is about teatime food but it's also about tea, the beverage, the cup that cheers and all that: Earl Grey, lapsang souchong, keemun, even green tea or rooibus, the South African red bush tea. If you must have alcohol – and this may suggest a little problem! what about Pimm's No. 1 with lots of chilled lemonade, a slice of lemon and sprigs of mint and borage? It's light in alcohol and very refreshing, especially in summer.

the cheese course

We've now got so many delicious farmhouse cheeses to choose from in these islands that we're totally spoiled for choice. To round off a meal, serve one cheese in perfect condition with a few homemade crackers and crusty bread or a piece of Membrillo, plump dates, cob nuts… Better still, what could be easier than a farmhouse cheese supper? Choose a selection of gorgeous cheeses. Lay them out on a bed of fresh fig or vine leaves or on timber boards or a flat basket. Provide lots of really good bread and crackers. Open a bottle of wine and enjoy.

Parmesan and Gruyère Cheese Soufflé

SERVES 8–10   (P: 20 MINS/C: 25 MINS)

Guests are always wildly impressed by a well-risen soufflé and believe me it's not rocket science so don't imagine for one moment that you can't do it. A soufflé is simply a well-flavoured sauce enriched with egg yolks and lightened with stiffly beaten egg. Soufflés are much more good humoured than you think and can even be frozen when they are ready for the oven. The French do infinite variations on the theme, both sweet and savoury. I love to make this recipe with some fresh Irish or local farmhouse cheese e.g. Desmond or Gabriel or a mature Coolea.

For the moulds:
melted butter
10g (¹/₂oz) Parmesan cheese,

For the soufflé:
45g (1¹/₂oz) butter
25g (1oz) flour
300ml (¹/₂ pint) milk
4 free-range, organic eggs
50g (2oz) Gruyère cheese, finely grated
50g (2oz) Parmesan, grated
salt and freshly ground pepper
pinch of cayenne pepper
freshly grated nutmeg

8 individual soufflé dishes, 7 x 4 cm
(2¹/₂ x 1¹/₂in) high or 1 large dish 15 x 6.5cm
(6 x 2¹/₂in) high

First prepare the soufflé dish or dishes: brush evenly with melted butter and if you like sprinkle with a little freshly grated Parmesan.

Preheat the oven to 200°C/400°F /gas mark 6 and warm a baking sheet. Melt the butter in a heavy-bottomed saucepan, stir in the flour and cook over a gentle heat for 1–2 minutes. Take off the heat and whisk in the milk, return to the heat, whisk as it comes to the boil, cover and simmer gently for 3–4 minutes. Remove from the heat.

Separate the eggs and put the whites into a large copper, glass or stainless steel bowl, making sure it is spotlessly clean and dry. Whisk the yolks one by one into the white sauce, add both cheeses, season with salt, pepper, cayenne and a little freshly grated nutmeg. It should taste hugely seasoned at this point because the egg whites will dull the seasoning. Stir over a gentle heat for just a few seconds until the cheese melts. Remove from the heat (this can be made ahead up to this point).

Whisk the egg whites with a little pinch of salt, slowly at first and then faster until they are light and voluminous and hold a stiff peak when you lift up the whisk. Stir a few tablespoons into the cheese mixture to lighten it and then carefully fold in the rest with a spatula or tablespoon. Fill the mixture into the prepared soufflé dish or dishes (if you fill them three-quarters full you will get about 10 but if you smooth the tops you will have about 8). Bake in the oven for 8–9 minutes for the individual soufflés or 20–25 minutes for a large one. For the large one you will need to reduce the temperature to 180°C/350° F/gas mark 4, after 15 minutes and a bain marie (put soufflé in baking tray of hot water) is a good idea. Serve immediately.

Top Tip: If you fill the soufflé dishes to the top, smooth off with a palette knife then run a washed thumb around the edge of the dishes before they go into the oven to help to get the 'top hat' effect when the soufflé is well risen.

Individual frozen soufflés can be baked from frozen but they will take a few minutes longer to cook.

Cheese Soufflés with Salad Leaves:

Just before the soufflés are cooked, toss a mixture of salad leaves and divide between the plates. Carefully turn the soufflés out onto the leaves and serve immediately.

Ardsallagh Goat's Cheese with Lavender Honey and Figs

SERVES 4   (P: 10 MINS)

4 fresh fig or vine leaves
round of Ardsallagh goat's cheese, or similar fresh soft goat's cheese
2 tablespoons lavender honey (see right)
4 fresh figs

To garnish:
sprigs of lavender (optional)
fresh fig or vine leaves

Place a fig or vine leaf on each plate and place one small or a quarter of a larger cheese on each one. Drizzle with lavender honey.

Serve with fresh figs. Cut each fig into quarters, almost to the base, then pinch so the fig opens to resemble a flower. Decorate with a few sprigs of lavender (if using) and fresh fig or vine leaves.

Lavender Honey

Put 2–3 teaspoons of dried lavender flowers into a pot of good honey. Allow to infuse for at least a week.

Raclette

A raclette party is so easy and such fun –
just provide cheese, boiled potatoes and
pickles. Guests do their own cooking and
there is a minimum of washing up. If you do
a great deal of impromptu entertaining, a
raclette stove is really worth having.

raclette cheese, about 175g (6oz) per person
freshly boiled potatoes, 3–4 per person
lettuce, such as Little Gem, cut in half
  lengthwise, or a good green salad
cornichons or slices of dill pickle, 3–4 per person
radishes
tiny spring onions (optional)
sea salt and freshly ground black pepper

Put the raclette stove in the centre of the table and turn on the heat. Cut the cheese into
slices a scant 5mm (1/4in) thick, and put a slice on each little pan.

While the cheese is melting, serve onto each person's heated plate freshly boiled potatoes
and 3–4 leaves of crisp lettuce, such as Little Gem, or a green salad. As soon as the cheese
melts, each guest spoons it over the potato and puts another piece on the pan to melt.

Serve with pickles and radishes, and maybe a few tiny spring onions as an accompaniment.

Ballymaloe Cheese Fondue

SERVES 2   (P: 10 MINS/C: 5 MINS)

A fondue is such a retro dish and it can be
great fun. When you sit at the table, choose
your seat carefully, because if you drop your
piece of bread into the fondue, you must
kiss the person on your right (this could be
your big chance!). My mother-in-law, Myrtle
Allen, devised this recipe using Irish Cheddar
cheese. The fondue is a meal in itself, but
even so it can be made in minutes. A fondue
set is obviously an advantage if you own
one, but if not, it is not essential. The
quantities given here are perfect for a
romantic supper for two. Each diner will
need a fondue fork and an ordinary fork.

2 tablespoons white wine
2 small garlic cloves, crushed
2 teaspoons Ballymaloe Country Relish or
  tomato chutney
2 teaspoons chopped parsley
175g (6oz) mature Cheddar cheese, grated

To serve:
crusty white French bread, or other white bread

Put the white wine into a fondue pot or a
small saucepan. Add the crushed garlic,
tomato relish or chutney, chopped parsley
and cheese, and stir.

Just before serving, place on a low heat until
the cheese melts and begins to bubble. Put
the pot on the fondue stove and serve
immediately.

Provide each diner with fresh, crusty French
bread. Alternatively, the fondue may be
served with cubes of ordinary white bread
crisped up in a hot oven.

Camembert with Caramel and Walnuts

SERVES 6–8   (P: 5 MINS/C: 15 MINS)

A complete sacrilege in some cheese lovers'
opinion, but a fun way to use a less-than-
totally gorgeous Camembert.

1 ripe Camembert cheese
7 whole walnuts, shelled
110g (4oz) granulated sugar

To serve:
watercress leaves and crusty bread

Unwrap the Camembert, place on a serving plate and arrange the walnuts on top.

Put the sugar into a heavy stainless steel saucepan over a medium heat, and stir until the
sugar dissolves and starts to caramelise. It will look lumpy and peculiar at first but will
eventually melt. When the syrup turns to a chestnut-coloured caramel, spoon it evenly over
the top of the cheese and walnuts – it will solidify into a shiny crust.

To serve, crack the caramel with a knife and serve the cheese in slices, with some peppery
watercress leaves and lots of crusty bread.

Saganaki (Greek Fried Cheese)

SERVES 6–8   (P: 5 MINS/C: 5 MINS)

This is a meal made in minutes. Fried cheese cooked in a little round aluminium frying pan is called a saganaki. Greek kasseri cheese is traditionally used, but it can be made with various hard cheeses, including halloumi, kefalotiri Greek and Cypriot cheeses, and even French gruyère. It must be served piping hot – Greek waiters occasionally run to get it to the customer while it is still bubbling.

225g (8oz) hard Greek or Cypriot cheese, such as kefalotiri or halloumi
butter or extra virgin olive oil, for frying
lemon juice, to sprinkle
cracked black peppercorns

To serve:
crusty white bread
green salad

Cut the cheese into slices about 1cm (¹/₂in) thick. Melt a little butter or olive oil in a small frying pan, put in a few cheese slices in a single layer, reduce the heat and let the cheese cook for 1 or 2 minutes until it begins to bubble. It should not brown. Sprinkle with a few drops of lemon juice and some freshly cracked pepper, rush it to the table, and eat with crusty white bread. Follow with a good green salad.

Melted Cooleeney Cheese in a Box

SERVES 6–8   (P: 5 MINS/C: 20 MINS)

Cooleeney cheese is a delectable Camembert type of farmhouse cheese made by Breda Maher from the milk of her Fresian cows.

1 Cooleeney cheese, slightly underripe, or brie, Camembert, or any farmhouse cheese sold in a wooden box
crusty white bread, or homemade Potato Crisps (see recipe below)

Preheat the oven to 180°C/350°F/gas mark 4.

Remove the labels from the box and the wrapper from the cheese. Ensure that the box is stapled, or it may fall apart in the oven. Put the cheese back in the box and bake in the oven for about 20 minutes, by which time it should be soft and molten in the centre.

Cut a cross in the centre of the cheese and serve immediately, with crusty white bread, or homemade potato crisps.

Potato Crisps

YOU WILL NEED 3–4 CRISPS PER PORTION.

2 very large potatoes
olive oil, for deep frying
salt

Scrub the potatoes and slice them as thinly as possible, preferably with a mandoline grater, to make long, thin slices. Deep-fry the potato slices until crisp and drain on kitchen paper. These can be cooked ahead of serving time and kept in a warm place. Sprinkle with salt.

Melted Gubbeen Cheese with Winter Herbs

SERVES 6–8   (P: 5 MINS/C: 30 MINS)

Farmhouse cheese-maker Giana Ferguson gave me this little gem of a recipe for her washed salt rind cheese, which she makes on the family farm near Schull, in West Cork.

1 baby Gubbeen (or any washed rind cheese), 450g (1lb) weight, 12cm (4¹/₂in) diameter
2 teaspoons chopped thyme
1 large or 2 small garlic cloves, finely chopped
freshly ground black pepper

To serve: crusty bread, green salad

Preheat the oven to 180°C/350°F/gas mark 4. Cut a piece of aluminium foil about 30cm (12in) square.

Split the baby Gubbeen cheese in half around its 'equator'. Put the base on the centre of the foil, generously sprinkle the cut surface with the thyme, garlic and lots of black pepper. Top with the other part of cheese. Gather up the edges of the foil, but leave a little vent for the steam to escape. Bake for 20–30 minutes or until soft and melting.

Open the parcel. Lift off the rind and eat the soft, herby, melting cheese with lots of crusty bread or boiled potatoes and a green salad. Exquisite!

Note: Cooleeney Irish cheese may also be used for this recipe. It will be perfect after baking for about 10 minutes.

Soft Yogurt Cheese (Labne)

This is so easy and wonderfully impressive. Use whole-milk yogurt to make a creamier cheese. Labne is a traditional yogurt cheese from Lebanon.

Line a sieve or colander with a double thickness of clean muslin and place it over a bowl. Pour in the yogurt. Tie the four corners of the cloth to make a loose bundle. Suspend the bag of yogurt over a bowl to allow it to drip, and leave for 8 hours.

Remove the cheesecloth. Refrigerate in a covered plastic container. It will keep for 4–5 days in the fridge.

Soft Yogurt Cheese with Chives and Parsley

SERVES 4–6   (P: 10 MINS + 8 HOURS TO DRIP)

Dry the chives and parsley thoroughly before chopping.

450ml (16fl oz) whole-milk natural yogurt
3–4 tablespoons double cream (optional)
1/2 teaspoon very finely sliced chives
1 teaspoon finely chopped parsley
salt and sugar to taste

Follow the instructions for making Soft Yogurt Cheese (see recipe above) with the natural yogurt, and allow to drip for 8 hours.

In a stainless steel or glass bowl, mix the yogurt cheese with the remainder of the ingredients. Mix well and adjust the seasoning to taste. Cover and refrigerate for at least 1 hour. If some liquid accumulates, just discard it before you serve.

Lemon balm or chervil may also be used, and a little garlic if you like. Alternatively, add chopped mint, dill or marjoram and a drizzle of extra virgin olive oil; a little sea salt and some paprika is also good. Nasturtium flowers are another good addition.

Soft Yogurt Cheese with Fresh Berries

SERVES 4–6   (P: 10 MINS/C: 8 HOURS)

450ml (16fl oz) whole-milk natural yogurt
125ml (4fl oz) double cream
2–3 tablespoons caster sugar
fresh summer berries
Fresh Strawberry Sauce (see p250)

Follow the recipe above for Soft Yogurt Cheese. Add the cream and caster sugar to taste and serve with fresh summer berries and Fresh Strawberry Sauce.

Plate of Irish Goat's and Sheep's Milk Cheeses with Figs

Irish goat's milk cheeses include:
Croghan, Mine Gabhar, Ardsallagh, St Tola, Clonmore, Corleggy, Corbetstown, Oísin or Boilie.

Irish sheep's milk cheeses include:
Cratloe Hills, Knockalara, Crozier blue.

(If you cannot find Irish cheese, use a sheep's milk or goat's cheese of your choice.)

To serve:
fresh fig or vine leaves
fresh figs, 1 per person
crusty bread

Lay fresh fig leaves on a timber board, wicker tray or individual plates. Arrange a selection of fresh Irish goat's and sheep's milk cheeses on top. Serve with plump fresh figs – allow 1 per person – and lots of good, crusty bread.

Goat's Cheese in Grappa with Crusty Bread

SERVES 4–6
(**P:** 10 MINS + 24 HOURS TO MARINATE)

The lovely Australian cook Maggie Beer gave us this recipe, when she taught at the school. She says that 'the strength of the grappa gives a wonderful balance to the creaminess of the goat's cheese in this dish, and although you could substitute brandy, the "kick" of the grappa is hard to beat.'

350g (12oz) fresh soft goat's cheese (we use
  Ardsallagh, our local goat's cheese)

For the marinade:
2 tablespoons grappa, or brandy
65ml (2¹/₂fl oz) extra virgin olive oil
1 large garlic clove, finely sliced
2 tablespoons roughly chopped flat parsley
freshly ground black pepper

To serve:
rocket salad, dressed with extra virgin olive oil
  and balsamic vinegar
bread slices, brushed with extra virgin olive oil
  and toasted in the oven

Make the marinade by mixing all the ingredients together in a bowl.

Pour a little of the marinade into a shallow pottery dish. Lay the goat's cheese on top and spoon the remaining marinade over. Cover with clingfilm and refrigerate for 24 hours, turning the cheese over once or twice.

About an hour before serving, leave the cheese to warm to room temperature. Serve with a rocket salad; slabs of bread, brushed with olive oil and toasted in the oven, are a must!

Manchego with Membrillo and Sardinian Parchment Bread

Serve triangles of aged Manchego cheese with quince cheese or jam and Sardinian parchment bread or another crusty white bread.

Some Good Things to Serve with Cheese

A cheese plate with complimentary nuts, dried fruit, relishes, perhaps a little salad and some crackers or flavoured breads makes such a yummy end to a meal.

Nuts
Fresh walnuts, pecans, almonds, hazelnuts, cob nuts, macadamia nuts, brazil nuts

Dried Fruit
Plump dried Turkish figs, dried peaches, pears, Medjool dates

Relishes
Beetroot and ginger, tomato relish, jalapeño, pimento

Honey
Particularly good with blue cheese

drinks

Tom Doorley has given some brilliant advice on wine matching, but here are some lovely aperitifs and out-of-the-ordinary soft drinks. I do also recommend my mulled apple juice, elderflower champagne and sweet lassis. For a really special touch, fill ice cubes with seasonal berries and fresh herbs.

Elderflower Champagne

MAKES ABOUT 5 LITRES (9 PINTS)
(**P:** 10 MINS + 24 HOURS + 2 WEEKS)

This magical, non-alcoholic recipe transforms perfectly ordinary ingredients into a delicious sparkling drink. My family make it religiously every year and then share the bubbly with their friends.

1 unwaxed, organic lemon
2 heads of elderflowers in full bloom
600g (1¼lb) sugar
2 tablespoons white wine vinegar
4.5 litres (8 pints) water

With a swivel-top peeler, remove the zest from the lemon and reserve, then extract the juice from the lemon. Put the elderflowers into a bowl and add the lemon zest and juice, sugar, vinegar and water. Cover and leave in a cool place for 24 hours.

Stir the liquid and sieve it into a bowl or jug, then funnel into screw-top bottles and seal tightly. Lay them on their sides in a cool place. After 2 weeks the elderflower champagne should be sparkling and ready to drink.

Elderflower Syrup

MAKES ABOUT 700ML (1¼ PINTS)
(**P:** 10 MINS + 24 HOURS)

Great for elderflower lemonade, or add a dash in a flute of champagne or a gin and tonic. It also adds magical flavour to fruit dishes, such as fruit salad.

175g (6oz) caster sugar
600ml (1 pint) water
6 heads of elderflowers in full bloom
zest and juice of 2 unwaxed, organic lemons

Put the sugar and water into a saucepan over a medium heat. Stir until the sugar dissolves, add the elderflowers, bring to the boil and boil for 5 minutes. Remove from the heat and add the lemon zest and juice. Cover and set aside to cool. Leave to infuse in a cool, dry place for 24 hours.

Strain and bottle in gin or vodka bottles. Seal well. Dilute as desired.

Rosemary Syrup

MAKES 770ML (1 PINT 7FL OZ)

Use as the basis of lemonades or fruit compotes.

450g (1lb) sugar
600ml (1 pint) water
2 rosemary sprigs

Put the sugar and water into a saucepan, add the sprigs of rosemary. Bring slowly to the boil, allow to cool, strain and store in a fridge. It will keep for weeks.

Good Things to have with Champagne, Sparkling Wine or Prosecco

Add a teaspoon of one of these per glass:
Elderflower Syrup (see above)
Sloe Gin (see p290)
Crème de Fraises
Murs
Framboises
Cassis
Peches
Abricot

Or drop a fresh strawberry, a few blackberries, raspberries or blackcurrants, or a slice of peach or apricot into each glass.

Maybe float a sprig of mint, lemon balm, lemon verbena or sweet cicely on top to really guild the lily.

Herb flowers, violas or violets also look darling floating in a glass of bubbly.

Bucks Fizz

Half fill a champagne flute with some fresh orange juice. Top up with champagne, sparkling wine or prosecco. Ruby grapefruit juice also makes a mouth-watering drink.

Granita Fizz

Drop an ice cube of your favourite granita or sorbet into a glass and top up with sparkling wine, champagne or prosecco.

Prosecco with Violet Syrup

Pour a little violet syrup into a glass, top up with prosecco or sparkling wine. Float a few fresh violets on top of each glass if available. Enjoy.

Homemade Lemonades

We always keep some chilled Stock Syrup in the fridge, to make a variety of lemonades. They contain no preservatives so they should be drunk within a few hours of being made.

Orange and Lemonade

juice of 2 oranges
juice of 4 lemons
450ml (16fl oz) Stock Syrup
about 1.5 litres (2¹/₂ pints) water
ice cubes
sprigs of mint or lemon balm, to garnish

In a large jug, mix together the citrus juices, the stock syrup and water to taste. Add ice, garnish with sprigs of mint or lemon balm and serve.

Limeade

juice of 5 limes
750ml (1¹/₄ pints) water
300ml (¹/₂ pint) Stock Syrup
ice cubes
sprigs of fresh mint or lemon balm, to garnish

Make and serve as above.

Ruby Grapefruit Lemonade

juice of 2 lemons
juice of 4 ruby grapefruit
450ml (16fl oz) Stock Syrup
water or sparkling water, to taste
Mint Ice Cubes (see below)

Mix together the citrus juices and the syrup, and add water or sparkling water to taste. Serve chilled, with mint ice cubes.

Rosemary Lemonade

A delicious thirst-quenching lemonade with a grown-up flavour!

juice of 3 lemons
225ml (8fl oz) Rosemary Syrup (see p286)
670ml (1 pint 4fl oz) water

Mix all the ingredients together. Taste and add more rosemary syrup if needed.

Elderflower Lemonade

Add 1 part Elderflower Syrup (see p286) to 6 parts water and ice.

Ice-Cubes with Mint, Herbs, Lemon Verbena, Flowers and Berries

Fill ice cube trays with:
1. Sugared cranberries
2. Redcurrants and mint leaves
3. Lemon segments
4. Pomegranate seeds
5. Star anise
Cover with water and freeze

Summer Parties
Take empty ice trays and in each hole put mint leaves, lemon balm leaves, sweet geranium leaves or sweet cicely leaves. Cover with water and freeze.
1. Raspberries and mint
2. Wild strawberries
3. Violas or violets, rose petals or marigold petals

Christmas Drinks
Pop Kumquats in Brandy into a glass, top up with champagne or Sloe Gin (see p290).

Funky tip: Soak lemon segments in elderflower cordial, freeze into ice cubes and use in gin and tonics.

Sorbet Cubes
Use your favourite sorbet to make ice cubes and drop them into sparkling wine or prosecco. Strawberry sorbet, elderberry, rhubarb, blackcurrant...all are delicious.

Blackberry Ice Cubes
Pop a juicy blackberry into each section of an ice cube tray, add a tiny sweet geranium or mint leaf. Fill with cold water and freeze. Pop into a glass of dry white wine or lemonade.

Lassi

SERVES 1   (P: 5 MINS)

In India we came across many different types of lassi (a yogurt drink), some sweet and some salty. They are drunk with meals or as a refreshing beverage on a hot afternoon. In India the yogurt is rich and wonderful, so don't dream of using low-fat yogurt – use the best you can find, or make your own (see p33)

Salty Lassi

SERVES 1   (P: 5 MINS)

50ml (2fl oz) best-quality natural yogurt
175ml (6fl oz) water and ice mixed
tiny pinch of salt
mint leaves (optional)

Whizz all the ingredients together in a blender for a few seconds. Serve in a chilled glass, scatter with a few mint leaves if you like, and serve immediately

Sweet Lassi

SERVES 1   (P: 5 MINS)

50ml (2fl oz) best-quality natural yogurt
175ml (6fl oz) water and ice mixed
1/4–1 tablespoon caster sugar
1/8–1/4 teaspoon rose water or kewra (Indian
  essence)
rose petals (optional)

Whizz all the ingredients together in a blender. Pour into a chilled glass, scatter with rose petals if you like, and serve immediately.

Sharbat

SERVES 2–4   (P: 10 MINS)

This is an apple-milk drink and one of the many cooling summer drinks from Morocco.

2 red dessert apples
2 tablespoons granulated sugar
2 scant teaspoons rose water or orange-flower
  water

Laxmi's Lassi

SERVES 1   (P: 5 MINS)

Laxmi Nair, whose family owns the gorgeous Leela Palace Hotel in Mumbai, gave me this recipe.

75ml (3fl oz) best-quality natural yogurt
175ml (6fl oz) water and ice mixed
1/2 green chilli, deseeded and chopped
2 fresh curry leaves
4 mint leaves
pinch of salt

Whizz all the ingredients together in a blender for a few seconds. Pour into a chilled glass and serve immediately.

Leela Palace's Lassi

SERVES 1   (P: 25 MINS)

tiny pinch of saffron strands
225ml (8fl oz) best-quality natural yogurt
1 tablespoon roughly chopped pistachio nuts
1 teaspoon sugar
1 teaspoon chopped mint

Put the saffron strands in a tiny bowl, pour in 1 tablespoon of water and soak for 10–15 minutes. Put the remainder of the ingredients in a liquidiser and whizz. Pour into a tall glass, drizzle the saffron over the top and serve.

450ml (16fl oz) milk
shaved ice (optional)

Peel and cube the apples. Put them into a liquidiser, along with the sugar, rose water or orange-flower water, and milk. Whizz at high speed for 15 seconds. Serve, with some shaved ice if you like, in small glasses.

Fresh Herb Tisanes

From spring onwards, when the herb garden is full of abundance, we make lots of tisanes and herb teas. All you need to do is pop a few leaves into a teapot and pour on the boiling water – infinitely more delicious than the dried herb tea-bags.

A Paris restaurant I dined in recently served herb infusions in the most delightful way. The waiter came to the table with several china bowls of fresh herbs on a silver salver. With tiny silver tongs he put the guest's chosen herb into a little china teapot, poured on boiling water and served it with a flourish. Exquisite.

choice of herb, e.g. lemon verbena, rosemary,
  sweet geranium, lemon balm, spearmint,
  peppermint
water

Bring fresh cold water to the boil and scald a china tea pot.

Take a handful of fresh herb leaves and crush them gently. The quantity will depend on the strength of the herb and how intense an infusion you enjoy. Put them into the scalded teapot. Pour the boiling water over the leaves, cover the teapot and allow to infuse for 3–4 minutes.

Serve immediately in china teacups.

Mulled Red Wine

SERVES 8   (P: 5 MINS/C: 30 MINS)

Just before the festive season we make up lots of little packages with the sugar, spices and thinly pared lemon rind, so when guests arrive, it's just a question of opening a bottle of wine and warming it in a stainless steel saucepan with the spices. Leftover mulled wine keeps for a few days and reheats perfectly.

100–110g (3¹/₂–4oz) sugar
1 bottle of good red wine
thinly pared zest of 1 lemon
1 small piece of cinnamon stick
1 blade of mace
1 whole clove

Put the sugar into a stainless steel or cast-iron saucepan, pour in the wine and add the lemon zest, cinnamon, mace and clove. Heat over a gentle heat, stirring often to ensure the sugar is fully dissolved. Serve hot but not scalding, otherwise your guests will have difficulty holding their glasses.

Mulled White Wine

SERVES 8   (P: 5 MINS/C: 30 MINS)

110g (4oz) sugar
1.5 litres (2¹/₂ pints) chardonnay or
   other white wine
3 cinnamon sticks
6 whole cloves
4 star anise
2–3 sprigs of thyme
1 thinly pared zest of orange

Put the sugar into a stainless steel or cast-iron saucepan, pour in the wine and add all the other ingredients. Heat over a gentle heat, stirring often to ensure the sugar is fully dissolved. Allow to infuse for 10 minutes. Serve warm.

Sloe Gin

Sloes are very tart little purple berries that grow on prickly bushes, often draped over the top of stone walls. They are in season in September and October. It's great fun to organise a sloe-picking expedition and have a sloe-gin-making party. Sloe gin makes a terrific Christmas present.

700g (1¹/₂lb) sloes
340g (12oz) white granulated sugar
1.2 litres (2 pints) gin

darning needles, for pricking
sterilised glass jars and bottles

Wash and dry the sloes, prick in several places (we use a clean darning needle). Put them into sterilised glass jars and cover with the sugar and gin. Seal the jars tightly and set aside in a cool, dry place.

Shake every couple of days to start with, and then every now and then for 3–4 months, by which time it will be ready to strain and funnel into bottles.

Sloe gin will improve on keeping so try to resist drinking it for another few months.

Damson gin can be made in the same way.

Classic Margarita

SERVES 2   (P: 5 MINS)

One sip of margarita and I'm transported to my beloved Mexico. I close my eyes and see the swirling colours and hear the lively music. Fine-grained dairy salt, unlike table salt, has no additives. This will help keep the liquid from clouding.

dairy salt
¹/₂ lime, plus 2 tablespoons lime juice
125ml (4fl oz) white tequila
2 tablespoons orange liqueur,
   such as Cointreau or Triple Sec
6 ice cubes

2 cocktail glasses

Pour some dairy salt into a saucer or small plate. Rub the rims of the two cocktail glasses with the lime, then dip the rims of the glass into the salt and spin to frost.

Put the tequila, orange liqueur, lime juice and ice cubes into a jug and mix well. When thoroughly chilled, strain and divide between the two glasses. Serve immediately.

Granita Cocktail

To a glass of prosecco or sparkling wine, add a scoop of your favourite granita or water ice. Try watermelon, strawberry, lemon verbena… Sublime!

Mojito

MAKES 1   (P: 10 MINS)

1 tablespoon granulated sugar
3–4 fresh mint leaves
freshly squeezed juice of 1 lime
2 ice cubes, crushed
25ml (1fl oz) white rum
splash of soda water

Put the sugar and fresh mint leaves in a chilled glass, muddle or crush with a wooden pestle or the thick handle of a wooden spoon. Add the freshly squeezed lime juice and rum, then add the ice, stir and top up with soda water. Add a straw and enjoy!

Banana Daiquiri

SERVES 2   (P: 5 MINS)

100ml (3¹/₂fl oz) light rum, such as
  Havana Club
25ml (1fl oz) orange liqueur, such as Cointreau
2 ripe bananas, diced
60ml (2¹/₄fl oz) lime juice
2 cups ice

Whizz all the ingredients in a blender. Pour into chilled glasses and enjoy!

Watermelon Juice

SERVES 8–12   (P: 20 MINS)

250ml (8fl oz) water
10–12 tablespoons sugar
1 large watermelon
zest and juice of 4 limes
ice cubes
sprigs of mint, to garnish

Put the water and sugar in a saucepan and bring to the boil. When the sugar has dissolved, remove the pan from the heat.

Cut the watermelon flesh into 5cm (2in) chunks and pick out the seeds. Working in batches, put the chunks into a food processor and purée. Stir the sugar syrup,

Mulled Apple Juice

SERVES 8   (P: 5 MINS/C: 10 MINS)

750ml (1¹/₃ pints) pure apple juice
750ml (1¹/₃ pints) bottled water
1 orange, preferably unwaxed
12 whole cloves

3 small cinnamon sticks
6 allspice berries or pimento berries
¹/₂ teaspoon grated nutmeg
75g (3oz) golden caster sugar

Caipirinha

MAKES 1   (P: 10 MINS)

Brazil's national cocktail and so hip.

1 lime, well washed
2 teaspoons granulated sugar
3 tablespoons Cachaca (Brazilian white rum)
  or white rum
crushed ice

Cut the lime in quarters. Pop into a tumbler. Sprinkle with sugar and crush with a wooden pestle until the juice comes out of the lime and the zest infuses the sugar. Add the Cachaca or white rum and some crushed ice. Stir and enjoy.

Pink Grapefruit and Pomegranate Cocktail

Mix freshly squeezed pink grapefruit juice with grenadine syrup. Sweeten to taste with Stock Syrup (see p288) and dilute with still or sparkling water. Add ice cubes and garnish with pomegranate seeds and mint leaves.

lime zest and juice into the melon pureé. Dilute with water to taste and add a few ice cubes and a sprig of fresh mint to each glass.

Watermelon Granita
Proceed as above but do not dilute with water at the end. Freeze the watermelon liquid in a sorbetière in the usual way.

Pour the apple juice and water into a stainless steel saucepan. Wash the orange well in warm water, and peel the rind thinly. Add to the pan, along with the rest of the spices and the sugar. Heat gently. Adjust the spicing or sugar if needed, and serve hot.

basics

Guacamole

1 ripe avocado
1–2 tablespoons freshly squeezed lime juice
1 tablespoon extra virgin olive oil
1 tablespoon freshly chopped coriander or
   flat parsley
sea salt and freshly ground pepper

Scoop out the flesh from the avocado. Mash
with a fork or in a pestle and mortar, add the
lime juice, olive oil, coriander and salt and
freshly ground pepper to taste. Serve
immediately. Otherwise, cover the surface of
the guacamole with a sheet of plastic to
exclude the air. Keep cool until needed. A
little finely diced chilli or tomato may be
added to the guacamole.

Tomato and Coriander Salsa

**This sauce is ever present on Mexican tables
to serve with all manner of dishes. Salsas of
all kinds, both fresh and cooked, have now
become a favourite accompaniment to
everything from pangrilled meat to a piece of
sizzling fish.**

6 very ripe tomatoes, chopped
2 tablespoons finely chopped red onion
1 garlic clove, crushed
1/2–1 chilli, deseeded and finely chopped
2 tablespoons chopped fresh coriander
freshly squeezed lime juice – about 1 lime
salt, freshly ground pepper and sugar

Mix all the ingredients together. Season with
salt, freshly ground pepper and sugar. Taste
and adjust the seasoning if necessary.

Tomato and Red Onion Salsa

4 very ripe but firm tomatoes, cut into dice
1 small red onion, cut in half and thinly sliced
1/2–1 green chilli
1 tablespoon lime juice

1 tablespoon extra virgin olive oil
1–2 tablespoons chopped coriander leaves
salt, freshly ground pepper and sugar to taste

Mix all the ingredients gently in a bowl. Taste
and adjust the seasoning if needed.

Mango Salsa

2 ripe mangoes, cut into 5mm (1/4in) dice
2 tablespoons Sweet Chilli Sauce (see p296)
2 tablespoons lime or lemon juice
2 tablespoons chopped coriander leaves

Mix all the ingredients together in a bowl.
Taste and adjust seasoning if needed. Cover
and chill until ready to use – it's best fresh, so
eat it within a day.

Banana and Cardamom Raita

**This is delicious served with spicy vegetable
stews, mild Madras curry or pangrilled chicken
breast. Perhaps surprisingly, it keeps for days
in the fridge and we've also enjoyed it as a
pudding.**

50g (2oz) raisins and/or sultanas
25g (1oz) almonds, blanched and slivered
200ml (7fl oz) natural yogurt
100ml (31/2fl oz) cream
100ml (31/2fl oz) soured cream
1 tablespoon pure honey, plus extra to taste
4–6 cardamom pods
3 firm ripe bananas
pinch of salt

Pour boiling water over the raisins or sultanas
and leave for 10 minutes, then drain.

Meanwhile, toast the almonds.

Mix the yogurt with the creams, add the
honey, taste and add more honey if needed.
Add the raisins and almonds, reserving a few
almonds for the garnish.

Remove the seeds from the cardamom
pods, crush using a pestle and mortar, and
stir into the yogurt mixture.

Slice the bananas, season with a pinch of
salt and add to the yogurt. Stir thoroughly,
turn into a serving bowl and scatter with the
reserved toasted almonds. Chill for an hour
if possible before serving.

Tomato Purée

**Tomato Purée is one of the very best ways of
preserving the flavour of ripe, summer
tomatoes for winter. We make lots of
homemade tomato purée at the end of the
Summer when the tomatoes are really ripe –
it's brilliant to have in the freezer for tomato
soup, stews, casseroles etc.**

900g (2lb) very ripe tomatoes
1 small onion, chopped
1 teaspoon sugar
a good pinch of salt
a few twists of black pepper

Cut the tomatoes into quarters, put into a
stainless steel saucepan with the onion,
sugar, salt and freshly ground pepper.

Cook on a gentle heat until the tomatoes
are soft (no water needed). Put through the
fine blade of a mouli-legume (food mill) or
a nylon sieve. Allow to get cold then
refrigerate or freeze.

Homemade Veg Stock

**Basically you can make a vegetable stock
from whatever vegetables you have available
but try not to use too much of any one
vegetable unless you particularly want that
flavour to predominate.**

1 small white turnip
2 onions, peeled and roughly sliced
green parts of 2–3 leeks

3 celery sticks, washed and roughly chopped
3 large carrots, scrubbed and roughly chopped
1/2 fennel bulb, roughly chopped
110g (4oz) mushrooms or mushroom stalks
4–6 parsley stalks
bouquet garni
few peppercorns
2 1/2 litres (4 pints) cold water

Put all the ingredients into a large saucepan, add the cold water, bring to the boil, then reduce the heat, cover and simmer for 1–2 hours. Strain through a sieve. Keeps for a week in the fridge or may be frozen.

Homemade Chicken Stock

Keep your carcasses, giblets and vegetable trimmings and use them for your stock pot. Nowadays some supermarkets and poulterers are happy to give you chicken carcasses and often giblets as well just for the asking because there is so little demand.

2–3 raw or cooked chicken carcasses or a
  mixture of both
giblets from the chicken, i.e. neck, heart,
  gizzard (Save the liver for another dish)
1 onion, sliced
1 leek, split in two
1 outside stick of celery (not the heart, the
  coarser outside stalks) or 1 lovage leaf
1 carrot, sliced
few parsley stalks
sprig of thyme
6 peppercorns
3.4 litres (6 pints) cold water

Chop up the carcasses as much as possible. Put all the ingredients into a saucepan and cover with cold water. Bring to the boil and skim the fat off the top with a tablespoon. Simmer for 3–5 hours. Strain and remove any remaining fat. If you need a stronger flavour, boil down the liquid in an open pan to reduce the volume by one-third or one-half. Do not add salt.

Note: stock will keep for several days in the refrigerator. Stock also freezes perfectly. For cheap containers use large yogurt cartons or plastic milk bottles, then you can cut them off the frozen stock without a conscience if you need to defrost it in a hurry!

The above recipe is just a guideline. If you have just one carcass and can't be bothered to make a small quantity of stock, why not freeze the carcass and save it up until you have 6 or 7 carcasses plus giblets, then you can make a really good sized pot of stock and get the best value for your fuel.

There are some vegetables which should not be put in the stock, e.g. potatoes because they soak up flavour and make the stock cloudy; parsnips – too strong, beetroot – they are too strong also and the dye would produce a red stock – great for beetroot soup. Cabbage or other brassicas give an off-taste when cooked for a long time. A little white turnip is sometimes an asset, but it is very easy to overdo it. I also ban bay leaf in my chicken stocks because I find that the flavour of bay can predominate easily and add a sameness to soups made from the stock later on.

Basic Fish Stock

MAKES ABOUT 1.8 LITRES (3 PINTS)

Fish stock takes only 20 minutes to make. If you can get lots of fresh fish bones from your fishmonger it's well worth making two or three times the recipe, because it freezes well.

1kg (2 1/4lb) fish bones, preferably sole, turbot
  or brill
5–10g (1/4–1/2oz) butter
100g (3 1/2oz) onions, finely sliced
125–250ml (4–8fl oz) dry white wine
4 peppercorns
bouquet garni containing a sprig of thyme,
  4–5 parsley stalks, small piece of celery and
  a tiny scrap of bay leaf

Wash the fish bones thoroughly under cold running water until no trace of blood remains and chop into pieces. In a large stainless steel saucepan, melt the butter, add the onions, toss and sweat on a gentle heat until soft but not coloured. Add the bones to the saucepan, stir and cook very briefly with the onions. Add the dry white wine and boil until nearly all the wine has evaporated. Cover with cold water, add the peppercorns and the bouquet garni. Bring to the boil and simmer for 20 minutes, skimming often. Strain. Allow to cool, degrease if necessary and refrigerate.

Hollandaise Sauce

2 free-range, organic egg yolks
110g (4oz) butter, cut into dice
1 teaspoon freshly squeezed lemon juice

Put the egg yolks in a heavy stainless steel saucepan on a low heat, or in a bowl over hot water. Add 1 dessertspoon of cold water and whisk thoroughly. Add the butter one piece at a time, whisking all the while. As soon as one piece melts, add the next. The mixture will gradually thicken, but if it shows signs of becoming too thick or of scrambling, remove from the heat immediately and add a little cold water if necessary. Do not leave the pan or stop whisking until the sauce thickens to coating consistency. Remove from the heat and add the lemon juice to taste.

Note: A low heat is crucial when making hollandaise sauce in a saucepan directly over the heat: it should be possible to put your hand on the side of the pan at any stage – if it feels too hot for your hand it is also too hot for the sauce. However, if the sauce is very slow to thicken it may be because you are being excessively cautious and the heat is too low. Increase the heat slightly and continue to whisk until the sauce thickens to coating consistency.

Top Tip: If you are making hollandaise sauce for the first time, keep a bowl of cold water close by so you can plunge the bottom of the saucepan into it if it becomes too hot and the sauce becomes too thick or scrambles.

Béarnaise Sauce

SERVES 6–8

Substitute mint for French tarragon and the name changes to sauce paloise; delicious with roast or pangrilled lamb. If you do not have tarragon vinegar to hand, use a wine vinegar and add some extra chopped tarragon.

4 tablespoons tarragon vinegar
4 tablespoons dry white wine
2 teaspoons finely chopped shallots
pinch of freshly ground pepper
2 free-range, organic egg yolks
110–175g (4–6oz) butter, salted or unsalted

depending on what it is being served with
1 tablespoon freshly chopped French
tarragon leaves

Boil the first 4 ingredients together in a shallow heavy bottomed stainless steel saucepan until completely reduced and the pan is almost dry but the shallots are not browned. Add 1 tablespoon of cold water immediately. Pull the pan off the heat and allow to cool for 1–2 minutes.

Whisk in the egg yolks and add the butter bit by bit over a very low heat, whisking all the time. As soon as one piece melts, add the next piece; it will gradually thicken. If it shows signs of becoming too thick or scrambling, remove from the heat immediately and add a little cold water. Do not leave the pan or stop whisking until the sauce is made. Finally add the freshly chopped French tarragon and taste for seasoning.

Sweet Chilli Sauce

3 large red chillies, finely chopped (seeds
and all)
1 garlic clove, crushed
185g (6^1/$_2$oz) granulated sugar
125ml (4fl oz) rice vinegar
1 teaspoon salt

Put all the ingredients into a little saucepan over a low heat. Stir to dissolve the sugar. Bring to the boil and continue to cook, stirring from time to time, for 5–6 minutes or until the mixture thickens to a syrupy texture. Cool and pour into a jam jar or bottle.

Onion Sauce (Sauce Soubise)

SERVES 8–10

Great with roast lamb or pangrilled lamb chops. Onion sauce is a sort of 'forgotten flavour' which makes a delicious change from the more usual mint jelly.

50g (2oz) butter
3 onions, about 450g (1lb) in weight, thinly
sliced or finely chopped
^{1}/$_2$ teaspoon salt
^{1}/$_4$ teaspoon freshly ground pepper
^{1}/$_2$ tablespoon flour

300ml (^{1}/$_2$ pint) milk, or 250ml (9fl oz) milk
and 30ml (1fl oz) cream

Melt the butter over a gentle heat, add the onions and cook in a covered saucepan on a low heat until really soft but not coloured. Season with salt and freshly ground pepper. Stir in the flour, add the milk and simmer gently for a further 5 minutes.

This sauce keeps for 3–4 days covered in the fridge and may of course be reheated.

Onion and Mint Sauce
Add 2–3 tablespoons freshly chopped mint to the Onion Sauce before serving.

Mayonnaise and Variations

Mayonnaise takes less than 5 minutes to make by hand, faster than in a food processor. All the ingredients should be at room temperature if possible. As ever the quality of the eggs matters. Fresh free-range eggs will create a better, more stable emulsion.

2 free-range, organic egg yolks
^{1}/$_4$ teaspoon Dijon mustard or pinch of
English mustard
^{1}/$_4$ teaspoon salt
1 dessertspoon white wine vinegar
225ml (8fl oz) oil (sunflower, arachide or olive
oil or a mixture). We use 175ml (6fl oz)
arachide oil and 50ml (2fl oz) olive oil;
alternatively use 7:1 sunflower oil to olive oil

Put the egg yolks into a medium-size bowl with the mustard, salt and the white wine vinegar (keep the whites to make meringues). Put the oil into a measuring jug with a good pouring spout. Take a whisk in one hand and the oil in the other and drip the oil onto the egg yolks, drop by drop, whisking at the same time. Within a minute you will notice that the mixture is beginning to thicken. When this happens you can add the oil a little faster, but don't get too cheeky or it will suddenly curdle because the egg yolks can only absorb the oil at a certain pace. Taste and add a little more seasoning and vinegar if necessary.

If the mayonnaise curdles it will suddenly become quite thin, and if left sitting the oil will start to float to the top of the sauce. Should this happen you can quite easily rectify the situation by putting another egg

yolk or 1–2 tablespoons of boiling water into a clean bowl, then whisk in the curdled mayonnaise, half a teaspoon at a time until it re-emulsifies.

Food processor method
Mayonnaise may be made in a food processor, however 4 egg yolks are the minimum because even in the smallest capacity bowl the blades are unable to pick up two egg yolks. Even in the food processor the oil must be added slowly at first to establish the emulsion, thereafter the oil may be added in a steady stream.

If the oil is added too slowly the heat generated by the blades whizzing around can curdle the mayonnaise, so try not to be too cautious.

White wine vinegar is the classic seasoning but lemon and lime juice is sometimes used. It keeps for a minimum of 5–7 days, covered in a fridge. Bring back to room temperature before stirring otherwise it may curdle.

Which oil?
Many mayonnaise recipes call for olive oil, however, if extra virgin olive oil is used the sauce will be too strong for most tastes. We use 7 parts sunflower or peanut oil and 1 part extra virgin olive oil or 6 to 2 for a more distinct olive flavour.

Aioli or Garlic Mayonnaise
Ingredients as above, plus:
1–4 garlic cloves, depending on size
2 teaspoons chopped parsley

Crush the garlic and add to the egg yolks just as you start to make the mayonnaise. Finally add the chopped parsley and taste for seasoning.

Coriander Mayonnaise
Add 1–2 tablespoons of chopped coriander to the basic Mayonnaise recipe.

Basil Mayonnaise
Pour boiling water over 20g (^{3}/$_4$oz) of basil leaves, count to 3, drain immediately and refresh in cold water. Chop and add to the egg yolks and continue to make the Mayonnaise in the usual way.

Tomato and Basil Mayonnaise

Add 1–2 tablespoons of aromatic Tomato Purée (see p294) to the Basil Mayonnaise.

Chilli Basil Mayonnaise

Add a good pinch of chilli powder to the egg yolks when making Garlic Mayonnaise, omit the parsley and add the basil instead. Great with salads and sandwiches.

Spicy Mayonnaise

Add 1–2 teaspoons Ballymaloe Tomato Relish or a good tomato chutney to the basic Mayonnaise. Add 1/2–1 teaspoon chilli sauce to taste.

Wasabi Mayonnaise

Add 1–2 tablespoons wasabi paste to the eggs instead of mustard.

Roasted Red Pepper Mayonnaise

Add 1–2 roast red peppers (see p298), seeded and peeled (do not wash). Purée the red pepper flesh, add the purée and juices to the Mayonnaise. Taste and correct seasoning.

Wholegrain Mustard Mayonnaise

Add 1–2 tablespoons wholegrain mustard to the basic Mayonnaise.

Lemon Mayonnaise

Use lemon juice instead of vinegar in the basic Mayonnaise.

Fennel Mayonnaise

Rick Stein introduced me to this delicious sauce. Add 3 teaspoons Pernod and 2 tablespoons of finely chopped fennel bulb to the basic mayonnaise recipe.

Dill Mayonnaise

Add 2–3 tablespoons of freshly chopped dill to the basic Mayonnaise recipe.

Asian Mayonnaise

Add 2 teaspoons of Wasabi paste, 2 tablespoons of Sweet Chilli Sauce (see p296), 3 tablespoons of freshly chopped coriander and the juice of 1/2 a lime to the basic Mayonnaise recipe.

Tapenade Mayonnaise

Add 3–4 tablespoons of Tapenade (see p75) to the basic Mayonnaise recipe.

Croûtons

SERVES 4

Sprinkle over salads or serve with soups.

1 slice of slightly stale bread, 5mm (1/4 in) thick
sunflower or olive oil

First cut the crusts off the bread, next cut into 5mm (1/4in) strips and then into exact cubes.

Heat the sunflower or olive oil in a frying pan, – the oil should be at least 2cm (3/4in) deep and almost smoking.

Add the croûtons to the hot oil. Stir once or twice, they will colour almost immediately. Put a tin sieve over a pyrex or stainless steel bowl. When the croûtons are golden brown, pour the oil and croûtons into the sieve. Drain the croûtons on kitchen paper.

Note: Croûtons may be made several hours ahead or even a day. The oil may be flavoured with sprigs of rosemary, thyme or onion.

Croûtons may be stamped out into various shapes, hearts, stars, clubs, diamonds, etc…

Pesto

MAKES 2 JARS

If you any have difficulty getting basil, use parsley, a mixture of parsley and mint or parsley and coriander – different but still delicious. Pesto keeps for weeks, covered with a layer of olive oil in a jar.

110g (4oz) fresh basil leaves
150ml (5fl oz) extra virgin olive oil
25g (1oz) fresh pine kernels (taste when you buy to ensure they are not rancid)
2 large garlic cloves, peeled and crushed
50g (2oz) Parmesan cheese, freshly grated
salt to taste

Whizz the basil with the olive oil, pine kernels and garlic in a food processor or pound in a pestle and mortar. Remove to a bowl and fold in the Parmesan. Taste and season. Pour into sterilised jars. Cover with a layer of olive oil. Screw on the lid and store in the fridge.

Pesto also freezes well but for best results don't add the Parmesan until defrosted.

Top Tip: Each time you use some pesto, clean the top and sides of the jar and make sure the pesto is covered with a layer of extra-virgin olive oil before replacing in the fridge. Otherwise the pesto will darken and go mouldy where it is exposed to the air.

Dill Tzatziki

This delicious cucumber and yogurt mixture is a Greek speciality, literally made in minutes, and is served with grilled fish or meat or as an accompanying salad.

1 crisp cucumber, peeled and cut into 3–5mm (1/8–1/4in) dice
1–2 garlic cloves, crushed
dash of lemon juice
425ml (3/4 pint) Greek yogurt or best-quality natural yogurt (not low fat)
4 tablespoons cream (optional)
2 heaped tablespoons chopped dill
salt, freshly ground pepper and sugar to taste

If you have time, put the cucumber dice into a sieve, sprinkle with salt and allow to drain for about 15 minutes. This drains out extra moisture. Put into a bowl and mix with the crushed garlic, a dash of lemon juice, the yogurt and cream if you like a really creamy texture. Stir in the dill, taste and season.

Roast Peppers

There are three ways to roast peppers:

1. Preheat the grill, or better still, use a charcoal grill or barbecue. Grill the peppers on all sides, allowing them to become quite charred.
2. Preheat the oven to 240°C/475°F/gas mark 9. Place the peppers on a baking tray and bake for 20–30 minutes until the skin blisters and the flesh is soft.
3. Put a wire rack over a mild gas jet, then roast the pepper on all sides until charred.

When the peppers are roasted, put them into a bowl and cover tightly with clingfilm for a few minutes to make them much easier to peel. Pull the skin off the peppers and remove the stalks and seeds. Do not wash the peppers or you will lose the precious sweet juices. Divide each pepper into 2 or 3 pieces along the natural division. They will keep for 1–2 days in the fridge.

Onion Marmalade

MAKES 450ML (16FL OZ)

This is especially delicious with patés and terrines of meat, game, poultry and goat's cheese. It will keep for months.

50g (2oz) butter
675g (1¹/₂lb) onions, thinly sliced
150g (5oz) caster sugar
1 teaspoon salt
¹/₂ teaspoon freshly ground black pepper
7 tablespoons sherry vinegar
250ml (9fl oz) full-bodied red wine
2 tablespoons crème de cassis

Melt the butter in a saucepan until it becomes a deep nut brown colour. Toss in the onions and sugar, add the salt and pepper and stir well. Cover the saucepan and cook for 30 minutes over a gentle heat, stirring from time to time with a wooden spatula.

Add the sherry vinegar, red wine and crème de cassis. Cook for a further 30 minutes uncovered, stirring regularly.

Spicy Tomato Jam

MAKES 1 LITRE (1³/₄ PINTS)

Tomatoes must be very ripe for this delicious recipe, which is even better when made with a mixture of heirloom tomatoes. Serve with crostini, bruschetta, cold or cured meats, homemade sausages, on toast…

1.5kg (3lb 5oz) very ripe tomatoes
285g (10¹/₂oz) sugar
1 orange
1 lemon
3 star anise
3 green cardamom pods
1 teaspoon coriander seeds
1 teaspoon juniper berries
3 cloves
1 teaspoon black peppercorns
1 vanilla pod

Core the tomatoes and cut a cross into the base of each one. Put the tomatoes in a deep bowl and pour boiling water over, then count to ten and drain gently. Peel off the skins.

Chop roughly then transfer to a stainless steel saucepan and add the sugar. Grate the zest of the orange and lemon, then juice the citrus fruit. Add the zest and juice to the pan.

Warm a heavy frying pan on a medium heat. Put the star anise, cardamom pods, coriander seeds, juniper berries, cloves and peppercorns into the pan, and stir for 2–3 minutes until fragrant. Turn into a mortar and grind with a pestle. Discard the cardamom husks, then add the ground spices to the tomatoes. Split the vanilla pod and add it to the saucepan.

Cook the mixture over a low heat for about 30 minutes, until all the tomatoes have softened. When the jam thickens slightly, pour into small clean jars. Cover and seal.

Allow the jam to mellow for a few days before using. It will keep in a cool, dark place for several months but store it in the fridge after opening.

Pickled Lemons

This is a brilliant unorthodox method which Claudia Roden showed us a few years ago when she taught a class with Diana Kennedy at the Cookery School

8 lemons
8 tablespoons salt
Sunflower or arachide oil

With a good sharp knife make 8 fine superficial, not deep incisions into the lemon skin from one end of the lemon to the other. Put the lemons into a large stainless steel saucepan and cover with salted water. Put a plate or smaller lid on top of them to keep them down, otherwise they float. Cover and boil for 25-30 minutes or until the peels are very soft. When cool enough to handle, scoop out the flesh, pack the skins into a glass jar and cover with oil.

Polenta

SERVES 6–8

Cornmeal or polenta can be served the moment it's ready, while it's still soft and flowing, or it can be poured into a dish and allowed to get cold. When cold, it can be sliced and chargrilled, pangrilled or fried, and served with all sorts of toppings. It can even be cut into thin slices and layered with a sauce, just like lasagne. When cooking and stirring polenta I use a whisk at the beginning, but as soon as it comes to the boil I change to a flat-bottomed wooden spoon.

1.8 litres (3 pints) water
1 level dessertspoon sea salt
225g (8oz) coarse polenta flour (if using quick-cook polenta, follow the instructions on the packet)

Pour the water into a deep heavy-bottomed saucepan and bring to the boil. Add the salt, then very thinly and gradually sprinkle in the polenta flour, whisking all the time – this should take you 3–4 minutes. Bring to the boil, stirring continuously and when it starts to bubble and 'erupt' like a volcano reduce the heat down to the absolute minimum – use a heat diffuser mat if you have one. Simmer, stirring regularly, for about 40 minutes.* The polenta is cooked when it is very thick but not solid, and comes away from the sides of the pot as you stir.

* If, after the polenta has come to the boil, you reduce the heat to medium and stir continuously, the cooking time can be reduced to about 20 minutes, but polenta is more digestible if cooked more slowly over a longer period.

Soft, Wet or Creamy Polenta

Wonderful with game birds or juicy meat or vegetable stews. It can also be served with a rich tomato sauce and spicy sausages.

polenta as cooked in previous recipe
110g (4oz) butter
75g (3oz) Parmesan cheese, grated
sea salt and freshly ground pepper
sage leaves, fried briefly

As soon as the polenta is cooked, add the butter, parmesan and some pepper. Taste and add a little salt if needed. The polenta should be soft and flowing; if it is a little too stiff add a few tablespoons boiling water. Serve immediately. A few fried sage leaves are a delicious addition.

Polenta with Fresh Herbs
Add 2–4 tablespoons of freshly chopped herbs, such as parsley, chives, thyme leaves, sage and rosemary into the polenta when it is cooked.

Chargrilled Polenta

Cold polenta can be cut it into squares, diamonds or slices and stored, covered, in the fridge for several days. Grilled or fried, it makes the most delicious snacks or accompaniment to meat or fish dishes, or you can make a sophisticated starter for a dinner party in just a few minutes.

Make the polenta in the usual way (see opposite).

Sprinkle water over a dish – I use a lasagne dish (23 x 18cm/9 x 7in), which is just perfect for this quantity, but a Swiss roll tin is also good. Pour in the cooked polenta and leave to cool. When cold, cut it into slices 1–2cm ($1/2$–$3/4$in) thick. The slices can be reheated immediately, or covered and stored in the fridge until needed.

To reheat, chargrill, pangrill or pan-fry the slices. If grilling, put the slices directly on to the bars of the grill at the highest heat, without oil, and cook until hot through and grill-marked on each side. If the polenta is to be sautéed use a little olive oil or butter.

storecupboard standby

Busy people who want to be able to whizz up quick and easy meals in minutes will need to make sure that their store cupboard is always well stocked. The following are some suggestions for items that we find invaluable.

Storecupboard
Ballymaloe Cucumber Pickle
Ballymaloe Tomato Relish
Butter
Carrots
Chicken stock/cube
Cream crackers or Carrs Water Biscuits
Dried fruit, especially apricots
Eggs, free-range and organic if possible
English mustard powder
Extra virgin olive oil
Flour, e.g. plain, self raising, strong brown, strong white, coarse brown
French mustard
Garlic
Good-quality dark chocolate
Grains, e.g. cous cous, bulgar, quinoa
Ground nut and sunflower oil
Harissa or chilli sauce
Homemade jam
Honey
Maldon or Halen Mon sea salt
Marmalade
Mature Cheddar cheese
Nam pla (fish sauce)
Nuts, e.g. hazelnuts, walnuts and almonds

Oatmeal
Olives
Onions
Oyster Sauce
Parmesan cheese
Pasta/noodles/macaroni/shells/penne etc.
Pesto
Pitta bread (in the freezer)
Plum sauce
Polenta
Potatoes
Red and white wine vinegar
Rice, e.g. basmati, Thai fragrant
Salami, chorizo
Sardines, tuna fish, anchovies
Sesame oil
Tinned beans, chickpeas
Tortillas

Easy Entertaining Equipment
Fondue set
Paella cooker
Raclette set
Waffle iron

index

credits

The author and publisher would like to thank the following for their kind help with props and locations:

Red plastic bowls on pl04–105: **Guzzini** (Tel: 020 8646 4141).
Red suede cushions on p102–103: **Alma Leather** (Tel: 020 7375 0343).
Daisy curtains, metal trays with wooden handles on p191: **Dotcomgiftshop.com** (Tel: 020 8746 2473).

PVC tablecloth, lace glasses, paper doilys on party bags and under cupcakes on p190–195: **Lovely, Lovely at Selfridges**. Green plastic 3-tier cake stand, pink metal jug, paper party bags on p190–195: **Urchin** (Tel: 0870 720 0709).
Striped candles, star-shaped and heart-shaped sparklers on p192–195: **Talking Tables** (Tel: 020 8767 6000).
Striped 'Happy' cushions on p191: **Life at Nettlebed** (Tel: 01491 640923)

Indian umbrella on p261: **Source** (Tel: 020 8505 6697).
Cushions on p26: **Life at Nettlebed** (Tel: 01491 640923).
Flask on p261: **Dotcomgiftshop.com** (Tel: 020 8746 2473).
Location on p46–49 through **Olive Locations** (Tel: 020 8647 7800)